Categories of the verb in natural la... (mood) and voice. Among these, voice, in its rich and diverse manifestations, is perhaps the most complex. But most prior research concentrates on only certain types, predominantly passives.

Voice expresses relations between a predicate and a set of nominal positions – or their referents – in a clause or other structure. *Grammatical voice* is the first typological study of voice systems based on a multi-language survey. It introduces a threefold classification of voice types, in the first place distinguishing passivization phenomena (derived voice) from active–middle systems (basic voice); and further, distinguishing each of these from pragmatically grounded voice behaviors, such as focus and inverse systems.

As the first comprehensive study of voice systems and voice typology, this book makes a significant contribution to current research in linguistics and grammatical theory.

CAMBRIDGE STUDIES IN LINGUISTICS

General Editors: B. COMRIE, R. HUDDLESTON, R. LASS,
D. LIGHTFOOT, J. LYONS, P. H. MATTHEWS, R. POSNER,
S. ROMAINE, N. V. SMITH, N. VINCENT

Grammatical voice

In this series

52 MICHAEL S. ROCHEMONT and PETER W. CULICOVER: *English focus constructions and the theory of grammar*
53 PHILIP CARR: *Linguistic realities: an autonomist metatheory for the generative enterprise*
54 EVE SWEETSER: *From etymology to pragmatics: metaphorical and cultural aspects of semantic structure*
55 REGINA BLASS: *Relevance relations in discourse: a study with special reference to Sissala*
56 ANDREW CHESTERMAN: *On definiteness: a study with special reference to English and Finnish*
57 ALESSANDRA GIORGI and GIUSEPPE LONGOBARDI: *The syntax of noun phrases: configuration, parameters and empty categories*
58 MONIK CHARETTE: *Conditions on phonological government*
59 M. H. KLAIMAN: *Grammatical voice*

Supplementary volumes

BRIAN D. JOSEPH: *The synchrony and diachrony of the Balkan infinitive*
ANNETTE SCHMIDT: *Young people's Dyirbal: an example of language death from Australia*
JOHN HARRIS: *Phonological variation and change: studies in Hiberno-English*
TERENCE MCKAY: *Infinitival complement clauses in German*
STELLA MARIS BORTONI-RICARDO: *The urbanization of rural dialect speakers: a socio-linguistic study in Brazil*
RUDOLF P. BOTHA: *Form and meaning in word formation: a study of Afrikaans reduplication*
AYHAN AKSU-KOC: *The acquisition of aspect and modality: the case of past reference in Turkish*
MÍCHEÁL Ó SIADHAIL: *Modern Irish: grammatical structure and dialectal variation*
ANNICK DE HOUWER: *The acquisition of two languages from birth: a case study*

Other titles also available

GRAMMATICAL VOICE

M. H. KLAIMAN

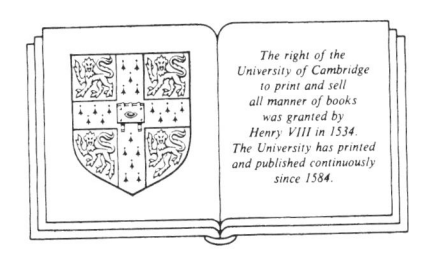

CAMBRIDGE UNIVERSITY PRESS
Cambridge
New York   Port Chester
Melbourne   Sydney

CAMBRIDGE UNIVERSITY PRESS
Cambridge, New York, Melbourne, Madrid, Cape Town, Singapore, São Paulo

Cambridge University Press
The Edinburgh Building, Cambridge CB2 2RU, UK

Published in the United States of America by Cambridge University Press, New York

www.cambridge.org
Information on this title: www.cambridge.org/9780521360012

© Cambridge University Press 1991

This publication is in copyright. Subject to statutory exception
and to the provisions of relevant collective licensing agreements,
no reproduction of any part may take place without
the written permission of Cambridge University Press.

First published 1991
This digitally printed first paperback version 2005

A catalogue record for this publication is available from the British Library

Library of Congress Cataloguing in Publication data
Klaiman, M. H.
Grammatical voice/M. H. Klaiman.
    p.   c.m. – (Cambridge studies in linguistics: 59)
ISBN 0 521 36001 3
1. Grammar, Comparative and general–Voice.   I. Title.
II. Series.
P281.K537   1991
415–dc20   91-6383   CIP

ISBN-13 978-0-521-36001-2 hardback
ISBN-10 0-521-36001-3 hardback

ISBN-13 978-0-521-36904-6 paperback
ISBN-10 0-521-36904-5 paperback

To Madan

न प्रेम ।
न प्यार ।
न काम ।
न रति ।
न आदर ।
न स्नेह ।
यह कार्य है
मदन के लिये ॥

Contents

List of figures	*page* xi
Preface	xiii
List of abbreviations	xviii

1	**The study of voice**	1
1.0	Preliminaries	1
1.1	Voice in traditional grammar	2
1.2	Role-remapping voice	11
1.3	Voice as alternation in subject's participant status	23
1.4	Voice as marker of pragmatic salience assignment	31
1.5	Argument structure and voice	35
2	**Middle voice and basic voice systems**	44
2.0	Preliminaries	44
2.1	Fula	47
2.2	Tamil	69
2.3	Indo-European	82
2.4	Basic voice as patterning of the verbal lexicon	104
3	**Control and voice**	110
3.0	Preliminaries	110
3.1	Perspectives on the control construct	112
3.2	The grammar of control	117
	3.2.1 Agency, undergoing and intransitive predicate classification: unaccusativity	121
	3.2.2 Active–stative systems	124
	3.2.3 Morphologically marked lexical classes in Cupeño	132
3.3	The control construct and basic voice	137
3.4	Affectedness, attribution of control and submissive verb constructions	140

x *Contents*

    3.5 Attribution of control and verbal derivation   146
    3.6 The grammaticization of control   156

4 Inverse voice systems   161
    4.0 Preliminaries: ontology, head-marking and the inverse type   161
    4.1 Korean   171
    4.2 Apachean languages   175
    4.3 Passive vs inverse voice   182
    4.4 Algonquian languages   185
    4.5 Tanoan languages   200
        4.5.1 Arizona Tewa   204
        4.5.2 Other Tanoan languages   211
        4.5.3 Tanoan systems and the inverse type   222

5 Information-salience voice systems   227
    5.0 Preliminaries: clausal pragmatics and informational salience   227
    5.1 Mayan languages   228
    5.2 Philippine languages   245

6 Toward a theory of voice   260

    Notes   272
    Bibliography   296
    Index   315

Figures

1.1	Clause-level and logical-level structure correlations	page 5
1.2	Unmarked and marked voice configurations	10
1.3	Some basic clause-structure correlations of semantic roles and grammatical relations	15
1.4	Some basic and remapped relational configurations	16
1.5	Some definitions of thematic relations	40
2.1	Summary of Fula verbal conjugation, based on Arnott 1956: 131, Table 1	48
2.2	Three-voice, two-voice, and one-voice valence classes of simple radicals in Fula	55
2.3	Semantic classification of some Fula radicals with middle primary voice, based on Arnott 1956 and 1970, Appendices 11, 12	58
2.4	Some diatheses, based on Geniušienė 1987	66
2.5	Ergative, active and active–middle argument-structure organization	108
3.1	Natural predicate classification according to the control construct	111
3.2	Non-control predicate subclasses according to Thalberg 1972	119
3.3	Potentiality of agency scale (animacy hierarchy)	120
3.4	Tentative classification of unergative vs unaccusative predicate concepts, based on Perlmutter 1978	122
3.5	Representative instances of intransitive verb classes in Chocho, based on Mock 1982 (1980)	126
3.6	Subgroups of zero-marked lexical verbs in Cupeño, based on Hill 1969: 353	134
3.7	Prototype functions of basic voice categories	139
4.1	Some Arizona Tewa person prefix paradigms, based on Kroskrity 1985	205

xii *List of figures*

4.2	Some Picurís person prefix paradigms, based on Zaharlick 1982	216
4.3	Some Southern Tiwa person prefix paradigms, based on Rosen 1990	221
4.4	Some Towa (Jemez) person prefix paradigms, based on Myers 1970	221
5.1	Mappings of nominal functions, case categories, verbal voices and form classes in Cebuano, based on Shibatani 1988a	249
5.2	Focus-, actor- and actor-/focus-sensitive properties in Philippine languages, based on Shibatani 1988a: 125, 1988b: 107	257

Preface

Throughout my career as a linguist, I have been interested in categories of meaning in natural languages and their expression through cross-linguistically recurrent structural patterns and behaviors. Over the past several years my research interests have come to focus on certain behaviors that, at the outset, seemed difficult to classify under any well-defined grammatical category. In fact, when I embarked on their study, all that these behaviors seemed to have in common was that somewhere and at some time, some grammarian has referred to them under the rubric of grammatical voice. Now, on two grounds, the time seems ripe for bringing to light my research on these behaviors in the form of a monograph on voice as a grammatical category. And so, by way of accounting to the reader for the lengthy text below, I risk overburdening it with this preface explaining how it has come to be.

In the first place, a comprehensive work on this subject seems desirable in light of the current diversity of views on voice. In fact, grammarians presently use the term voice in reference to no fewer than three distinct classes of grammatical behaviors. The term is invoked, firstly, in reference to systems where regular alternations in verbal morphology signal alternate allocations of nominals among positions in structural configurations. This class of voice systems is termed derived voice* in the present study. It encompasses behaviors prominent in current grammatical theories, usually treated under the general rubric of passivization*. Included are ordinary transitive (personal) passives plus such other varieties as impersonal passives, oblique passives, antipassives and so on.

However, there is a second, much older tradition of identifying voice with verbal oppositions which, in certain languages, signal alternations in the participant roles of subjects. Generally, they express the coincidence or noncoincidence of a clause's subject with the locus of the principal effects of the action or situation denoted by the verb. Systems of this type are best known from active/middle* alternations in classical languages, such as Latin, Greek and Sanskrit. Nonetheless, they are also found in languages neither Indo-European nor ancient. They are discussed in the main text below under the rubric of basic* (as contrasted with derived*) voice.

Thirdly and finally, some writers invoke the term voice in reference to systems in which alternations of verbal morphology signal the alternating assignment among a clause's nominals of some pragmatic status or salience, such as informational or ontological salience. Systems of this type, below termed pragmatic voice* systems, are perhaps best known from recent treatments of Philippine language such as Tagalog. However, such systems are not confined to a single genetic group or family, but are also manifested elsewhere, such as in Mayan languages, which are among the pragmatic voice systems discussed in the main text. Also, pragmatic voice encompasses Algonquian and other systems of the inverse* type, which the main text likewise surveys.

The present work aims to clarify the idea of voice by adopting a typological approach to voice phenomena. In the course of the presentation, it has been necessary to invoke some technical terms. Where they are introduced, such terms are marked with an asterisk (*).

Aside from the need for greater clarity in the conceptualization of voice, an additional impetus for the present work has been the success of recent titles on other major verbal categories. In recent years, Cambridge University Press has produced Bernard Comrie's *Aspect* (1976) and *Tense* (1985) and F. R. Palmer's *Mood and modality* (1986). Voice has lately been the only major verbal category for which there has been no up-to-date comprehensive treatment, making the present seem a propitious time for such a work. I never seriously considered submitting my project proposal to any publisher other than Cambridge University Press. I am indebted to the Cambridge University Press Syndicate for its acceptance of this work, which made that effort unnecessary.

And so to the pleasant task of thanksgiving. I wish to acknowledge my friends on the Cambridge University Press staff who have assisted in this project, headed initially by Penny Carter and subsequently by Marion Smith and Judith Ayling, for their expeditious and painstaking handling of the work, by which they have made me feel as supported and valued as any author could desire. I am grateful for the generosity of the anonymous reviewers who furnished a favorable evaluation of my proposal to the Cambridge University Press Syndicate, as well as to two reviewers who subsequently broke anonymity to discuss the proposal with me in person, Arnold Zwicky and Bernard Comrie.

I should acknowledge, however, that the proposal was not the project's true beginning; it was about three years before the proposal stage that the work began. Since that time, numerous scholars have lent their assistance, many by commenting on my published and unpublished research related to voice or by furnishing copies of their own. While most of these individuals are acknowledged at some point in the main text, I should like to take this opportunity to particularly name and thank the following: B. J. Allen, P. K. Anderson, D. W. Arnott, Glenn Ayres, Joan Bresnan, William Cowan, Bill Croft, Amy Dahlstrom, Bill Davies, Donald Frantz, Emma Geniušienė, Ives Goddard, John Haiman, Heather Hardy, George Hewitt, Jane Hill, Eloise Jelinek, M. Dale Kinkade, Paul Kroskrity, Sir John Lyons, Steve Marlett, Anthony Mattina, Carol Mock, Doris Payne, David Perlmutter, Paul Riesman, Carol Rosen, Jerrold Sadock, Janine Scancarelli, William Schmalstieg, George Sheets, Masayoshi Shibatani, Thom Smith-Stark, Bob Sprott, Yero Sylla, Laurence and Terry Thompson, and Bob Van Valin. I apologize for any omissions in this list; the number of individuals I have found willing to lend lesser or greater degrees of assistance has been gratifyingly large. Of course, when it comes to the results, I alone am responsible for any shortcomings.

During the last three years of this project, after it came under contract, logistical obstacles arose owing to constraints on time and resources. For instance, enrollments at the last two institutions where I have been employed have put limits on the time and energy available for research (I have been teaching over two hundred students per year). Also, the project has received sparse financial assistance, proposals for same having been turned down by, *inter alia*, the National Science Foundation. However, the work has benefited from research grants in the amounts of $500 and $1000 awarded respectively by California State University-Fullerton and Oakland University in 1989 and 1990. Both institutions also assisted by making personal computers available for use in my office, for which I wish to express thanks. In addition, I wish to acknowledge Susan Kroon, former Oakland University student, for proof-reading assistance.

Another and much valued source of support has been the Department of Linguistics at the University of Minnesota. Under the capable chairmanship of Dr Michael Kac, the department has routinely offered me the status of Honorary Fellow since 1986, thereby permitting me to access the collections of the University of Minnesota Libraries. The librarians and staff have also contributed to the completion of this work. Among them, I especially wish to thank Jane Riedel and her colleagues in the Interlibrary Loan Office at the University of Minnesota's Wilson Library for their incalculable assistance in locating requested materials, however arcane the source or sloppily scrawled the request.

I have embarked on this, the largest research project thus far of my career, with the objective of making a worthwhile contribution to my discipline. Time will tell if I have succeeded, but should I fail, it will not have been for want of cooperation from speakers of the languages represented in the present work, speakers who have contributed their time and assistance to make possible the numerous references cited in the main text below. Yet I have an ever higher regard for the languages themselves. One thing of which my experience as a linguist has absolutely convinced me is that language is more than a natural object.

Language is organic. As a linguist who works routinely with languages, I cannot imagine thinking about them in any other way. A language has structure, function and design. It arises, it has a lifespan, and ultimately – possibly leaving heirs – it disappears. Language has nothing if not patterning and logic, yet every language I have ever taken the trouble to become acquainted with has confirmed my conviction that a language also has personality, a way of going about its purposes. No longer can I begin to investigate a new language without expecting to find within it a wonderful and companionable spirit. I have met language speakers I did not like, but never a language.

At a time when many so-called departments of linguistics have more or less gone out of the business of teaching about languages, it becomes a cherished pleasure to encounter others who share an enthusiasm for them and a serious fondness for their study. Among such colleagues is one, Bernard Comrie, to whom I owe an obligation difficult to state in words. Professor Comrie has supported this project with his counsel and encouragement since its beginnings, serving as a content advisor to this work on behalf of Cambridge University Press. I can't imagine having carried out the project without the sustaining interest of Professor Comrie. His timely and well-stated comments and suggestions have steered the text out of cul-de-sacs and blind alleys again and again. Even before this work was conceived, he has for years been an esteemed friend and advisor to me.

Nevertheless, Professor Comrie's contributions go beyond his assistance to individuals or individual projects, since he works actively with publishers and institutions on behalf of linguistics at large, benefiting directly or indirectly all who labor in our field. Of all the linguists of my acquaintance, I admire Bernard Comrie most. But it is for the service you perform on behalf of our discipline, Bernard, that I thank you most of all.

And for providing a nucleus of sanity, it goes without saying – last but foremost – I couldn't have managed without Madan Madhav Sathe.

Abbreviations

A	transitive subject
A voice	actor voice
ABL	ablative
ABS	absolutive
ACC	accusative
AI	animate intransitive
ANTI	antipassive
AT	Arizona Tewa
AUX	auxiliary
CAUSE	causative
D voice	directional voice
DAT	dative
DU	dual
EMPH	emphatic
ERG	ergative
F	focus
FEM	feminine
G voice	goal voice
GEN	genitive
I voice	instrumental voice
II	inanimate intransitive
INF	infinitive
INST	instrumental
ITR	intransitive
LOC	locative
MASC	masculine
NEUT	neuter
NOM	nominative
OBJ	object
OBL	oblique

OBV	obviative
OC	out-of-control
OPT	optative
P	transitive object
PL	plural
PROX	proximate
PTCPL	participle
R	Reflexive (or Reflexive-retaliative) extension
RN	relational noun
S	intransitive subject
SAP	speech act participant; first or second person
SG	singular
ST	Southern Tiwa
SUBJ	subject
T	topic
TA	transitive animate
TI	transitive inanimate
TR	transitive
VP	verb phrase

1 *The study of voice*

1.0 Preliminaries

In the history of grammar, the study of voice dates at least to the Sanskrit grammar of Pāṇini (*ca* 500 BC). In this work, entitled *Aṣṭādhyāyī* ('Eight-Chaptered'), are described the distinctions of inflectional paradigms and of meanings associated with the opposition of active and middle in the Sanskrit verb. Voice analysis is thus one of the most ancient topics in the tradition of descriptive grammar. Nevertheless, many recent writers seem to invoke the concept of voice in an intuitive or pretheoretical sense, rarely offering clearcut standards to determine whether specific behaviors are to be included in or excluded from the category.

Grammatical voice* refers to a category of the verb. Its status is thus comparable with that of other verbal categories such as tense, aspect, and mood/modality.

Grammatical voice is manifested in systems in which alternations in the shapes of verbs signal alternations in the configurations of nominal statuses with which verbs are in particular relationships. Voice differs in this respect from case*, a nominal category whereby the relationship of some particular nominal to some verb is signaled.

The present work is intended to broaden and lend clarity to the current understanding of grammatical voice and voice systems by advancing a typological scheme for their description; that is, by proposing grounds, behavioral and structural, for characterizing voice phenomena as conforming to types. The present chapter furnishes a descriptive overview of a variety of voice behaviors. The chapter presupposes some familiarity with voice accounts in current grammatical theory, although it does not address the content of recent proposals for the formal treatment of voice.[1]

Chapter 1's objective is to overview classes of natural language behaviors which descriptive grammars often handle under the rubric of voice. Section 1.1 concerns historical foundations for analyzing these behaviors, i.e. traditional and posttraditional conceptions and definitions of voice. Sections 1.2–1.4 survey three kinds of behaviors which match traditional and posttraditional views of voice alike; these are termed derived voice* systems, basic voice* systems, and pragmatic voice* systems. Section 1.5 concerns some concepts of grammatical organization foundational to the further study of voice.

An outline of the contents of the complete work is deferred until the close of the present chapter.

1.1 Voice in traditional grammar

Current treatments of voice reflect earlier traditions of grammatical scholarship. For the purposes of the present discussion, one of the most significant traditions is that of classical language studies. Works representative of this tradition include descriptive and pedagogical treatments of the structures of ancient European languages, chiefly Greek and Latin.

In the classical tradition, the structures of these languages are usually analyzed in terms of two factors. The first is the language items themselves, which are organized according to lexical classes (parts of speech). The second factor is the paradigmatic variation in the forms of items according to certain functions called grammatical categories*. As noted above in Section 1.0, voice is recognized, along with tense, aspect, and mood/modality, as a grammatical category of the lexical class of verbs. Since this view has its origins in traditional grammar, it is fair to say that voice is traditionally regarded as a parameter of morphological variation in the verb.[2]

Some terms for the category of voice reflect this. That is, traditional terminology alludes to the different ways a verb might be, so to speak, sounded (Latin *vox* 'voice'), i.e. to its repertoire of forms; or to variation in the verb's disposition (Greek *diathesis*) according to alternations in its relations with sentential arguments.[3]

English grammarians usually treat the active/passive alternation under the rubric of voice, although there are noteworthy exceptions. Pre-eminent among them, the great Otto Jespersen speaks of the active and passive "turn" in the English verb, refusing to identify this alternation with voice "as found, for instance, in Greek" (1965: 168). In

Jespersen's view, the latter term is more appropriate to the description of verbal alternations in classical Indo-European languages.

In part, Jespersen's may be a reaction to an inaccuracy perpetuated in many treatments of voice in traditional grammars. In classical literary languages such as Greek and Latin, voice alternations are not restricted to transitive verbs. However, there is a tradition of describing voice alternations in terms of relations within transitive structures.[4]

Moreover, many traditional grammars associate the functions of voices with alternations in viewpoint encoded in structures that are both formally as well as logically transitive. Transitivity* in the logical sense means that the situation denoted in a predication involves two participants; while formal transitivity (for purposes of the present discussion) can be regarded as meaning that the predication includes nominals in at least two semantic roles*, such as Agent and Patient (as these roles are often termed traditionally). According to this view of voice, a transitive situation can, in principle, be projected grammatically from either of two viewpoints, corresponding to two voices of the sentential verb.

One of these voices is said to encode the doing of an action (Michael 1970: 374–5). This voice is called active* because the action notionally devolves from the standpoint of the most dynamic, or active, party involved in the situation, typically the Agent. The second voice encodes action which notionally devolves from the standpoint of a nondynamic, typically static participant in the situation, such as the Patient of a transitive verb. This voice is called passive* because the verb is portrayed as "signifying the *state* of 'being acted upon' or 'suffering the effects of the action'" (Lyons 1968: 372; emphasis in original).

Traditional grammars also recognize a third or middle* voice category. Originally, the middle seems to have been conceived as a compromise category displaying characteristics of both the active and the passive. In a middle construction, the viewpoint is active in that the action notionally devolves from the standpoint of the most dynamic (or Agent-like) participant in the depicted situation. But the same participant has Patient-like characteristics as well, in that it sustains the action's principal effects.

A typical instance is the Classical Greek *loúomai khitôna* 'I wash (middle) the shirt (for myself),' i.e. 'I am washing my shirt' (Lyons 1968: 373). Here the middle is appropriate, since the Agent both performs and benefits from the action. According to one writer, "The Greek construction is called middle because it is semantically intermediate between the active and the passive: the subject does the action to or for him/herself . . ." (van Oosten 1977: 469, fn. 1)

In posttraditional linguistics, many treatments of voice dispense both with the notion of participant viewpoint (the idea of action devolving from some participant's standpoint) and with the concept of a middle voice, in the sense of a construction which displays both active-like and passive-like characteristics. Some recent accounts suggest a mapping between clause-level verb–nominal structure and logical-level predicate-argument structure* roughly as shown in Figure 1.1. This figure depicts a correspondence between a clause-level configuration, consisting of a verb or verbal element in a network of syntactic configurations with nominals, and a logical-level configuration, consisting of a predicate in a network of relations with arguments. These logical-level arguments are of two kinds: those essential to form a predication, or core arguments* (called "inherent arguments" by Marantz 1984); and other arguments that are optional (noncore). (In the figure, optional or noncore arguments correspond to numbered xs enclosed in parentheses.)

The number and type(s) of its core or essential argument(s) is an idiosyncratic property of an individual predicate and plays a role in determining the valence* of the corresponding (clause-level) verb or verbal element. A one-place (univalent) predicate, or predicate in an essential relation with exactly one argument, corresponds to an intransitive* verb; a two-place (bivalent) predicate corresponds to a transitive* verb; a three-place predicate to a ditransitive* verb; and so on. In Figure 1.1, following a convention introduced by Dixon 1979 and reaffirmed by Comrie 1978, core or essential clause-level nominals/logical-level arguments are indicated as follows: the symbol S corresponds to the core argument of a typical univalent predicate/intransitive verb, while A and P correspond to the two core arguments of a typical bivalent predicate/transitive verb.

Here we do not pause to discuss the assignment of semantic roles* to core arguments/nominals, although obviously, several of the symbols in Figure 1.1 do suggest specific semantic content (for instance, "A" is reminiscent of Agent and "P" of Patient). For present purposes, it is merely assumed that S is a univalent structure, A and P in a multivalent structure are each in a direct relation with the predicate/verb. A structural configuration which meets this description may be called normal.

Given this background of assumptions, a normal structural configura-

grammatical structure verb $\sim$ S (x_1) (x_2) ... (x_n) 　　　　　verb $\sim$ A $\sim$ P (x_1) (x_2) ... (x_n)

logical structure predicate $\sim$ S (x_1) (x_2) ... (x_n) 　predicate $\sim$ A $\sim$ P (x_1) (x_2) ... (x_n)

a. univalent　　　　　　　　　　　　b. multivalent

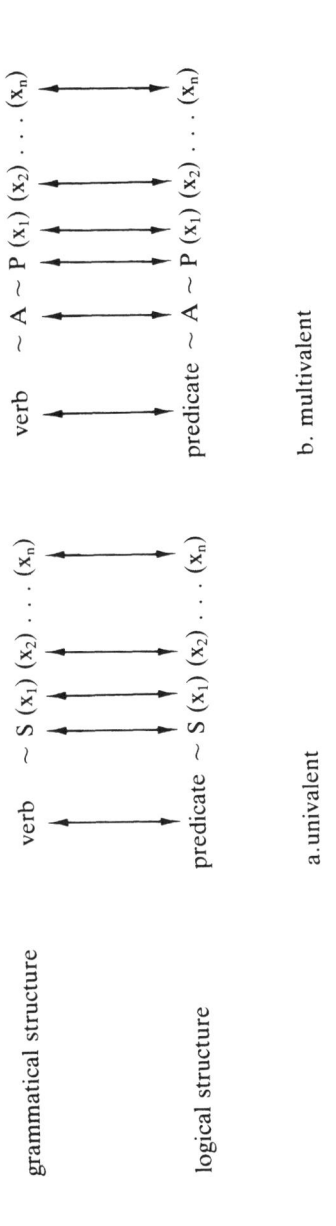

Figure 1.1 Clause-level and logical-level structure correlations

tion, e.g. that of a clause, corresponds to one which is in an unmarked voice. Moreover, a marked voice results from any alternation in or deviation from the normal relations – depicted in Figure 1.1 – between a predicate/verb and its core arguments/nominals.

This conception of voice and voice alternations has many proponents. One of the best known is Fillmore 1968. In his view (and that of writers who share a common perspective), the function of voice marking, or overt verbally encoded manifestations of voice, is to signal the intactness or disruption of the basic relation(s) of a verb to its core nominal(s).[5]

This view of voice is consistent with the possibility of several distinct types of disruptions in verb–nominal relations, corresponding to several marked voice configurations. For instance, a core argument of an unmarked or basic configuration may be eliminated, resulting in its being suppressed in a corresponding marked voice construction. When this occurs, the marked voice may be said to encode or reflect omission of a core argument.

Examples (1)–(3) below illustrate this point. In Bengali (ex. 1), omission of the core argument, the S, of an intransitive (*se* in 1a) results in a marked construction (1b). Here the basic verb is nominalized and followed by a finite form of the verb *jaa-* 'go.' However, in (1b), this verb does not have the conventional lexical sense; rather, it serves as a grammatical marker, signaling omission of the basic S. The result is a structure in which the S is suppressed, or a subjectless clause. Moreover, syntactically speaking, clause (1b) has zero valence, or is said to be impersonal*.

Omission of either core argument, A or P, of a transitive may be signaled by distinct marked voices. (2) illustrates P-omission in the Mayan language Tzeltal (from Jacobsen 1985: 182).[6] In (2b), the omission of the P is signaled both by the addition of the verbal suffix -*awan* and by the loss of the P-agreement morpheme (the suffix -*on* in 2a).

A-omission is illustrated in the Spanish examples of (3). Example (3b) is marked relative to (3a), reflecting omission of the A (*ellos* 'they' in 3a). Moreover, while the argument corresponding to the P in the basic structure of the clause (*la ventana* 'the window') appears in (3b), the basic A is suppressed, or obligatorily unexpressed. In (3b), the element *se* marks this omission. (Taken up in Chapter 2 is the fact that this *se* also has other functions, particularly in marking the reflexive*.)

(1) a. Se okhaane bɔse
       he there   sits
       'He sits there'
    b. Okhaane bɔsaa   jaay
       there   sitting goes
       '(literally) It is sat there/It can be sat there'
(2) a. La   s-   tiʔ -on te   ȼ'iʔ e
       tense 3SG A bite 1SG P the dog demonstrative
       'The dog bit me'
    b. Tiʔ -awan -∅   ȼ'iʔ e
       bite -awan 3SG A dog demonstrative
       'The dog was biting'
(3) a. Ellos rompieron la ventana
       they broke-3PL the window
       'They broke the window'
    b. Se rompió   la ventana
       se broke-3SG the window
       'The window broke/was broken'

Omission of a core argument is just one type of disruption in basic verb–nominal relations. Another type is core argument rearrangement. This occurs when a core argument's basic structure relation to the verb is ceded, or reassigned to another nominal, usually entailing an alteration of basic verbal valence* (defined as the number and types of nominal positions with which a verb is lexically associated). The German example (4b) is based on a univalent (intransitive) structure corresponding to (4a); while the English example (5b) is based on a transitive structure corresponding to (5a).

(4) a. Die Kinder   schlafen
       the children-NOM   sleep
       'The children sleep'
    b. Es wird (von den Kindern)   geschlafen
       it is (by the children-DAT)   slept
       '(literally) It is slept by the children'
(5) a. Babe Ruth throws baseballs
    b. Baseballs are thrown (by Babe Ruth)

First consider the alternation in (4a, b). The S in (4a), *die Kinder* 'the children', may or may not appear in (4b). Either way, the verb in (4b) appears in a special, or marked, shape preceded by an auxiliary, and the S, if expressed, fails to agree with it. This is evidence that the relation of the S to the verb in (4a) is not preserved in (4b), or to put it another way, the corresponding nominal is no longer a core nominal. An additional piece of evidence for this is that, if expressed, the S appears in an oblique shape; the parenthesized form in (4b) is in a nondirect (nonnominative) case governed by a preposition (*von*). Moreover, it is in a marked position within the sentence, appearing clause-finally (compare the S's clause-initial positioning in ex. 4a).

In addition to all this, (4b) includes a clause-initial element *es*. It is what some writers term a dummy*, or a syntactic placeholder with neither thematic nor referential content (similar to *there* in the English *There were children sleeping*). Expressions such as (4b) are often termed impersonal passive*; they will be further considered below (Section 1.3; Section 2.3). For the present, it may be noted that (4b) is impersonal because, like the earlier (1b), it is nonvalent, having no nominal in a core relation to the verb.

Now consider the alternation in (5a, b). Example (5a) corresponds to a basic transitive configuration with a verb in relation with two core nominals, A and P. The corresponding marked construction (5b) has one core nominal corresponding to the P in (5a), but in (5b) this nominal has evidently assumed the syntactic relation basic to the A, or the relation borne by the A in (5a). Evidence for this is the fact that the (logical-level) P in (5b) both occupies the usual linear position of the A and also takes its case form, the nominative. For its part, the nominal corresponding to A is either suppressed in (5b) or, if expressed, occurs in a marked position – sentence-finally – and in an oblique shape (governed by the postposition *by*). The totality of evidence indicates that the A's basic relation to the verb is disrupted in (5b), being, in fact, reassigned to the basic P.

The sort of marked voice construction illustrated in (5b) is, of course, commonly called passive*. Notice that in (5b) the verb, which is basically transitive (*throws*), appears in a marked shape and is intransitive (*are thrown*). Examples (4b) and (5b) reaffirm the point made earlier that the basic valence is typically altered when a voice alternation disrupts the verb's basic relations with core nominals. In particular, one typically observes a reduction in transitivity*, here meaning the number of nominal positions associated with a lexical verb.[7]

1.1 Voice in traditional grammar

To summarize the present discussion, one posttraditional view of voice is based on the assumption that in basic structural configurations, verbs occur in relations with core nominals that are normal, or unmarked. Nonbasic, marked structural configurations arise by alterations in these normal relations. The function of voice marking is to signal intactness or disruption of normal relations.[8]

Disruptions are of two major types: omissions (of core nominals) and rearrangements (of core nominal relations within clausal configurations). Figure 1.2 presents a scheme for the disruptions – or marked voice configurations – covered in the above discussion.[9]

The scheme summarized in Figure 1.2 presupposes an explicit theory of mapping between grammatical and logical levels of structural analysis; this has been provided for earlier in Figure 1.1.

In evaluating the above model of voice alternations, one issue to take into consideration is whether it accurately summarizes the range of types into which voice behaviors are organized cross-linguistically. A perusal of various language-particular accounts suggests that it may not. In fact, there seem to be entire classes of behaviors that conform either partially or not at all to the scheme just outlined, although they are widely regarded as voice behaviors. As it turns out, the above model is of questionable validity particularly for classical languages, those languages for whose description voice was originally posited as a grammatical category. There are even certain limitations in the above view of voice when it comes to languages to which it is relatively suited, as will be noted in the following section.

One recent writer comments on the current state of voice analysis as follows: "In traditional Indo-European grammar, the voices of a verb are morphologically distinct forms which indicate various relations between the subject and the verbal idea; however, the manner in which the term 'voice' should be applied outside of that language family is not always a straightforward, uncontroversial issue" (Ayres 1983: 20). In fact, the term voice is currently invoked in reference to systematic alternations in predicate–nominal relations of at least three distinguishable types.

In the first place, the term voice is perhaps most widely invoked today in reference to systems in which an alternation in verbal shapes signals alternate assignments of nominals to positions in structural configurations. This has been reviewed above. However, there is also a second, more traditional use of the term voice in reference to systems in which

basic configuration	VI ~ S (exs. 1a, 4a)	VT ~ A ~ P (exs. 2a, 3a, 5a)
omission of core argument	V_0 (ex. 1b)	VI ~ S (= A) (ex. 2b) VI ~ S (= P) (ex. 3b)
rearrangement of core argument(s)	V_0 (oblique S) (ex. 4b)	VI ~ P (oblique A) (ex. 5b)
	a. basic univalent configuration	b. basic multivalent configuration

Key
VI = intransitive verb
VT = transitive verb
V_0 = nonvalent verb (lacking core arguments)

Figure 1.2 Unmarked and marked voice configurations

verbal alternations reflect alternations of the subject's status *vis-à-vis* the denoted action, in terms of whether or not the principal effects of the action devolve upon the subject. And finally, some writers invoke the term voice in reference to systems in which verbal marking signals alternating assignments to nominals of some status of clause-level pragmatic salience, such as topichood, focus, or some other kind of informational prominence; or where alternations in verbal marking otherwise interact with some independent scheme for allocating salience among a predication's core nominals. Each of these respective types of voice behaviors will be briefly surveyed in Sections 1.2, 1.3 and 1.4. The purpose of this survey is to make more explicit the diversity in current understandings of the concept of voice.

1.2 Role-remapping voice

According to the preceding section, nominals in structural configurations may correspond to logical-structure arguments, and may be in either of two classes of relations with the verb: core (essential) and noncore (optional). Presumably, if a nominal corresponds to some logical-structure (core or noncore) argument, then it has semantic content, or can be identified with some semantic role*. In the previous section, examples of typical semantic roles which may be borne by core arguments, Agent and Patient, have been alluded to. Noncore arguments often represent such roles as Location, Instrument, Beneficiary and others.

It is assumed that the content of all semantic roles can be specified in a grammatical theory. However, the definitions of various roles remain provisional at the current stage of research, as do some other issues in semantic role theory (see below, Section 1.5). But for present purposes, semantic roles are spoken of as if having specifiable content.

Another assumption is that there is no indeterminacy in linking*. This term refers to the identification of semantic roles, which are assigned in logical-level predicate-argument structures, with particular nominal positions (such as S, A, P) in clause-level structures which are basic, or in which the relations of verbs to nominals are normal, as discussed earlier. It may be assumed that, in any language, linking is accomplished through some regular process, although what this specifically consists of remains to be worked out in detail (regarding some recent proposals, see Klaiman in preparation).

Semantic roles are a feature of valence*, the particular number and kinds of nominal positions which are lexically associated with a given verb. Since (according to the model of voice in the preceding section) marked voices alter a verb's basic valence, it follows that they also entail alterations in the semantic roles associated with verbs in basic structural configurations.

Under the account discussed in the preceding section, then, voice alternations entail restructuring in the linking of semantic roles with nominal positions.

However, as to the specifics of how this comes about, the model is inexplicit. What the model claims is that, in rearrangement type marked voices, one core argument's basic (or normal) relation with the verb is assumed by some other argument. It is unspecified how this reassignment interacts both with linking and with the specification of basic nominal positions in predicate-argument structures. In general, the model is inexplicit as to what rearrangement of a basic configuration entails, or what it means in terms of grammatical theory for one argument to assume the core relation basic to another.[10]

As a step toward remedying this limitation, some additional assumptions will now be introduced. Let it be assumed that there exists a set of grammatical relations*, including "subject-of," "object-of," "indirect object-of," and others. Let it also be assumed that, in basic configurations, these relations map onto nominals that are semantically specified, or have thematic content assigned through linking. It can be assumed, further, that the set of relations in question has significance for the organization of the grammar – i.e., that semantically linked arguments can (in principle) be remapped from one grammatical relation to another by syntactic rules. This amounts to assuming that syntactic processes may refer to grammatical relations, rather than directly targeting either semantic roles (such as Agent, Patient, etc.) or nominal positions in predicate-argument structure (such as S, A, P). Such an assumption is referred to henceforth as the relational hypothesis*.

The relational hypothesis responds to the question of what it means for one argument to assume the relation basic to another argument. Provided grammatical relations map onto semantically specified nominals in basic structural configurations, it can be simply assumed that, when normal verb–nominal relations are disrupted, one argument assumes the grammatical relation which is basic to another. For instance, one cannot appropriately say that the Patient nominal in (5b) acquires the Agent role, nor that the P becomes an A or transitive subject; but one may say that the nominal linked to the Patient role assumes the grammatical relation basic to the nominal linked to the Agent role – the Subject relation.[11] The process whereby this occurs remaps some semantically specified nominal, or argument, onto a grammatical relation other than that to which it is mapped in a basic structural configuration. Such a rule or process can be called role-remapping*.

A brief excursus concerning the place of grammatical relations in syntactic theory seems appropriate at this juncture. In recent years, concomitant with a change in emphasis in formal models of grammar, there has been a burgeoning interest in the study of grammatical relations. The change of emphasis has been occasioned by a growing concern with the study of universal grammar*. This term refers to the investigation of the principles underlying the organization of all languages.[12] While a detailed discussion of the rationale for universal grammar could take one far afield, the motives for its study, concisely, are (a) practical, since an inventory of universal rules eliminates redundancy in individual language grammars; (b) descriptive, since universal grammar can be expected to reveal the patterns underlying recurrent language-particular behaviors; and (c) metatheoretical, given that universal grammar has a potential to be explanatory in a way that particular-language grammars generally are not – since its purpose is, ultimately, to relate language behaviors to language's fundamental properties as a species-specific faculty.

In recent research on universal grammar, the relational hypothesis is one of the major topics. It is the crux of an ongoing debate over the relative merits of two varieties of grammars, termed monostratal* and multistratal*. Proponents of the relational hypothesis (multistratalists) argue that, in the absence of a level of relational structure in syntactic representations of clauses and sentences, certain universals of grammatical organization fail to be captured. Particularly at stake are the statements of a number of recurrent syntactic processes, including voice rules. The study of grammatical relations and their role in formal syntax is especially associated with an ongoing program of research into a framework of grammatical description known as relational grammar.[13]

Below will be outlined a theory of voice which assumes a level of relational-structure representation. The presentation is informal, and does not aim for the provision of a standard relational grammar treatment. Nor does it strictly follow the theoretical premises of relational grammar.

Let it be assumed that, in some class of predicate-argument structures, there occur core nominals corresponding to logical-level arguments to which three specific semantic roles, Agent, Patient and Experiencer, are assigned through linking. Assume, also, that the basic grammatical relation of Agent is Subject; of Patient, Object; and of Experiencer, Indirect Object. It will be further assumed that there exist noncore nominals, also corresponding to logical-level arguments, that are linked with a different set of semantic roles, including Location, Instrument, Beneficiary and others. The grammatical relations to which these noncore nominals are mapped in basic structures are termed Oblique relations. For nominals linked to the semantic roles just mentioned, the respective corresponding basic-level grammatical relations would be Oblique–Locative, Oblique–Instrumental, Oblique–Benefactive, and so on. A sketch of the theory thus far appears in Figure 1.3.

An additional assumption of this theory is that the basic grammatical relations assigned to particular nominals may be altered through role-remapping rules, as outlined above. A specific example, already discussed, is a rule reassociating the Patient role, assigned in basic structure to the Object relation, with the relation basic to the Agent, the Subject relation. A second role-remapping rule would be one associating the Experiencer, assigned in basic structure to the Indirect Object relation, with some other relation, such as that basic to the Patient, the Object relation. A third kind of role-mapping rule might associate an Oblique, such as an Oblique–Instrumental or Oblique–Locative, with the grammatical relation basic to some core nominal, such as the Subject relation. Figure 1.4 is a scheme of the remappings respectively occasioned by these three hypothetical role-remapping rules.

Given this much theoretical machinery, a revised account of voice alternations is feasible as follows: marked voices consist, essentially, of syntactic rules which have the effect of altering the assignments of nominals in basic structural configurations to the grammatical relation of Subject. This view of matters can be illustrated with actual-language data instantiating each of the remappings schematized in Figure 1.4.

For this purpose, data will be furnished from Southern Tiwa, a language of the Tanoan family spoken in present-day New Mexico. The analysis of the following Southern Tiwa examples should be construed

semantic roles   Agent   Patient   Experiencer   Location   Instrument   Beneficiary
                        ↕   ↕   ↕   ↕   ↕   ↕
grammatical relations Subject Object   Indirect   Oblique–   Oblique–   Oblique–
                                         Object   Locative   Instrumental Benefactive

a. core arguments   b. several noncore arguments

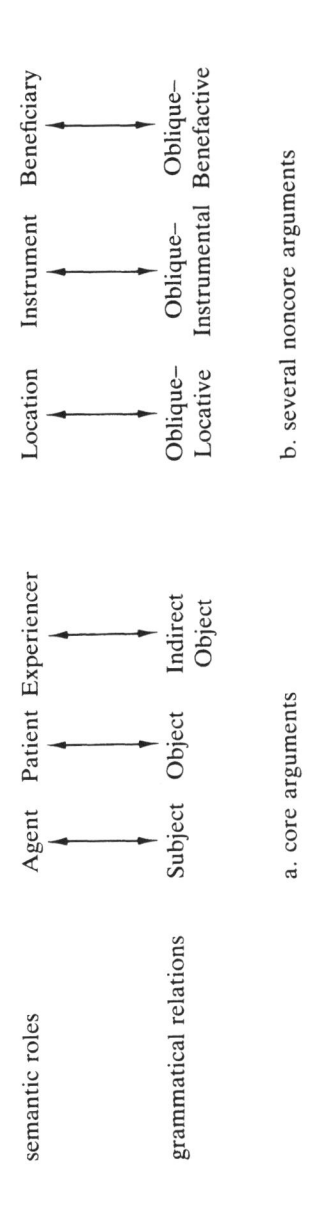

Figure 1.3 Some basic clause-structure correlations of semantic roles and grammatical relations

(i) basic configuration	Subject = A	Object = P	Indirect Object = E	X	Y Z ...
(ii) Patient assumes Subject relation	Subject = P	Object =	Indirect Object = E	X	Y Z ...
(iii) Experiencer assumes Object relation	Subject = A	Object = E	Indirect Object =	X	Y Z ...
(iv) Oblique assumes Subject relation	Subject = X	Object = P	Indirect Object = E		Y Z ...

a. core arguments   b. oblique arguments

Key
A = Agent, P = Patient, E = Experiencer
X, Y, Z = oblique arguments, e.g. Oblique–Locative = Location, Oblique–Instrumental = Instrument, Oblique–Benefactive = Beneficiary, etc.

Figure 1.4 Some basic and remapped relational configurations

as provisional. (In particular, the account shortly to be given of examples 6a, b will undergo a radical revision in Chapter 4 below.)

Examples (6a, b) (from Allen & Frantz 1983a: 5–6) respectively illustrate a sentence corresponding to a basic transitive structure, and the corresponding form after application of the rule schematized in Figure 1.4, (ii), whereby the Patient, or basic Object, assumes the Subject relation. (7a, b) (from Allen & Frantz 1983b: 306) respectively illustrate a sentence corresponding to a basic ditransitive structure containing an Agent, Patient and Experiencer, and the corresponding form after application of the rule schematized in Figure 1.4, (iii), whereby the Experiencer, as basic Indirect Object, assumes the Object relation basic to the Patient. Finally, (8a, b) (from Allen, Gardiner & Frantz 1984: 304–5) respectively illustrate a sentence corresponding to a basic structure containing an Oblique nominal – specifically, an Oblique–Locative – and the corresponding form after application of the rule in Figure 1.4, (iv), whereby the Oblique assumes the Subject relation.

(6) a. Hliara -n   ibi-   'u'u- mu -ban
       lady   PL animate 3PL:3PL baby see past
       'The ladies saw the babies'
    b. 'u'u -n   i-   mu -che -ban hliara -n   -ba
       baby PL animate 3PL see -che past lady   PL animate OBL
       (gloss as in 6a)
(7) a. Ti-   khwien- wia -ban 'ĩ   -'ay
       1SG:3SG animate dog   give past you   to
       'I gave the dog to you'
    b. Ka-   khwien- wia -ban
       1SG:2SG/3SG animate dog   give past
       'I gave you the dog'
(8) a. Seuan -ide   ∅-   wan -ban na -'ay
       man   SG animate 3SG animate come past I   to
       'The man came to me'
    b. In-   seuan- wan -ban (na)
       1SG/3SG animate man   come past (I)
       (gloss as in 8a)

To clarify these examples, a few points should be noted concerning Southern Tiwa morphosyntax. In this language, core nominals are sometimes incorporated, or situated in the verbal complex between an inflectional prefix and the verbal base. Frequently, incorporated nominals represent Objects, as in (6a) and (7a). On the other hand, animate Subjects cannot incorporate; thus in (6a), compare unincorporated *hliara-n* 'ladies' as Subject with incorporated *'u'u* 'baby/babies' as Object. (For more on the particulars of Southern Tiwa noun incorporation, see Allen, Gardiner & Frantz 1984; Frantz 1985; and Rosen 1990.) Noun incorporation has effects on inflectional morphology; for instance, the animate singular/plural suffixes *-(i)de/-n* appear only on unincorporated nominals (compare *'u'u* in 6a with *'u'u-n* in 6b).

Southern Tiwa verbal agreement also calls for a brief exegesis. Inflectional prefixes on verbs index the person, number and noun class (e.g., animate vs several classes of inanimates) of arguments. In transitive verbs, the shapes of prefixes vary for the reference of the Subject and for that of an Object. Intransitive verbs assign a distinct agreement paradigm (Allen & Frantz 1978: 11; Allen & Frantz 1983b: 304; for the paradigms, see Allen & Frantz 1986: 402–03; Allen, Frantz, Gardiner & Perlmutter 1990; and Rosen 1990). It is said that transitive verbs may be detransitivized, i.e. undergo syntactic rules that result in reduced valence. According to recent accounts, the effects of such rules are to leave a marker of detransitivization within the verbal complex and to assign prefixes of the intransitive, rather than transitive, paradigm. With this, it is now feasible to return to examples (6)–(8) and to the voice alternations that each pair represents.

Examples (6a, b) ostensibly illustrate the first kind of role-remapping rule discussed earlier. (6a) represents a basic transitive structure. The inflectional prefix indexes a plural third person Subject, "ladies," and a plural third person animate Object, "babies." This Object, *'u'u*, bears no animate suffix and is incorporated, indicating that it represents a nonsubject relation. However, in (6b), this argument is unincorporated and appears as an independent noun in sentence-initial position, similar to the Subject *hliara-n* 'ladies' in (6a). Notice that the latter appears in (6b) postverbally and in an oblique shape, as the object of the postposition *-ba* which (according to Allen & Gardiner 1981: 293) ordinarily marks nominals representing the Oblique–Instrumental relation. In addition, the element *i-* in (6b) is identical to the prefix which indexes third person plural Subjects of intransitive verbs. The implication is that the verb in (6b), although corresponding to a basic transitive verb of the same shape (shown in 6a), has only one core argument, "babies." This seems to be confirmed in the verbal complex of (6b) by the special marker *-che*, evidently a detransitivizing marker. The weight of the evidence suggests that the basic transitive structure corresponding to (6a) is susceptible to a role-remapping rule. Under this rule, the effects of which are seen in (6b), the basic Subject's relation is assumed by the basic Object. This is shown schematically in Figure 1.4, (ii). (See Allen & Gardiner 1981 for further details of this analysis; but also see below, Section 4.5.2, for a reanalysis.)

Examples (7a, b) illustrate the second role-remapping rule discussed earlier. In (7a), the inflectional prefix indexes a first person singular Subject in construction with a third person singular animate Object, "dog." The latter, *khwien*, is incorporated. Nothing in the shape of the verbal prefix, however, indexes the Indirect Object, which appears post-verbally as an independent nominal in an oblique shape, governed by the postposition *-'ay* 'to.' In (7b), on the other hand, the prefix indexes a nominal corresponding to the Subject of (7a) (first person singular) and a nominal corresponding to the Indirect Object of (7a) (second person). Since the prefix is from a transitive paradigm, indexing both Subject and Object,[14] it would appear that the basic Indirect Object status of "you" in (7a) has been altered in (7b). Moreover, this argument is not expressed as an Oblique in (7b), again suggesting that its basic relational status is altered. On the other hand, there seems to be no alteration in the grammatical relation of the basic Subject, as it neither happens that this argument is expressed by a marked nominal in (7b), nor that the verb of (7b) is marked for detransitivization (compare 6b). On the basis of these facts and others, Allen & Frantz 1983b: 306–9 argue that a sentence such as (7b) arises from a reorganization of the structure basic to a sentence such as (7a) through a process like that schematized in Figure 1.4, (iii). In other words, (7b) comes about through a rule whereby the Indirect Object of a ditransitive structure assumes the relation basic to an Object. (See the cited authors for more details of this analysis.)

Finally, (8a, b) illustrate an alteration in a nominal's basic assignment to an Oblique grammatical relation. In (8a), the argument concerned indexes the first person. Its Oblique relation is indicated by its being governed by a postposition *-'ay* 'to' and by the fact that this nominal is excluded from the reference of the agreement prefix. This agreement prefix, having zero shape, indexes a third person singular nominal *seuan-ide* 'man,' apparently the sole core nominal of the intransitive verb "come." But in (8b) there is a different agreement prefix, one that indexes both first person as well as third person singular animate. Also, if the first person is expressed in (8b), it is not oblique, but appears as an independent nominal in a direct shape. In fact, the optionality of the independent first person nominal in (8b) may be ascribed to the fact that its reference is carried redundantly in the prefix. The weight of the evidence, then, is that in (8b) the first person argument, corresponding to an Oblique Object in (8a), assumes the relation of the basic Subject. In addition, the nominal which bears this relation in the corresponding sentence (8a), "man," does not maintain this relation in (8b), since in the latter it is incorporated (whereas "man" as Subject in 8a cannot be incorporated). That is, the Subject relation basic to "man" in (8a) seems to be assumed by the first person in (8b). Accordingly, (8b) instantiates a role-remapping rule which reassigns a basic Oblique to Subject, a rule schematized in Figure 1.4, (iv). (For additional discussion, see Allen, Gardiner & Frantz 1984 and Allen & Frantz 1986.)

Among the rules which are depicted schematically in Figure 1.4, and which have been illustrated with Southern Tiwa data in (6)–(8), are two which alter the assignment of the Subject relation to some nominal in a basic structural configuration. These rules are schematized in Figure 1.4 as (ii) and (iv), and illustrated in Southern Tiwa by (6a, b) and (8a, b), respectively. If such is considered the essence of a voice rule, then one way of viewing voice is as what Barber 1975: 16 calls "a strategy to move NP's in and out of subject position." Furthermore, if marked voices reflect syntactic rules of the role-remapping sort,[15] then every marked voice is associated with an alteration in the semantic role basic to Subject.[16]

Before the present discussion is concluded, two topics should be addressed, the first having to do with justifying the grammatical relation Subject; the second concerning the status of what are called role-remapping rules above.

As regards the first topic, the identification of Subject and other grammatical relations in a clause, sentence or other predication may depend partially on particulars of morphology, as in the Southern Tiwa examples just discussed. More generally, however, it depends on the clustering upon some particular nominal position of properties which may be morphological (sometimes termed coding properties) or syntactic (sometimes termed behavior and control properties) (Keenan 1976a). Morphological properties of Subject, while varying from language to language, typically include direct case marking (in a language which marks nominals for case) and government of verbal agreement (in a language having verb–nominal concord). Syntactic properties of Subject also vary cross-linguistically, but typical ones include omissibility under conjunction reduction and government of cross-clausal nominal coreference in control constructions (such as those termed Equi and Subject Raising in traditional generative-transformational syntax). In English, both morphological and syntactic Subject properties devolve upon Agents of active structures and Patients of passives, as respectively illustrated below in (9) and (10) (from Comrie 1988: 13).

(9) a. We are running
   b. The man danced and (the man) ran away
   c. We persuaded Mother to leave (= that Mother leave)
   d. We believe Mother to have left (= that Mother has left)
(10) a. We were hit by him
   b. The man was hit by the woman and (the man) ran away
   c. We persuaded Mother to be examined by the doctor (= that Mother be examined by the doctor)
   d. We believe Mother to have been examined by the doctor (= that Mother has been examined by the doctor)

That the same cluster of properties characterizes active Agents and passive Patients to the exclusion of other nominals – e.g., active Patients, passive Agents, and Obliques of any sort – indicates that, in English, one grammatical status is shared by just these two entities. This is clear motivation for proposing a grammatical relation Subject independent of and noncoterminous with any other nominal status, such as the semantic role Agent.[17] However, the relation Subject, as defined by the properties illustrated in (9) and (10), is particular to English. While grammatical relations such as Subject are often said to be universal, attempts to define them cross-linguistically in terms of some specific set of morphological and/or syntactic properties have not been successful in the past (for some discussion see Johnson 1977a), although it may, nonetheless, be feasible to conceive of Subject in terms of prototypical properties (Keenan 1976a). Nevertheless, it remains undetermined at this time whether Subject and other grammatical relations have a constant identity across languages (Rosen 1984). Moreover, grammatical relations do not necessarily have a significant role in the grammatical

22 *The study of voice*

organization of every language (Foley & Van Valin 1984).[18] These facts have implications for voice typology and the characterization of voice rules, some of which will be enlarged upon below.

Concerning the second topic mentioned above, the status of role-remapping rules, it is worth noting that several writers have recently proposed an alternative to accounting for alternate mappings of nominals to grammatical relations through rules of syntax. This is achieved by treating voice rules as applying in lexical rather than syntactic representations. Under this view, rules of voice apply in the predicate-argument structure assigned in a verb's lexical entry. Lexical voice rules provide for alternations in the linking* of semantic roles with the Subject relation. For instance, the linking alternation schematized in the relation between (11a) and (11b) below is analogous in its effects to either of the syntactic role-remapping rules (ii) or (iv) in Figure 1.4.

(11) a.   <semantic role$_1$ semantic role$_2$ ...>
             | |
             Subject   non-Subject

     b.   <semantic role$_1$ semantic role$_2$ ...>
             | |
             non-Subject   Subject

The rule whose effects are schematized in (11) applies in the lexicon to specify alternate predicate-argument structures which a given verb may satisfy in distinct voices, rather than altering the assignments of grammatical relations to nominal positions in syntactic structures. The latter format of role-remapping rules is consistent with a multistratal* theory of syntax, while the former is consistent with a monostratal* theory. But this opposition of theoretical approaches cannot be pursued in detail here (see Ladusaw 1988; Klaiman in preparation; Section 3.2.1 below).

Regardless of approach, however, the kind of voice alternations considered in the present section comprise only one class of voice behaviors. For reasons to be clarified in the following section, this class of behaviors is termed derived voice*. As it turns out, a comprehensive theory of voice cannot be limited in its scope to processes of this type alone. Whether captured formally through role-remapping rules in syntax, or through alternate linking rules in the lexicon, this conception of

1.3 Voice as alternation in subject's participant status

voice behaviors is irrelevant to the systems which first inspired the concept of voice in grammars of antiquity.

1.3 Voice as alternation in subject's participant status

According to the preceding section, current grammatical treatments of voice concentrate, by and large, on rules which affect the semantic role content of the Subject position in structural configurations. The term usually applied to voice rules of this type is passive*. For instance, the type of voice alternation schematized in Figure 1.4 (ii), corresponds to an ordinary passive, or one in which the argument mapped to Object in a basic structural configuration assumes the Subject relation in a corresponding, nonbasic configuration. Another type, schematized in Figure 1.4, (iv), is called an oblique passive, or a passive in which a basic Oblique nominal assumes the Subject relation in a corresponding, nonbasic configuration. The particular variety of oblique passive illustrated in (8b) is a locative passive; but instrumental passives, benefactive passives, and other sorts of oblique passives are all possible. Another variety of passive is one that alters the mapping of a nominal to the Subject relation in a basic intransitive structure. This type is termed impersonal passive*; its properties have been discussed earlier (Section 1.1). In addition, another kind of derived voice closely related to passive, antipassive*, is discussed later (in the following section and in Chapters 3, 5).

Irrespective of the variety, passive presupposes a mapping from structures which are basic, hence unmarked (active), to structures which are nonbasic, or derived, hence marked (passive). Whether the structures in question are syntactic or lexical depends on which of two theoretical stances one chooses (see the conclusion of the preceding section). Nonetheless, either stance is consistent with one conception of the active/passive alternation: that it arises from a rule which maps from basic onto nonbasic, or derived, structures. This type of voice alternation can be termed derived voice*.

But in the classical literary Indo-European languages described in traditional grammars (see above, Section 1.1), the characteristic voice alternation, as Lyons 1968: 373 points out, is not active/passive. Only in two Indo-European stocks does a specific formal passive occur (Indo-Iranian and Hellenic). Rather, the characteristic Indo-European voice

24 *The study of voice*

alternation is active/middle. According to Lyons, "The implications of the middle (when it is in opposition with the active) are that the 'action' or 'state' affects the subject of the verb or his interests."

The Indo-European active/middle alternation can be illustrated with the Classical Sanskrit examples (12a, b). In this language, there are separate inflectional paradigms for active and middle categories of the verb. All finite, and some nonfinite, verbal forms obligatorily express the distinction. Many verbs, such as *kr̥-* 'make, do' in (12), inflect in either voice.

(12) a. Devadattaḥ   kaṭam   karoti
       Devadatta-NOM mat-ACC makes-SG **ACTIVE**
       'Devadatta makes a mat'
    b. Devadattaḥ   kaṭam   kurute
       Devadatta-NOM mat-ACC makes-SG **MIDDLE**
       'Devadatta makes (himself) a mat'

In both (12a) and (12b), *devadattaḥ* is semantically an Agent and *kaṭam* is semantically a Patient. In addition, *devadattaḥ* appears to have the same grammatical relation in each example, and the same is true of *kaṭam*. Specifically, *devadattaḥ* has the same set of formal properties (nominative case marking, government of verbal concord), appearing to be Subject in each example. Likewise, *kaṭam* appears in the accusative case, apparently maintaining the same grammatical relation, the Object relation, in each example.

It follows from this that active/middle alternations are to be distinguished from passivization. That is, the alternation of voices in (12a, b) reflects no remapping or reassignment of arguments among relational-structure statuses. Moreover, there is no ground for considering (12a) derivationally more basic – or, for that matter, derivationally less basic – than (12b). *Devadattaḥ* is both Agent and Subject of each example, and *kaṭam* is both Patient and Object of each example. The choice of active vs middle verbal marking correlates with no necessary alternation in the semantic roles linked to grammatical relations or core nominal positions in the structure of a clause. Accordingly, active–middle systems are of a distinct type from derived voice systems. Since rules of derived voice relating basic structural configurations to nonbasic or derived configurations seem inappropriate to their analysis (see discussion below), they are referred to as basic voice* systems.

While classical Indo-European languages such as Latin, Greek and

1.3 Voice as alternation in subject's participant status

Sanskrit may be the best-known examples, they are not the only examples of the basic voice type. Active–middle (basic) voice systems also occur in languages neither Indo-European nor ancient. Chapter 2 is devoted to a survey of systems of the basic voice type, although a few illustrations will not be out of order here.

Consider first modern Tamil, a Dravidian language of southern India. In this language, verb stems display a distinction of geminated vs single obstruents, as illustrated in (13a, b) (from Paramasivam 1979: 95). European-language writers on Tamil usually describe this as an opposition of "Strong" and "Weak" verbal forms.

(13) a. Kuzantai   ennai   utai -kkir   -atu
       child-NOM   me-ACC   kick present **STRONG** SG NEUT
       'The child is kicking me'
    b. Kuzantai   kālai   utai -kir   -atu
       child-NOM   leg-ACC   kick present **WEAK**   SG NEUT
       'The child is kicking its legs (in the air)'

Formally, the Tamil verbal voice opposition resembles the Classical Sanskrit alternation illustrated in (12a, b) in various respects. In Tamil, the Weak/Strong opposition is marked on all finite and on some non-finite verbal forms, like the alternation of active and middle in Sanskrit. Again, many verbal bases in each language admit both forms; a Tamil instance in point is *utai* 'kick' in (13a, b). Finally, like active/middle in Indo-European, the opposition of Strong/Weak in Tamil involves no necessary alteration in the assignment of semantic roles to nominal positions. In both (13a) and (13b), "child" is Agent as well as Subject (it takes nominative case and governs verbal concord), so that there is no alteration in the semantic content of the Subject. Rather, the selection of voice depends on whether the denoted situation comprises what Tamil traditional grammars label a "self-act" as opposed to an "other-act," i.e., whether the principal effects of the action accrue to the logical subject as contrasted with some other participant.

While the Tamil voice alternation amounts to an active–middle system, and thus pertains to the basic voice type, it is historically and functionally distinct from the other well-known voice system of the Indian subcontinent, that of Sanskrit. This will be emphasized in the detailed overview of basic voice given below in Chapter 2. At this point, however, to dispel any lingering doubt as to the existence of basic voice systems independent of Indo-European influence, one additional system will be illustrated. Unlike Tamil, the language concerned has had no significant history of contact with Indo-European languages until the most recent times.

Modern Fula (Fulani) contrasts with both Tamil and Sanskrit in having neither written records of its archaic stages, nor an indigenous grammatical tradition. It is a member of the West Atlantic group of Niger-Congo languages, spoken in Senegal, Gambia, and other areas of western and northern Africa.

Fula has three voices, each associated with a distinct inflectional paradigm of the verb. Over half the verbal bases can inflect in more than one paradigm – active, middle or passive – while about a fifth of the lexical verbs, such as ɓorn 'dress' in (14a–c) (from Arnott 1970: 260), can inflect in all three.

(14) a. 'o ɓorn -ii   mo   ŋgapalewol
        he dress past **ACTIVE** him gown
        'He dressed him in a gown'
    b. 'o ɓorn -ake   ŋgapalewol
       he dress past **MIDDLE** gown
       'He put on a gown'
    c. 'o ɓorn -aama   ŋgapalewol
       he dress past **PASSIVE** gown
       'He was dressed in a gown'

Among the three voices in Fula, passive seems secondary, since no verb inflects exclusively in the passive. Certain verbs inflect in the middle alone, others in the active alone; accordingly, these seem to be primary voices. In addition, many verbs inflect in just the active and middle. A typical instance is *res-* 'deposit,' illustrated in its respective active and middle forms in (15a, b) (from Arnott 1970: 255).

(15) a. 'o res   -ii   ɗum
        he deposit past **ACTIVE** it
        'He set it down, deposited it on the ground'
    b. 'o res   -ake   ɗum
       he deposit past **MIDDLE** it
       'He put it on deposit (for his own future use)'

As in the earlier Sanskrit and Tamil examples (12a, b) (13a, b), so in (15a, b) there is no alteration in the allocation of semantic roles to

1.3 Voice as alternation in subject's participant status

nominal positions. The voice opposition appears to be basic, not derived.

Now that a few illustrations have been furnished, something should be said about traditional and posttraditional approaches to the structural analysis of basic voice systems, or systems of active/middle alternations.

Traditionally, as noted earlier, the middle in opposition to the active is said to express a distinction of meaning relating to alternate views of the logical subject's participation in the denoted action. The middle, in contrast to the active, signals the subject's coincidence with the locus of the action's principal effects. This is borne out in Classical Sanskrit (12b), Tamil (13b) and Fula (15b).

While acknowledging that active/middle and active/passive alternations are traditionally considered distinct types, some writers have proposed accounting for the former, like the latter, through rules of derivation operating upon grammatical relations in clausal syntax (Barber 1975, Hubbard 1985). This is an important departure from the traditional view, and so deserves a brief examination. The account of Barber 1975 will be cited for this purpose.

Barber argues that alternations of verbal voice marking in Classical Greek "flag" identities of Subject and non-Subject nominals. According to her, "The middle voice . . . seems to function fundamentally as a strategy for marking identities between the surface subject and other NP's in the sentence proposition" (p. 17).

In support of this, Barber (pp. 18–19) offers the following examples (16)–(19). She states that, where a verb is transitive and its Object is expressed, as in (16), the use of the middle voice indicates an identity between the Subject and an unexpressed Indirect Object. In the structure underlying (16b), then, there supposedly occurs an unexpressed non-Subject (Indirect Object) coreferential to the Subject; while in (16a), this argument is absent. Barber also claims that, if a transitive Object is unexpressed, then the middle indicates its coreference with the Subject. As a result, the sentence either has reflexive* meaning (Subject does action to self) as in (17); or reciprocal* meaning (referents of plural Subject do action to each other), as in (18) (second gloss). Finally, if a sentence is intransitive, then the middle in contrast to the active is said by Barber to mark an identity between the Subject and, again, an unexpressed Indirect Object; she provides the illustration in (19b).

(16) a. Hair -ō   moiran
       take **ACTIVE** share
       'I take a share'
    b. Hair -oumai   moiran
       take **MIDDLE** share
       'I choose (take for my own benefit) a share'
(17)   Lou -omai
       wash 1SG **MIDDLE**
       'I wash myself'
(18)   Lou -ometha
       wash 1PL **MIDDLE**
       'We wash ourselves' OR
       'We wash each other'
(19) a. Politeu   -ō
       be-citizen 1SG **ACTIVE**
       'I am a citizen/have civic rights'
    b. Politeu   -omai
       be-citizen 1SG **MIDDLE**
       'I act as a citizen/carry out my civic rights for myself'

In Barber's analysis, there is little to contest if the argument identities she speaks of are interpreted loosely – that is, if the middle is construed merely as expressing "the fact that the agentive subject is also affected in some way by the action," in her phrasing (p. 17). One Greek grammar puts it as follows: "The middle voice shows that the action is performed with special reference to the subject ... The middle represents the subject as doing something in which he is interested" (Smyth 1974: 390).

However, Barber evidently wishes to portray middle voice specifically as a strategy for signaling a syntactic process, since she speaks (pp. 23–4, fn. 7) of particular "NP positions" as "accessible to this identity-marking operation in Greek." Among these positions she includes "direct object, indirect object, and genitive (possessor) of direct object" (the last of these being illustrated by her example *lou-omai* [I-wash **MIDDLE**] *tas* [the] *kheiras* [hands] 'I am washing my hands'). Barber states, further, that there is no functional difference between the use of middle voice in instances such as (17)–(18) and the alternative use of reflexive and reciprocal pronouns, respectively, for marking Subject/non-Subject identities.

1.3 Voice as alternation in subject's participant status

Barber's analysis treats middle as distinct from passive, since middle does not involve reassignments of arguments among nominal positions. Nonetheless, middle voice purportedly marks a syntactic process which, like passive, operates over nominals mapped to grammatical relations in basic structural configurations. It is worth considering whether this account is both correct for early Indo-European languages, such as Greek, as well as apt for active–middle or basic voice systems in general.

On analysis it turns out that, in a number of particulars, the account does not apply to certain active/middle alternations. For instance, according to this account, one middle voice function is to mark reflexives and reciprocals. Some kinds of reflexives and reciprocals do take middle marking in some basic voice systems, such as Classical Greek and Classical Sanskrit (see Section 2.3). But not in all. In modern Tamil, for instance, verbs which alternate for both voices occur in the active (Strong) as contrasted with the middle (Weak) in reflexive and reciprocal expressions. This is illustrated in (20a, b) (from Klaiman 1982b: 269; cf. examples 13a, b above). In both examples, the reflexive/reciprocal marker is an independent morpheme, the pronoun *taṉ*; this is the only marker specific to reflexive/reciprocal function in the language. (For further discussion of Tamil, see Section 2.2.)

(20) a. Avaṉ   taṉṉai   utaittuk
       he-NOM self-ACC kick-PTCPL **STRONG**
       (*utaintu)   koṇṭāṉ
       (kick-PTCPL **WEAK**) took-SG past MASC
       'He kicked himself'
   b. Paiyaṇkaḷ oruvarai oruvar   utaittuk
       boys-NOM one another-ACC kick-PTCPL **STRONG**
       (*utaintu)   koṇṭārkaḷ
       (kick-PTCPL **WEAK**) took-PL past
       'The boys kicked one another'

Further evidence that middle voice may not specifically mark reflexive meaning occurs in Fula. Fula has a set of suffixes which modify the transitivity and voice potential – i.e., the valence* – of verbal bases. In Arnott 1956, 1970, these suffixes are referred to as extensions. One extension is Reflexive *-i(t)*. A verbal base marked with this extension invariably takes middle inflections. However, middle transitive verb forms are not semantically equivalent to extended Reflexive forms. In

(21)–(23), for instance, the b-examples, illustrating transitive middles, have distinct glosses from the c-examples, which are the corresponding forms marked with the extension.[19] (These examples are from Arnott 1970: 342–3.)

(21) a. femmb -a
 shave **ACTIVE**
 'shave'
 b. femmb -o
 shave **MIDDLE**
 'get oneself shaved'
 c. femmb -it -o
 shave R **MIDDLE**
 'shave oneself'
(22) a. moor -a
 dress hair **ACTIVE**
 'dress someone's hair'
 b. moor -o
 dress hair **MIDDLE**
 'get one's hair dressed'
 c. moor -it -o
 dress R **MIDDLE** hair
 'dress one's own hair'
(23) a. (no active)
 b. saah -o
 be generous **MIDDLE**
 'be generous to/present to'
 c. saah -it -o
 be R **MIDDLE** generous
 'be generous to in return/present in return'

Given the contrasting glosses of the b- and c-examples in (21)–(22), it seems inappropriate to claim that the semantic function of middle voice is to mark reflexivity *per se*, as this seems to be the function of the extension. (This is taken up again in Section 2.1.)

In Indo-European as well, there are middle voice functions which defy the analysis proposed by Barber. For instance, in Classical Sanskrit there are various verbs whose status in basic structural configurations is transitive, but which occur in the middle when used intransitively for expressing spontaneous actions – events that occur, as it were, of their

1.4 Voice as marker of pragmatic salience assignment

own accord, without the control* or instigation of an Agent. Consider the verb *nam-* 'bend' in (24) (from Speijer 1973: 240). This verb is active and transitive in (24a), middle and intransitive in (24b). Example (24b) expresses spontaneous action, and is not passive. (Ordinary passives in Sanskrit permit the Agent to be expressed; but **namate daṇḍaḥ devadattena* 'The stick bends by Devadatta', as a variant of ex. 24b, is impossible.)

(24) a. Devadatto   namati   daṇḍam
       Devadatta-NOM bends-SG **ACTIVE** stick
       'Devadatta bends the stick'
    b. Namate   daṇḍaḥ
       bends-SG **MIDDLE** stick-NOM
       'The stick bends'

Incidentally, (24b) is parallel to the earlier Classical Greek example (19b). If one applies Barber's analysis of (19b) to (24b), it would follow that the function of the middle voice in the latter is to indicate the coreferentiality of "stick," the Subject, with an unexpressed Indirect Object – making the basic meaning of the sentence "The stick bends for itself." Not only is this inaccurate, but it is also illogical, since basic Indirect Objects (bearing the semantic role Experiencer) are characteristically animate, while "stick" is not.

The comparison of basic and derived voice types is pursued further in Chapter 2. For the present, it is worth reiterating that basic type, not derived type systems are those whose description first prompted grammarians to posit a voice category in grammars of classical Indo-European languages. In general usage, the term voice refers to either basic or derived systems, but the two are typologically distinct. And as we are about to observe, there is a third typologically distinct class of alternations in verbal marking to which the term voice is sometimes applied.

1.4 Voice as marker of pragmatic salience assignment

Apart from the derived and basic voice types discussed in the two preceding sections, there is another class of phenomena occasionally treated under the rubric of voice. This third voice type, pragmatic voice*, is manifested when alternations in verbal marking signal the variable assignment to sentential arguments of some special pragmatic status or salience. At least two varieties of pragmatic salience* are signaled in this way.

First, there are systems in which verbal marking signals the relative ontological* status of nominal referents. As pointed out by several writers (e.g. Dixon 1979 and Comrie 1980: 61–3), speakers and hearers tend to assign salience to nominals on the basis of their referents' relative real-world capacities to control situations, or in terms of their likeness or even their physical proximity to the participants in the speech event. For instance, a dog has less salience in the mental universe of a typical speaker/hearer than do members of the human species, and much less salience than a group of humans that includes the speaker and/or the hearer. Actions are regarded naturally as proceeding from relatively more salient to relatively less salient participants, rather than in the reverse direction.

In some languages, these facts are grammaticized through special marking of verbal bases when sententially denoted actions proceed from ontologically less salient to more salient participants. A system in which verbs are marked in this way is often termed an inverse system*. Other terms associated with systems of this sort are obviative and fourth person.

The following illustrations (25a, b) (due to Wolfart 1973: 25) are from a North American language of the Algonquian family, Plains Cree. In (25a) the verb is marked with an element -ā. This element, termed a direct theme sign, signals that the action proceeds in the ontologically plausible or expected way, with the argument "we" acting on the argument "dog." On the other hand, in (25b) there appears a marked or inverse theme sign -iko, indicating that the action proceeds in the inverse manner, or with the ontologically less salient "dog" acting on the more salient "we."

(25) a. Ni- sēkih -ā   -nān atim
       1   scare theme **DIRECT** 1PL dog
       'We scare the dog'
    b. Ni- sēkih -iko   -nān atim
       1   scare theme **INVERSE** 1PL dog
       'The dog scares us'

In Algonquian linguistics, the alternation illustrated in (25) is traditionally termed direct/inverse. Alternations of this sort are characteristic

1.4 Voice as marker of pragmatic salience assignment

not only of the Algonquian family, but are also ascribed to some Wakashan languages such as Nootkan (Whistler 1985) as well as to Chukotko-Kamchatkan languages of Siberia (Comrie 1980, 1981a: 115). Possibly there are other language groups in which the same or similar behavior is manifested (Whistler 1985: 255–6).

A noteworthy feature of direct–inverse systems is that, apart from the alternation of voice marking, there is no formal mechanism for signaling which of the participants encoded by core arguments in a clausal structure acts on which – as is obvious from a comparison of (25a, b).

Another point worth emphasizing is that, except in certain rare instances (discussed below in Chapter 4), pairs of expressions such as (25a, b) do not freely alternate. In an inverse language, a situation such as that in (25a), in which "we" acts on "dog," can be encoded only in a direct (noninverse) voice of the verb, while the converse situation denoted in (25b) can be encoded only in an inverse, not a direct, voice. In this respect, direct–inverse is unlike the kinds of systems discussed in the preceding sections. For instance, it differs from a system of derived voice, in which marked voice forms arise from, and alternate with, basic or unmarked forms. (This point is elaborated on below in Section 4.3.)

It has been observed that, in a direct–inverse system, alternations of verbal marking reflect the relative ontological salience of nominal referents in clausally or sententially denoted situations. Because ontological salience is defined in relation to the viewpoint of participants in a discourse, the voice type concerned may be called pragmatic voice*.

The same voice type also encompasses a second class of voice behaviors related to another type of pragmatic salience. In this type, alternations of verbal marking reflect the relative importance or prominence of nominal referents in the information structure* of the discourse. This kind of salience, too, is pragmatic, since it is based on the informational needs of hearers and the expressive intentions of speakers.

In some languages, alternations in verbal marking signal alternate assignments to nominals of statuses of informational salience, such as topic*. Such information-salience encoding systems are sometimes called focus systems*. They are treated as voice alternations by some writers. Examples (26a, b) (from Ayres 1983: 42) illustrate an alternation in the assignment of informational salience in the Mayan language Ixil.

(26) a. A-   k'oni   in   ta'n uula
       2SG ERG shoot   1SG ABS with sling
       'You shot me with a sling'
    b. Uula a-   k'oni -b'e   in
       sling 2SG ERG shoot index 1SG ABS
       'With a sling you shot me' (Chajul dialect)

In (26a), an oblique nominal linked to the Instrument role appears sentence-finally and is governed by the preposition *ta'n* 'with'. However, in (26b), this argument appears fronted in the clause and stripped of the preposition. According to Ayres, the suffix *-b'e* which appears on the verbal base in (26b) is an index of instrumental focus, meaning that the Oblique–Instrumental nominal is the locus of informational salience in the clause. Ayres states that Ixil also has markers for focusing or assigning informational salience to other nominal statuses.

Ayres emphasizes the distinctness of focus, as illustrated in (26b), from other processes in Mayan languages which can be termed voice processes. According to Ayres, processes of the latter group are distinct from focus constructions both formally and functionally.

Formally, the non-focus voices entail alterations in the coding (morphological) relations between a verb and one or more nominals of the clause. For instance, the sort of voice alternation shown below in (27a,b) (from Ayres, p. 27), called an antipassive* voice, involves both changes in nominal case as well as an alteration in the agreement marking on the verb. It is to be distinguished from focus voice because it involves reassignments of arguments among nominal positions, thus comprising a kind of derived voice.

(27) a. Kat a-   q'os   in
       aspect 2SG ERG hit   1SG ABS
       'You hit me' (Chajul and Nebaj dialects)
    b. Kat   q'os -on   axh   (s   wi')
       aspect hit voice 2SG ABS (on me)
       'You hit (me)' (Chajul and Nebaj dialects)

However, in a focus voice construction, such as (26b), there is no evidence of alterations in coding. In both (26a) and (26b), the second person is indexed by an agreement prefix in an ergative case form; and the first person, similarly, is indexed in both examples by an enclitic pronoun in an absolutive case form. Also, in (26b), the verb carries no marker of agreement with the focus "sling." This suggests that the voice alternation entails no alteration in morphosyntactic relations between the verb and its nominals.

The contrasting characteristics of derived and focus voices in Mayan languages are further discussed below in Section 5.1. But here it is worth noting that voice alternations signaling variable assignments of informational salience are not found in Mayan languages alone. Similar voice systems are also documented in certain Austronesian languages, particularly in Philippine languages of the Malayo-Polynesian subgroup of Austronesian.

The formal analysis of these systems is currently controversial. There is a decades-old tradition of treating Philippine focus alternations as voice variation. This tradition is followed by some recent writers, such as Foley & Van Valin 1984. However, there are also writers who treat Philippine focus constructions as passives. And according to a third viewpoint, Philippine focus alternations manifest a special type of case, not voice, patterning called ergative*. (Ergativity is further discussed in Chapters 3 and 5 of the present work.) Philippine voice, for its part, will be explored in detail in Section 5.2.

For the present, it is worth observing that in Mayan and Philippine languages alike, informational salience is usually assigned to nominals that are relativized or questioned. Moreover, in Philippine focus systems, focused nominals tend to have definite reference, and indefinite nominals are not focused. This is significant, since referential definiteness is a natural manifestation of the information-structure salience encoded in these systems.

Both information-salience and inverse systems are evinced in alternations of verbal marking which reflect the assignment to sentential arguments of some salience whose basis is in the situation of speaking, or pragmatic salience. As mentioned above, systems of this type are discussed in both current and traditional literature under the rubric of voice, although they are distinct from the voice types surveyed in the two preceding sections. Along with derived and basic voice systems, then, pragmatic voice* systems comprise a third voice type.

1.5 Argument structure and voice

Although the voice behaviors discussed in the preceding three sections are typologically diverse, they resemble one another in that all are signaled by morphological oppositions in the verb. Functionally, too, they can be said to share a characteristic, albeit one which is difficult to formulate precisely. However, pretheoretically, one can state that all the above-described voice behaviors involve variability in the ways in which nominal positions in basic structural configurations are assigned to or correlate with roles that pertain to the structures of events or actions in the world. Such roles can be called participant roles*.

Here it is assumed that ontological or other pragmatic statuses (as discussed in Section 1.4), participant statuses (as discussed in connection with middle voices in Section 1.3) and semantic roles (as alluded to in Section 1.2) all represent kinds of participant roles. It is assumed, further, that participant roles of each sort correlate with categories of participants in the real-world situations which are encoded through linguistic structures.

The principal purpose of this section is to clarify what is meant by participant roles. Of chief concern is the idea of logical-argument structure and the definition of the semantic roles which accrue to arguments thereof. The need to clarify this motivates several recent theories of argument structure.

Section 1.1 above mentions a premise common to these theories: that every verb can be assigned a lexical representation, a predicate-argument structure*, in which relations that the corresponding logical predicate bears to essential or core arguments are mirrored by the verb's relations with a set of core nominal positions. Core arguments correspond to the logically required participants in the situation denoted by the verb, and, as such, can be identified with logical statuses of subject, object, and so on.

Also, within a verb's predicate-argument structure, core arguments are essential to defining what might be called the verb's argument frame*. This refers to a representation of what a verb's inherent characteristics contribute to the interpretation of clauses in which it appears. Valence, the specification of the number and types of nominal positions with which a verb combines to form a predication, is a factor in the verb's argument frame.

For immediate purposes, a more detailed treatment of the components of verbal predicate-argument structures is unnecessary. However, it is worth noting that nominal positions in predicate-argument structures – or, properly speaking, those nominal positions that correspond to logical-level arguments – may be associated with a variety

1.5 Argument structure and voice

of semantic roles. Semantic roles are part of a grammatical system, not part of the structures of events. They can be thought of as the contents of nominal positions in predicate-argument structures. Conversely, one can say that, at the logical level, each argument of a predication is assigned a certain semantic role by virtue of the corresponding nominal's position in the predicate-argument structure of the verb.

For instance, the English verb "build" is assigned a predicate-argument structure with two core nominal positions (both corresponding to logical arguments) that may be designated x and y. The corresponding semantic roles consist of what each argument respectively contributes to the interpretation of a predication having "build" as its predicate. The role of the x-argument may be termed the "builder" role and that of the y-argument the "built" role. As this suggests, the number of distinct semantic roles in any language is a factor of the combined valences of all the verbs in the language.

However, most formal theories of argument structure assume that types can be identified over the range of semantic roles in a system or, putting it another way, "that the agent arguments of two different verbs have something in common" (van Riemsdijk & Williams 1986: 241). This assumption is foundational to the concept of thematic relations*. In the 1960s, serious interest in thematic relations seems to have arisen due to research on case grammar as a model of structural representation. In more recent grammatical theory, they are discussed under the rubric of theta-roles* (or for maximum brevity, θ-roles).

Dowty 1989: 74ff. outlines a heuristic (formal procedure) for defining theta-roles. This involves taking the intersection of what he terms the "lexical entailments" of particular positions in the argument frames of verbs. For instance, there is an assumed correspondence between the "builder" position in the argument frame of the verb "build" and some position in the argument frames of other verbs such as "bake," "sculpt," and so forth. Further, it is assumed that certain properties devolve upon core nominals by virtue of their occupying a common position in the argument frames of various verbs.

Dowty explains how the lexically entailed properties of a nominal position are identified as follows: "if a sentence x *builds* y is true, then it is necessarily also true that x performs purposeful actions, that as a result of these actions a structure or other artifact y comes into existence, and so on" (p. 75). Thus a semantic role "builder" is defined by the set of properties that necessarily hold of x if the sentence x *builds y* is true. Similarly, the lexical entailments of "bake," sculpt," etc. identify properties of corresponding nominal positions in these verbs' argument frames. A thematic relation or theta-role, then, amounts to the semantic role type which is shared across a set of argument frames by corresponding nominal positions. Putting it another way, the theta-role, or semantic role type, arises at the intersection of the lexically entailed properties attributable to a particular nominal position. For instance, the semantic role type of the *x*-argument for the class of verbs comprising just "build," "bake," and "sculpt" consists in the shared, lexically entailed properties *x performs some action*, *x by virtue of acting effects some state of affairs*, and so on.

It has been noted in Section 1.1 that typical theta-roles which devolve upon core nominal positions S, A and P in structural configurations are Agent and Patient, while typical noncore theta-roles include Experiencer, Location, Instrument and Beneficiary. Given a heuristic for defining theta-roles such as that proposed by Dowty, one might anticipate that each of the roles just mentioned has some definition upon which researchers in grammatical theory agree. However, as Dowty observes, "two problems with thematic roles remain persistently vexing: (i) lack of agreement among linguists as to which thematic roles exist, and the absence of any obvious way to decide this question, and (ii) the lack of any effective way to independently justify the assignment of noun phrases to thematic roles in particular sentences" (p. 70).

Dowty's (ii) comprises the problem of linking*, which is alluded to above (Section 1.2). However, less tractable (in the present writer's view) is (i), the absence of a consensus as to which theta-roles universal grammar requires and how the required roles are to be defined. As another writer comments, "Many different theories make reference to θ-roles (under one name or another) yet there is unfortunately no presently available theory of what the range of possible roles is and how you might tell in a given context which one you're dealing with; one must, for the present, rely on intuition in large part" (Sells 1985: 35).

One limitation of the above-described heuristic in resolving questions of how to define theta-roles is that it is based on an *a priori* assumption, the assumption that nominal positions in argument frames can be independently identified. That is, according to the heuristic, a theta-role comprises the intersection of the properties which, by lexical entailment, accrue to some particular nominal position in the argument frames of a class of verbs. Hence, to define a theta-role, the analyst must know in advance which verbs have in common a particular nominal position in their argument frames, thereby comprising a lexical class. In turn, this presupposes some procedure for comparing argument positions across the predicate-argument structures of verbs.

Rather than formally defined theta-roles, many writers presently work with informal characterizations of their content. Several working characterizations of various theta-roles are furnished in Figure 1.5 (for others not given in this figure, consult Andrews 1985, Geniušienė 1987: 39ff., and Dowty 1989). Note that Agent has contradictory characterizations (some writers associate volitionality with this semantic role type, others do not), indicating the arbitrariness in current conceptions of thematic relations.

Present grammatical theory awaits a consensus as to how argument frames are organized. At this moment, a growing number of theorists appear inclined to believe that argument frames are organized according to a template or theta-role (theta-) hierarchy*.[20] A theta-hierarchy orders arguments according to a scale of markedness, thereby predicting, for each theta-role represented in an argument frame, its relative likelihood of linking* with core nominal positions such as subject, object, and so on.

Not all present theories of argument structure posit theta-hierarchies, however. Further, among those that do, there is currently no agreement regarding what theory-independent principles one may appeal to in order to establish which theta-roles are required, let alone their precise ordering within the theta-hierarchy.

There is also currently no consensus on the well-formedness conditions that apply in argument frames, constraining the allocation of theta-roles to nominal positions. Dowty 1986, 1989 points out that two conditions are posited in recent argument structure theories.

One is a condition of independence*; any theta-role must be characterizable independent of the representation of verbal lexical structures, and, accordingly, must exist independent of the meanings of individual verbs. This means that theta-roles must not be redundantly implicated by verbal semantics, since this would make their inclusion in lexical structures superfluous.

A second condition is completeness*: any argument in a predicate-argument structure must be associated with a theta-role. To be sure, in predicate-argument structures, nonargument positions may occur. (A standard instance is an idiom nominal such as "tabs" in the expression

Agent

a participant which the meaning of the verb specifies as doing or causing something, possibly intentionally (i.e. because (s)he wants to) (Andrews 1985: 68).

The Agent NP is identified by a semantic reading which attributes to the NP will or volition toward the action expressed in the sentence (Jackendoff 1972: 32).

the role of an active, animate being who intentionally causes something (Marantz 1984: 32).

Patient

a participant which the verb characterizes as having something happen to it, and as being affected by what happens to it (Andrews 1985: 68).

roles of objects that bear the brunt of the action described by the verb (Marantz 1984: 32).

Theme

a participant which is characterized as being in a state or position, or changing its state or position (Andrews 1985: 70).

With verbs of motion the Theme is defined as the NP understood as undergoing the motion . . . With verbs of location, the Theme is defined as the NP whose location is being asserted . . . (Jackendoff 1972: 29, 30).

roles of objects which the verb specifies to undergo a changed state or location or of which the verb indicates a location (Marantz 1984: 32).

Experiencer

a participant who is characterized as aware of something (Andrews 1985: 70).

Location

the location of a participant . . . the place where something is done (Andrews 1985: 70).

the thematic relation associated with the NP expressing the location, in a sentence with a verb of location (Jackendoff 1972: 31).

Instrument

a participant that the Agent uses to act on the Patient (Andrews 1985: 70).

Beneficiary

the person for whom something is done (Andrews 1985: 69).

Figure 1.5 Some definitions of thematic relations

1.5 Argument structure and voice

"keep tabs on." Since it is considered a non-argument nominal, it is assigned no thematic relation in the lexical representation of the verb "keep.")

Most theories of argument structure concur about these two fairly elementary principles, but beyond them, there is some vacillation as to what further well-formedness conditions constrain argument frames. One current formalism, lexical–functional grammar, stipulates as part of its argument structure theory a condition of biuniqueness*: every argument position must be assigned a unique theta-role, and vice versa.

Other current theories forgo this rather strong condition in favor of a weaker condition such as uniqueness* or distinctness*. These are differentiated according to the view one takes of argument structure. To clarify, consider example (28):

(28) John likes himself

According to Dowty 1989, the analysis of argument structure in this example depends on which view one adopts of its thematic organization. Either theta-roles are individuated relative to argument positions in lexical structures, or they are individuated relative to the denotata of arguments; that is, to participants in verbally encoded events.

Under the first of these views, *John* and *himself* in (28) are distinct arguments by virtue of representing distinct positions in the argument frame of "like." Given this assumption, there is no inconsistency in distinguishing properties that accrue to *John* in respect of its theta-role (Agent) from properties that accrue to *himself* in virtue of its theta-role (Patient). In particular, the fact that these arguments are coreferential does not contravene their individual identity as arguments. On the contrary, *John* and *himself* are assigned different theta-roles. This occurs in conformity with a condition of distinctness* which stipulates that no particular theta-role can be borne by two different arguments (where "arguments" refers to nominal positions in an argument frame). This condition is weaker than the above-discussed biuniqueness, since it does not specifically rule out the possibility of one argument position bearing two theta-roles.

On the other hand, under the second view, with theta-roles individuated to the denotata of arguments, (28) has not two distinct arguments, but one. The two inherent or core theta-roles of the verb, Agent and Patient, are regarded as devolving jointly upon one argument. Under this view, the structure of (28) nonetheless conforms to uniqueness*, a condition that no particular theta-role can accrue to two different arguments (where "arguments" refer to participants in a verbally denoted situation). This condition, too, is weaker than biuniqueness, in that it allows one argument to be associated grammatically with more than one theta-role.

Firm criteria for deciding among the several hypothetical argument structure conditions outlined above (biuniqueness, distinctness, uniqueness) await formulation at the present time. It is not inconceivable, however, that some indeterminacy or range of options in the organization of argument structure is a fact of grammatical organization across languages. For example, it will be observed below, Section 2.2, that alternative criteria for argumenthood (along the lines just discussed) are actually useful in accounting for variability of voice functions in basic (active–middle) systems. Further research may clarify this possibility.

However, even assuming future advances in research on the theory of argument structure, there remain fundamental problems for the analysis of voice. In a comprehensive voice theory, theta-roles such as Agent, Patient and so on may have applicability to some systems – for instance, those of the derived voice type – but they are out of correspondence with the theoretical machinery needed to characterize others. It is doubtful, for instance, that the pragmatic salience which is encoded in inverse and focus systems – discussed in Section 1.4 above – can be treated as a feature of the lexical entailments of verbs. Similarly, it is far from obvious that in basic voice systems, discussed above in Section 1.3, the factor of subject affectedness arises from the lexical entailments of middle verbs. This factor seems, rather, to be implicated through an analysis of situations encoded by the middle construction (as discussed below in Chapter 2). Accordingly, it is not certain that theta-roles, as conceived in current formal grammar, represent fundamental argument statuses – participant roles – that figure in the organization of all types of voice systems. Chapter 6 of the present work discusses how grammatical theory might take account of the various kinds of nominal statuses, or participant roles, needed for a comprehensive account of voice.

The balance of the present work is devoted to exploring the typology of voice, with emphasis both on the varying functions of particular voice systems, as well as on the category's status in the grammatical organization of languages. In this chapter, groundwork for what follows has been laid by discussing grammatical concepts essential to the description of voice systems (Sections 1.0, 1.1, 1.5) and by introducing a tentative,

1.5 Argument structure and voice 43

broadly conceived typological classification of voice systems (Sections 1.2–1.4). The plan for the remainder of the work is as follows.

Chapter 2 overviews the functions of voices in various active–middle or basic voice systems. Chapter 3 brings up significant observations concerning the lexicon and voice. It proposes a scheme for the classification of predicates in terms of certain features of inherent lexical meaning, and places basic voice among a larger set of recurrent patterns which reflect a particular organization of the verbal lexicon.

Chapters 4 and 5, respectively, deal with inverse and informational salience (focus) systems as two subtypes of pragmatic voice. Finally, Chapter 6 attempts to formally and theoretically unify the findings of the survey of voice types.

2 Middle voice and basic voice systems

2.0 Preliminaries

Systems of active/middle voice alternations have been briefly surveyed in Section 1.3, where they are assigned to a voice type called basic*. They have been contrasted with a second class of voice systems termed derived*.

As discussed in Chapter 1, derived voice encompasses several types of passives* and certain (often lexically restricted) alternations of valence*. In the analysis of derived voice systems, marked voice categories implicate reallocations of arguments among positions in structural configurations. By contrast, basic voice has so far been portrayed principally in terms of its being unamenable to such an analysis; that is, in terms of characteristics it lacks.

This chapter is intended to lay the groundwork for a positive characterization of the functions of basic voice alternations, with emphasis on the middle voice category. In the following sections, three basic (active–middle) voice systems will be surveyed. The findings will support a view of the basic voice type as a particular pattern of organization of a language's verbal lexicon. The basis of this organization criss-crosses the distinction between transitivity and intransitivity, comprising a counterpart to the organization of the lexicon in ergative* and active* languages (the details of which are considered in Chapter 3).

The following are the major points of the present chapter. In system after system, verbs which alternate for active and middle voices are basically transitive, not intransitive. However, any system with alternating active/middle verbs also has a class of exclusively middle verbs and a class of exclusively active verbs.

There is a tendency for exclusively middle verbs to be intransitive, but the correlation is not absolute. Exclusively middle and exclusively active

2.0 Preliminaries

verbs may be either transitive or intransitive. Contrastingly, middle forms of alternating active/middle verbs tend to be intransitive.

For variably active/middle inflecting verbs, the middle in opposition to the active implicates the logical subject's affectedness* in a variety of ways which may vary from system to system. However, verbs of the exclusively middle class tend to be deponent*, expressing physical states or mental dispositions presupposing the subject's animacy and control*. By contrast, exclusively active verbs are rarely deponent.

To recapitulate, this chapter develops a view of basic voice as a kind of patterning over the lexical verbs of a system. This is different from the views of some previous writers, particularly as regards the functions of the middle category.

One of these views is that the middle signals lowered transitivity*. Consistent with this, Kuryłowicz 1964: 74 states, "The middle voice is by its origin nothing else than a development of . . . [an] etymological *intransitive* value . . ." Kuryłowicz states that in Indo-European languages this value is a "secondary function of the passive" (emphasis in the original).

Passive, of course, is a type of derived detransitive construction. An association between middle and passive voice function is reflected in some writers' use of the term mediopassive* to refer broadly to nonactive voices. This term also reflects a view many hold that, diachronically, the middle category has extended its functions in some Indo-European stocks so as to take on passive meaning.[1]

A different, though related, view held by others (such as Barber 1975) is that the middle functions as a marker of valence* alternations (polyadicity*), especially valence reduction ("recession" in the terminology of Geniušienė 1987). Also, various writers are prepared to extend the term middle to reductions in the valence of lexical verbs even where no particular morphological marking is involved, as in the English alternation *Max is cooking the rice* vs *The rice is cooking*.

A third view expressed by a number of writers is that there exists an association between middle and reflexive*. In numerous languages, a reflexive morpheme is associated with various kinds of reductions in valence, marking such functions as passive, inchoative* meaning, detransitive* meaning, and reciprocal* meaning, in addition to reflexive meaning proper or the basic function of the reflexive (i.e., referent of subject does action to self; this meaning will also be referred to below as the semantic reflexive*). The valence-reducing functions a reflexive morpheme may encode arise, presumably, by extension of the reflexive's basic function, since any morpheme which expresses reflexivity automatically marks the verb as having one less referentially distinct argument than the number of arguments it is lexically assigned (for some discussion see Haiman 1976).

Aside from writers who view the middle's basic or central function as reflexive (Woodcock 1959: 14; and see citations in Geniušienė 1987: 8; 61, fns. 2, 3),[2] there are also those who see extensions in the functions of reflexive morphemes as evidence of middle voice behavior even when there is no inflectional middle voice as such (Croft, Shyldkrot & Kemmer 1987). Also, certain writers identify middleness with reflexive morphology even when it does not express reflexive meaning proper. For instance, when a reflexive morpheme marks a passive construction (the reflexive passive; see Siewierska 1984: 162ff.; Langacker & Munro 1975; Andersen 1987: 13), some writers (see e.g. Geniušienė 1987: 112) invoke the term "mediopassive." Incidentally, reflexive marking also encodes the antipassive*, a derived voice, in a number of ergative–absolutive languages (see Paterson 1983, Levin 1987).

Middle voice's relations with transitivity, valence and reflexivity will be critically examined below. However, the present chapter does not specifically concern detransitive, passive or reflexive constructions. Rather, in what follows, middle voice and the basic voice type are studied through systems where the middle serves as one term of a formal opposition in the morphology of the verb.

Such systems are, of course, well known in classical Indo-European, the languages which first inspired the concept of voice in Western grammar. Nonetheless, active–middle systems are by no means confined to languages that are ancient or Indo-European. Section 1.3 has discussed systems of this kind in Fula, a West Atlantic (Niger-Congo) language, and Tamil, a Dravidian language of southern India.

The next three sections comprise a survey of the functions of the middle category in these systems. We begin in Section 2.1 with Fula, a language far remote from classical Indo-European. Fula seems worth first examination not only because its voice system is presumed free of Indo-European influence, but also because, among the languages to be discussed, it has the richest inventory of different functions associated with the formal middle category.

Subsequently, Section 2.2 deals with basic voice in Tamil, and Section

2.3 with basic voice in certain branches of Indo-European. Finally, Section 2.4 discusses verbal organization in relation to the middle category and to the basic voice type.

2.1 Fula

Among languages of the West Atlantic group of Niger-Congo, Fula is currently the best researched and has the largest number of speakers. Most of its speakers are dispersed over an enormous area extending from the Atlantic coast around Senegal and Gambia eastward as far as northern Nigeria, southern Chad, and even the Sudan. Bibliographies on Fula and the other West Atlantic languages appear in Sapir 1971 and in Westermann & Bryan 1970.

Regional varieties of Fula show many mutual differences (see Arnott 1970: 3–5 for some discussion). The following sketch of voice behaviors is based principally upon Arnott 1956, 1970, which deal with the Fula of Gombe Division of northern Nigeria. From time to time, however, a western Fula dialect will be cited, that of Fuuta Tooro in northern Senegal, which is described by Sylla 1979, 1982. Data below is from Gombe Fula unless specifically noted otherwise.

One remarkable feature of the Fula system of verbal conjugation is the organization of virtually all finite, and even most nonfinite, inflections into three categories, schematized in Figure 2.1 (this is a simplified and regularized version of Table 1 in Arnott 1956: 131).

Arnott refers to the categories represented in the three columns of Figure 2.1 as voices. He comments (p. 130, fn. 4):

The term Voice has been used in the past because of the general resemblance between the behaviour of the affix series of Fula and those of Greek. It is retained here, without any desire to emphasize the resemblance. A comparison of the Middle Voice in Fula with the Greek middle, and also with the French reflexive, does indeed show a striking number of similarities, even in detail, but there are equally conspicuous differences which must not be overlooked.

It will be shown below that, as Arnott suggests, the Fula paradigm labeled Middle in Figure 2.1 is like the Greek inflectional middle in certain major respects. First, invariant middle verbs in Fula, as in Greek, express a particular range of meanings called deponent*. Deponency relates to actions of physical or mental disposition presupposing the logical subject's animacy and control*. Second, like the Greek middle, the Fula middle is associated with nonpunctual temporal

48 Middle voice and basic voice systems

	Active	Middle	Passive
Affirmative tenses			
Past			
General	-ii	-ake	-aama
Emphatic	-∅/-u	-i	-a
Narrative	-i	-ii	-aa
Future/Habitual			
General	-ai	-oto	-ete
Indefinite	-ma/-uma	-ooma	-eema
Narrative	-(a)ta	-(o)too	-(e)tee
Nonpunctual			
Stative	ɗon- . . . -i	ɗon- . . . -ii	ɗon- . . . -aa
Progressive	ɗon- . . . -a	ɗon- . . . -oo	ɗon- . . . -ee
Nonindicative			
Subjunctive	-a	-oo	-ee
General Imperative	-∅/-u	-a	
Habitual Imperative	-atai	-atai	
Negative tenses			
A. Past and Stative	-aayi	-aaki	-aaka
B. Future/Habitual/ Process	-(a)taa	-(a)taako	-(a)taake
C. Quality	-aa		

Figure 2.1 Summary of Fula verbal conjugation, based on Arnott 1956: 131, Table 1

categories of the verb. Finally, the functions of the Fula middle, when in contrast to the active, are similar to many of the functions of the Greek middle, although (contrary to Arnott, quoted above) the semantic reflexive is not a specifically middle function.

To begin the discussion, some examples of Fula lexical verbs (or, as Arnott terms them, radicals) in different voices are presented in (1) (cf. examples 14a–c in Chapter 1 above), in (2) (from Arnott 1956: 130), and in (3) (in Fuuta Tooro dialect; from Sylla 1979: 254, 253).[3] Each of (1)–(3) illustrates a radical which is capable of inflecting in all three voices. Three-voice radicals form a substantial proportion of Fula's inventory of simple radicals. (Nonsimple, or derived, radicals are discussed later.)

(1) a. 'o ɓorn -ii   mo ŋgapalewol
       he dress General Past **ACTIVE** him gown
       'He dressed him in a gown'
    b. 'o ɓorn -ake   ŋgapalewol
       he dress General Past **MIDDLE** gown
       'He put on a gown'
    c. 'o ɓorn -aama   ŋgapalewol
       he dress General Past **PASSIVE** gown
       'He was dressed (by someone) in a gown'

(2) a. 'o loot -ii   ɓiyiko
       she wash General Past **ACTIVE** child
       'She washed the child'
    b. 'o loot -ake
       she wash General Past **MIDDLE**
       'She washed (herself)'
    c. 'o loot -aama
       she wash General Past **PASSIVE**
       'She was washed by someone'

(3) a. nyamlu   -∅   -de
       loan/borrow **ACTIVE** INF
       'to loan (to someone)'
    b. nyaml   -aa   -de
       loan/borrow **MIDDLE** INF
       'to borrow, receive something as a loan'
    c. Ali nyaml   -aama   kaalis
       Ali loan/borrow General Past **PASSIVE** money
       'Ali has been loaned some money'

In discussing the categories active, middle and passive, Arnott distinguishes between what he calls differential* and inherent* meanings or semantic functions. The distinction relates to whether a particular voice is respectively nonprimary or primary for a given radical. Fula radicals which occur in all three voices, such as those illustrated in (1)–(3), are termed by Arnott AMP radicals. Their primary voice is the active. The active is also the primary voice of radicals which occur in the active alone; those which alternate between the active and the middle; and those which alternate between the active and the passive. These are respectively called A, AM and AP radicals.

In the case of AMP or three-voice radicals such as those illustrated in (1)–(3), the middle and the passive are nonprimary voices, and their functions are differential as opposed to inherent. A differential function shared by both of these, according to Arnott 1956: 135, is valence reduction or lowered transitivity (detransitivization*): "the Active verbal is capable of supporting one more object than the Middle and Passive verbal with the same radical." This is borne out in each of (1)–(3), since the b- and c-examples each have one less object than the corresponding active or a-examples.

In the case of some AMP radicals, Arnott 1956: 136 associates a second differential function with the middle voice, reflexive*. Example (2b) above is furnished by Arnott to illustrate the middle's differential reflexive function.

The Fula middle's putative association with each of the above-noted differential functions will be examined critically in the present section. In some instances, nonsimple or derived radicals formed by applicative* stem extensions will be cited. These will prove useful for evaluating what meanings are proper to the middle, as contrasted with meanings inherent to various classes of radicals with which the middle voice conjugation merely happens to be compatible.

Inherent functions of the Fula middle are also discussed below. Inherent, as opposed to differential, functions are those encoded by a voice when it is the primary voice of some class of radicals. The Fula middle's inherent functions are of particular concern for the present discussion. However, before either they or the differential functions of the middle can be discussed in detail, a digression is necessary concerning the relationship between voice and valence.

In Fula any simple radical is associated with a basic valence. In a corresponding derived radical this valence is altered in some way, sometimes with effects on voice potential. We will now consider, in order, altered valence and altered voice potential.

In Fula every simple radical belongs to a valence class. A simple radical assigning a single core argument (subject) is intransitive. A simple radical assigning more than one core argument is transitive; the radicals illustrated in (1)–(3) are all transitive.

Transitive radicals with one nonsubject core argument (as illustrated in 2a) are bivalent; while transitive radicals with two nonsubject core arguments (as in 1a and 3a) are trivalent. (Arnott 1970's respective terms are "one-object" and "two-object.")

A derived radical may be formed by suffixation to a simple radical of one or more special elements. These suffixes are termed radical extensions.[4] Certain extensions, when added to a simple radical, affect neither its valence nor its voice potential (the inventory of voice categories in which the radical inflects).

But there are also extensions which do alter both the valence and voice potential of a simple radical. One class of these is the applicative* extensions. Extension of a simple radical by an applicative results in a derived verbal stem with an increased valence.[5]

Fula has three applicative extensions. One is the *-an* extension illustrated in (4c) (this is a Fuuta Tooro form, cited from Sylla 1979: 283 and Marantz 1982b: 330). Sylla and Marantz term this extension Benefactive, although Arnott 1970 refers to it as the Dative extension. The simple radical corresponding to the extended stem in (4c) is illustrated in (4a), while the ungrammatical (4b) shows that the increase in the simple radical's valence is contingent upon the extension.

A second extension, *-ir*, is termed by Arnott the Modal extension and is illustrated in (5c) (from Arnott 1970: 348). This extension has the effect of adding to the valence of the simple radical (illustrated in 5a) an instrumental argument. The added argument may be expressed either as a prepositionally marked oblique as in (5b), or alternatively as a prepositionless core nominal (object), as in (5c). (On derived object status in applied constructions, see below.)

Cross-linguistically, the most common applied construction is the morphological causative. A construction can be classed as a morphological causative when there is specific morphological encoding of causativity within the verb. Moreover, a causative is associated with an additional core argument, a causer or causal agent, added to the set of core arguments assigned by the corresponding noncausative verb. Therefore the morphological causative is a kind of applicative.

Fula has both a morphological and a nonmorphological, or periphrastic, causative. These are respectively illustrated in the Fuuta Tooro examples (6b) (from Sylla 1979: 368) and (7b) (from Sylla 1979: 330 and 1982: 160). The periphrastic causative (7b) is superficially complex and biclausal, having two overt predicates. However, the morphological causative in (6b), with the extension *-n*, has only one predicate and is overtly monoclausal.[6]

(4) a. Takko def -ii   gergotal
       Takko cook General Past **ACTIVE** chicken
       'Takko cooked chicken'

    b.*Takko def -ii sukaaɓe
       Takko cook General Past **ACTIVE** children
       ɓe   gergotal
       determiner chicken
       'Takko cooked chicken for the children'
    c. Takko def -an -ii sukaaɓe
       Takko cook DAT General Past **ACTIVE** children
       ɓe   gergotal
       determiner chicken
       'Takko cooked chicken for the children'

(5) a. 'o haɓɓ -ii gujjo
       he tie   General Past **ACTIVE** thief
       'He tied up the thief'
    b. 'o haɓɓ -ir -ii gujjo 'e ɓoggol
       he tie   Modal General Past **ACTIVE** thief with rope
       'He tied up the thief with rope'
    c. 'o haɓɓ -ir -ii gujjo ɓoggol
       he tie   Modal General Past **ACTIVE** thief rope
       'He tied up the thief with rope'

(6) a. Aali am -ii
       Ali dance General Past **ACTIVE**
       'Ali danced'
    b. Aamadu am -n -ii Ali
       Aamadu dance CAUSE General Past **ACTIVE** Ali
       'Aamadu made Ali dance'

(7) a. Aali dar -iima
       Ali stop General Past **MIDDLE**
       'Ali stopped'
    b. Mi wad -ii Aali dar -aa -de
       I make General Past **ACTIVE** Ali stop **MIDDLE** INF
       'I made Ali stop'

While both nonactive voices and applicative extensions are associated with alterations in basic valence, only applicative extensions mark augmented valence. Unlike nonactive voices, moreover, applicative extensions are not associated with valence reduction. Also, Fula applicative extensions are unlike nonactive voices formally in that they consist of stem extensions, which never terminate morphologically complete words. By contrast, the markers of voice in Fula comprise the system of verbal conjugation, and may terminate morphologically complete words (verbs). For these reasons, an analysis of Fula morphosyntax must distinguish between applicatives and voices. (Also see Chapter 1, note 16.)

Nonetheless, the applicatives just discussed do interact with voice, since they affect not only the valence of a simple radical, but also its voice potential. A nonsimple radical derived by addition of a Dative or Modal applicative suffix has one more passive than the corresponding simple, nonextended radical. While some simple radicals ordinarily cooccur with two postverbal, prepositionally unmarked nominals (such as the verbs "send" and "loan"), these radicals are not trivalent and do not have two passives. Nonsimple radicals with applicative extensions, by contrast, are trivalent, and do have two passives.[7]

Thus, compare the bivalent unextended radical illustrated in (8a), which cannot passivize in the way shown by the ungrammatical (8b) (but can passivize in the way shown by the earlier ex. 3c), with the applicative extended radicals illustrated in (9)–(10). These have multiple passives. (Ex. 8a is from Arnott 1956: 137; 8b is due to Arnott, personal communication [and see Sylla 1979: 262ff.]; 9a–c are due to Arnott 1970: 355; and 10a, b are due to Arnott 1970: 349.) In addition to the Dative and Modal applied passive forms below in (9) and (10), causative extended radicals also passivize, according to Arnott 1970: 346 (and they take middle inflections too "where appropriate," although in Arnott's work no relevant illustrations are furnished).[8]

(8) a. Mi   wu'y   -ii   mo   deptere
        I   loan/borrow General Past **ACTIVE** him book
        'I loaned him a book'
   b.*Kaalis nyaml   -aama   Ali
        money loan/borrow General Past **PASSIVE** Ali
        'Money has been loaned (to) Ali'

(9) a. ɓe   kirs   -an   -ii   min   ŋgaari
        they slaughter DAT   General Past **ACTIVE** us   bull
        'They slaughtered a bull for us'
    b. ŋgaari hirs[9] -an   -aama   min
        bull   slaughter DAT General Past **PASSIVE** us
        'A bull has been slaughtered for us'
    c. Min   kirs   -an   -aama   ŋgaari
        we   slaughter DAT   General Past **PASSIVE** bull
        'We have had a bull slaughtered (for us)'

(10) a. Wudere nden   loot -ir   -aama
       cloth   determiner wash Modal General Past **PASSIVE**
       saabunde
       soap
       'The cloth has been washed with soap'
    b. Saabunde nde'e   loot -ir   -aama
       soap   determiner wash Modal General Past **PASSIVE**
       'This soap has been washed with'[10]

As shown above, extension of a simple radical by an applicative may increase its voice potential, i.e. its passivizability. An extended Dative or Modal radical has a larger number of passives than the simple radical on which it is based.

The effects of passivization in Fula are as follows. First, the verb inflects in the conjugation listed in the rightmost column of Figure 2.1. In addition, the logical subject of the corresponding simple radical is suppressed; it cannot be expressed overtly. Some logical nonsubject must occupy the syntactic position ordinarily assigned to the subject, and in case passivization applies to an extended Dative or Modal radical, there is more than one possible nominal (re)assignment to subjecthood.

But ordinarily, there is not more than one middle construction which can be derived from a simple radical upon addition of an applicative extension. In fact, a radical extended in this way does not necessarily inflect for the middle voice at all. Thus unlike the passive, the middle does not always signal detransitivization. Although some derived applicatives inflect in the middle, they are not detransitive (see n. 8, examples ib, iib for illustrations). But this finding is inconsistent with the middle's supposed differential function of detransitivization, alluded to earlier. An alternative possibility is that the middle, while not a marker of detransitivization *per se*, expresses a meaning or class of meanings that happen to be oftentimes consistent with intransitivity, as in (2b) above.

To weigh this possibility, it will be useful to proceed to the earlier-promised examination of Fula primary voice functions, especially those of the middle.

Figure 2.2 lists the valence classes of simple radicals in Fula. (This is a simplified version of a table in Arnott 1970: 188, fn. 5, based on a survey of 1,500 simple radicals.) The classes in which the middle is a non-

Three-voice radicals

AMP	A(M)P
transitive (20%)	transitive (24%)

Two-voice radicals

AM	AP	MP
transitive/intransitive	transitive	transitive
(less than 1%)	(1%)	(10%)

One-voice radicals

A	M	P
intransitive	intransitive	intransitive
(31%)	(13.5%)	(less than 0.5%)

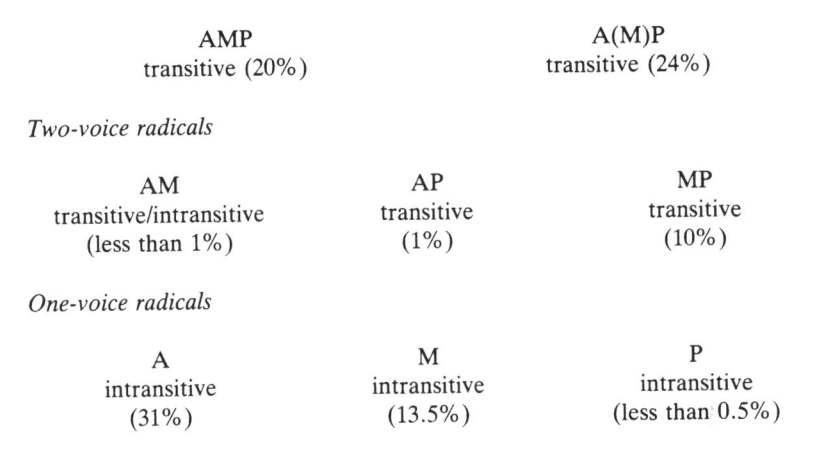

Figure 2.2 Three-voice, two-voice, and one-voice valence classes of simple radicals in Fula

primary voice, expressing differential rather than inherent meanings, are the AMP, A(M)P, and AM classes. Here A, M and P respectively designate active, middle and passive inflection; the parenthetical (M) in A(M)P will be explained below. The figure also shows the valence classes in which the middle is a primary voice, expressing inherent middle meanings. These are the M and MP classes.

Arnott provides percentages of the total proportion of each class of radicals from among the 1,500 surveyed. These percentages are included in Figure 2.2. The figure also lists correlations between a radical's valence class (which relates to its voice potential) and its transitivity. Although not in Arnott's original table, this information is culled from his published work and included in the figure.

Figure 2.2 reveals that valence reduction (or detransitivization) relates to voice potential in a particular way. While all one-voice radicals are intransitive, they do not all inflect in any one voice. One-voice radicals can be invariantly passive (P radicals), invariantly middle (M radicals) or invariantly active (A radicals). Accordingly, it is not the case that A radicals are transitive and other one-voice radicals intransitive.

On the other hand, all two- and three-voice radicals are basically transitive (multivalent). Moreover, the structures in which they occur are nearly always transitive when these radicals inflect in their primary voice. If this primary voice is the middle (as in the case of MP radicals), then radicals inflected in this voice are transitive.

In this connection, it bears note that among the limited set of AM radicals are some exceptional verbs which are intransitive when inflected in the active but transitive when inflected in the middle.[11] This adds evidence that valence reduction or detransitivization is not a specific function – differential or inherent – of the middle.

The evidence also indicates that there is no regular alternation of active and middle voices. Rather, each appears to represent a distinct basic voice category. However, active and middle each frequently alternate with the passive. Passive voice is always associated with a reduction in the valence that a given radical assigns in its primary voice. Moreover, unlike active and middle, the passive is almost never a primary voice. Although a P class is listed in Figure 2.2, its membership is negligible.[12]

The conclusion is that passive is a derived rather than a basic voice (in the sense of a voice that a radical assigns in a basic structural configuration). Middle and active, by contrast, are basic voices, each capable of being associated with a variety of valences. Thus there are intransitive, bivalent, and trivalent simple radicals which assign primary middle voice, just as there are intransitive, bivalent and trivalent radicals which assign primary active voice. Below, (11a–c) respectively illustrate trivalent, bivalent, and monovalent (intransitive) radicals with primary active voice; (12a–c) are corresponding illustrations of radicals with primary middle voice. (11a–c and 12a–c are from Arnott 1956: 135.)

(11) a. 'o holl -ii   mo ɗ um
       he show General Past **ACTIVE** him it
       'He showed it to him'
    b. 'o nodd -ii   mo
       he call General Past **ACTIVE** him
       'He called him'
    c. 'o maay -ii
       he die General Past **ACTIVE**
       'He died'
(12) a. 'o ug   -ake   mo nde
       he throw General Past **MIDDLE** him it
       'He threw it at him'

b. 'o sal- ake nde
   he refuse General Past **MIDDLE** it
   'He refused it'
c. 'o dar -ake
   he stop General Past **MIDDLE**
   'He stopped'

Since valence reduction does not seem to be a true middle function, some positive characterization of the Fula middle's functions remains to be discovered. One can anticipate that at least some of these functions will be compatible with the reduced valence or intransitivity so often associated with this voice.

According to Arnott, the inherent meanings of the middle as a primary voice (i.e., a voice of M and MP radicals) comprise "various semantic categories covered by the generalization: 'deliberate activity with the body or mind, or part of the body, particularly in relation to another person or thing'" (1970: 412). This class of radicals assigns logical subjects whose referents have two faculties, animacy and control*.

Animacy is a fairly straightforward concept. The term control*, for the time being, is used in the sense of the capacity and potential of a participant to both engage in and withdraw from engaging in a verbally denoted action. (This concept will be further elaborated upon in the following chapter.) Control thus inheres in a lexical verb's semantics. It is neither directly correlated with nor determined by the verb's valence or transitivity.

Figure 2.3 lists some radicals of the M and MP classes which are representative of semantic categories consistent with Arnott's generalization "deliberate activity with the body or mind." In the asterisk notes at the foot of the figure are listed some contrasting meanings which accrue to some Fula *activa tantum* or A radicals.

Meanings which, according to the figure, are characteristic of middle primary voice radicals are worth comparing with some characteristic meanings of A radicals, such as those cited in the asterisk notes to the figure. According to Arnott 1956: 141, 1970: 412, Appendix 12, many A radicals of his sample fit into one of two semantic groups.

One group comprises some 100 radicals that express "acquisition or possession of a quality" (Arnott 1970: 412). Instances include *ranw-* 'be white' (and other color verbs); *mawn-* 'be big,' *tedd-* 'be heavy,' *nayw-*

Class 1   Psychological and affective actions
(a) Mental activities, frames of mind and attitudes, excluding uncontrollable or reflex actions*

M	hiim-	'think, reflect'	MP	maand-	'bear in mind'
	miil-	'ponder'		huunj-	'know by heart'
	hiis-	'calculate'		hinn-	'have pity on'
	duŋg-	'be content'		hool-	'trust'
	sun-	'be sad'		saah-	'be generous (toward)'

(b) Speech reflecting some particular mental attitude

MP	barr-	'threaten'
	yaas-	'condole with'
	jaɓɓ-	'welcome'
	sal-	'refuse'
	siid-	'joke with'

Class 2   Physical actions
(a) Intransitives expressing particular bodily postures**

M	jooɗ-	'sit'
	tur-	'stoop'
	'oppin-	'squat'
	dicc-	'kneel'

(b) Bodily actions, excluding uncontrollable or reflex actions***

M	yin-	'swim'	MP	wakk-	'carry on shoulder'
	ficc-	'buck'		'yell-	'balance on head'
	yuurn-	'peep'		ɗaf-	'cling to'
	nisɓ-	'sniff'		baas-	'dodge'
	dar-	'stop, stand'			

(c) Telic (goal-presupposing) verbs of bodily motion, aim, or physical assault****

M	yott-	'arrive'	MP	ma'y'y-	'climb, mount'
				ɓad-	'approach'
				'yaɓɓ-	'overstep'
				saal-	'go past'
				'udd-	'fall on, attack'
				faag-	'pursue'
				'ug-	'throw at'

   * such as the A(M)P radicals 'annd- 'know,' faam- 'understand'
  ** as contrasted with transitive AMP radicals such as depp- 'set down/sit down,' wuur- 'incline/bend,' hipp- 'invert/lie face downwards,' fukk- 'throw down/lie down,' ɓamt- 'raise up/raise oneself up'
 *** such as the A radicals ɗisl- 'sneeze,' moos- 'smile,' and the A(M)P radicals nan- 'hear,' yi'- 'see'
**** as contrasted with atelic or non-goal-presupposing verbs of physical motion such as the A radicals war- 'come,' yah- 'walk,' dill- 'go,' dogg- 'run'

Figure 2.3 Semantic classification of some Fula radicals with middle primary voice, based on Arnott 1956 and 1970, Appendices 11, 12 'be old,' *hall-* 'be wicked,' *'yo'y-* 'be cunning,' and *tekk-* 'be thick, fat.' These verbs are compatible with, but do not require, animate logical subjects. They generally express either uncontrollable states or dispositions not related to momentary acts of will.

The other group consists of radicals expressing natural cries, such as *woy-* 'cry,' *wodd-* 'roar, bellow,' *siik-* 'creak, chirp,' *hur-* 'snort,' *'uum-* 'groan,' *sony-* 'tinkle.' Some of these radicals, likewise, do not require animate logical subjects. However, those taking animate subjects express what may be characterized as instinctive or reflex actions. Neither group of A radicals expresses actions which are both controllable and characteristically animate.

Thus to the extent that exclusively active-inflecting (A) radicals and primary middle (M and MP) radicals each display congruity in their semantics, one observes a contrast in their characteristic meanings. Radicals of the latter group express deponent* meanings, while those of the former group express nondeponent meanings.[13]

Traditionally, the term deponent refers to any *media tantum* or invariant middle verb with active meaning (see below, Section 2.3). However, in the present context, deponency means the expression of action presupposing the logical subject's animacy and control, and relating either to physical state or attitude, or to mental disposition. Deponent semantic functions contrast with the expression of reflex physical states or postures and noncontrollable mental dispositions, which as a class comprise nondeponent semantic functions.

Apart from its inherent deponent meanings or semantic functions, the Fula middle is associated with several differential functions, functions it characteristically expresses when the middle-inflecting verb has some other primary voice. Several groups of differential middle functions will now be considered.

One group of differential middle functions relates either to the temporal characteristics of the denoted action or to its modality*.

For instance, there is a differential middle function related to Aktionsart*, the verb's inherent temporal sense. Aktionsart contrasts with tense* and aspect*, temporal characterizations of action which are not inherent to the sense of the verb.

Fula has two nonpunctual temporal categories termed Stative and Progressive. They are included in the conjugations listed in Figure 2.1. Both are encoded by a characteristic *don-* prefixed to the radical. As the table shows, verbs in the Stative and Progressive can inflect in any of the three Fula voices.

60 *Middle voice and basic voice systems*

But for AMP or three-voice radicals, Arnott 1970: 280 notes a statistical correlation of differential middle voice with nonpunctual categories, especially the Stative. Thus while an A or active-only radical such as *tekk-* 'be thick, be fat' may characteristically occur in the Stative (see below, example 13), an AMP radical such as *loot-* 'wash' when in the Stative usually assigns the middle inflection (14a). The corresponding Stative passive (shown in 14b) implicates a suppressed noncoreferential Agent. (Examples 13 and 14a, b are from Arnott, pp. 280, 281.)

(13) 'o   ɗon-   tekk   -i
      he   nonpunctual be thick Stative **ACTIVE**
      'He is fat (in a state of having thickened)'
(14) a. 'o   ɗon-   loot -ii
        he   nonpunctual wash Stative **MIDDLE**
        'He is clean (in a state of having washed)'
     b. ŋgel   ɗon-   loot -aa
        it-diminutive nonpunctual wash Stative **PASSIVE**
        'It (e.g. the child) is washed'

Aside from its affinity for nonpunctual temporal categories, the differential middle is also associated with irrealis modality. Categories listed in Figure 2.1 which express this modality are the Future/Habitual and the Negative (particularly, within the latter, the Negative B, which has a nonpunctual semantics). Arnott 1956: 138, 1970: 257 notes that the middle characteristically combines with the General Future and Negative B categories in expressing meanings of potentiality and impossibility, respectively. These are illustrated in (15a, b) (from Arnott 1970: 257, 295). Also, in the Negative A category (which has a past nonpunctual semantics), middle and passive alternate in encoding durative or nonpunctual meanings, as illustrated in (16a, b) (Arnott 1970: 293). One can compare the (affirmative) use of the Stative (also shown in these examples).

(15) a. Nde loot -oto   na
        it wash General Future **MIDDLE** particle
        'Can it be washed?'
     b. Nde loot -ataako
        it wash Negative B **MIDDLE**
        'It cannot be washed'

(16) a. 'i ɗon-   jog -ii   sawru na
       he nonpunctual hold Stative **MIDDLE** stick particle
       'aa'aa 'o jog -aaki
       no   he hold Negative A **MIDDLE**
       'Is he holding a stick? – No, he is not holding (one)'
    b. Mi tammii 'o ɗon-   haɓɓ -aa
       I think   he nonpunctual tie   Stative **PASSIVE**
       'aa'aa 'o haɓɓ -aaka
       no   he tie   Negative A **PASSIVE**
       'I think he is tied up. – No, he is not tied up'

One of the middle's differential functions, then, appears to be the expression of noneventuality*, or action which is irrealis and/or nonpunctual.

The radicals listed in Figure 2.2 as A(M)P radicals provide additional evidence for this. A(M)P radicals are listed as a distinct class in Arnott 1970 owing to the discovery that nearly all verbs earlier classed in Arnott 1956 as AP radicals do accept middle inflections when noneventuality* is expressed. Middle inflections accrue to these radicals when they appear in the Stative; in the General Future expressing potentiality of action; and in the Negative B expressing impossibility. Some illustrations are given in (17) (from Arnott 1970: 258). Incidentally, the fact that nearly a quarter of Fula radicals are transitive and accept middle voice inflections only in the specialized temporomodal category of noneventuality suggests that this category is a middle voice function.[14]

(17) a. Mi winnd -ii   'innde maako
       I write General Past **ACTIVE** name his
       'I wrote down his name'
    b. 'innde maako ɗon-   winnd -ii
       name his   nonpunctual write Stative **MIDDLE**
       'His name is written down'
    c. 'innde maako winnd -ataako
       name his   write Negative B **MIDDLE**
       'His name can't be written'

It will be recalled that Arnott 1970 posits an association between valence reduction, or detransitivization, and the Fula middle voice. However, none of the middle voice functions – inherent or differential –

which have been critically examined thus far account for this association. At the present stage of the discussion it remains unaccounted for.

In order to pursue this matter, we will now consider other differential functions of the Fula middle. There are two groups of functions that bear particular scrutiny. One is a detransitivizing function which Arnott has discussed in especial detail. The other consists of several differential middle functions which have affinities with reflexivization. To complete the examination of the Fula middle, we will take up each of these groups of functions in turn.

Arnott distinguishes one differential middle function under the rubric of neuter*. It is illustrated below in (18b) (examples 18a, b are from Arnott 1970: 256). He also recognizes a group of differential middle voice functions which he classes as reflexive. They are distinguished into three subclasses termed direct, indirect, and causative reflexive. The b-examples of (19)–(21) are Arnott's respective illustrations of these middle reflexive functions. (Examples 19a, b are repeated from 2a, b above; 20a, b are repeated from Chapter 1, 15a, b; and 21a, b are from Arnott 1956: 137.)

(18) a. 'o ɓill -ii ɗum
he squash General Past **ACTIVE** it
'He squashed it'
b. 'o/ɗum ɓill -ake
he/it squash General Past **MIDDLE**
'He got squashed/it squashed'
(19) a. 'o loot -ii ɓiyiko
she wash General Past **ACTIVE** child
'She washed the child'
b. 'o loot -ake
she wash General Past **MIDDLE**
'She washed (herself)'
(20) a. 'o res -ii ɗum
he deposit General Past **ACTIVE** it
'He set it down, deposited it on the ground'
b. 'o res -ake ɗum
he deposit General Past **MIDDLE** it
'He put it on deposit (for his own future use)'
(21) a. Mi moor -ii mo
I braid hair General Past **ACTIVE** him/her
'I dressed his/her hair'

b. Mi moor -ake
I braid hair General Past **MIDDLE**
'I got my hair dressed'

Although Arnott does not class the middle's neuter function illustrated in (18b) as reflexive, it is reflexive-like in a certain sense to be explained shortly. (The next chapter further discusses the general phenomenon of neuter verbs and their semantics.) Arnott does label as reflexive the functions illustrated in the b-examples of (19)–(21). But these functions are not all the same.

In order to clarify the reflexive or reflexive-like character of these several middle functions, there is a need at this point in the presentation for a more precise understanding of reflexivity. For this purpose it will now be useful to briefly outline Fula's formal strategies for encoding reflexivity.

One strategy involves the use of an independent pronoun meaning "self." An illustration is (22), in the Fuuta Tooro dialect (from Sylla 1979: 36).

(22) Takko moor -ii hooremun altine
Takko braid hair General Past **ACTIVE** self Thursday
'Takko dressed her own hair on Thursday'

As (22) shows, in such forms, the usual voice assigned is the active. Another way of encoding reflexive and reflexive-like meaning, and one that is of greater interest for the succeeding discussion, is by the use of stem extensions.

It will be recalled that Fula has applicative extensions, stem formants which signal an increase in a simple radical's valence. Fula also has two stem extensions which, in contrast with the applicatives, are associated with valence reduction. Arnott terms these extensions Reflexive and Reciprocal.[15] The former is illustrated in (23b) (examples 23a, b are from Sylla 1982: 116) and (24b) (examples 24a, b are from Arnott 1956: 137). The latter is illustrated in (25b) and (26b) (examples 25a, b and 26a, b are from Arnott 1970: 358, 359).

(23) a. War ɓe
kill-imperative **ACTIVE** them
'Kill them!'
b. War -t -o[16]
kill R imperative **MIDDLE**
'Kill yourself!'

64 *Middle voice and basic voice systems*

(24) a. Mi   moor   -ii   mo
     I   braid hair General Past **ACTIVE** him/her
     'I dressed his/her hair'
   b. Mi   moor   -it   -ake
     I   dress hair R General Past **MIDDLE**
     'I dressed my own hair'
(25) a. 'o   hokk -ii   Bello ŋgapalewol
     he   give   General Past **ACTIVE** Bello gown
     'He gave Bello a gown'
   b. ɓe   ndokk -indir   -ii   ŋgapaleeji
     they give   Reciprocal General Past **ACTIVE** gowns
     'They gave each other gowns' (see n. 9)
(26) a. 'o   ɗon-   yerd -ii   mo
     he   nonpunctual trust Stative **MIDDLE** him
     'He trusts him/has trust in him'
   b. ɓe   ɗon-   ŋgerd -ootir   -i
     they nonpunctual trust   Reciprocal Stative **ACTIVE**
     'They trust each other/have trust in each other' (see n. 9)

As these examples show, reflexive and reflexive-like semantic functions can be encoded in Fula by middle voice and/or by affixation to a simple radical of a valence-reducing extension. In order to discern a basis for distinguishing the reflexive and reflexive-like meanings encoded through these formal alternatives, it will be helpful at this point to briefly consider one recent theory of the structure of reflexives.

Geniušienė 1987: 53ff. proposes a theory of reflexives according to which every lexical verb is associated with a structure represented by a three-level diagram, called a diathesis*. The diathesis accounts for interconnections among referential structure, semantic role (thematic) structure, and syntactic (grammatical relations, i.e. relational) structure. According to Geniušienė, a theory incorporating diathesis representations facilitates a viable typology of reflexive constructions, since reflexive semantic functions generally presuppose coincidence in a verb's core nominals at some level of its diathesis.

For instance, the diathesis of a nonreflexive transitive verb, such as *outwit*, is shown below in Figure 2.4, (Ai); while a related reflexive diathesis for this verb might be either (Aii) or (Aiii). The first reflexive diathesis, (Aii), involves suppression of the object relation. It might correspond to an example such as Spanish *Pepe se despista* 'Joe outwits himself.' The second reflexive diathesis, (Aiii), can be instantiated by the English *Joe outwits himself.* The first kind of reflexive, (Aii), can be referred to as a diathetical reflexive*, meaning a reflexive involving modification in a diathesis at more than the referent level alone; while the reflexive type (Aiii), by contrast, is nondiathetical.

Whether diathetical or nondiathetical, the type of reflexive shown schematically in Figure 2.4 (Aii, Aiii) is defined by one core referent's omission and the consequent assignment of the other to two semantic roles. Geniušienė refers to this type as a semantic reflexive*. However, reflexive marking also cross-linguistically encodes other meanings or semantic functions which are distinct from the semantic reflexive; and these, too, Geniušienė attempts to account for in her theory.

For example, the reciprocal*, schematized in Figure 2.4 (B), involves a modification of the basic transitive diathesis (Ai). Although distinct from the semantic reflexive, the reciprocal diathesis may be considered a structural reflexive in the sense that nominal positions assigned by the verb coincide in reference.

On the other hand, another diathesis, schematized in (C) of Figure 2.4, is not a structural reflexive at all. Geniušienė terms this diathesis objective decausative*, noting that the corresponding function is sometimes referred to by traditional writers as "intransitive-middle." Although in many languages this diathesis is formally encoded as reflexive, it is not structurally reflexive because no referential coincidence of nominals is involved.

Finally, to mention just one further type (not shown in the figure), reflexive morphology cross-linguistically often accrues to transitive verbs of body-part motion or action, such as *comb one's hair* or *lick one's lips*. In treating this type, Geniušienė posits diathesis with two semantic roles, Actor and Part. Since the diathesis involves identity at the referent level between the former role and the latter (or, properly speaking, a role representing the possessor of the latter), this type does comprise a structural reflexive.

The above summarizes Geniušienė's theory of reflexives adequately for a consideration of reflexive and reflexive-like functions and their formal encoding in Fula. It has been noted that Fula has three specific formal devices expressing this class of functions: the Reflexive extension, the Reciprocal extension, and the middle voice. The first of these, the Reflexive, is illustrated in the b-examples of (23)–(24), while the second, the Reciprocal, is illustrated in the b-examples of (25)–(26). The former is compatible with middle inflections, as the examples show.

However, the Reciprocal extension and the middle voice do not co-

A. (i)

Person 1	Person 2
Agent	Patient
Subject	Object

Ordinary transitive diathesis

(ii)

Person 1	
Agent	Patient
Subject	

(iii)

Person 1	
Agent	Patient
Subject	Object

Semantic reflexive diatheses

B.

Person 1	Person 2
Agent/Patient	Patient/Agent
Subject	

Reciprocal diathesis

C.

—	Referent 2
—	Patient
—	Subject

Objective decausative diathesis (neuter)

Figure 2.4 *Some diatheses, based on Geniušienė 1987*

occur. As (25b) and (26b) illustrate, extended radicals formed by the Reciprocal accept only active inflections, even when the corresponding simple radical takes middle primary voice (compare 26a, b; the verb concerned, *trust*, is a middle primary voice radical). As this indicates, functions involving structural reflexivity, in the sense of identities of core nominal positions or core semantic roles at the referent level (see again Figure 2.4 [B], are not always encoded by the middle; the Fula reciprocal function is an exception.

The Fula middle voice does, however, occur in many constructions expressing reflexive-like meanings, sometimes cooccuring with the Reflexive extension, but other times not. Arnott carefully distinguishes the classes of radicals which behave in each of these ways. The reflexive-like functions of the Fula unextended middle will now be considered (later the discussion returns to middle voice in combination with the Reflexive extension).

Numerically, according to Arnott, the majority of instances in which the unextended middle voice encodes reflexive-like meaning are typified by (18b) above. Arnott terms this semantic function the neuter*. The diathesis corresponding to this function is the objective decausative, shown schematically in Figure 2.4 (C). As noted earlier, this diathesis is not structurally reflexive. Rather, it arises when there is suppression of a core referent in a verb's lexically assigned diathesis (and suppression as well of the corresponding semantic role and grammatical relation). The core argument available for subjectivization in this diathesis corresponds semantically to a Patient, as the figure shows.

It follows that structural reflexivity has no bearing on the assignment of the unextended middle in the neuter function. Rather, this use of the middle could be attributed to the fact that the neuter function implicates the affectedness of the argument which the verb assigns as subject. More instances of the middle's affinity with semantic functions implicating subject affectedness will be observed shortly.

Another function of the unextended middle, the function illustrated in (19b), does comprise a structural reflexive. This is because the diathesis involves referential coincidence of two nominal positions, corresponding to the roles Actor and Part (or, properly speaking, Actor and Part-Possessor), as discussed above. Arnott 1956: 137, 1970: 255 calls this function of the Fula middle the direct reflexive. He comments (1970: 255) that it "is found with a considerable number of radicals denoting actions which are commonly performed on the body or a part of it."[17] Although it represents a structural reflexive, this type does not arise from strict referential coincidence of two core nominals, and thus is not a semantic reflexive in Geniušienė's terms. However, the unextended middle's use in this function is, again, consistent with the logical subject's affectedness.

Example (20b) illustrates another function of the Fula unextended middle – one which, according to Geniušienė, is encoded by a formal reflexive in numerous languages. However, the diathesis to which this example corresponds is not structurally reflexive. Geniušienė refers to it as transitive* because the core nominals are distinct at all levels of the diathesis, referential, semantic, and syntactic (relational). Arnott labels the corresponding semantic function indirect reflexive. He comments that the middle is assigned in this function "where the action is not on a person's body, but in his own interest, for his own benefit" (1970: 255).

As stated, this diathesis is not structurally reflexive.[18] Accordingly, there must be some other ground for the assignment of the middle. Here again, as in the earlier cases, the middle seems to be consistent with an implication of the subject's affectedness.

Finally, (21b) illustrates another unextended middle voice function. This function is smaller to that shown in (19b), since body-part action is expressed. However, Arnott 1956: 137, 1970: 256 distinguishes this type from the preceding one, remarking that the semantic function in (21b) "is found mostly with radicals referring to operations which a Fulani does not normally perform on himself, such as shaving, dressing the hair, etc." He terms this function causative reflexive. Geniušienė, for her part, posits a corresponding diathesis which she labels reflexive-causative*. Structurally the diathesis is reflexive since there is a coincidence of Subject and Object referents, although this coincidence is relative to a context in which a body or body-part referent must be present or represented in the diathesis. Again, this use of the unextended middle voice is consistent with the fact that the logical subject represents the participant principally affected in the denoted situation.

As shown, the unextended middle voice is assigned in Fula to a variety of reflexive and reflexive-like functions. However, one function not discussed in any detail so far is the semantic reflexive, the expression of coincidence in the referents of a lexical verb's core arguments. This function does not seem to be encoded in Fula by the unextended middle.

The semantic reflexive function is exemplified in Fula by (23b) above. In every such example available to the present writer, middle voice does occur. However, in each such instance, the middle inflection is preceded by the Reflexive extension, as in (23b). All extended radicals derived by this extension that appear in Arnott 1970, moreover, inflect in the middle.

In view of this, it appears that the expression of semantic reflexive meaning in forms such as (23b) is not a function of middle voice as such, but a function of the extension. Apparently, the middle voice cooccurs with the extension in the case of Reflexive-extended radicals because middle is consistent with diatheses, and with the corresponding semantic functions, which implicate the subject's affectedness. Hence one may conclude that semantic reflexive meaning is consistent with, but not explicitly encoded by, the middle voice.

The functions of Fula middle voice surveyed in the present section can be summarized as follows. As a primary voice, the middle expresses an inherent semantic function, deponency*. In addition, the middle encodes differential functions when suffixed to radicals whose primary voice is other than middle. One of these functions is the expression of a particular temporomodal category, noneventuality*. Also, the middle is associated with a second differential function, that of affectedness*, or the encoding of the logical subject's status as the locus of the denoted situation's principal effects. However, coincidence in the referents of core nominal positions assigned by a lexical verb – the semantic reflexive – appears to be neither an inherent nor a differential function of the Fula middle voice.

2.2 Tamil

Tamil is a Dravidian language of South India, unrelated to Indo-Aryan languages such as Sanskrit, yet resembling Sanskrit in having an ancient indigenous tradition of grammatical description. In this and the following section, both of these traditions will be referred to from time to time, particularly for purposes of comparing voice behaviors in these systems.

In both ancient and modern Tamil, an essential component of verbal conjugation is the system of stem alternations. Through this system, most finite as well as nonfinite verb forms in Tamil are overtly marked for one of two conjugational categories. In describing this alternation, Western-language grammarians (e.g. Arden 1969) posit "Weak" and "Strong" verbal classes, although most lexical verbs derive stems alternately in either class.[19] There are a limited number of Western-language linguistic studies concerning this. Some useful information is furnished by Manickam 1972: 77–108 and, even more so, by Paramasivam 1979 (1977).[20]

According to Paramasivam 1979: 81, 82, fns. 18, 19, the Weak/Strong opposition is not reported in the earliest Classical Tamil grammars, such as the *Tolkāppiyam* (third century AD). Only from the seventeenth century AD do indigenous grammars acknowledge it, referring to the Weak and Strong categories respectively as *taṉviṉai* and *piṟaviṉai*, "self-act" and "other-act." These terms seem modeled on the traditional Sanskrit terms for the middle and active categories, respectively *ātmanepadam* and *parasmaipadam* ("self-word" and "other-word"; see below, Section 2.3). However, as will be clarified below, the Tamil system has features which make it distinctive, not only from the system of voice alternations in Sanskrit, but also from other systems of the same type, including that of Fula discussed in the preceding section.

None of the modern writers on Tamil cited above assigns the Weak/Strong opposition to any particular grammatical category. Although no system precisely like the Tamil Weak/Strong opposition has been identified elsewhere, behaviors reminiscent of it are known to occur in other Dravidian languages as well as in some non-Dravidian languages of the South Asian language area (see n. 23 below; also Zide 1972, Saksena 1980, Klaiman 1982c). Among works in which the Tamil Weak/Strong alternation seems to be first treated explicitly as a voice behavior are Klaiman 1982a, 1982b and Klaiman 1988 (see also Steever 1981: 134ff.).

The present work assumes that Tamil Weak/Strong is a voice behavior. Moreover, the Tamil system is assigned to the basic voice type on the following grounds.

First, Tamil instantiates the organization of the verbal lexicon which is characteristic of active–middle systems; it has both invariant middle (Weak) and invariant active (Strong) lexical verbs, in addition to a class of alternating active/middle verbs. Second, to the extent that the members of each nonalternating verb class are semantically congruent, they contrast in expressing deponent* and nondeponent meanings, respectively; this typifies basic voice system. Finally, verbs which do alternate for both voices implicate the subject's affectedness* when inflected in the middle (Weak), although in Tamil the middle or Weak voice does not encode reflexivity*.

The Tamil Weak/Strong alternation has been illustrated in Section 1.3 (13a, b) and (20a, b). The first of these pairs is repeated below as (27a, b). Additional examples are (28)–(30). All these examples illustrate lexical verbs that alternate as Weak and Strong.

Tamil verbs form inflecting stems in different ways. In some instances, the verbal base is suffixed by alternate stem formants encoding tense and voice, as in (27a, b). In other cases, the shape of the verbal base itself alternates, as in (29a, b). Each Tamil verb can be placed in a conjugational class according to the manner in which it forms tensed stems (for details, see Arden 1969: 145ff. and Paramasivam 1979: 75ff.). However, for the purposes of the succeeding discussion, the precise morphological formation of the Weak and Strong alternates is not of crucial significance, and glosses to examples do not delineate voice markers with precision. For immediate purposes, what is significant is just that the alternation is marked in some fashion.

(27) a. Kuẓantai   kālai   utai -kir̠   -atu   (95)
       child-NOM leg-ACC kick present **WEAK** SG NEUT
       'The child is kicking its legs (in the air)'
    b. Kuẓantai   en̠n̠ai   utai -kkir̠   -atu   (95)
       child-NOM me-ACC kick present **STRONG** SG NEUT
       'The child is kicking me'

(28) a. Māṭu   pullai   mēyn -t   -atu   (85)
       cow-NOM grass-ACC graze **WEAK** past SG NEUT
       'The cow grazed (on) the grass'
    b. Avan̠   māṭṭai   mēy -tt   -ān̠   (85)
       he-NOM cow-ACC graze **STRONG** past SG MASC
       'He grazed the cow'

(29) a. Piḷḷai   cōru   uṇ -ṭ   -ān̠   (87)
       son-NOM rice   eat **WEAK** past SG MASC
       'The son ate rice'
    b. Ammā   piḷḷaikkuc cōru ūṭṭ -in̠   -āḷ   (87)
       mother-NOM son-DAT rice eat **STRONG** past SG FEM
       'The mother fed the child rice'

(30) a. Avan̠   cen̠n̠aiyil vaḷar -v   -ān̠   (74)
       he-NOM Madras-LOC grow **WEAK** future SG MASC
       'He will grow up in Madras'
    b. Nāṅkaḷ   oru nāy vaḷar -pp   -ōm   (75)
       we-NOM one dog grow **STRONG** future 1PL
       'We will raise a dog'

Several Western-language treatments prior to Paramasivam propose accounts of the grammatical opposition which the a- and b-examples in (27)–(30) illustrate. Paramasivam 1979: 81–90 reviews several of these proposals.

According to one, the Weak/Strong opposition formally encodes a grammatical opposition involving transitivity, i.e. intransitive/transitive. However, Paramasivam rejects this proposal on the basis of various alternates, such as (27a, b), in which both Weak and Strong forms are of equivalent transitivity. Note that in each of (27a, b) the verb assigns one object, and this object behaves as grammatical objects generally do in Tamil, being assigned a specific case, the accusative.

According to a second account, a Strong alternate is the causative of a corresponding Weak form. Examples such as (28)–(30) seem to support this. However, Paramasivam rejects this analysis, again on the basis of examples such as (27a, b). Furthermore, he notes that Tamil has both periphrastic and morphological causatives, the latter distinct from Strong verbal forms. As he observes, stems formed by the morphological causative are invariably Strong, never Weak (Paramasivam, pp. 123ff.).

A third proposal is that Weak and Strong respectively encode nonvolitional and volitional meanings. Paramasivam rejects this on the ground that many Weak and Strong alternates, such as (29a, b), express volitionality in equivalent degrees. He also notes and rebuts a fourth proposal to the effect that Strong and Weak respectively represent ergative and nonergative alternates (p. 90).

Paramasivam's own proposal is that Weak/Strong encodes an alternation in the subject's relation to the action denoted by the verb. According to him, the Tamil system centers on a distinction affective/effective, where an affective verbal form "is one the subject of which undergoes the action (or state or change of state) described by that verb stem," while an effective verbal form "can be negatively described as one the subject of which does not undergo the action denoted" (pp. 90–1, 93).

Paramasivam's use of the term "undergo" in the preceding definitions seems inapt, since the subject of a verb, Weak or Strong, need not be the semantic undergoer. The true basis of the Weak/Strong alternation seems to be that, in Weak alternates, the subject referent corresponds to the locus of the principal effects of the verbally denoted action; while in corresponding Strong alternates, the denoted action's principal effects devolve upon some other argument. (The functions of voice in invariant or nonalternating Weak and Strong verbs will be separately considered below.)

At the outset of the present work, voice has been characterized as encoding some alternation in the relationship between a configuration of lexically assigned nominal positions and the verb. According to this characterization, Weak/Strong appears to be a voice system. Moreover, the type of Tamil's Weak/Strong system appears to be basic rather than derived. This is supported by (27a, b) and by (31)–(33) below. Each of these examples shows that the alternation of voices does not necessarily entail suppression or reassignment of arguments (semantic roles) among verbally assigned nominal positions.

(31) a. Kūṭṭam   avaḷai   neruŋk -iṉ   -atu   (86)
       crowd-NOM her-ACC approach **WEAK** past SG NEUT
       'The crowd approached her'
    b. Kūṭṭam   avaḷai   nerukk -iṉ   -atu   (86)
       crowd-NOM her-ACC approach **STRONG** past SG NEUT
       'The crowd pushed in on her'
(32) a. Avaḷ   kaṭavuḷai vaṇaŋk -iṉ   -āḷ   (85)
       she-NOM God-ACC   submit **WEAK** past SG FEM
       'She worshipped (submitted to) God'
    b. Avaṉ   puliyai   vaṇakk -iṉ   -āṉ
       he-NOM tiger-ACC submit **STRONG** past SG MASC
       'He subjugated the tiger'
(33) a. Racikarkaḷ naṭikaiyai valain   -tu
       fans-NOM   actress-ACC surround **WEAK** PTCPL
       (*valait   -tuk)   koṇṭu   āṭ -iṉ -ārkaḷ (96)
       (surround **STRONG** PTCPL) take-PTCPL danced
       'The fans surrounded the actress and danced'
    b. Racikarkaḷ naṭikaiyai valait   -tuk
       fans-NOM   actress-ACC surround **STRONG** PTCPL
       (*valain   -tu)   koṇṭu   aṭi -tt -ārkaḷ (96)
       (surround **WEAK** PTCPL) take-PTCPL beat
       'The fans surrounded the actress and beat her up'

In each of the a, b alternates of (31)–(33), the number of core arguments and their assignment to particular structural positions remain constant. Therefore, accepting that Weak/Strong is a voice opposition, it pertains to the basic rather than the derived type because it involves no necessary reorganization of arguments among structural positions. Rather, Weak/Strong encodes an alternation in the locus of the action's principal effects. In the above a-examples, the denoted action is construed as principally affecting the referent of the subject, while in the b-examples, the principally affected participant is other than the subject.

Like the middle in Fula, then, the Tamil Weak voice has a differential function of encoding subject affectedness.[21]

In other respects, however, differential functions of the Tamil Weak and Strong voices are unlike differential voice functions in Fula. For instance, in Tamil the Weak (middle) voice does not seem to correlate with any particular temporomodal category, and has no particular association with noneventuality, as the middle does in Fula (see the preceding section).

To be sure, where Weak and Strong alternates vary for transitivity, the Weak form often has an inchoative* sense, denoting events which occur spontaneously, or without the specific intervention of a semantic Agent or instigator. Illustrations are the a-examples of (34) and (35). However, many Weak alternates are not intransitive (36a) nor do they necessarily have inchoative meaning (36b) (compare the Strong alternate 36c).

(34) a. Nāṭu   iraṇṭākap pirin -t   -atu (84)
       country-NOM bilaterally divide **WEAK** past SG NEUT
       'The country divided into two'
   b. Avan̲   kuẓantaiyait tāyiṭamiruntu piri   -tt
      he-NOM   child-ACC   mother-ABL   divide **STRONG** past
      -ān̲ (85)
      SG MASC
      'He separated the child from the mother'

(35) a. Avaḷ   en̲ matiyil   utkārn -t   -āḷ (90)
       she-NOM my lap-LOC sit   **WEAK** past SG FEM
       'She sat on my lap'
   b. Avaḷ   en̲n̲ai utkār -tt   -āḷ
      she-NOM me-ACC sit   **STRONG** past SG FEM
      'She seated me'

(36) a. Avaḷ   kamyūn̲isṭ kaṭciyil   cērn -t   -āḷ (87)
       she-NOM communist party-LOC join **WEAK** past SG FEM
       'She joined the communist party'
   b. Avan̲   avaḷai   cērn -t   -ān̲
      he-NOM her-ACC join **WEAK** past SG MASC
      'He joined her'
   c. Avan̲   paṇam cēr -tt   -ān̲
      he-NOM money join **STRONG** past SG MASC
      'He collected money'

Also, unlike other languages where structural reflexive or reflexive-like functions may accrue to the middle (e.g. Fula as discussed in the preceding section, and classical Indo-European languages as discussed in the section below), Tamil has no structural reflexive or reflexive-like middle (Weak) voice functions.

Theoretically this may be due to Tamil's being a language in which semantic roles are not individuated relative to referents of nominal positions, but relative to argument positions (semantic roles in a verb's argument frame). A contrast in argument-structure types along these lines has been discussed earlier in Section 1.5. Individuation of semantic roles to argument positions means that, where a lexical verb assigns distinct core semantic roles, they count as two separate arguments, even if they happen to coincide referentially.

In Tamil, regardless of any referential relationship between the two core arguments, if a transitive verb inflects in both the Strong and the Weak categories, then the selection of voice in any individual instance depends on whether the verb assigns a subject argument upon whose referent the denoted action's principal effects devolve. The Weak voice is assigned if there is such an argument, and the Strong voice is assigned if there is not. It should be reiterated that the term argument here means a verbally assigned role, not the referent thereof. Accordingly, the Strong voice is selected over the Weak if the action is semantically reflexive (referent of subject does action to self; see 37); if the action is reciprocal (referents of plural subject do action to one another; see 38); if the action is of the body-part variety, as discussed in the previous section (see 39); or in an instance such as (40a), which evinces one of the diatheses mentioned in the preceding section, the transitive reflexive*.[22]

(37) Avan̲   tan̲n̲ai   utai -ttuk
 he-NOM self-ACC kick **STRONG** PTCPL
 (*utain -tu)   kon̲ṭān̲
 (kick   **WEAK** PTCPL) took
 'He kicked himself'

(38) Paiyan̲kaḷ oruvarai oruvar   utai -ttuk
 boys-NOM one another-ACC kick **STRONG** PTCPL
 (*utain -tu)   kon̲ṭārkaḷ
 (kick   **WEAK** PTCPL) took
 'The boys kicked each other'

(39) Avan̲   tan̲ kālai   utai-tt   -ān̲
     he-NOM own leg-ACC kick STRONG past SG MASC
     (*utain -t   -ān̲)
     (kick   WEAK past SG MASC)
     'He kicked his own leg (kicked himself in the leg)'
(40) a. Avan̲   tan̲akkup paṇam cēr   -tt
        he-NOM   self-DAT money collect STRONG past
        -ān̲   (*cērn -t   -ān̲)
        SG MASC (collect WEAK past SG MASC)
        'He collected money for himself'
     b. Avan̲   paṇam cēr   -ttuk   (*cern
        he-NOM money collect STRONG PTCPL (collect
        -tu)   kon̲ṭān̲
        WEAK PTCPL)   took
        'He gathered up the money'

The reason active (Strong) voice occurs in the above instances seems to be that the middle (Weak) voice cannot be assigned when the subject referent's affectedness arises in virtue of its referential coincidence with some nonsubject argument position. Rather, when assigned differentially or in contrast to the Strong voice, the Weak signals that the subject referent acts and is affected purely in consequence of acting. Frequently this is consistent with intransitivity, as in several earlier examples (30a, 34a, 35a). But in view of the very large number of instances of differential Weak voice which are transitive, it would be problematical to ascribe a detransitivizing or valence-reducing function to the Weak category in Tamil.

How can Weak and Strong voice assignments be accounted for formally? One possibility may be to invoke a status Affectee which is assigned to nominal or argument positions at some structural level. Affectee is not, however, to be construed as a theta-role. Rather, it is a status that can combine with the theta-role of either a logical subject or logical object. If Affectee is assigned to an argument linked with subject, then the Weak form of the verb is selected; if not, the Strong form is selected. Although not specifically formulated for Tamil, a treatment of lexical structure embodying features such as [±affected] has been proposed elsewhere (Rappaport & Levin 1986).

For such an analysis to be tenable in Tamil, one question that would need to be resolved is the level of grammatical organization to which the status Affectee pertains. In some instances the inherent semantics of a verb cannot exhaustively specify which core argument has Affectee status. The verb *valai* 'surround' in (33a, b) is a case in point. There seems to be no basis for claiming that the lexical sense of the verb assigns one argument and only one argument the Affectee role. Rather, which argument is construed as affected appears to depend on inferences about the involvement of the core participants (core argument referents) in the denoted situation. Accordingly, Affectee status does not seem to be assigned at the level of the lexically specified argument frame.

This point is reinforced by (41a–d) below, in which the odd and even examples illustrate the respective Weak and Strong variants of the verb *anai* 'embrace.' The referential relations between the embracer and embracee are irrelevant to the selection of voice, as (41a, b) show. Rather, which voice is selected evidently depends on which referent the speaker intends to portray as the most affected participant in the act of embracing. Thus in (41c), the Weak voice is selected because the situation is so portrayed as to emphasize or focus on the emotive involvement or affectedness of the subject; while in (41d), the Strong voice is chosen consistent with a nuance of the object as the most affected party.

(41) a. Murukan   tan/Rāmanin   manaiviyai anain
    Murukan-NOM own/Raman's wife-ACC   embrace
    -t   -ān
    WEAK past SG MASC
    'Murukan embraced his own/Raman's wife'

   b. Murukan   tan/Rāmanin   manaiviyai anai
    Murukan-NOM own/Raman's wife-ACC   embrace
    -tt   -ān
    STRONG past SG MASC
    'Murukan embraced his own/Raman's wife'

   c. Tāy   kuẓantaiyai anain   -tu
    mother-NOM   child-ACC   embrace **WEAK** PTCPL
    kontu   aẓutāḷ
    take-PTCPL   cried
    'The mother, embracing the child, wept'

d. Tāy   kuẓantaiyai aṉai   -ttu
   mother-NOM child-ACC embrace **STRONG** PTCPL
   nerukkiṉāl̤
   engulfed
   'The mother, embracing the child, engulfed it'

There is a further difficulty with assigning an Affectee status in lexical representations. Suppose that, in a lexical structure, this status is assigned to some nominal linked to the grammatical status of object. Then a relinking of subjecthood to the Affectee argument might be expected to trigger selection of the Weak over the Strong form if the verb is one which alternates for voice. Thus the passive based on an alternating verb's Strong shape might be expected to be assigned Weak (middle) voice. As a note of comparison, it is indeed the middle voice which is invariably assigned when an active verb passivizes in classical Indo-European languages such as Greek and Sanskrit (see the following section).

However, for Tamil this prediction is not borne out. In this language, it is possible, in principle, for transitive verbs both Weak and Strong to passivize. (However, the Weak forms of some alternating verbs fail to passivize – see examples 42–4, and compare, respectively, 27a, 36b, and 41c.) Under passivization, a verb appears in a nonfinite shape followed by a passive auxiliary verb *paṭu* 'suffer, happen.' What is most noteworthy is that, under passivization, verbs are assigned just the voice that they have in the corresponding nonpassive. Accordingly, passive counterparts of Strong nonpassives are formally Strong, as confirmed by (45c) (derived from a form like 45b, not 45a) and (46) (cf. 28a); while passive counterparts of Weak nonpassives are formally Weak, as shown in (47b) (cf. 47a) and (48) (cf. 32a):

(42) *Kāl   kuẓantaiyāl utai   paṭṭatu
     leg-NOM child-INST kick-**WEAK** suffered-SG NEUT
     'The (his) leg(s) was/were kicked (in the air) by the child'
(43) *Aval̤   avaṉāl   cērap   paṭṭāl̤
     she-NOM him-INST join-**WEAK** suffered-SG FEM
     'She was joined by him'
(44) *Kuẓantai   tāyāl   aṉai   paṭṭatu
     child-NOM mother-INST embrace-**WEAK** suffered-SG NEUT
     'The child was embraced by its mother'

(45) a. Caṉṉal   uṭain -t   -atu
       window-NOM break WEAK past SG NEUT
       'The window broke'
    b. Avaṉ   caṉṉalai   uṭai -tt   -āṉ
       he-NOM window-ACC break STRONG past SG MASC
       'He broke the window'
    d. Caṉṉal   ciṟu paiyaṉāl uṭai -kkap   paṭṭatu
       window-NOM little boy-INST break STRONG suffered-SG
                                                    NEUT
       'The window was broken by a little boy'
(46) Pul   māṭṭiṉāl   mēyap   paṭṭatu
     grass-NOM cow-INST graze-WEAK suffered-SG NEUT
     'The grass was grazed (on) by the cow'
(47) a. Avaṉ   avaṉai   Rājiv eṉṟu   kūppi -tt
       he-NOM him-ACC Rajiv saying call   WEAK past
       -āṉ
       SG MASC
       'He called him Rajiv'
    b. Avaṉ   Rājiv eṉṟu   kūppiṭap   paṭukirāṉ
       he-NOM Rajiv saying call-WEAK suffers-SG MASC
       'He is called Rajiv'
(48) Puli   avaṉāl   vaṇaṅkap   paṭṭatu
     tiger-NOM him-INST worship-WEAK suffered-SG NEUT
     'The tiger was worshipped by him'

To recapitulate, the passivization facts do not support treating Affectee as a status assigned to nominals in predicate-argument structures since, were this so, Affectee status could be expected to transfer upon passivization to the Affectee argument's reassigned status or grammatical function, that of subject. As a result, all passives might be expected to be assigned Weak voice. But as shown, the facts of voice assignment in Tamil passives do not bear this out. An alternative possibility might be to treat affectedness not as a grammatical status but as a kind of agrammatical status, one that accrues to participants in sententially denoted situations (as contrasted with arguments in lexical or syntactic structures).

But pursuing the details of such an account in this chapter would entail a digression of impractical proportions. Rather than embark on it here, we shall leave it until later (Section 3.6; Chapter 6). For the present, the discussion will now turn to inherent (as opposed to differential) functions of the Tamil Weak or middle voice.

Previous research does not systematically deal with the inherent functions of Tamil voices, i.e. the semantic characteristics of verbs which comprise Tamil's invariant Weak or *media tantum* class as opposed to those of the invariant Strong or *activa tantum* class. However, for present purposes, some tentative conclusions can be reported from a modest survey. This survey is based on a small and unsystematic sample consisting of 60 invariant Weak and 46 invariant Strong verbs. The verbs included in the sample have been isolated from a listing of 223 verbal roots in Arden 1969: 150–69 and checked against dictionary entries in Burrow & Emeneau 1961 and the *Tamil lexicon* (1926–36).

One thing the survey suggests is that detransitivization or valence reduction is not a Weak or middle voice function. Both invariant Strong and invariant Weak verbs may be transitive or intransitive. Most of the Weak verbs sampled, moreover, happen to be transitive.

A second fact which emerges from the survey is that certain invariant Strong and invariant Weak verbs are close in meaning. However, it appears that in some instances, the invariant Strong verb has an effective or nonaffective sense, while the sense of the semantically related invariant Weak verb is affective.

An instance in point consists of two verbs meaning "dress." The invariant Strong verb *utu* is glossed 'put on clothes, surround, encircle,' while the invariant Weak *pūṇ* is glossed 'wear, put on (ITR), be yoked.' A similar contrasting pair is invariant Strong *para* 'fly, hasten' vs invariant Weak *eẓu* 'rise, ascend (by one's own effort or buoyancy).' In each of these pairs, the Weak verb implicates the subject's state of affect resulting from the action, while, contrastingly, the sense of the Strong verb is nonaffective.

In addition, various invariant Weak verbs in the sample denote actions which naturally entail the subject referent's affectedness, e.g. *paṭu* 'suffer, endure, occur' (compare the invariant Strong *poru* 'suffer, tolerate, condone'); *nō* 'ache, be in pain'; *ī* 'give to an inferior, confer, give as alms' (compare the invariant Strong *koṭu*, which more neutrally means 'give'); *vāṅku* 'get, buy'; *vil* 'sell (give for profit)'; *peṟu* 'get, obtain'; *tiruṭu* 'steal'; *aṭai* 'get, gather'; *kōru* 'desire, request'; and *tēṭu* 'seek, inquire after, attempt (something).'

The survey also reveals that a special affective semantics accrues to one subclass of invariant Weak verbs. These verbs, mostly transitive, denote actions of taking something in, either physically or psychically. Instances include: *ari* 'understand, know' (compare the invariant Strong *mara* 'forget'); *kēḷ* 'hear'; *cāppiṭu* 'eat'; and *viẓaŋku* 'swallow.'[23] By comparison, some invariant Strong transitive verbs denote actions that impinge on a nonsubject's psychic or physical state; for instance, *eccari* 'warn,' *ari* 'sift, filter (e.g. to remove chaff).'

A number of Tamil invariant Weak verbs, also mostly transitive, express actions presupposing the animacy and control* of the logical subject referent. One subclass includes verbs of speaking or other acts of communication; a second subclass includes verbs of mental abilities or attitudes. These subclasses are respectively illustrated in the left- and right-hand columns of (49).

(49) pēcu 'speak, tell, make vocal sounds' tēr 'pass a test, inquire into, understand'
col 'say' tavaru 'blunder, fail in duty'
eṉ 'say' aruḷ 'be gracious, grant'
eẓutu 'write' nampu 'trust, hope, long for'
tērru 'comfort, console, clarify' eṇṇu 'think, reckon, compute'
pāṭu 'sing'
talḷu 'reject'

Semantically, the verbs in (49) are consistent with the previous section's characterization of deponency*. That is, these verbs express mental or physical dispositions presupposing the logical subject's animacy and control*.

Interestingly, Tamil has a contrasting class of invariant Strong verbs. These verbs, generally intransitive, denote situations that accrue to inanimate logical subjects or occurrences which are otherwise non-controllable; that is, their semantics is nondeponent. Among these verbs are, again, two subclasses. One subclass denotes qualities. Instances include *koẓu* 'grow fat, be rich, prosper' and *veḷu* 'whiten, become bright (ITR), bleach (TR).' A second and larger subclass is comprised of nonqualitative verbs assigning subjects whose referents are alive or animate. They include: *pira* 'be born,' *iru* 'be,' *piẓai* 'survive,' *ira* 'die, elapse (e.g. time),' *ciri* 'laugh, smile,' *pū* 'bloom, blossom,' and *paẓu* 'ripen.' As stated, each of these invariant Strong verbal subclasses denotes non-controllable actions and events. In other words, their semantics is nondeponent.

As in Fula, then, so too in Tamil, the middle (Weak) and active (Strong) voices have certain inherent semantic functions. And the contrasting semantic classes with which these inherent voices are associated are very reminiscent of those identified earlier in Fula. That is, these classes appear to comprise deponent and nondeponent verbs, respectively.

The functions of Tamil basic voice categories surveyed in this section can be summarized as follows. The Tamil Weak or middle voice expresses both differential* and inherent* functions. The differential function most consistently associated with the Weak or middle voice (i.e. its typical function as a voice of verbs which alternate as Strong or Weak) is to encode affectedness*, or situations the principal effects of which devolve upon the referent of the logical subject, as opposed to some other participant. This function is often, but by no means always, consistent with intransitivity.

The Weak or middle voice also has an inherent function associated with its invariant marking on nonalternating or *media tantum* verbs. Verbs of this class are usually, though not invariably, transitive. To the extent that they are semantically coherent, the meanings they express are deponent*. Moreover, verbs of the invariant Weak class contrast with a distinct class of invariant Strong or *activa tantum* verbs. The latter tend to be intransitive, and to the extent that they are semantically coherent, the meanings they express are nondeponent*.

Finally, functions for which the Tamil Weak or middle voice seems to have scant if any affinity are (a) the expression of noneventual or other special temporomodal semantics; and (b) the encoding of reflexive-like semantic functions or structural reflexive diatheses.

2.3 Indo-European

The study of voice and its functions is part of a long tradition pre-dating modern grammatical analysis. In fact, the conception of the middle as a verbal category seems to be as old as the tradition of grammatical description in Indo-European (IE) languages. Rules specifying the selection of middle vs active inflections appear in the Classical Sanskrit grammar attributed to Pāṇini, the *Aṣṭādhyāyī*. There seems no compelling reason to overlook the potential contributions this work can make to our understanding of voice, or to assign lesser weight to premodern grammars as contrasted with modern grammars in sorting out and evaluating the IE middle's functions. Accordingly, the indigenous Indian grammar (in the edition of Vasu 1962) will be invoked in support of some findings of the present section.

The middle voice and its functions are, of course, also examined by many latter-day writers on classical IE languages. As a result, several differential functions, functions that the middle expresses when in opposition to the active, have been identified. Two differential functions which receive especially prominent mention in prior works are detransitivization* (or valence reduction) and reflexivity*. Another concern of some writers is the relationship between the middle and derived voice, or the passive*.

The present section examines the question of the IE middle's affinity with passivization and discusses the middle's differential functions. Subsequently, as in the previous sections, it will shift focus to the middle's inherent functions, or meanings it expresses as a voice of *media tantum* or middle-only inflecting verbs (in contrast to functions of the active as the invariant voice of *activa tantum* or active-only inflecting verbs). Some topics mentioned in previous sections, such as the temporomodal category of noneventuality*, neuter* semantic function, and deponency*, will recur below.

The discussion begins with the IE passive. In the basic voice systems surveyed in the preceding sections, Fula and Tamil, the passive is formally distinguished from the middle category.

Also, in these systems, middle voice does not encode passive meaning or the passive semantic function proper. Passive meaning or semantic function involves the suppression or downgrading of a nominal which is assigned in the verb's valence* as logical subject, concomitantly resulting or not resulting in the subjectivization of some other status, such as logical object. Despite the downgrading or suppression of the subject-linked nominal, however, its argument status, or semantic roles, remains part of the valence; it may or may not be assigned to another nominal, but it is not eliminated.

Passive contrasts in this respect with the neuter* semantic function (shown schematically in Figure 2.4 as diathesis C). In the neuter, two lexical verbs alternate in such a way that one verb assigns a logical subject referent, together with a corresponding semantic role and a corresponding nominal position, which the other verb does not. The first verb is transitive; the intransitive alternate is termed a neuter. Semantically, a neuter verb can be characterized as inchoative*, or expressing spontaneous events, i.e. situations presupposing no participant's control*. The semantics of the passive, by contrast, may be non-inchoative.

In the non-IE systems earlier discussed, middle and passive are formally distinct, and the functions encoded by the former may include neuter* meaning (as in Fula). But in these systems, as mentioned, the middle voice does not specifically encode the passive semantic function.

However, in classical IE languages, the situation is different. Indo-Europeanists concur that a formal passive did not exist in the protolanguage. Rather, in the protolanguage there occurred one nonactive voice; its meanings or values included the expression of the passive semantic function.

Nonetheless two IE daughter stocks, Greek and Indo-Iranian, did evolve morphologically distinct passive forms of the verb. Still, in neither stock are passive verbal forms distributed throughout the system of verbal conjugation. In Classical Greek, according to Barber 1975: 23, fn. 2, only in the aorist and sometimes the future tenses do specific passive forms occur (their respective characteristics, according to Smyth 1974: 180–1, are *-thē* and *-ē*); while in earlier Homeric Greek, the passive is confined to the aorist alone. In Classical Sanskrit, the passive occurs only in the present tense system (including the imperfect past), where its characteristic is the stem-forming suffix *-ya*, and in one person of the aorist; it is excluded from the future and perfect tense systems. And in earlier Vedic, only the present tense system has a passive verbal form.

It is significant that both intransitive as well as transitive basic verbs passivize in Greek and Sanskrit. The second of these is illustrated in the b-examples of (50) (examples 50a, b are from Chapter 1, n. 18) and in (51). (Note that 51b, a passive of an intransitive, is impersonal*.)

(50) a. Devadattaḥ   kaṭam   karoti
       Devadatta-NOM mat-ACC makes-3SG **ACTIVE**
       'Devadatta makes a mat'
   b. Kaṭo   Devadattena   kri   -ya -te
       mat-NOM Devadatta-INST make -*ya* 3SG **MIDDLE**
       'A mat is made by Devadatta'

(51) a. Sa   śete
       he-NOM sleeps-3SG **MIDDLE**
       'He sleeps, is sleeping'
   b. Tena   śay -ya -te
      by him-INST sleep -*ya* 3SG **MIDDLE**
      '(literally) It is slept by him'

In Greek and Sanskrit alike, the formal passive is typically encoded by stem formants (e.g. Sanskrit -*ya*) added to verbal bases, deriving inflecting stems. Also, the inflections added to passive stems are generally middle rather than active, as (50b) and (51b) illustrate.[24] This in itself suggests that the middle does not directly express passive meaning; rather, the semantic function or functions it encodes happen to be compatible with the meaning of the passive. As noted above, passive meaning may involve subjectivization of a logical nonsubject, typically the notional undergoer or affected* participant in the denoted action.

As we now turn to functions particular to the IE middle, it will be convenient to continue citing Greek and Indo-Iranian (Sanskrit) data. This is because these languages evince a formal opposition (albeit restricted to certain parts of the verbal conjugation) between middle and passive, making it relatively easy to isolate those functions that are middle voice functions proper. Moreover, the two stocks in question are among the relatively few IE stocks which are well attested at archaic stages of their development, and they are also the two stocks with the earliest known indigenous grammatical traditions. For these reasons, and to make manageable the task of surveying voice behavior in a family with nine or more major branches, the focus will remain on these stocks in the discussion below.

It has been observed earlier that one of the differential functions some writers attribute to the IE middle is the encoding of reflexive meaning. In certain IE stocks, in fact, the middle or nonactive voice morpheme is said to have had an original meaning of reflexivity*. To clarify this, it is useful to briefly consider the history of the IE middle inflection.

The middle's forms as attested in the early IE daughter stocks are "remarkably heterogeneous" (Burrow 1973: 316). One group of stocks has a series of middle voice inflections dating back to the Proto-IE stage. These stocks include Old Germanic (e.g. Gothic), Indo-Iranian (including Old Persian and Sanskrit) and Greek. Bopp 1862: 649 provides a comparative table of middle inflections showing that many of the forms are cognate in some or all of these stocks. The similarities are particularly strong in Greek and Sanskrit (Burrow 1973: 314–17).

However, in a second and distinct group of stocks, there appears in nonactive verbal forms an element r̥. Among stocks displaying the r̥ element are Tocharian, Celtic (such as Old Irish, see Thurneysen 1970: 328, 365–7) and Italic (Latin, see Wheelock 1963: 84, 97, 132, 136). In Latin, the r̥ element is the characteristic of a verbal conjugation usually called passive.

Hittite is significant because many of its middle inflections are cognate to those of languages of the first group, but are oftentimes added to verbal bases displaying the r̥ stem marker. Burrow 1973: 316–17 concludes from this that the r̥ element is an archaic feature that "must have been . . . optional in Indo-European, and . . . in the further course of development it became established as a necessary element in Italo-Celtic and Tocharian, and on the other hand went out of use in that dialectal area of Indo-European from which Indo-Iranian and Greek derive." There are several theories as to the original function of the r̥ element. One is that this element derives from an archaic marker of reflexivity (Bopp 1862: 661ff.).

Regardless of the accuracy of this theory, two things are clear: first, that some IE middle functions are reflexive-like (in the sense in which this term has been used earlier in the present chapter); and second, that a number of IE languages have developed neo-middle constructions marked by originally reflexive morphemes.

For instance, according to Entwistle & Morison 1964: 102, in Common Balto-Slavic a neo-middle construction evolves from reflexive clitic pronominals added to active-inflecting verbs. Middle conjugations arising from the grammaticization of such patterns occur in some languages descended from Common Balto-Slavic, such as Old Norse (see Gordon 1957: 298, 303–4 for tables of active and middle conjugations). These forms have been perpetuated in modern North Germanic languages such as Swedish, illustrated in (52a–c) (from Geniušienė 1987: 264, 250, and Andersen 1987: 13). It is also well known that in the development of Romance languages, verb–clitic collocations have come to encode a variety of neo-middle functions (see Grimshaw 1982; Croft, Shyldkrot & Kemmer 1987, and references therein).

(52) a. Äng   -en   slog   -s   fort
       meadow article mowed reflexive fast
       'The meadow mowed fast'
   b. Kon stångar alla / Kon stånga -s
      cow butts   all / cow butts reflexive
      'The cow butts everyone' / 'The cow butts'
   c. Jag avunda -s   honom
      I   envy   reflexive him
      'I envy him'

Although originally reflexive markers may extend their functions in striking ways, this does not necessarily entail that the resulting constructions, called "neo-middle" above, encode exactly the same functions as are encoded by conjugational middle voices. Nor does it establish that the original function of the IE nonactive voice forms was reflexive. We will concentrate for the moment on the semantic reflexive function, or the expression of referential coincidence between core nominal positions assigned by a transitive verb. This is the prototypical or central function of any reflexive (but see below, n. 33), making it appropriate to consider whether such is actually a meaning encoded by the Classical Greek and Sanskrit middle.

Consider the Greek examples (53a–f) and the Sanskrit example (54) below. (Example 53a is repeated from Chapter 1, example 17; 53b and 54 are from Speijer 1973: 238; 53c–f are from Smyth 1974: 390.)

(53) a. Lou -omai   d. kosmei -sthai
        wash 1SG **MIDDLE**   adorn **MIDDLE** INF
        'I wash myself'   'to adorn oneself'
     b. Kalupt -omai   e. stephanou -sthai
        wrap   1SG **MIDDLE**   crown   **MIDDLE** INF
        'I wrap myself'   'to crown oneself'
     c. aleiphe -sthai   f. gymnaze -sthai
        anoint **MIDDLE** INF   exercise **MIDDLE** INF
        'to anoint oneself'   'to exercise (oneself)'
(54) Satyakāma   eva Jābālo   bravī -thāḥ
     Satyakama-NOM   just Jabala-NOM   call OPT 2SG **MIDDLE**
     'You must call yourself Satyakama Jabala'

Examples (53a–f) and (54) respectively illustrate typical middle voice

88 *Middle voice and basic voice systems*

functions in Greek and Sanskrit. Yet none appears to exemplify the semantic reflexive.

To clarify this, all the Greek examples in (53a–f) are instances in which one core referent in an identity relation with the subject comprises either the latter's body or body part. Earlier in the present chapter, similar instances have been referred to as body-part reflexives. This function is distinct from the semantic reflexive function, which is not expressed in any of (53a–f). It is noteworthy that in the *Greek grammar* of Smyth 1974: 390, virtually only instances like (53a–f) are offered as supposed illustrations of the "direct reflexive middle" which "represents the subject as acting directly *on himself*" (emphasis in original).

In the *Sanskrit syntax* of Speijer 1973, example (54) is the only instance provided to illustrate the reflexive function of the middle voice. Yet this example seems incorrectly glossed. It would appear more appropriately construed as a middle with passive function ("You must *be called* Satyakama Jabala"), since the logical object "Satyakama Jabala" does not appear in the accusative case and is, accordingly, not a grammatical object. Rather, it appears in the nominative case, indicating that it is a grammatical subject (or more correctly, is in apposition with the understood subject "you").

It is interesting that, apart from the writers just cited, a number of Greek and Sanskrit grammarians are either silent about the middle's expressing reflexive meaning (such as Whitney 1973 on Sanskrit), or deny outright that it has any meaning corresponding to the semantic reflexive. For instance, after reviewing the middle's reflexive-like functions in Sanskrit, Burrow 1973: 295 comments: "One sense that the middle does not normally express is that of a direct reflexive, which is expressed by means of the accusative [pronoun] *ātmānam* 'self.' " Similarly, while offering various instances of reflexive-like middles (including a small number of genuine semantic reflexive middles, such as *paraskeuaze-sthai* 'prepare oneself'), Smyth 1974: 390 issues the qualification, "The direct reflexive idea is far more frequently conveyed by the active and a reflexive pronoun." Also, Geniušienė 1987: 245 notes that middle voices in Greek and Sanskrit, as well as Latin r̩ forms, do not characteristically express the semantic reflexive function. She states, "In all these languages, a reflexive pronoun was the main means of expressing semantic reflexivity." (See also Gonda 1960: 43ff.)

In light of the association many writers posit between reflexive mean-

2.3 Indo-European   89

ing and the IE middle voice (see again Section 2.0), it may seem surprising that the semantic reflexive should have been encoded tangentially, at best, by the IE middle. However, this result is consistent with an otherwise unexplained fact about the indigenous Sanskrit grammar, the *Aṣṭādhyāyī*. The work, a compendium of some 4000 rules organized into eight chapters (*aṣṭa* 'eight' + *adhyāya* 'chapter'), describes with utmost systematicity and in exhaustive detail the classical language of North-Central India approximately five centuries before the Christian era. The grammar includes 65 rules (I.iii.13–77) governing the use of middle inflections, plus sixteen rules (I.iii.78–93) governing active inflections. Yet among these there is no rule sanctioning the middle's use in the expression of reflexivity. Given the detail and the precision of the grammar, as well as the early, highly evolved tradition of grammatical scholarship it reflects, it would be surprising were this to have resulted from oversight or negligence. The more plausible explanation seems to be that no reflexive function is described because semantic reflexivity is not a Sanskrit middle voice function.

To be sure, the middle in both Greek and Sanskrit does have certain functions of the sort earlier referred to as reflexive-like, e.g. the neuter function. The IE middle also is associated with structural reflexive functions other than the semantic reflexive.

One relevant function discussed previously is the reciprocal*. It will be recalled that reciprocal function proper involves coincidence in the referents of verbally assigned core semantic roles. Accordingly, like the semantic reflexive, the reciprocal is a structural reflexive diathesis, one that embodies identities of core nominals at the referential level (see above, Figure 2.4 [B]).

It is true that some middles in early IE have meanings resembling the reciprocal. Some voice rules of the ancient Sanskrit grammar refer to these middle meanings (I.iii.14 *kartari karma vyatihāre*, I.iii.15 *na gati hiṃsārthebhyaḥ*, I.iii.16 *itaretarānyonyopapadācca*). Also, in his grammar of Greek, Smyth 1974: 392 states that middle verb inflections of the dual and plural numbers may express reciprocity. Pāṇini's grammar and Smyth's alike state that such middle meanings are alternatively expressed by active verbs in construction with pronominals meaning "each other" or "one another."

Nevertheless, it does not seem that reciprocal function proper is expressed by the IE middle. This is because most reciprocal uses of the middle in Sanskrit and Greek do not correspond to a structural reflexive diathesis. To clarify this, consider the typical Sanskrit example (55) (from commentaries to Pāṇini's grammar) and the typical Greek instance (56) (from Smyth 1974: 392).

(55) Vyati- paca -nte[25]
    preverb cooks 3PL **MIDDLE**
    'They cook for one another'
(56) Tauta dia- nemou -ntai[26]
    this preverb divide up future 3PL **MIDDLE**
    'They will divide this up among themselves'

Although these examples express reciprocal meaning, they do not involve coreference of core arguments as such; in neither example do the core semantic roles assigned by the verb coincide referentially. For instance, were the middle to have that function in (55), the gloss would be 'They cook one another.'

Rather, the sense of both (55) and (56) is that there devolve mutually upon the subject referents the effects of action carried out jointly or in concert. In view of this, Geniušienė 1987: 253ff. remarks that the use of the middle to encode reciprocal function proper is "represented only by a few isolated instances" in Classical Sanskrit and Greek; otherwise such a function of the middle is uncommon in early IE.

In general, reflexive-like differential functions of the middle in Greek and Sanskrit do not entail identities of core arguments. The Greek body-part middles illustrated in (53a–f), for instance (similar examples are also common in Sanskrit; see Burrow 1973: 294), involve identities between one core argument and the possessor of the other. Moreover, a relation of possession between two core arguments, neither of which is a body part, is also sometimes encoded by the middle. For instance, in Greek, Smyth 1974: 390–1 notes a tendency for middle voice to be selected over active in expressions such as "give one's vote" and "set forth one's opinion." Commentaries on the ancient Sanskrit grammar (rule I.iii.56 *upādyamaḥ svakaraṇe*) mention a similar tendency instantiated in the contrast between active "Devadatta has relations with Yajnadatta's wife" vs middle "Devadatta has relations with his (own) wife." Another and related Sanskrit middle function involves body-part action in which the referent of the subject participates, but not as the instigator. To refer to this function in Greek, Barber 1975 coins the term catalytic middle. In Sanskrit, a middle verb which encodes this function may be formally causative, such as *aroh-aya-te hastī svayameva* (mount-

CAUSE-3SG-**MIDDLE** elephant-NOM on-its-own) 'The elephant lets itself be mounted, mounts (by a human) on its own' (from commentary to rule I.iii.67 *neraṇau yat karma ṇai cet sa kartānādhyāne*).

None of the middle functions just cited is structurally reflexive. Moreover, the IE middle has other functions which are even more obviously neither reflexive nor reflexive-like. For instance, in both Greek and Sanskrit, the middle tends to be selected over the active when a verb which inflects in either voice expresses action implicating the logical object referent being brought nearer to or farther from the logical subject referent's "sphere" (in the phrasing of Smyth 1974). Klaiman 1988 labels this differential middle voice function nucleonic, since the subject referent furnishes a figurative nucleus for the path of the object referent. Greek examples (from Smyth 1974: 391) appear in (57), while Sanskrit examples (from commentary on the ancient grammar) are furnished in (58)–(59).[27] Note that, in the a-examples of (57)–(59), the object referent moves figuratively nearer the subject referent, while in the b-examples, it moves away.

(57) a. lambane -sthai   tinos
     seize   **MIDDLE** INF something
     'to seize or put one's hand upon something'
   b. logon   poiei   -sthai
     speech deliver **MIDDLE** INF
     'to deliver a speech'
(58) a. Vidyām   ādatte
     knowledge-ACC takes-3SG **MIDDLE**
     'He acquires knowledge'
   b. Vikrīnīte
     sells-3SG **MIDDLE**
     'He sells (disposes of by sale) something'
(59) a. Māṇavakam   upanayate
     Manavaka-ACC leads near-3SG **MIDDLE**
     'He initiates (literally, brings near to himself) Manavaka'
   b. Manyum   vinayate
     anger-ACC dismisses-3SG **MIDDLE**
     'He dismisses his (own) anger'

In light of the above, it seems implausible that referential or other nominal identities can account for the range of differential functions that accrue to be IE middle. For instance, there seems no compelling reason to argue that the basic subject of a verb which expresses a differential middle voice meaning is necessarily in some covert identity relation with a nonsubject nominal. As already discussed in connection with (19b) in Section 1.3, there is no concrete evidence that a verb like the Greek *politeu-* 'be a citizen, have civic rights' assigns any nonsubject nominal function or status. (Regarding a similar instance in Fula, see again n. 18 in this chapter.) There likewise seems to be no particular motivation for invoking in lexical representations a status Affectee which may coincide with nominal positions, assigning basic voice when coinciding with subject. Reasons against this have been discussed in the preceding section.

Instead, the solution which seems to provide the most plausible account of IE differential middle functions is this: the middle, in opposition to the active, encodes situations having principal effects upon the referent of the nominal which the verb assigns as subject. This is not only true of the differential middle voice functions just discussed, but also is borne out by the middle's use as the inflectional voice of passives.

A number of grammarians characterize the meaning of the IE middle in just this way. For instance, in the phrasing of Lyons 1968: 373 (earlier cited in Section 1.3), "The implications of the middle (when it is in opposition with the active) are that the 'action' or 'state' affects the subject of the verb or his interests." A similar view is sometimes propounded in premodern, even indigenous, grammars. Thus Pāṇini's rule I.iii.72 *svaritañitaḥ kartrabhiprāye kriyāphale* specifically sanctions the middle's selection over the active when the verbally denoted action is interpreted as affecting the *kartṛ* or, loosely translated, the referent of the logical subject (sometimes translated by Western writers as "agent"), rather than some other participant.

This conclusion is further strengthened by a consideration of another IE middle voice function. A highly typical (in the view of some writers, the most typical) IE differential middle function is the neuter*. As discussed above, the neuter function relates corresponding transitive and intransitive lexical verbs. Its diathesis is represented schematically in Figure 2.4 (C), and has been characterized as structurally nonreflexive. At this point we will consider the neuter function of the IE middle in some detail.

Detailed discussion is in order because of the prominence of the neuter as a middle function in early IE. The alternation between active transitives and middle (intransitive) neuters is instantiated in various IE daughter stocks. Latin illustrations appear in (60a, b) (from Geniušienė 1987: 257); a Gothic example appears in (61b) (61a, b are also from Geniušienė); and a Sanskrit example is furnished in (62b). Note that the b-examples of (60)–(62) are reminiscent of the English intransitive verbs which participate in middle* alternations (see Chapter 1, n. 7).

(60) a. Stellae ne   move -ntur
        stars   not move 3PL r̲-voice
        'The stars do not move'
    b. Dirump -or[28]
        torment 1SG r̲-voice
        'I suffer'
(61) a. inmaidjan
        change-**ACTIVE** INF
        'to change something'
    b. Allai inmaidja -nda
        all   change   1PL **MIDDLE**
        'We shall all change'
(62) a. So   namati   daṇḍam
        he-NOM bends-3SG **ACTIVE** stick-ACC
        'He bends the stick'
    b. Namate   daṇḍaḥ
        bends-3SG **MIDDLE** stick-NOM
        'The stick bends'

As the above examples, especially (61a, b) and (62a, b) illustrate, the middle's differential neuter function is manifested in alternations of corresponding transitive and intransitive verbs respectively inflecting in the active and the middle. Also, as noted, the intransitive alternates tend to be semantically inchoative*, denoting spontaneous events presupposing no participant in the role of Agent or instigator.

Geniušienė 1987: 257 states that the neuter is among the most common of IE middle voice functions, being (along with passive) the "main function" of r̲ forms in Latin, as well as a "central" function of the middle in Greek, Hittite and Sanskrit.

In Sanskrit, the neuter middle has some especially interesting properties. Two subclasses of neuter middle verbs are formally distinguished. One subclass is illustrated by the active/middle alternating verbs shown respectively in (63a, b) (from Burrow 1973: 294).

(63) i. a. dṛmhati   'makes firm'
         b. dṛmhate   'becomes firm'
      i. a. vardhati   'increases, makes bigger'
         b. vardhate   'increases, becomes bigger'
    iii. a. vahati   '(chariot) carries man'
         b. vahate   '(man) rides (in chariot)'

Sanskrit neuter verbs of the subclass illustrated in (63b, i–iii) are marked solely by the use of the middle inflection in opposition to the active. However, the active forms with which these middles alternate are of a special set.

The characterization of this set centers on an opposition involving Aktionsart*, or a verb's inherent (lexical) temporal sense. Aktionsart has been alluded to earlier (Section 2.1) in connection with inherent active and middle voice functions in Fula. Aktionsart plays a role in the formation of Sanskrit neuters in terms of an opposition telic/atelic*.

Telic refers to the inherent sense of a lexical verb as goal-presupposing, or encoding action that presupposes an endpoint or definite point of termination. Atelic, by contrast, refers to an inherent verbal sense as goal-nonpresupposing (see Hopper & Thompson 1980).

In Sanskrit, where two verbs vary as transitive and detransitive neuter alternates as shown in (63), the transitive generally has an atelic temporal sense. By contrast, for transitive verbs whose lexical sense is telic, the formation of the neuter middle alternate is different. Illustrations are (64) and (65) (respectively from Speijer 1973: 239 and Rosen 1984: 56). A listing of some alternating telic transitive and neuter middle (intransitive) verbs appears in (66) (from Gonda 1951: 95).

(64) a. Odanam   pac -āmi
        rice gruel-ACC cook 1SG **ACTIVE**
        'I boil the rice gruel'
     b. Pac -ya   -te   odanam
        cook passive SG **MIDDLE** rice gruel-NOM
        'The rice gruel is boiling'
(65) a. Devadattaḥ   kusūlam   bhinat -ti
        Devadatta-NOM   pot-ACC   breaks 3SG **ACTIVE**
        'Devadatta breaks the grain pot'
     b. Kusūlo   bhid -ya   -te
        pot-NOM   break passive   3SG **MIDDLE**
        'The grain pot is breaking'

(66) i. a. inddhe
　　　b. idhyate (root *idh*-) 'kindle, ignite'
　　ii. a. pṛṇāti
　　　b. pṛcyate (root *pṛc*-) 'mix'
　　iii. a. riṇakti
　　　b. ricyate (root *ric*-) 'empty, discharge, use up'
　　iv. a. vinakti
　　　b. vicyate (root *vic*-) 'separate, sift'
　　v. a. pṛṇāti
　　　b. pūryate (root *pṛ*-) 'fill'
　　vi. a. vivakti
　　　b. ucyate (root *vac*) 'call (*heissen*)'

Semantically, the neuter middles in (66b, i–vi) are unlike those in (63b, i–iii), because the corresponding active transitive verbs (66a, i–vi) are telic. Formally, these neuter middles are distinguished from those in (63b) by the fact that they are not marked by the middle inflection alone. Rather, the neuters in (66b) are marked by the middle inflection added to a verbal stem with the formant *-ya*. This coincides with the stem formant of the passive in the Sanskrit present tense system, alluded to earlier. Thus the neuter verbs in (66b, i–vi) are formally indistinguishable from passives.[29]

The fact that middle voice alone encodes the neuter, a detransitivizing function, just in the case of atelic verbs seems significant. Cross-linguistically, there is a tendency for lowered transitivity to be associated with atelic verbs, as contrasted with telic verbs (Hopper & Thompson 1980). There is also a tendency for lowered transitivity to be associated with irrealis and nonpunctual temporomodal categories of the verb. Irrealis and nonpunctual have already been discussed in connection with one of the middle's differential functions, noneventuality*, in Fula (see above, Section 2.1). There is a logical affinity between noneventual categories, especially the nonpunctual, and atelic Aktionsart.

It has been observed earlier that the IE middle, in its differential functions, is traditionally associated with lowered transitivity or detransitivization. This is observed particularly in one temporomodal category, the perfect. Evidently this category goes back to the protostage of IE. Both Greek and Sanskrit have a perfect conjugation, and by the classical stage of both languages, its value was that of a preterite or present perfect. An example is the Classical Greek active infinitive *graphō* 'write' contrasted with the perfect middle (first person singular) *gegrapha* 'I have written.'

The original value of the IE perfect seems to have been stative. Many perfects in archaic, or preclassical, Greek and Sanskrit are translated into English by present tense forms with stative sense. Instances in Homeric (from Perel'muter 1988: 277) include *hénnymai* 'to get dressed, dress oneself,' perfect *heîtai* 'he is dressed'; *pynthánomai* 'to learn,' perfect *pépystai* 'he knows.' Sanskrit examples include *cit-* 'to perceive,' present *cetati* 'notices,' perfect *ciketa* 'knows'; *pṛ-* 'to fill,' present *pṛṇāti* 'he fills (something),' perfect *pupūre* '(something) is full.'

In IE the middle has an especial affinity with the stative value of the perfect. Correspondingly, some telic transitive verbs express detransitive neuter meanings only in their middle perfect forms. Homeric illustrations, from Perel'muter 1988: 284, include the following.

(67) a. askéō 'to make beautiful, adorn':
éskētai '(the chariot) is adorned (with gold and silver)'
b. níptō 'to wash':
néniptai '(the blood) has been washed off (the dead body)'
c. syrrégnymi 'to crush':
synérrēktai '(he) is crushed (by many misfortunes)'

This IE behavior is reminiscent of the Fula middle's association with nonpunctual temporomodal categories. As noted in Section 2.1, in Fula this association is particularly strong in one basic transition radical class, the A(M)P class. Fula has many transitive radicals of this class. They accept middle inflections only when their sense is irrealis or, alternatively, when their sense is nonpunctual. In IE the corresponding pattern, just illustrated, is for certain transitive verbs to have detransitive alternates that inflect in the middle voice, these alternates being largely confined to a particular nonpunctual temporomodal category, the perfect.

In Greek, moreover, a large number of verbs (many of which express bodily actions) are invariantly middle-inflecting in one tense category, the future (see Smyth 1974: 219 for a lengthy listing of examples). This is further evidence for the affinity of the middle with the temporomodal semantics of noneventuality*.

These observations suggest that the IE middle's central differential function, that of encoding the affective character of a verbally denoted situation, is more readily achieved if the temporomodal semantics of the verb is nonpunctual. Consistent with this is the fact, observed above, that Sanskrit transitive verbs having inherent atelic or non-goal-presupposing meaning form neuters solely by the assignment of the middle inflection, not by marking for any special temporomodal category. By contrast, neuter middle alternates of transitive verbs which have inherent telic or goal-presupposing meaning are marked with the passive stem formant, which in turn is associated with a specific temporomodal category, the present tense.

In sum, there is evidence that, in its differential neuter function, the IE middle has an affinity both for nonpunctual temporomodal categories or meanings and for detransitivization or valence reduction.

Having concluded the examination of differential functions of the IE middle, the discussion now turns to its inherent functions, functions it encodes as an invariant voice of *media tantum* or middle-only inflecting verbs. Below, these middle functions will be contrasted with inherent functions of the active as an invariant voice of *activa tantum* or active-only inflecting verbs.

Both active-only and middle-only inflecting verbal classes are recognized by traditional grammarians. In some Latin grammars, special emphasis is placed upon the *media tantum* class. This class consists of verbs which occur invariantly in the r conjugation. Traditionally, such verbs are characterized as nonactive in form although active in meaning. Prominent examples include: *hort-* 'urge,' *fate-* 'confess,' *sequ-* 'follow,' *experi-* 'try,' and *pati-* 'suffer.'

Although these verbs are treated here under the rubric *media tantum*, most traditional Latin grammarians refer to them as deponents. This terminology emphasizes the fact that these verbs have a particular semantics contrasting with the passive meaning that accrues in the r conjugation to variably active/middle verbs. As Wheelock 1963: 161, fn. 1, explains, " 'Deponent' derives from **dē-pōnō**, *lay aside*. Though passive in form, these verbs have 'laid aside' their passive meaning and taken an active one."[30]

In contrast to Latin, Greek and Sanskrit do not have a voice marked with the characteristic r. However, like Latin, each of these languages does have verbs which ordinarily do not inflect in the middle, called *activa tantum* verbs; and each has verbs which ordinarily do not inflect in the active, called *media tantum* verbs. The latter class is, again, referred to by some traditional grammarians as deponent. However, in contrast to the deponent verbs in Latin, the Greek and Sanskrit verbs of this class are capable of alternating for voice. They occur either in the middle or the passive – the latter in tenses from which the formal passive is not restricted (for an illustration, see examples 51a, b). Thus the designations *media tantum* or middle-only inflecting, and *activa tantum* or active-only inflecting, are not strictly valid, since Sanskrit and Greek verbs of both these classes do, in principle, passivize.[31]

To evaluate what meanings *activa tantum* and *media tantum* verbs characteristically express, it will be useful to examine a listing of typical members of each class. Accordingly, some examples of Greek verbs belonging to each of these classes are provided in the respective left- and right-hand columns of (68). The larger class, listed in the right-hand column, comprises the *media tantum* verbs. Its members are grouped into two semantic subclasses consisting of (i) *physical actions* and (ii) *mental/emotive actions*. The listings in (68) are based on Schwyzer 1950: 225ff. and Smyth 1974 and are representative only of the language's classical stage. For comparison, a few Sanskrit *activa tantum* and *media tantum* verbs are listed below in (69), due to Burrow 1973: 295.

(68) **activa tantum**   **media tantum**
　　　　　　　　　　　　(i) *physical actions*
　　bainō 'go'　　　　　ēmai 'sit' (occurs in present tense
　　eimi 'go'　　　　　　　only)
　　pēdaō 'leap'　　　　keimai 'lie, be laid'
　　edō 'eat' (cf. Sanskrit *ad-*) oichomai 'be gone'
　　pīnō 'drink'　　　　ereugomai 'belch'
　　chezō 'defecate'　　gignomai 'become, be'
　　omicheō 'urinate'　　petomai 'fly'
　　oureō 'spew, spit'　orchoumai 'dance'
　　emeō 'vomit'　　　　derkomai 'see, look'
　　kluō 'hear'　　　　　phtheggomai 'speak', utter sound'
　　herpō 'creep'　　　　hallomai 'jump, leap'
　　　(cf. Sanskrit *sṛp-*) hepomai 'accompany'
　　　　　　　　　　　　　(cf. Sanskrit *sac-*, Latin *sequ-*)
　　zō 'live'　　　　　　ossomai 'see, fancy, foresee'
　　ethelō 'wish'　　　　theaomai 'see, observe, consider'

akroaomai 'hear'
neomai 'go, come' (occurs in present and imperfect only)

(ii) *mental/emotive actions*
achnumai 'be troubled'
olophuromai 'bewail, lament'
aideomai 'respect; be modest'
achthomai 'be vexed'
memphomai 'blame'
ganumai 'rejoice'
hēdomai 'be pleased'
lilaiomai 'desire eagerly'
boulomai 'wish, will, prefer'
aisthanomai 'perceive'
euchomai 'pray; boast'
skeptomai 'view, regard'
dunamai 'be able, can'
oiomai 'think, conjecture'
phebomai 'fear, be afraid'

(69) **activa tantum**   **media tantum**
    ad-   'eat'   labh- 'receive'
    as-   'be'   ās-   'sit'
    kṣudh- 'be hungry'   kṣam- 'endure'
    bhuj- 'bend, curve'   vas-   'put on, wear (e.g.
    sṛp–   'creep, slink,   clothing)'
           slither'   sac-   'accompany'

Let us consider whether identifiable semantic congruences exist among the active-only and middle-only inflecting classes in Greek and Sanskrit, beginning with Greek.

From the data in (68) it seems that not all verbs in either column conform to any one semantic class. For instance, some verbs in each column converge in meaning, such as active-only *pēdaō* 'leap' and middle-only *hallomai* 'jump, leap'; also active-only *kluō* 'hear' and middle-only *akroaomai* 'hear.' Moreover, each class includes some verbs denoting actions that presuppose the animacy of logical subjects.

However, in (68), the number of active-only verbs which express mental or emotive actions is very small, compared with the number of such verbs in the middle-only class. Moreover, if one compares one of the infrequent active-only verbs of this sort, *ethelō* 'wish,' with the semantically similar middle-only verb *boulomai* 'wish, will, prefer,' a difference of sense is noted. The middle-only verb "wish" denotes a controlled action, one which the participant concerned may choose to engage in or abstain from. The sense of the active-only verb, on the other hand, is that of a reflex, or an action that, as it were, overtakes or occurs to the participant.

A similar contrast in lexical sense is found in some verbs denoting physical or bodily actions. Again, there are verbs denoting such meanings both in the active-only class and in the middle-only class. However, active-only verbs more often express physical or bodily actions that tend to be performed reflexively, such as defecating, urinating, vomiting and the like. By contrast, middle-only verbs of physical or bodily action more often express actions which are ascribable to animate participants and presuppose their control.

To cite one instance, the middle-only Greek verb *hepomai* (corresponding to Sanskrit *sac-*) means 'coincide' or 'follow', but not in the sense of an action which is not controlled or intended by the actor. Rather, the sense of this verb is closer to 'accompany,' i.e. a controlled act of being with or going with another participant. Other middle-only verbs in (68) also denote typically controlled, nonreflex actions presupposing animate logical subjects. Instances include "dance," "speak," "blame," and others.

In sum, to the extent that there is semantic congruity in each of the Greek middle-only and active-only verbal classes, the meanings of these verbs tend to be consistent with an opposition which, as suggested by earlier sections of the present chapter, repeats itself from one active–middle system to another. At the heart of this opposition is the expression of physical and mental attitudes and dispositions presupposing the control of an animate logical subject, as contrasted with reflex, uncontrolled actions; that is, deponent*, as contrasted with nondeponent*, verbal meanings.

Turning to Sanskrit, for the sake of comparison with Greek, only a few examples of active-only and middle-only verbs have been provided in (69). However, in his list of Sanskrit roots, Whitney 1885 furnishes an extensive corpus, yielding some 34 additional verbs which inflect in the middle only, plus more than three times that number of active-only roots. Some discussion of these is now in order.

Whitney's list reveals that the greatest concentration of active-only and middle-only roots alike occurs in just one of the ten Sanskrit conjugational classes, Class Four. This class is made up principally of intransitive verbs, to which belong most of the telic neuter verbs illustrated above in (66b, i–vi). The class in question has been discussed above (n. 29) in regard to the origins of the -*ya* passive, since roots of this class, whether active- or middle-inflecting, form stems in -*ya*. Many active-only and middle-only verbs shortly to be cited belong to this class.[32]

According to Whitney 1973: 273, of the 130 or more Class Four roots, most of which are intransitive, the largest subgroup (over fifty roots) "signify a state of feeling, or a condition of mind or body." Examples include *kṣudh-* 'be hungry,' *tṛṣ-* 'be thirsty,' *kup-* 'be angry,' *klam-* 'be weary,' *muh-* 'be confused,' *lubh-* 'be lustful,' *śuṣ-* 'be dry,' and others. The primary voice of most verbs of this subgroup is active, with some inflecting in the active only, such as the first verb cited, *kṣudh-* (this verb also appears in 69). Semantically, verbs of this class tend to be nondeponent.

According to Whitney, the second-largest subgroup of Class Four verbs, having some forty members, comprises the telic neuters discussed earlier (see 66). As already stated, verbs of this subclass alternate formally with non-Class Four verbs which are transitive and, in most instances, active (with some exceptions; see e.g. ex. 66a, i; a middle). Class Four intransitive neuters themselves are, however, invariantly middle. Gonda 1951: 95 characterizes their semantics thus: "These -*yá*-words denote something happening or befalling a subject, they are 'eventives': a process takes place, by which the subject is, in some way or other, affected. The same processes may also be conceived in a transitive sense; then they are denoted by the active verb."

Gonda, p. 99, observes that Class Four also includes a third, and still smaller, subgroup of invariantly inflecting verbs. All of these roots pertain to a semantic set "which may be called 'Schallwörter'," verbs denoting cries and noises. Examples include *tan-* 'roar,' *dṛp-* 'rave, be mad,' and (questionably Class Four) *rai-* 'bark.' There are also quite a few verbs of the same semantic set outside Class Four. They include: *kvaṇ-* 'tinkle, hum, sound,' *kṣvid-* 'hum, growl,' *kharj-* 'creak (as a wheel),' *guñj-* 'buzz, hum,' *dhvan-* 'make sound, roar,' *mlech-* 'speak indistinctly, blather,' *raṭ-* 'howl,' *raṇ-* 'ring, tinkle,' *rap-* 'talk, chatter,' *stan-* 'thunder,' and *sphūrj-* 'rumble, thunder, crash.' All of these verbs are active-only.

It will be recalled that semantically similar verbs also occur among the active-only classes in other basic voice systems (see the discussion of invariant Strong verbs in Tamil at the end of the preceding section, as well as the comments on Fula A radicals earlier in Section 2.1). Sanskrit verbs of this semantic set express either situations that presuppose inanimate logical subjects, or reflex or noncontrolled actions of animates. Accordingly, like the corresponding active-only verbs in other basic voice systems, these verbs can be characterized semantically as nondeponent. It might be mentioned in passing that a few Sanskrit verbs denoting cries and noises do alternate for both active and middle voices (one instance is *rud-* 'weep, cry'). However, hardly any such verbs are middle-only. One exception, the middle-only verb *vad-* 'tell, say,' is interesting in that it expresses a nonreflex action of speaking articulately. Hence it contrasts semantically with the above-cited verbs, since it is deponent.

Outside Class Four, too, there occur semantically deponent middle-only verbs. Among these are the verbs listed in the right-hand column of (69). Occasionally, middle alternates of active/middle verbs also express deponent or deponent-like meanings. One example is the verb *ut-sthā*, which means 'rise' in the active (e.g. *āsanād uttiṣṭhati* 'he rises from the seat') but has the deponent sense 'strive' in the middle (e.g. *gehe uttiṣṭhate* 'he strives for the house') (these examples are from commentary to Pāṇini's rule I.iii.24 *udonūrdhvakarmaṇi*). In light of this, it might be too extreme to characterize deponent meaning as a strictly inherent, never differential middle voice function.

Neuter meaning, which has been characterized earlier as a differential middle voice function, is likewise occasionally expressed by middle-only verbs in Sanskrit. A Class Four middle-only verb *liś* 'become small, diminish' seems to share the inchoative* semantics characteristic of neuter verbs; the same holds for several non-Class-Four middle-only verbs, including *sphāy-* 'swell,' *pru-* 'spring up, reach to, flow,' and *khall-* 'be loose, shake, be slack.' It must be acknowledged, however, that some active-only verbs are ambiguous, expressing both transitive and detransitive-neuter readings without any alteration of shape or voice. Instances include *śrā-* 'mature, boil, cook, ripen' and *pī-* 'increase, grow, fatten.'

As a counterpart to middle-only verbs with deponent semantics, there also occur in Sanskrit a number of active-only verbs which are nondeponent, expressing either reflex actions presupposing animate subjects, or actions whose logical subjects are characteristically inanimate. Aside from the *Schallwörter* verbs cited earlier, instances include: *ṣṭhiv-* 'spit out, expectorate,' *sas-* 'sleep, be inactive,' *dal-* 'split open, bloom,' *lul-* 'move to and fro, dangle, be tremulous,' *sriv-* 'fail, miscarry,' *sridh-* 'fail, blunder' and *dhraj-* 'glide, move, fly.'

Finally, a number of Sanskrit middle-only verbs denote actions that in some way implicate the logical subject's affectedness. Correspondingly, certain active-only verbs are semantically effective, denoting actions whose principal effects ordinarily devolve upon a participant other than the logical subject. Verbs of the former class, invariant middles, include: *īḍ-* 'implore, ask for,' *kḷp-* 'be adapted, accommodate oneself to, be suitable,' *ghaṭṭ-* 'grope, rub the hands over a thing,' *bhikṣ-* 'accept alms, beg,' *maṃh-* 'bestow e.g. as alms, be beneficent, be liberal.' Verbs of the latter class, invariant actives, include: *turv-* 'overcome, overpower,' *tsar-* 'steal up to, sneak up on,' *dhūrv-* 'bend, injure,' *pā-* 'protect,' *pṛ-* 'rescue,' *snath-* 'pierce, strike, injure' and *vrasc-* 'hew, fell, cut down.'

The findings of the present section can now be recapitulated, beginning with a summary of the IE middle's differential functions.

First, the IE middle has an affinity with various semantic functions consistent with affectedness*, or denoting situations the principal effects of which devolve upon the referent of the logical subject. This applies to a number of the middle's differential functions, such as the earlier-discussed nucleonic and body-part middle functions. It also occasionally holds of the middle as an inherent voice of certain verbs which do not inflect in the active. However, in classical IE languages, two functions which would seem logically consistent with the middle's affective semantics, the semantic reflexive (referent of subject does action to self) and the reciprocal (referents of plural subject do action to each other), are, at best, marginal functions of the middle voice.

In a second differential function, the middle is associated with neuter* verbs, a special subcategory of intransitives. Verbs of this subcategory tend to be semantically inchoative*, and they alternate with formally related transitives.

In addition, in its neuter function the IE middle is associated with noneventuality*, especially as a voice of verbs expressing inherent nonpunctual* or atelic* temporomodal senses. Also, both in its function of encoding the neuter and as the inflectional category of the formal passive, the middle in languages such as Greek and Sanskrit has an affinity with detransitivization*.

Lastly, a large number of IE verbs belong to invariant-inflecting classes. These classes, *media tantum* and *activa tantum*, provide evidence that the middle and the active have contrasting inherent functions. To the extent that each of these classes is semantically congruent, certain patterns are in evidence.

First, verbs of the former class, middle-only inflecting verbs, characteristically express deponent* meanings. Frequently they denote postures or states of body or mind that presuppose the animacy as well as the control* of the logical subject.

By contrast, the inherent function of the active is nondeponent*, with active-only inflecting verbs characteristically expressing non-controlled/reflex actions, as opposed to animate/controlled actions.

2.4 Basic voice as patterning of the verbal lexicon

This chapter has had two objectives. One has been to establish the character of active/middle alternations in basic voice systems, with particular emphasis upon characteristic cross-linguistic functions of the middle. Among these, particular emphasis has been placed on detransitivization* (valence reduction) and reflexivity*.

The present chapter's other major objective has been to establish some positive characterization of voice behavior in basic voice systems. Some consistency of organization in the verbal lexicon does manifest itself in languages with productive alternations of active/middle morphology in the verb; this will be elaborated upon shortly.

In regard to the first objective, the survey of active–middle systems in Sections 2.1–2.3 reveals several findings.

First, the functions of middle voices and reflexives are not coterminous, similarities notwithstanding. Cross-linguistically, the number of distinct functions associated with reflexives is large (over fifteen are distinguished by Geniušienė 1987) and far exceeds the number of distinct functions of the morphological middle voice. An examination of reflexive in comparison with middle voice reveals that the two categories, reflexive and middle, characteristically overlap in only a few functions, such as the neuter and body-part functions; also, in some languages, the possessive–objective and catalytic functions, as well as the indirect or transitive function (illustrated above in 20b). The proto-

2.4 Basic voice as patterning of the verbal lexicon 105

typical meaning of reflexives is, however, the structural reflexive, involving coincidence in the referents of verbally assigned core nominal positions. Two especially typical structural reflexive functions, often encoded by reflexive markers, are the semantic reflexive and the reciprocal.[33]

But neither semantic reflexive nor structural reciprocal meaning are specifically encoded by the morphological middle voice. In fact, in some of the languages surveyed above, these functions are either invariably or characteristically active.

Second, the middle, when in contrast with the active, cross-linguistically displays an association with various kinds of noneventuality*, e.g. with atelic, nonpunctual, and/or irrealis temporomodal categories of the verb. This is manifested either overtly (through the middle's affinity for particular tense–aspect categories in some languages) or covertly (through the middle's affinity with particular verbal Aktionsart classes in other languages).

Third, the middle, when in contrast with the active, correlates with valence reduction or detransitivization* in the particular respects summarized in (70):

(70) a. In every surveyed system, middle-inflecting verbs demonstrate a greater statistical tendency than active-inflecting verbs to be intransitive.
   b. Neuter meaning is expressed by middle verbs in every surveyed system. Generally, such verbs are intransitive. In the majority of systems (Fula and IE), neuters comprise a subclass of middle-only inflecting verbs; while elsewhere (i.e. in Tamil), they comprise middle alternates of alternating active/middle verbs.
   c. Each surveyed system evinces a distinction among three subclasses of lexical verbs: active-only (non-middle inflecting), middle-only (non-active inflecting), and alternating active/middle. Among these, the basic valence of verbs of the third class is nearly always transitive, making intransitivity more characteristic of verbs which either are incapable of forming middles, or verbs whose primary voice is middle rather than active.

Finally, either as a characteristic voice of middle-only as contrasted with active-only verbs, or in opposition to the active voice for active/middle inflecting verbs, the middle implicates the logical subject's affectedness*. That is, the middle encodes a range of specific meanings, which vary from system to system, such that the referent of the nominal which a verb assigns as logical subject coincides with the locus of the principal effects of the verbally denoted action. This point will be returned to below.

As regards the present chapter's second objective, that of providing a positive characterization of the patterning of active and middle voices in basic voice systems, some intriguing parallels have been observed among the systems surveyed above. These are summarized in (71a–d).

(71) a. Every basic voice system is organized into classes of active-only, middle-only, and alternating active/middle inflecting lexical verbs (as noted in 70c).
b. Among the three verbal classes listed in (a), in every basic voice system surveyed, the alternating active/middle class is the largest.
c. The two nonalternating verbal classes of a basic voice system are characteristically of unequal size. One of the two classes, whether the active-only or the middle-only, is larger than the other. In Fula and Sanskrit, the former class is larger. Fula active-only (A) verbs outnumber middle-only (M) verbs by about two-to-one; in Sanskrit the corresponding ratio is about three-to-one. By contrast, in Tamil the middle (Weak)-only verbs appear to comprise the larger class, although the survey reported on above, Section 2.2, is too limited for this to be claimed with certainty.
d. While the middle demonstrates some affinity with intransitivity (70a–c), the active/middle opposition criss-crosses distinctions of lexical transitivity and intransitivity.

The characteristics listed in (71a–d), especially (c) and (d), are highly reminiscent of other, currently better-studied systems, which are identified cross-linguistically on the basis of specific patterns of organization of the verbal lexicon. Accordingly, in studying verbal organization in basic voice systems, it may be useful to invoke a typological comparison with systems of the ergative* (ergative–accusative) and active* (active–stative) types.

More will be said concerning ergative and active in the following chapter. But at this point, as a prelude to that discussion, it may be worthwhile to examine schemes of argument-structure organization in

2.4 Basic voice as patterning of the verbal lexicon

ergative and active languages, comparing a parallel scheme for active–middle languages.

This comparison is provided in Figure 2.5. In the figure, (i) is a schematic representation of an ergative–absolutive system, while (ii) is a schematic representation of an active–stative system. (The former is due to Comrie 1978: 332; the latter to Mock 1980: 10.) A corresponding scheme tentatively representing the organization of an active–middle system is proposed in part (iii) of the figure.

As part (i) of the figure shows, in an ergative system a single set of marking behaviors (and possibly other behaviors as well) devolves upon S and P (intransitive logical subjects, transitive logical objects) in opposition to A (transitive logical subjects). Also, of the two nominal groupings, A tends to be more marked grammatically. The specific manifestations of this markedness may differ from system to system, but typically include such devices as phonologically null (S, P) vs nonnull (A) case assignments, greater restriction in linear positioning of marked class (A) nominals, and others. Moreover, a common feature of all ergative systems is that subjects of intransitives (S) coalesce in formal properties with one of the core nominal positions assigned by transitives (specifically, with P).

Active–stative systems as schematized in part (ii) of the figure also involve a formal coalescence of S with some transitive core nominal position, A or P. However, in these systems, S coalesces in some instances with the former and in others with the latter. An active–stative system, then, will have intransitive verbs whose subjects are A- or subjective-inflecting, as well as intransitive verbs whose subjects are P- or objective-inflecting. Often there also occurs a third class of intransitives whose subjects are variably A- or P-inflecting (these sometimes vary in lexical meanings according to the inflection).

In an active–stative system, the basis of the subjective-inflecting/objective-inflecting distinction in intransitives typically has to do with the degree of control* over the action ascribed to the referent of S. Relatively controlling intransitive subjects tend to be A-inflecting; relatively noncontrolling, P-inflecting. However, the precise membership of the A-inflecting and P-inflecting intransitive subclasses varies greatly from one active system to another. Moreover, as in the case of active–middle systems, so too in active–stative systems, there is a tendency for one intransitive subclass, either the A-inflecting or the P-

(i) **ergative–absolutive**

Markedness		−	+
transitive	V	P	A
intransitive	V	S	

(ii) **active–stative**

Markedness		+	−
transitive	V	A	P
intransitive	V	S_a	S_p

(iii) **active–middle**

Argument affectedness		−	+
active			
(i) intransitive	V	S	
(ii) transitive	V	A	P
middle			
(iii) transitive	V	P	A
(iv) intransitive	V		S

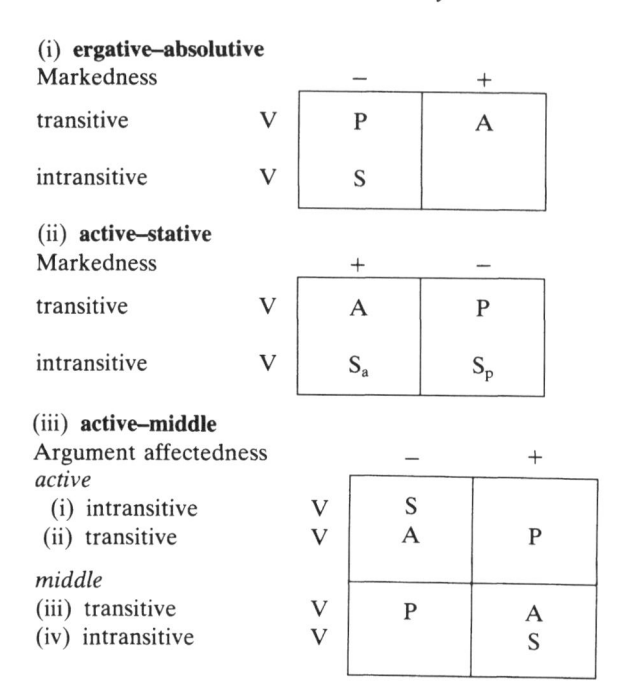

Figure 2.5 Ergative, active and active–middle argument-structure organization

inflecting, to be larger than the other. Active–stative verbal organization is discussed in greater detail in the next chapter.[34]

In the schematic representation of an active–middle system given in part (iii) of Figure 2.5, it is assumed that argument affectedness underlies the pattern of verbal organization. This again occurs in such a way as to presuppose – but not coalesce with – transitivity distinctions.

As (iii) shows, none of active S, active A or middle P is positively specified for affectedness. However, the active P, in contradistinction to the active S or A, is positively specified for this property. On the other hand, in the middle voice, it is the S or A as opposed to the P which is positively specified for affectedness.

Further, (iii) is consistent with the fact that the verbs which most tend to be variably active-/middle-inflecting are basically transitive. Also, the scheme is consistent with the fact that both active-only and middle-only verbs may in principal be either transitive or intransitive. Some facts, however (such as the fact that a minority of variably active/middle verbs

2.4 Basic voice as patterning of the verbal lexicon

are intransitive, e.g. Greek *politeu-*, which has been illustrated in example 19 of Chapter 1; and the fact that the middle has a greater affinity for intransitivity) are not captured in the scheme.

Figure 2.5, part (iii), reflects a view of basic voice as a specific type of organization of the verbal lexicon of a language. As a crude model, such a scheme may not be without merit. However, under this scheme, certain matters are not addressed.

One is the problem of positively specifying what comprises affectedness*, the semantic function associated in a variety of ways, cross-linguistically, with morphological middle voices. Another problem is to establish what this function represents in terms of grammatical theory. The second of these problems is returned to in Chapter 6 below. The first problem is taken up in the next chapter.

3 Control and voice

3.0 Preliminaries

According to the previous chapter, basic voice, the voice type exemplified by active–middle systems, reflects a pattern of lexical predicate classification. To account for this pattern in a typological perspective, the present chapter proposes a natural semantic classification for lexical predicates. The hypothetical universal basis of the classification is a control construct* schematically represented in Figure 3.1.

Figure 3.1 is to be interpreted as follows. Universally, some predicates pertain to a natural class denoting events with respect to which control is attributed to no argument (or properly speaking, to no argument-encoded participant). In some instances, the meaning of a predicate may associate absence of control with one or more nominal positions. Accordingly, absence of control may be considered a participant role* as defined above, Section 1.5.

Predicates of the class which ascribe control to no argument, non-control predicates, occur in two subclasses shown in the figure (to be discussed later). Non-control predicates contrast with a complementary class of predicates, control predicates, which denote actions. Here the term action* specifically refers to any verbally encoded event implicating the involvement of some participant to whom or which control is attributed.

Control predicates are, in turn, organized into two natural subclasses. One subclass comprises predicates to whose logical subjects (or properly speaking, to whose logical subject referents) control is attributed. The other subclass comprises predicates to whose logical subjects control is not attributed. In the latter instance, attribution of control may devolve instead upon a nonsubject core argument, or upon an argument mapped to a suppressed, or null, nominal position.

The term logical subject* is used here in reference to the argument of

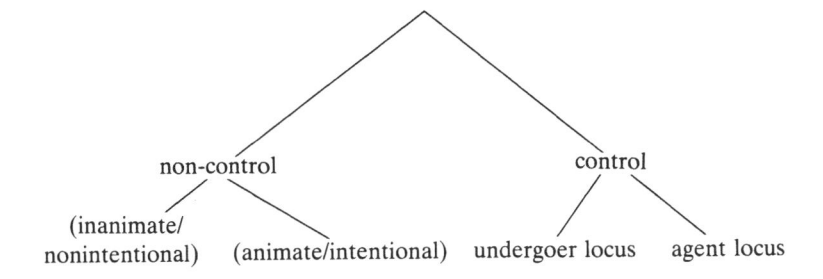

```
                    ╱╲
                   ╱  ╲
            non-control    control
             ╱    ╲         ╱    ╲
   (inanimate/
  nonintentional) (animate/intentional) undergoer locus  agent locus
```

Figure 3.1 Natural predicate classification according to the control construct

a lexical verb's predicate-argument structure which is thematically superior (according to a theta-hierarchy* along the lines discussed in such works as Bresnan 1987 and Kiparsky 1987; a simplified version might be agent > beneficiary > experiencer > theme/patient > location). A logical subject to which control is ascribed will be understood as having the participant role of agent*; while a logical subject of an action predicate which is non-controlling (e.g. outranked for control by some other thematic relation that the verb assigns) will be understood as having a distinct participant role, undergoer*.[1] Where its locus of control corresponds to an agent, a predicate will be said to have an agentive semantics; and where the locus of control corresponds to an argument distinct from the logical subject, the predicate will be said to have an undergoing semantics.

While hypothetically universal, the control construct may impinge upon the organization of the verbal lexicon in ways that vary from language to language. In this chapter, it will be shown that, in some languages, the control construct is relevant to verbal classification just among intransitive basic predicates; in other languages, just among basic (nonderived) predicates; whereas in still other languages, it plays a role in both basic and derived predicate classification.

According to the preceding chapter, the classification of verbs into active/middle, active-only, and middle-only inflecting subclasses in basic voice systems is similar in broad outline from system to system, but differs in particulars. Accordingly, the inflectional class of any given predicate is difficult to predict, and may vary from one basic voice system to another.

The case is similar for the control-encoding systems to be surveyed in this chapter. It is not suggested here that an individual predicate's lexical class – agentive, undergoing, or non-control – is cross-linguistically stable, or can be predicted with any degree of certainty. Rather, the aim of the survey below is to show how active–middle or basic voice conforms with and relates to an array of apparently universal strategies whereby a language's verbal lexicon is organized on the basis of the control construct.

The plan of the chapter is as follows. Section 3.1 presents an overview of the control construct and discusses its foundations in philosophy and the social sciences. Section 3.2 surveys lexical predicate classification according to the control construct in several distinct kinds of systems: unaccusative* (3.2.1), active–stative* (3.2.2), and overtly control-classifying (3.2.3). Section 3.3 returns to basic voice systems, suggesting a new perspective on the analysis of active–middle lexical patterning.

Thereafter the discussion turns to systems in which the grammatical significance of control extends beyond the organization of basic lexical predicates. Section 3.4 discusses attribution of control and the semantics of affectedness in certain complex constructions called submissive verb* constructions. Section 3.5 discusses verbal derivation and attribution of control. Lastly, Section 3.6 concerns the cooccurrence in individual systems of different verbal classification strategies. It also discusses theoretical implications of the chapter's findings.

3.1 Perspectives on the control construct

The literature of universal grammar includes some works dealing with attribution of control (e.g. Brennenstuhl 1976, Brennenstuhl & Wachowicz 1976, and Givón 1975). Attribution of control is also a topic in grammatical descriptions of some individual languages, several of which are cited below. However, attribution of control is not yet as extensively investigated in grammatical theory as in some other scholarly fields.

For instance, control and related issues of action, agency and undergoing have long figured prominently in philosophy. Moreover, philosophical writings furnish the intellectual antecedents for research on control in the social sciences. Attribution of control has recently been a prominent topic in psychology, particularly in social learning theory (on which see Phares 1976, Chapter 2).

In both philosophy and psychology, an effort has been made to dis-

3.1 Perspectives on the control construct

tinguish the concept of control from that of agency*. Agency and its converse, undergoing*, are concepts much discussed in linguistics, but their origins are not in the traditions of grammatical theory. They recur, rather, to a tradition of philosophical thought as old as Aristotle's discussion of the primacy of object vs action (McKinney 1981). As noted above, in philosophical usage, the term action* applies to verbally encoded events which implicate agency.

Davidson 1971: 7 proposes to define agency in terms of intention: "a man is the agent of an act if what he does can be described under an aspect that makes it intentional." The qualification "under an aspect" accommodates action intentionally undertaken but having an unintended outcome, as when one accidentally wrecks a car while driving. In addition, the view of agency Davidson proposes avoids the specious (but popular) association of action with activity and undergoing with passivity.[2]

Being a relation of intention, agency presupposes both animacy as well as awareness of the action of which one is author (Thalberg 1972: 91). It also implicates volitionality; an action, by definition, is both conscious and also nonreflex (Thalberg, p. 52). However, volitionality itself is a complex notion, less straightfoward than that of intention. For instance, volitionality is not simply absence of coercion, since one may act voluntarily even when one's situation or one's choices are affected by external manipulation; a person may voluntarily do what another obliges him to. Accordingly, Wertheimer 1987 proposes to characterize behavior as nonvolitional when it is in conflict with the individual's stable, long-term preferences and/or accepted principles of conduct. Therefore, bodily reflexes are not, properly speaking, involuntary (although they may be non-controlled).

Undergoing is popularly understood as the converse of agency, but an undergoer's participation in an action, in contrast to an agent's, need be neither conscious nor volitional. That agency and undergoing have reality in structural organization and comprise grammatically significant statuses is part of the lore of the Western grammatical tradition, particularly in the study of grammatical voice (Section 1.1). However, nonaction predicates, predicates which presuppose neither agency nor undergoing, are also significant in the descriptive analysis of some kinds of voice systems. They, too, have a place in the study of universal patterns of lexical organization (Thalberg 1972). More will be said concerning them in the following section.

Control* is different from both agency and undergoing. Unlike agent (and undergoer), the notion of controller is not predicated on the concept of action*. Moreover, control – unlike agency – entails neither awareness nor intention, although in some circumstances a controller may also be an agent.

Recently, several writers have propounded a view that control relates to a state of options or choices an individual may have in a given situation. A person is said to control an outcome if and only if the person can make a voluntary response that increases the probability of occurrence of that outcome, where by "voluntary response" is meant a response that increases in probability when rewarded and decreases when punished (Lacey 1979: 11). According to Brennenstuhl 1976: 62, "A process is uncontrollable for a person if after an appropriate number of attempts to prevent, to change, or to produce it he has not been able to narrow down the failures and to increase the success ratio above random." This view of matters is precise, but unfortunately has a limitation. Processes an individual cannot control may also be beyond his/her capacity to attempt; so in practice, under the above characterization, it may be difficult to determine the controllability of a given process.

In psychology, a number of significant insights are due to research on locus of control*. This term refers to a psychological construct, i.e. a pattern of construal of oneself and one's place in the world on the part of the individual.

The locus of control construct is defined as a pattern of expectancies as to the source or origin of reinforcement, i.e. what happens to one (McKinney 1981). Locus of control is said to be internal when there is an expectancy that reinforcement results from one's own behavior; external when there is an expectancy that reinforcement has some other origin, such as chance or powerful others (see papers in Lefcourt 1981). Such expectancies may be either situation-specific or generalized, amounting in the latter case to a feature of personality (Dyer 1976: 138ff.).

Although in philosophy, control is sometimes equated with the power to act or not as one chooses (Thalberg 1972: 16), psychological research draws a distinction between control and power. Power, like locus of control, is a construct. But whereas locus of control is a set of expectancies as to the source of reinforcement, power is understood as (a) a motivational state and (b) a set of expectancies as to the efficacy of one's behavior (Phares 1976: 71ff.).

Also, control is sometimes related to choice, i.e. capacity to choose; but properly speaking, this too is to be distinguished from control. Seligman & Miller 1979: 349–50 illustrate the distinction in terms of a situation of coerced choice: a thief offers a victim the choice between his money and his life. The victim who hands over his wallet makes a choice, but cannot be said to be in control. The example illustrates an important aspect of the difference between power and control, one that hinges on a distinction between outcome control vs agenda control. In making his choice, the victim of the above example exercises some control over the outcome of the situation, but it is the thief who wields control over the agenda, and is consequently seen as having power over the victim.[3] Apparently agenda, not outcome, control is the basis of the concept of power and also the concept of autonomy, the latter referring to the absence of a control relation between two social entities (Rosenbaum 1986: 113). In all likelihood, the concept of authority likewise arises from agenda control.

Distinct from, yet related to, locus of control is a second construct, locus of causality (McKinney 1981; DeCharms 1979, 1981). Like locus of control, locus of causality may be internal or external; but it differs in its basis from locus of control. DeCharms 1981: 344 characterizes internal locus of causality as "the person's experience of being the cause of his decisions, choices, activities, and attempts to solve problems as well as of the solutions to problems." External locus of causality would, conversely, be the experience of decisions, choices, etc. originating outside the individual.

By contrast, locus of control, as noted earlier, refers to the attribution of the source of reinforcement, i.e. *outcomes* to behavior. In addition, locus of causality, rather than locus of control, is considered closely related to the perception of freedom (Harvey, Harris & Lightner 1979, Perlmuter & Monty 1979: 271–3). Individuals may perceive themselves as unfree "yet realize that, at least up to a point, they retain control" (Phares 1976: 34), as when individuals live in a totalitarian situation wherein the outcomes of defiance are highly predictable.

A further contrast between outcome control and locus of causality is worth considering. Imagine a storm approaching a group of individuals enjoying a picnic. The approaching storm causes the picnickers to abandon their festivities. Nevertheless, they retain a degree of control, not over the storm, but over the situation of which the storm is an aspect – they can take steps to evade the storm's effects, and so avoid a drenching. This example illustrates how internal locus of outcome control may coexist with external locus of causality. It is easy to imagine other circumstances in which an individual may lack outcome control. For instance, little can be done to evade the grief occasioned by the death of an intimate. Outcome control seems to be significant to some patterns of lexical behavior, and will be mentioned again in later sections of this chapter.

The present section is not intended as a thoroughgoing summary of the philosophical and psychological literature on control. However, if one assumes that some grammatical behaviors may encode control distinctions, then a question arises as to the control construct's underlying mechanism: is the value people place on control culturally contingent and the product of social conditioning (such as learning), or is attribution of control an inborn aspect of perception?

Recent writers differ on this issue. For instance, some suggest that locus of control may be shaped and influenced by forces outside the individual (Renshon 1979, Reid & Ziegler 1981, Levenson 1981, Phares 1976: 156–9).

However, other writers suggest that locus of control relates to the individual's needs and perceptions at an extremely basic level. For instance, according to Seligman & Miller 1979, an array of experimental studies indicates dramatic correlations between control and physiological function. These include studies showing that significant physiological disorder arises in individuals who have limited control over stresses to which they and a yoked, passive partner are jointly subjected. These responses are observed not solely in humans, but, significantly, have been documented also in monkeys and other animals (Lefcourt 1982: 16–18).

Seligman & Miller 1979 report that the level of electric shock that individuals agree to experience under experimental conditions doubles in intensity when subjects expect to have control over the shock, as contrasted with a situation in which no control is expected. Control may consist of an "escape" button which nullifies the shock administered in response to error on a learning task. Subjects are often content to have the button at hand throughout the experiment without using it. Their behavior suggests that physiology makes adjustments to perceived control or its absence.

Another group of relevant experiments (cited in Seligman & Miller 1979: 361) involves young children as subjects. Offered a blind choice (such as a chance to be awarded the content of either of two closed, opaque tin cans), subjects usually prefer to exercise the choice (the selection of cans) themselves, rather than leave it up to the experimenter. The results of these experiments suggests that choice *per se* is intuitively valued, irrespective of its situational utility or meaninglessness.

Perlmuter & Monty 1979: 346 comment on this experimental literature, noting that while the mechanism underlying the findings is as yet dimly understood, the results are nonetheless suggestive. Perhaps most impressive are the findings on animals and yoked control. As Perlmuter & Monty remark, "The culture-free results of relevant animal experiments strongly support the idea that the need for control be considered axiomatic." It has been speculated, moreover, that there may be psychological prerequisites to the conceptualization of agency and undergoing and that these prerequisites may arise from a natural dichotomy of subjective vs objective self-awareness states (Duval & Wicklund 1972).

For purposes of the discussion to follow, it is assumed, on the basis of the preceding, that attribution of control is a fundamental and universal behavior in certain natural species, including humans. Given this, there seems no reason in principle to discount the possibility that attribution of control may be reflected in the mental structures which underlie grammatical behavior.

The balance of this chapter concerns the grammaticization of control through certain patterns of lexical predicate organization.

3.2 The grammar of control

Locus of agency* and undergoing*, two concepts discussed above, Section 3.0, devolve upon nominal positions assigned in a verb's predicate-argument structure*. Verbal classes can be defined according to whether and in what way individual predicates assign either or both of these statuses.

However, any predicate that assigns an agent*, whether or not in the logical role of subject, expresses an action* in the sense of a verbally denoted event presupposing some participant's control (see again Section 3.0). It follows from this that attribution of control is superordinate to both agency and undergoing. Accordingly, control is not a nominal status assigned by a verb, but a characteristic that inheres in the verb's semantics.

The following three subsections survey several different ways in which control and non-control basic predicate classes are organized in various systems. Section 3.2.1 discusses a classification of intransitive predicates known as the unaccusative/unergative* opposition. Section 3.2.2 concerns the classification of intransitives in active* (active–stative) systems. Section 3.2.3 surveys an extended basic predicate classification system in a Uto-Aztecan language, Cupeño.

As a preliminary to the survey, it is worth summarizing certain philosophical views on control semantics and the lexicon in universal grammar. Thalberg 1972, Chapter 2, distinguishes two classes of action* predicates, termed verbs of doing and verbs of undergoing (or of "having things happen to one"). Both types belong to a larger class of control-presupposing (or simply control) predicates.

In English, according to Thalberg, there are certain criteria for identifying control predicates. One is the predicate's ability or inability to cooccur with an adverb of volition or nonvolition (e.g. *deliberately* or *unwillingly*). (To be sure, these adverbs cooccur more felicitously with a control predicate having an agentive, not an undergoing, logical subject; note the oddity of ??*John was robbed on purpose*.)

For the remainder of the present discussion, it is assumed that every language has criteria for determining a given verb's membership in the control predicate class, although particular criteria may differ from language to language.

Thalberg goes on to observe, however, that in a given language, some predicates may not conform to the applicable criteria, thereby comprising predicates neither of doing nor of undergoing. Such predicates do not express actions. They can be called non-control predicates.

For instance, in English, inability to cooccur with expressions of control or of lack of control (e.g. volitionality-expressing and nonvolitionality-expressing adverbs) establishes the membership of a predicate in the non-control class. According to Thalberg (pp. 55ff.), English non-control predicates are distributed among three subclasses schematized in Figure 3.2.[4]

Class One

"Bodily process verbs," including: perspire, flush, pale, bleed, tremble, throb, grow, digest (food). Predicates of this class denote spontaneous behaviors of the body or its parts.

Class Two

"Reaction verbs," including: blush, shudder, yawn, hiccup, choke, wheeze, vomit, sneeze. Though semantically similar to Class One verbs, these differ in denoting events that cannot be predicated of the body or its parts, but must be predicated of persons (compare e.g. *Max's face flushed/bled/trembled* with **Max's face blushed/shuddered/yawned*).

Class Three

"Breakdown verbs," including: (a) fumble, stammer, trip, stagger, collapse; (b) snore, faint, die. Subgroup (a) predicates denote lapses in an individual's control over events other than bodily functions; subgroup (b) predicates denote lapses in bodily functioning.

Figure 3.2 Non-control predicate subclasses according to Thalberg 1972

All the predicates in Figure 3.2 presuppose animate subjects. In addition, referents of the logical subjects they assign have intention and awareness – faculties that (as noted in the preceding section) are characteristic of agents*.

The reason why the predicates in Figure 3.2 are non-control predicates is that the events they denote are not subject to the logical subject's control. However, there exists another, complementary class of non-control predicates not included in the figure. These are non-control predicates presupposing neither the intention nor the awareness of the logical subject. Examples include verbs which express natural occurrences, such as *rain*, *hail* and *thunder*, or behaviors and attributes of entities low in agency, e.g. *bloom*, *fructify* and so on. These verbs can be classed as non-control predicates of a special subclass, inanimate/nonintentional predicates.

The difference between verbs of this subclass and the predicates listed in the figure, animate/intentional non-control predicates, can be clarified by invoking a scale of potentiality of agency (sometimes called an animacy hierarchy). Such a scale has been proposed by Dixon 1979: 85; it is reproduced below as Figure 3.3. According to Dixon, the arrow in

120 *Control and voice*

| 1st person pronominal | 2nd person pronominal | 3rd person pronominal | proper noun | human common noun | animate common noun | inanimate common noun |

←───

Figure 3.3 Potentiality of agency scale (animacy hierarchy)

the figure represents increasing "likelihood of functioning as transitive agent" of an action predicate. The scale amounts to a ranking of nominal referent classes for ontological salience, each higher class being viewed as hypothetically more likely to act on some lower class than to be acted on by a lower class.

Notice that logical subjects of the two subclasses of non-control predicates shown in Figure 3.1 – inanimate/nonintentional and animate/intentional – align with opposite ends of the scale. That is, logical subjects of the inanimate/nonintentional class tend to have low potentiality of agency, and so cluster at the opposite end of the scale from logical subjects of the other class of non-control predicates, animate/intentional predicates, which have high potentiality of agency. To be sure, both subclasses have nonaction semantics; their logical subjects are nonagents. But the participant roles of these logical subjects differ in terms of potentiality of agency, as shown in the scale.

Notice that both classes of non-control (nonaction) predicates contrast with undergoing predicates. Undergoing predicates do denote actions, or events with respect to which there is some agent, a participant credited with control. They differ from agentive predicates in that the logical subjects they assign are not agents. Undergoing predicates include basic intransitive verbs such as *spread*, *melt*, *open*, etc.; i.e. neuter* verbs. They also include derived passives of predicates that assign agents as basic subjects. Thus both neuter and passive verbs are actional but nonagentive. By contrast, the verbs in Figure 3.2 and the inanimate/nonintentional verbs mentioned following the figure are neither agentive nor undergoing, but comprise non-control predicates.

It is hoped that this section has helped to clarify the natural semantic classification schematized in Figure 3.1. As the figure shows, non-control and control predicates represent a fundamental natural semantic opposition. Within the former, there is a further natural opposition of inanimate/nonintentional vs animate/intentional predicates; and within the latter, there is a further opposition of nonagentive, i.e. undergoing, vs agentive predicates. The figure represents each of these natural oppositions.

The three subsections that follow concern overt predicate classification behaviors in various languages which reflect the scheme of Figure 3.1 either in its entirety or in part.

3.2.1 Agency, undergoing and intransitive predicate classification: unaccusativity

One opposition schematized in the control construct, Figure 3.1, is that of agentive* vs undergoing* predicates. In numerous languages, the encoding of this opposition has scope only among the intransitive, not the transitive, basic (nonderived) lexical verbs.

One manifestation of this is unaccusativity*, a subclassification of lexical intransitives into two complementary subgroups, frequently called unaccusative* and unergative*. Unaccusativity consists in the grammatical subjects of certain intransitive verbs displaying behaviors characteristic of grammatical objects (Bresnan 1987: 3). It is manifested in an opposition of two complementary intransitive basic predicate classes, one class (unergatives) assigning subjects that conform to behaviors of transitive subjects (A); and a second class (unaccusatives) assigning subjects that conform to one or more behaviors of transitive objects (P).

The overt manifestations of unaccusativity vary from language to language. One well-known language-particular instance, found in Italian, involves a contrast in the selection of copular verbs *essere* and *avere* in the formation of participial predicates (Perlmutter 1982: 305).

Some recent analyses handle the unergative/unaccusative opposition by treating an unaccusative verb as assigning a sole core nominal which comprises not a subject, but an object, at some fundamental structural domain or level. In a multistratal* formalism, such as relational grammar, this level might be the initial stratum of a syntactic representation (see Klaiman in preparation); while in a monostratal* formalism, the same facts might be captured in the predicate's lexically assigned valence* (as in the lexical–functional treatment of unaccusativity proposed by Baker 1983). (On the distinction between multi- and monostratal grammars, see Ladusaw 1988.)

Although the precise membership of unaccusative and unergative subclasses is not uniform from language to language (Rosen 1984), there

(A) Unaccusatives

(a) "Predicates expressed by adjectives in English," including predicates expressing size and color
(b) "Predicates whose initial nuclear term is semantically a Patient," e.g. drip, shake, thrive, boil, and all inchoative* predicates, e.g. melt, freeze
(c) "Predicates of existing and happening," e.g. exist, occur, result, disappear
(d) "Non-voluntary emission of stimuli that impinge on the senses," e.g. shine, glitter, crackle, stink
(e) "Aspectual predicates," e.g. begin, cease, continue
(f) "Duratives," e.g. last, stay, remain

(B) Unergatives

(a) "Predicates describing willed or volitional acts," e.g. work, smile, joke, lie
(b) "Manner-of-speaking verbs," e.g. whisper, growl
(c) "Sounds made by animals," e.g. bark, chirp, roar
(d) Predicates of "certain involuntary bodily processes," e.g. cough, sneeze, belch, sleep

Figure 3.4 Tentative classification of unergative vs unaccusative predicate concepts, based on Perlmutter 1978

does seem to be some cross-linguistic semantic congruity. This is suggested by a scheme of unergative vs unaccusative predicate concepts tentatively proposed by Perlmutter 1978, partially reproduced in Figure 3.4.

Writers occasionally dispute details of the scheme in Figure 3.4 (see Chapter 2, n. 13 for an instance in point). Generally, however, it is accepted that unergatives and unaccusatives are organized cross-linguistically into complementary subclasses more or less along the lines indicated in the figure.

It is noteworthy that the pattern of semantic classification in the figure seems consistent with oppositions in the control construct (Figure 3.1). Verbs of the (A) group in Figure 3.4, unaccusatives, are intransitives whose logical subjects typically fall toward the right-hand side, the low side of the potentiality of agency scale in Figure 3.3. Among these are predicates of the inanimate/nonintentional subclass of non-control intransitives ([A] a, c, d in Figure 3.4). Also grouped with unaccusatives are intransitives corresponding to neuters* ([A] b in the figure). These have been characterized earlier (Section 3.2) as undergoing* predicates.

3.2 The grammar of control

The unergative intransitives of Figure 3.4 also correlate with oppositions in the control construct. One subclass of unergatives consists of intransitive non-control predicates which assign logical subjects high in potentiality of agency ([B] d in the figure); i.e. animate/intentional non-control predicates. The other subclasses consist of agentive intransitives ([B] a, b in the figure) and *Schallwörter* predicates ([B] c).

In sum, the organization of intransitives into unergative and unaccusative classes seems to proceed from a natural semantic opposition involving high vs low degrees of potentiality of agency.[5] One subclass of unergatives consists of agentive* verbs. These are in a direct semantic opposition with undergoing* intransitives, specifically neuter verbs, which belong to the opposing, unaccusative category. Given this, agentive vs undergoing could be construed as the core of the unergative/unaccusative opposition. However, within the unergative/unaccusative opposition, each of these core verbal classes is respectively supplemented by one of two subclasses of non-control intransitives – those presupposing logical subjects with high potentiality of agency (animate/intentional), which pattern with unergatives, vs those presupposing logical subjects with low potentiality of agency (inanimate/nonintentional), which pattern with unaccusatives.

Neuter verbs have just been characterized as quintessentially unaccusative, inasmuch as, semantically, they comprise undergoing predicates. In the previous chapter, the neuter is assigned a formal structure, or diathesis*, in which its logical subject corresponds to a logical object of some formally related (typically homophonous) transitive verb. The membership of the neuter class may vary from language to language. Rosen 1984: 53 has pointed this out, citing, among other instances, the Italian neuter/transitive lexical pair *calare* 'fall/lower' (there is no precisely equivalent pair in English). Of course, all languages need not manifest an opposition of transitives and corresponding neuters. But the same is also true of unaccusativity; membership in each of the unergative and unaccusative classes is not strictly uniform from language to language, and some languages altogether lack overt manifestations of unaccusativity.

Neuter verbs suggest a relationship between unaccusativity and middle voice, since (a) neuters tend to be unaccusative rather than unergative and (b) in basic voice systems, neuter verbs tend to be inflectionally middle (as the preceding chapter has shown). Moreover, even in a language lacking a productive morphological alternation of active and middle on the verb, there may be some lexically restricted set of verbs (such as English *drip*, *sink*, etc.) which are middle in the sense of being neuters; and many recent writers in fact refer to these as middle verbs (see Chapter 1, n. 7).

However, the functions of morphological middle voices, discussed in the preceding chapter, are not subsumed by the neuter alone, central and recurrent though this function may be to the middle category in basic voice systems. Unaccusativity is, to be sure, one manifestation of the control construct (Figure 3.1); and morphological oppositions of active vs middle voice are another. But before further commenting on the relationship of middle voice to the control construct (see below, Section 3.3), it is important to consider other ways in which the construct figures in lexical organization.

3.2.2 Active–stative systems

As discussed in the preceding section, one type of lexical organization in which the control construct is manifested is unaccusativity*. Unaccusativity is characterized by an opposition between two subclasses of basic intransitive verbs, one subclass including all agentive intransitives, the other including all undergoing intransitives. Basic or logical subjects of the latter, the unaccusative subclass, display one or more object behaviors, while basic subjects of the former, the unergative subclass, do not.

Given unaccusativity as one pattern of lexical organization, the next logical step would be for the intransitive predicates of a system to be organized into two classes such that predicates of one class construe with an overt grammatical subject, while predicates of the other class construe with an overt grammatical object.

Lexical organization along these lines has already been noted in Section 2.4. Although there seems little reason to treat this behavior as anything more than a special variety of unaccusativity (this is elaborated on below), most previous writers portray it as a distinct phenomenon under the rubric of active* nominal case organization, or the active–stative type.

The active–stative type can be very lavishly illustrated, since numerous languages manifest the relevant patterning (see e.g. languages cited in Merlan 1985, Payne 1984 and Dixon 1979). In the interest of brevity, however, just one system will be illustrated in the present section: Chocho, an Otomanguean (Uto-Aztecan) language of

3.2 The grammar of control

Mexico. One of the few works to discuss Chocho's active–stative patterning in detail is Mock 1982 (an English-language version, Mock 1980, has been kindly furnished by the work's author).

According to Mock, Chocho's active–stative patterning is manifested through an opposition of two kinds of pronominal elements which appear on verbal bases, indexing grammatical subjects and objects. Pronominal suffixes index logical subjects and possessors; while enclitics index logical direct and indirect objects. However, the formal distinction between enclitics and suffixes is only manifested in the first and second persons, so that the verbal forms encoding SAP or speech act participants (first person, second person) are critical to the system.

A subject-encoding suffix and an object-encoding enclitic may occur together on a transitive verbal base, as shown in (1a, b) (from Mock, pp. 21, 6).

(1) a. T-   ìng   -á rí
       aspect anoint 1 3
       'I anoint him'
    b. Bí-   kų̄ -ā má
       aspect see 2 1
       'You saw me'

Either type of pronominal may index an intransitive subject or S, but not interchangeably. The language has complementary sets of subjective-inflecting and objective-inflecting intransitive basic verbs. The distribution of the pronominals attests to the active–stative nature of Chocho verbal organization, as we will see.

In Figure 3.5, (A) and (B) respectively list exclusively subjective-inflecting and exclusively objective-inflecting Chocho basic verbs (A and B are respectively based on Mock, Tables 3 and 2, pp. 40, 39). (C) (from Mock, Table 4, p. 40) illustrates a few intransitive verbs which are variably subjective- or objective-inflecting (with concomitant variations in lexical meaning, as the glosses suggest).

It bears note that in some active systems, all intransitives are either exclusively subjective-inflecting or exclusively objective-inflecting, a pattern which Dixon 1979: 82 refers to as "split S-marking." However, Chocho represents an instance of what Dixon (p. 80) terms "fluid S-marking." This type is distinct, since such systems have a third subclass of intransitives, i.e. variably subjective-/objective-inflecting intransitives.

(A) **Subjective-inflecting intransitives, three conjugations**

déč–á	'I sleep'	tē-é	'I sing'	čík-á	'I dance'
dàsō-á	'I arrive'	tìngá	'I run'	sánūngí-á	'I whistle'
dá̧xú̧-á	'I fight'	tìtùšθì-ná	'I change'	čó-á	'I come'
dùng-á	'I cry'	tíkà̧θ-é	'I stand up'	θī-á	'I go'
				číkàng-á	'I get out of the way'

(B) **Objective-inflecting intransitives, three conjugations**

dá̧θē má	'I fall'	táší má	'I tremble'	ẓ̌ādoá mā	'I slip'
dé má	'I cough'	tášá̧ʔngā má	'I yawn'	ẓ̌útē má	'I boil (with anger)'
dábá má	'I howl'	tūxī má	'I am sleepy'	ṣindà má	'I go to pieces'
díkuȩ̀ má	'I get drunk'	tùndá má	'I faint'	xúʔngà má	'I sneeze'
dȩ̄'ȩ̄ má	'I die'	túc̨ueâ má	'I get lost'	čēngā má	'I burn (with anger)'
dāc̨ē má	'I get stuck'	tátá má	'I stay quiet'		
diāṣī má	'I am hidden from'	tīrī má	'I am (LOC)'		
dìrāṣ̌é má	'I manage (to)'	tác̨é má	'I glow (e.g. with anger)'		
dàṣē ʔ má	'I stay (LOC)'	tác̨êngā má	'I burn up (e.g. with anger)'		
		tátú̧xī̧ má	'I fall from a height'		

(C) **Alternately subjective/-objective-inflecting intransitives**

(i) Subjective-inflecting

dá̧ʔxí̧-á	'I get down'
dūʔngí-á	'I wash my hair'
tuāʔngí-á	'I grow on purpose'
tē'-é	'I place myself'
tùṣoà̧-ná	'I recover (and know it)'

(ii) Objective-inflecting

dá̧ʔxī̧ má	'I get lowered'
dúngí má	'My hair gets washed'
tuángí má	'I grow'
tē'ē má	'I am (LOC)'
túṣuȩ̄ʔ má	'I recover'

Figure 3.5 Representative instances of intransitive verb classes in Chocho, based on Mock 1982 (1980)

Figure 3.5 reveals that in Chocho, the core of the subjective-inflecting intransitives (A) consists of agentive verbs, or verbs which express actions* (agency-presupposing events) and which assign basic or logical subjecthood to agents* (in the sense in which this term is defined in

3.2 The grammar of control

Section 3.0 above). By contrast, the core of the objective-inflecting intransitives (B) seems to consist of undergoing* predicates. Some of these are neuters*, such as "boil," "burn," etc. This class includes, as well, non-control predicates that assign subjects with high potentiality of agency, earlier called animate/intentional non-control predicates (such as "cough," "slip"). Finally, the core of the alternating subjective-/objective-inflecting intransitives in (C) seems to comprise agentive* and undergoing* counterparts.

Significantly, items in the respective left- and right-hand columns of class (C) resemble corresponding transitives and neuters. One can compare transitive/neuter counterparts listed elsewhere in the present work (e.g. Chapter 2, example 63). In Figure 3.5 (C), most items in the left-hand column are agentive intransitives; each is paired with a corresponding nonagentive intransitive in the right-hand column. The main respect in which the verbs in (C) differ from transitive/neuter counterparts is the intransitivity of the agentive verbs on the left. Also, neuters in some other languages, e.g. English, differ from the intransitives in the right-hand column of (C) in that the latter comprise a special conjugational class (objective-inflecting).

It is interesting that Chocho transitive verbs likewise have objective-inflecting intransitive counterparts, although not as basic lexical alternates. Rather, Chocho has a strategy for deriving objective-inflecting intransitives from basic transitives. This strategy is a derived voice rule. Its effects are illustrated by the contrast between the basic transitive verb "buy" in (2a) and the corresponding objective-inflecting intransitive verb in (2b) (examples 2a, b are from Mock 1982 (1980): 17). The latter relates to the former by a special derivational rule, a detransitivizing rule.

Evidence supporting a detransitivization analysis comes from certain alternations in the shapes of verbal bases. Both (2a, b) and (3a, b) (from Mock, p. 18) illustrate this. The verbs in the a-examples of (2) and (3) belong to a class of basic transitives whose members take a special active prefix ē- or ē?-. This prefix is not added to basic intransitives. Therefore it is significant that the prefix disappears in the corresponding derived objective-inflecting constructions, the b-examples of (2) and (3), suggesting a reduction in valence, i.e. detransitivization.[6]

Note, too, that the nominal comprising the A of the basic verb is usually deleted in the corresponding derived form; this is shown in (2b). If it surfaces at all (as in 3b), then it occurs not as an object, but as an oblique.[7]

(2) a. D-   ē-   ʔnā má rí
       aspect active buy 1   3
       'He buys me'
    b. D-   ìʔnà má
       aspect buy 1
       'I get bought'
(3) a. B-   ēʔ-   ngā tàtá̧   -ná θē
       aspect active sow father 1   seed
       'My father sowed the seed'
    b. B-   íngā θē (dȩ̀ṣȩ̀ tàtá̧ -ná)
       aspect sow seed (by/for father 1)
       'The seed got sown (by/for my father)'

The relevance of derived voice processes to the description and analysis of active–stative systems will be clarified shortly.

In many respects, the pattern of basic predicate classification in Chocho is representative of active–stative systems in general. Accordingly, it would seem that the main difference between active patterning and unaccusativity resides in the overt encoding, rather than in the underlying organization. That is, unaccusative predicates comprise roughly the same semantic class or classes as objective-inflecting intransitives in an active–stative system such as Chocho; while unergatives fall into nearly the same semantic class or classes as subjective-inflecting intransitives. Given, then, that the basis of the classification is essentially the same, what differentiates the two kinds of systems seems to be the way in which the classification is encoded.

Essentially, an active–stative system is one in which unaccusativity is manifested not just in the distinct morphosyntactic behaviors of the two classes of intransitive verbs (as in ordinary unaccusative systems) but also in the overt case* marking of S or intransitive subjects. Functionally, however, an active–stative system remains unaccusative – or (viewing the matter from an alternative perspective) unaccusativity represents a covert type of active–stative patterning.

However, one further difference deserves note: an active–stative system (Chocho being a case in point) may have some formal means, e.g. derived voice, for augmenting the membership of some class of intransitives, the subjective- or the objective-inflecting class (see further discussion below). Such is not, however, usually the case with the covert active type, i.e. with unaccusativity.

3.2 The grammar of control

Since this perspective on matters is somewhat novel and diverges from some previous views of active–stative typology, a critical comparison of perspectives is in order at this point. In studies on the typology of case, the active–stative type has frequently been treated as a special kind or variant of the ergative* type. As noted at the conclusion of the preceding chapter, an ergative–absolutive case marking system is one in which S, the intransitive subject, formally allies itself with the object (P) rather than the subject (A) of a transitive predicate.

However, in all kinds of case marking systems, total consistency of patterning is unusual; and in ergative–absolutive systems, splits in the pattern of case marking are the norm. That is, in every system which manifests ergativity, there is some domain in which S aligns with A as opposed to P, a fact which Dixon 1979: 133 acknowledges by remarking that "some accusativity always exists" in ergative languages.

The most common factors conditioning ergative/accusative splits are three: syntactic level (subordinate clause case patterning may be accusative); tense/aspect (completive temporal categories of the verb may condition ergativity, noncompletive may condition accusativity); and person/number of logical subject (first and second person pronominals may pattern accusatively). Many traditional treatments of active–stative typology consider the alignment of S with P to be normative for active systems, and so view them as fundamentally ergative. Then it follows that every active–stative system involves a split, because some intransitive verbs are subjective-inflecting, and thus behave accusatively. Putting it another way, S is aligned with, i.e. marked like, A rather than P for some class of intransitives in every active system.

Some writers, however, take issue with the traditional view. For instance, Klimov 1974 (and see references therein) argues for a reexamination of active–stative typology. His lead is followed in some recent descriptive studies of active–stative systems (including Durie 1987, Merlan 1985, T. E. Payne 1984, Dahlstrom 1983, O'Connor 1985, and some of the contributions to Plank 1985, such as DeLancey 1985), where the perspective taken on the active type is incompatible with a split-ergative analysis.

A major factor prompting the change in view has been the recent discovery that subjective- and objective-inflecting intransitive subclasses vary greatly in relative size from one active system to another (see e.g. Merlan's 1985 and Payne's 1984 survey articles as well as Holisky 1987 on Tsova-Tush or Batsbi). Moreover, in some active systems, the objective-inflecting intransitive verbal class is extremely small. In such systems, the statistically dominant pattern may be S aligned morphosyntactically with A rather than P. In this case, it seems implausible to view the pattern as one of split ergativity. Where S and A coalesce more often than not, indeed, one wonders why one should not instead speak of split accusativity.

The conception of active patterning as a kind of defective ergativity also seems implausible given that many such systems have mechanisms making it possible to add to the membership of either the objective-inflecting or the subjective-inflecting intransitive class, or both. In many active languages, derived voice or voice-like processes have this effect. Such processes occur not just in Chocho, illustrated above in (2)–(3), but in other active languages as well – an instance in point being Acehnese, whose extensive system of verbal derivation is examined below, Section 3.5.

It follows that, in an active system with productive processes of verbal derivation, many if not theoretically all of the basic lexical verbs have a potential to be either subjective- or objective-inflecting, so that it becomes implausible to speak of such systems as having a "split" in the classification of basic lexical verbs. Rather, what seems to be going on is that there is a coherent semantic classification scheme which interacts with the system of verbal morphosyntax.[8]

Incidentally, consistent with the above, Dahlstrom 1983 provides several compelling arguments against an ergative analysis of active–stative behavior. She points out that the typical split in ergative–absolutive systems involves a partition into two domains, in one of which the morphosyntactic patterning is ergative, while in the other, the morphosyntactic patterning is accusative. But an active system does not have an accusative and an ergative domain. Rather, in an active system, some S or intransitive subjects look and behave like transitive subjects (A), while other S look and behave like transitive objects (P). According to Dahlstrom, p. 40, such a system "is not split between ergative and accusative, but is actually a coherent system in its own right."[9]

The traditional term active–stative* reflects a premise or perception that subjective- and objective-inflecting intransitives tend to have distinct temporomodal semantics, respectively expressing relatively nonstative vs relatively stative verbal meanings. Lately, however, this characterization, too, has been challenged (see Merlan 1985: 349).

3.2 The grammar of control

Dahlstrom proposes to replace the designation active–stative with "*agent/patient*", because the opposition in subclasses of basic intransitive predicates evidently depends on which of two core semantic roles verbs of each class assign as logical subjects, agent or patient. Dahlstrom thus concurs with the present writer than an agentive-subject vs nonagentive-subject distinction among intransitives is at the core of lexical oppositions and correlated morphosyntactic behaviors in active–stative systems.

Before concluding this section, it is worth briefly noting one system which might be characterized as extended-active. This system is organized not just on the basis of a dichotomy of subjective- vs objective-inflecting intransitives, but includes as well a third class of intransitives which inflect like indirect objects. The third class contrasts not just formally, but also semantically, with subjective- and objective-inflecting intransitives. While these respectively express agency and undergoing, the third intransitive class is associated with an intermediary control status, limited control.

According to Hardy & Davis to appear, the Muskogean language Alabama manifests the patterning just described. Hardy & Davis designate the subjective, objective and indirect object inflections respectively as I, II and III. The contrasting functions of I and II inflections are illustrated in the respective a- and b-examples of (4) and (5) (from Hardy & Davis, pp. 4, 5). Notice that (5a, b) suggest active–stative patterning.

Examples (6a, b) (from Hardy & Davis, pp. 11, 22) illustrate III inflectional behavior. The a-example illustrates III-marking indexing the indirect object of a ditransitive verb, while the b-example illustrates III-marking indexing an intransitive subject of intermediary control. (According to Hardy & Davis, III-marking also accrues to nominals representing inalienable possessors, while II-marking is assigned when possession is alienable.)

(4) a. Batatli -li
     hit   1SG I
     'I hit someone/him'
  b. Cha- batatli
     1SG II hit
     'Someone/he hits me'

132   *Control and voice*

(5) a. Waliika -li
    run   1SG I
    'I run'
  b. Cha-   tammi
     1SG II fall
     'I fall'
(6) a. Chin- niili -li
       2SG III nod 1SG I
       'I nod to you'
  b. Chim-   maali
     2SG III be right
     'You're right'

Some predicates can occur in any of the three inflections. The lexical sense usually varies accordingly. An instance in point (illustrated by Hardy & Davis, p. 34) is the verb "be high" (*abahli*). With logical subject I-indexing, this predicate means "climb (something), go high, rise"; with logical subject II-indexing, it means "be high up"; and with logical subject III-indexing, it means "(something) is high up for me."

Hardy & Davis compare the Alabama system of inflection to the control classification system in Salishan languages. However, there are limits to the comparison (see below, Section 3.5; and see Hardy & Davis). There seems to be a somewhat stronger affinity between the Alabama extended-active system and the system of control-encoding basic predicate classification in a different language, Cupeño. The Cupeño system is overviewed in the following subsection.

3.2.3 Morphologically marked lexical classes in Cupeño

In the present chapter so far, lexical alternations have been examined in which intransitive verbs alone pattern according to oppositions schematized in the control construct, Figure 3.1. The goal of the survey of systems in the present section is to give evidence for the construct's reality and, further, to demonstrate how the construct relates to the typology of basic voice systems, a topic to which we recur in the following section.

But before that, one system is worth examining all of whose basic or

3.2 The grammar of control 133

lexical predicates are organized and even overtly classified according to the construct. It is relatively rare to encounter a language in which verbs in general exhibit explicit morphological marking for degrees or categories of control, but such appears to be the case in Cupeño, a Uto-Aztecan language (Hill 1969).

Cupeño has three basic predicate categories, which Hill refers to as "natural," "volitional" and "nonvolitional." The characteristic of the first is zero, while verbs of the second and third categories are respectively marked by class suffixes *-ine* and *-yaxe*.

Verbs which occur exclusively in the natural, or zero-marked, class include several semantic subgroups shown in Figure 3.6. These subgroups are (A) predicates denoting states of mind; (B) predicates denoting mainly reflex, and occasionally nonreflex, bodily events and processes; (C) predicates assigning logical subjects low in potentiality of agency (generally inanimate); and (D) predicates which assign logical subjects high in potentiality of agency (usually animate), and which denote actions of a special character, i.e. culturally required, typically ritual behaviors.

In the figure, many of the verbs (classes A, B, C) encode characteristically non-control events. Among these, verbs of two subgroups (A, B) assign animate/intentional logical subjects; while verbs of a third subgroup, (C), generally assign inanimate/nonintentional subjects.

The remaining verbs in the figure, listed under (D), denote actions with respect to which a participant's intentions are irrelevant (e.g. rituals and ceremonies), since one engages in them as a matter of social rather than individual initiative and prerogative.

Verbs of the Cupeño zero-marked class, being non-control verbs, contrast semantically with verbs of the other two morphological classes. The latter generally express actions, or events presupposing some participant's control (and voluntary initiative as well).

The markers of the action predicate classes, the suffixes *-ine* and *-yaxe*, are in a highly productive mutual contrast. Many action predicates can be of either class. Depending on the basic denotation of the predicate, the alternation of morphological classes may encode either of two semantic oppositions.

In one group of instances, the *-ine/-yaxe* alternation expresses a contrast in action performed intentionally vs accidentally. Respective illustrations are the a- and b-examples of (7)–(9) (from Hill, p. 350).

(A) cáŋnewe-∅ 'be angry'
    hemáne-∅ 'be ashamed, embarrassed'
    ʔ'ayelu-∅ 'be crazy, delirious'

(B) ʔáṣqetu-∅ 'menstruate'
    helʸépe-∅ 'have hiccups'
    ʔetíse-∅ 'sneeze'
    kílme-∅ 'urinate'
    kʷáʔe-∅ 'eat'
    páʔe-∅ 'drink'

(C) ṣéʔe-∅ 'bloom (of plants)'
    tewe-∅ 'grow (of plants)'
    wéwe-∅ 'rain'
    yúye-∅ 'snow'
    cíʔe-∅ 'rattle (of rattlesnakes)'

(D) híimaye-∅ 'donate goods for a burning ceremony'
    ʔáʔalxi-∅ 'relate tribal history'
    ʔísexʷe-∅ 'sing men's funeral chants'
    weráʔpiʔe-∅ 'do the "war" dance'

Figure 3.6 Subgroups of zero-marked lexical verbs in Cupeño, based on Hill 1969: 353

(7) a. Neʔen pipíqnen
       'I touched it'
    b. Neʔen pipíqneyex
       'I bumped into it by accident'
(8) a. Neʔen pisílʸnen
       'I poured it out'
    b. Neʔen pisílʸneyex
       'I spilled it accidentally'
(9) a. Neʔen piwecáxnen
       'I threw it down'
    b. Neʔen piwecáxneyex
       'I dropped it accidentally'

It will be recalled that Hill 1969 labels the morphological classes illustrated in the respective a- and b-examples of (7)–(9) "volitional" and "nonvolitional." In terms of the control construct, however, both classes are agentive, since both encompass verbs which assign agents* as

3.2 The grammar of control

logical subjects. Moreover, some aspect of the agent's participation in the action is volitional, whether the action is accidental or not. Accordingly, the morphological alternation in (7)–(9) does not seem to encode whether the logical subject has or exercises a faculty of volition. Rather, we suggest it encodes a distinction in the character of the logical subject's involvement or participant role in the action – specifically, whether or not the logical subject's referent exercises outcome control, a concept defined earlier (Section 3.1).

A second, and very numerous, class of *-ine/-yaxe* alternates turns out to consist of transitive/neuter counterparts. Illustrations are (10)–(13) (examples 10–12 are from Hill, p. 349, and 13 is from p. 354):

(10) a. Ne?en cáwelnen keláweti
       'I shook the stick'
     b. Keláwet cáwelpeyex
       'The stick shook'
(11) a. Ne?en cipílnen kevá?meli
       'I broke the pot'
     b. Kevá?melem cípilpeyex
       'The pot shattered'
(12) a. Ne?en kic piyútnen
       'I built a house'
     b. Kíc yútpeyexwen
       'A house was standing'
(13) a. húme-ine
       'to spread a liquid, to paint'
     b. húme-yaxe
       'to be spread, painted'

In connection with the alternates in (10)–(13), Hill observes that *-ine* and *-yaxe* are respectively cognate with markers of transitive/causative function and intransitive/passive function in other Uto-Aztecan languages. However, in Cupeño, valence alternation is not characteristic of all *-ine/-yaxe* alternating verbs, as the earlier (7)–(9) attest. Moreover, according to Hill, "there are a number of examples of transitives marked with *-yaxe* and intransitives marked with *-ine*" (p. 349). Accordingly, the most useful way of thinking about the opposition in (10)–(13) seems to be in terms of corresponding agentive and undergoing predicates, which is exactly how transitive and neuter alternates have been characterized earlier in this chapter.

Besides the above, there are certain minor but significant patterns in Cupeño. For instance, Hill reports that a few Cupeño basic verbs alternate for all three morphological classes. The verbal base *húce-* in (14) illustrates this (from Hill, p. 351). In the zero-marked or "natural" shape, shown in (14a), this base denotes a non-controlled, i.e. culturally required act (one that is done at a certain point in a hunting sequence); while in its other shapes, the base has a control semantics, alternating for agentive (14b) vs undergoing (14c) readings.

(14) a. húce -∅
       'to skin'
    b. húce-ine
       'to take off'
    c. húce-yaxe
       'to be undone, untied'

Hill also notes instances, again relatively few, in which a particular basic verb appears only in the "natural" and "nonvolitional" (zero and *-yaxe*), or only in the "natural" and "volitional" (zero and *-ine*) classes. Respective illustrations are (15a, b) and (16a, b) (Hill, p. 351):

(15) a. Ne?en hiqsá?
       'I rested'
    b. Ne?en hiqsá?neyex
       'I caught my breath'
(16) a. ?eyúy?i pecúx
       'Ice melted'
    b. Nexánis cúxpen pehíñe?ay
       'The man spat his saliva'

Finally, there are basic predicates which invariantly pertain to just one of the three Cupeño morphological categories. However, according to Hill, p. 349, the majority of Cupeño lexical verbs alternate in two or more categories, the most productive alternation being that of *-ine* vs *-yaxe*, illustrated in (7)–(13).

To summarize briefly, the Cupeño system of basic verbal classes involves a fundamental opposition of unmarked, non-control predicates vs marked, control predicates. The latter class – the action predicates – are further subclassified into two distinctively marked groups based on an opposition of agency* vs undergoing*. This system of verbal classification is significant for the purposes of the present work, because it appears to bear out nearly in its entirety the scheme of oppositions in Figure 3.1, the control construct.

3.3 The control construct and basic voice

In Section 3.2, several systems have been surveyed, providing evidence that the control construct has reality in universal patterns of basic lexical predicate organization. Logically speaking, the construct might be manifested in any of a still greater variety of ways, not all of which have been illustrated. However, among all its hypothetical manifestations, the most costly in terms of marking would be a system in which every lexical predicate is assigned to some overtly indexed morphological class. Cupeño comes close to such a system, although it exploits zero as a marker of one of the three morphological classes. Presumably, the cost of such a system in terms of marking has something to do with its comparative rarity in natural languages.

Economy in the grammaticization of the control construct can be achieved in either, or in a combination, of two ways: by restricting the extent of the construct (so that the organization of predicates is sensitive only to a part of it, e.g. only to the agentive/undergoing opposition); or by restricting the domain of the lexicon in which the construct operates (e.g. to one particular subclass of verbs, such as intransitives).

Unquestionably, unaccusativity* and active* (active–stative) behavior (characterized above, Sections 3.2.1, 3.2.2, as variants of a single pattern) exemplify the second kind of economy. This follows since only intransitive predicates participate in an overt opposition. Moreover, the agentive/undergoing opposition is central to the organization of these systems, more so than is the opposition of non-control vs control, which is at the heart of the control construct.

Accordingly, unaccusative and active–stative languages exemplify, to some extent, economy both as regards the extent of encoding of the control construct, and as regards the extent of the verbal lexicon affected. However, these economies are achieved at a cost; such systems do not grammaticize the control construct in its entirety.

An intermediate degree of economy might be achieved in a system having two categories of equivalent morphological markedness, such that an individual predicate is generally marked for one category or the other, but may be classified in any of three different ways – as invariantly marked for category one, as invariantly marked for category two, or as alternating between categories one and two.

The thesis of the present section is that basic voice is a control-encoding system which works in this way. As observed in the preceding chapter, every basic voice system embodies an alternation of two overtly encoded verbal categories, active and middle; has alternating active/middle in addition to invariant active-only and middle-only lexical predicates; and encodes certain contrasting semantic functions. Figure 3.7 schematically represents the core or prototype of the functional oppositions in an active–middle system.

To clarify Figure 3.7, it must be reemphasized that, although every basic voice system has some unique features (as demonstrated by the systems survey in Chapter 2), some patterns are recurrent. In particular, in system after system, some functions are encoded through just one of the morphological classes (active-only, middle-only, variably active/middle), and certain semantic classes of predicates again and again pertain to one and the same morphological class. This suggests that basic voice is organized according to some core or prototype.

This core or prototype is what Figure 3.7 seeks to capture. It validates as central to basic voice organization each and all of the oppositions depicted in Figure 3.1, the control construct.

However, according to the preceding chapter, the semantic function central to basic voice is not control, but affectedness*. Affectedness relates to a logical subject's coincidence with the locus of a verbally denoted situation's principal effects. But it has just been averred that control, not affectedness, determines the pattern of verbal voice classes in a basic voice system.

A solution to this paradox depends on the observation that affectedness and control are ontologically related. Where actions are concerned – events presupposing the control of some participant – an undergoer, as opposed to an agent, is more likely to be construed as affected. An actional predicate is affective, then, in the case of the undergoer's coincidence with the subject.

On the other hand, in the case of a nonactional predicate, no participant is construed as controller. Therefore, like control in the case of actional verbs, affectedness in the case of nonactional verbs is closely related, ontologically, to potentiality of agency (as represented in Figure 3.3). That is, an entity assigned a relatively high position on the

Active-only

Non-control predicates

(a) Presupposed subject animate/intentional (nondeponent semantic function)
typical instances: *sneeze, be fat*
(b) Presupposed subject inanimate/nonintentional
typical instances: *bloom, thunder, creak*

Middle-only

Control predicates

Presupposed subject animate/intentional (deponent semantic function)
typical instances: *speak, think, sit*

Active/middle

Agentive predicates

typical instances: *increase* (TR), *bend* (TR)

Undergoing predicates (neuters)

typical instances: *increase* (ITR), *bend* (ITR)

Figure 3.7 Prototype functions of basic voice categories

animacy scale is more plausibly construed either as an agent (in contrast to undergoer) in the case of an action verb, or as the locus of the denoted action's effects in the case of a nonaction (non-control) verb. The participant role of affected entity, accordingly, more plausibly devolves upon higher animates as contrasted with lower animates. Correspondingly, lower animates are less plausibly credited with potentiality of affect, just as they are less plausibly credited with potentiality of agency.

Figure 3.7 sets up a core or prototype membership of basic predicates in each of the three morphological classes of an active/middle voice system: active-only, middle-only and variably active–middle. Such a core or prototype essentially assumes a scheme of basic voice organization centering on an opposition of non-control vs control natural predicate classes and, within the latter, subclasses of agentive vs undergoing predicates. Each natural semantic class may be expressed through somewhat varying domains of the verbal lexicon from system to system, but this need not contravene the validity of the prototype.

There is, in fact, a remarkable stability in the organization of basic voice systems, as shown in the preceding chapter. This stability seems to result from the fact that, at the foundation of every basic voice system, there is a common functional basis, affectedness*. As stated earlier, affectedness is an ontological construct, one that can be reinterpreted in terms of control*. (See Klaiman 1991a, Klaiman to appear, and below, Chapter 6.)

Understanding, then, that the construct schematized in Figure 3.1 comprises the basis of all active–middle systems, basic voice can be construed as one among various patterns in lexical organization which both encode and validate the control construct.

3.4 Affectedness, attribution of control and submissive verb constructions

Thus far, this chapter has surveyed systems in which control is foundational to the classification of basic, or nonderived, lexical predicates.

Alternations in attribution of control may, however, be encoded in other ways. For instance, derivational processes may generate nonbasic, augmented-control and decontrol variants of basic lexical predicates. Some particular instances are cited in the next section.

Alternatively, it is possible for inherent attribution of control to be altered by placing a predicate within the semantic and syntactic scope of some control-encoding verb or operator. An argument may be introduced or assigned by this control-encoding element, thus becoming associated with the construction, although it need not be specified in the basic predicate's valence. As a further effect, the basic predicate semantics may be altered, e.g. with regard to attribution of control.

Behaviors of the type just described are very widespread in languages of Southeast Asia. They are sometimes discussed under the rubric of submissive verb* constructions, although they have such alternative designations as adversative* or adversity passive*.

Semantically, grammatical subjects of these constructions can be characterized as sustaining the principal effects of the denoted action. Typically these effects are adverse (hence the labels "adversative" and "adversity"), although beneficial effects are sometimes encoded.

The markers of submissive verb constructions, submissive elements, usually belong to a limited (sometimes unary) set. Also, in the majority

3.4 Attribution of control and submissive verb constructions

of these systems, each submissive element corresponds to a basic lexical verb. This holds, for instance, of Vietnamese *bị* 'suffer,' illustrated as an ordinary predicate (of a monoclausal structure) in (17a) (from Thomas 1988: 377), and as a submissive verb in (17b) (from Emeneau 1951: 73).

(17) a. Hà-nội bị   một trân   bão
       Hanoi suffer one classifier typhoon
       'Hanoi suffered a typhoon'
    b. Tôi bị   [con   chó cắn]
       I   suffer classifier dog bit
       'I was bitten by a dog'

In addition to Vietnamese (on which see Thomas 1988, Emeneau 1951, Truitner 1972, Nguyen 1974a, Clark 1974b, and Le 1976), various other Southeast Asian languages have autonomous lexical verbs used as submissive elements. They include Thai (Filbeck 1973, Clark 1974a, Ekniyom 1977, Prasithrathsint 1983); Lao (Clark 1974a); Hmong (Fuller 1985); Cambodian (Clark 1974a); Mandarin Chinese (Clark 1974a, Hashimoto 1969, Kierman 1969, Chu 1973, Hsu 1974, Chappel 1986a, 1986b); and a number of (non-Mandarin) Chinese as well as geographically adjacent non-Chinese languages (see Hashimoto 1988: 344ff. for a survey and discussion of the origins of the submissive elements in these languages).

Since in such a large group of languages, submissive elements arise from autonomous verbs, several writers claim or assume that submissive verb constructions are biclausal. This is suggested in (17b), where the square brackets delineate the domain of the inner predicate, "bite," from that of the outer predicate, the submissive verb "suffer."

In Japanese, a functionally similar construction occurs in which a verbal base is extended by a bound element *-(r)are*. Published treatments of this construction are numerous (see Klaiman 1983, 1987b for some references). Although the Japanese submissive element *-(r)are* is not an autonomous verb, some writers do analyze the construction in question as biclausal (see below for references), in which case there would be a structural congruity between submissive constructions in Japanese and those of other Asian languages, such as Vietnamese.

The a-examples below in (18)–(19) illustrate Japanese basic lexical predicates, while the b-examples are corresponding forms with the *-(r)are* element. (These examples are from Klaiman 1983: 57–8.) Example (20) (due to McCawley 1972: 264) also illustrates the -(r)are construction.

(18) a. Sensei wa   Taroo o   sikatta
       teacher T-SUBJ Taroo objective scolded
       'The teacher scolded Taroo'
    b. Taroo wa   sensei   ni   sika -rare -ta
       Taroo T-SUBJ teacher indirect OBJ scold -(r)are past
       'Taroo was subjected to the teacher scolding (him)'
(19) a. Taroo wa   Hanako kara omotya o   nusunda
       Taroo T-SUBJ Hanako from toy   objective stole
       'Taroo stole a toy from Hanako'
    b. Hanako wa   Taroo ni   omotya o
       Hanako T-SUBJ Taroo indirect OBJ toy   objective
       nusum -are -ta
       steal -(r)are past
       'Hanako was subjected to Taroo stealing a toy (from her)'
(20) Okurete itta   node, (watasi wa)   saki ni kita hitotati
     late   arrived because (I   T-SUBJ) ahead came people
     ni   minna ii   sina o   mora   -rare
     indirect OBJ all   good thing objective receive -(r)are
     -te   simatta
     PTCPL completive verb
     'As I was late (getting to the store), I was subjected to other people who arrived earlier getting all the good things'

The grammatical subject of a verb marked with the element -(r)are may bear some core argument relation to the basic verb. For instance, *Taroo* in (18b) corresponds to the logical object of the basic predicate "scold" in (18a). However, in (19b), the grammatical subject *Hanako* is not a core argument of the corresponding basic verb "steal" in (19a), but is, rather, an oblique. Moreover, in some instances the grammatical subject of the -(r)are predicate may bear no argument relation at all, core or noncore, to the corresponding basic verb. McCawley 1972 persuasively argues this of (20). Here the grammatical subject *watasi* 'I' bears no argument relation to the basic predicate *mora-* 'receive.' (This example is plausible in the context of a dilatory bargain-hunter's lamentations after an unsuccessful visit to a department store sale.) Additional examples of a similar character are furnished by McCawley and by Klaiman 1983: 61–2.

3.4 Attribution of control and submissive verb constructions

It might be pointed out that parallel instances also sometimes occur in languages in which submissive elements correspond to autonomous verbs. For instance, the subject of the submissive verb *bèi* in the Mandarin example (21) (from Clark 1974a: 100; Hashimoto 1988: 335) is not an argument of the basic predicate "run":

(21) Kànshŏu bèi [fànɫen pǎo -le]
    guard   suffer criminal run perfect aspect
    'The guard was subjected to: the criminal ran away'

As noted above, some writers analyze submissive verb constructions as passives. Analyses of this sort usually center on examples such as Vietnamese (17b) and Japanese (18b), i.e. instances in which the subject of the submissive verb corresponds to an argument of the basic verb in a corresponding nonsubmissive construction. Given, however, examples such as Japanese (20) and Mandarin (21), derived voice does not seem like a plausible account for submissive verb constructions in general (see Klaiman 1983, 1987b for additional arguments to this effect for Japanese).

Lately a few writers, including Ishikawa 1985 on Japanese and Thomas 1988 on Vietnamese, have surmised that the structures of the two predicates or operators in a submissive verb construction may interact in a relation of anaphoric control. Anaphoric control means that some nominal, typically the grammatical subject, of the outer (submissive) predicate or operator furnishes the referential content of an empty nominal position in the structure or structural domain of the nonsubmissive verb. Under the anaphoric control analysis, submissive verb constructions are a subtype of control constructions (see below, n. 13).

Such an analysis is supported by the overt parallelism of submissive verb and Equi-type control constructions, e.g. in Vietnamese. Respective illustrations are (22a, b) (from Thomas 1988: 377, 378). The subscripted $_i$ in each example specifies the anaphoric control relation.

(22) a. Anh Tám$_i$ bị [∅$_i$ đi ra miền quê]
    brother Tam suffer go out region rural
    'Tam had to go out to the sticks'
  b. Cô ấy$_i$ sợ [∅$_i$ về nhà]
    she   fear   return house
    'She is afraid to go home'

According to the anaphoric control analysis, in submissive verb constructions such as (22a) – but not in other control constructions such as (22b) – the control relation is nonobligatory. This means that the subject of the submissive element antecedes a nominal position in the nonsubmissive verb's structure only if the two nominal positions are in a relation of coreferentiality. However, the control relation being nonobligatory, there is no requirement that the two nominal positions be coreferential. It is this that allows for instances such as (20) in Japanese and (21) in Mandarin. The account holds that such instances are acceptable provided certain conditions are met. These conditions have to do with the submissive subject's ontological relationship to the action denoted by the basic or nonsubmissive predicate.

Most writers on submissive verb constructions regard the ontological relationship in question as one of affectedness*, although few attempt to characterize what this consists of precisely. Nor is it proven that affectedness has the same content in all languages which have submissive verb constructions. Only in a few of the relevant languages have explicit criteria for attribution of affectedness been proposed.

In Japanese, one clear criterion for affectedness is non-control* in the following sense: the submissive subject (the grammatical subject of the -(r)are predicate) may not be construed as participating on its own initiative in the action or event denoted by the nonsubmissive or basic predicate. Therefore, in this language, derived submissive constructions based on such propositions as *X meets with Y* or *X marries Y* are generally ungrammatical.

On the other hand, parallel expressions may be grammatical in other languages, a case in point being (23b) in Vietnamese. But according to the source of this example, Thomas 1988: 385, such constructions are acceptable only where the action embodies an aspect (in this instance, an outcome) which one can construe as unintended from the submissive subject's standpoint. According to Thomas, this accounts for the contrast in grammaticality between (23a) and (23b).

(23) a.*Tám bị lầy   Lan
      Tam suffer marry Lan
      'Tam was subjected to marrying Lan'
    b. Tám bị lầy   một cô con   gái rất độc ác
       Tam suffer marry one she classifier girl very spiteful
       'Tam was subjected to: (he) married a very spiteful girl'

3.4 Attribution of control and submissive verb constructions

As (23b) illustrates, in submissive verb constructions the subject referent usually lacks outcome control (and in some instances also agenda control). Nonetheless, high potentiality of agency is characteristic of submissive subjects. Cross-linguistically, they tend to be animate, and are nearly always human. This is in accord with the submissive subject's participant role as affected entity. (In the phrasing of Thomas 1988: 387, the submissive subject tends to "control the speaker's empathy.") Invariably, the ontological capacity of this participant to control the outcome is never exceeded by that of any other participant in the denoted situation.

That the submissive subject is ascribed a capacity for outcome, but not necessarily agenda, control is borne out by the Japanese -(r)are constructions in (24)–(25) (from Klaiman 1987b: 409–11). Each of the basic predicates in (24a–d) construes with an inanimate logical subject and denotes any of certain non-control events, such as raining (a), snowing (b), getting too much sun (c), or getting one's foot caught in a mechanical object (d). In Japanese, submissive verb constructions expressing such mundane and alleviable mishaps are not uncommon. However, parallel constructions involving a different class of denoted situations may prove ungrammatical, as (25a–d) illustrate.

(24) a. Kodomotati wa   ame ni   hur -are -ta
        children   T-SUBJ rain indirect OBJ fall -(r)are past
        'The kiddies were subjected to it raining'
    b. Taroo wa   yuki ni   hur -are -ta
        Taroo T-SUBJ snow indirect OBJ fall -(r)are past
        'Taroo was subjected to it snowing'
    c. Hi ni   teras -are -te   ita
        sun indirect OBJ shine -(r)are PTCPL was
        'One was (subjected to being) shone on by the sun'
    d. Taroo wa   asi o   erebeetaa ni
        Taroo T-SUBJ foot objective elevator   indirect OBJ
        hasam   -are -ta
        catch   -(r)are past
        'Taroo got his foot caught in the elevator'
(25) a. *Taroo wa   bakudan ni   bakuhatu sare -ta
        Taroo T-SUBJ bomb   indirect OBJ explode -(r)are past
        'Taroo was subjected to a bomb exploding'

146 *Control and voice*

    b.*Kaminari ni   oti   -rare -ta
       lightning indirect OBJ strike -(r)are past
       'One was subjected to lightning striking'
    c.*Kiri ni   hur -are   -ta
       fog indirect OBJ fall -(r)are past
       'One was subjected to fogging'
    d.*Zisin   ni   okor -are -ta
       earthquake indirect OBJ occur -(r)are past
       'One was subjected to an earthquake occurring'

The contrasting grammaticality of (24a–d) and (25a–d) can be ascribed to a distinction in types of control. To be sure, no participant exercises agenda control over any of the events depicted in (24)–(25). Nonetheless, in the case of mundane inconveniences, like those expressed in (24a–d) (rain, snow, sun, malfunctioning elevators and the like), a participant *qua* individual is normally expected to be capable of mitigating the situations of which these inconveniences represent an aspect. This is done by having, so to speak, a defense at one's disposal. That is, such inconveniences can be anticipated and, accordingly, their outcomes can be mitigated.

On the other hand, in the case of such dramatic and unforeseeable, nonmundane non-controlled events as those depicted in (25a–d) (suffering a bombing, being struck by lightning, and the like), one is unlikely to be in a position not just to exercise agenda control, but to exercise outcome control either.

Accordingly, a distinction between potential vs lack of potential for outcome control over certain situations seems relevant to the contrasting grammaticality of instances such as (24a–d) vs (25a–d). Moreover, if this view is accurate, then it supports the hypothesis that participants' ontological statuses, i.e. their capacity for control, are crucial to a grammatical account of submissive verb constructions.

3.5 Attribution of control and verbal derivation

In the preceding section, attribution of control has been related to a special class of constructions found in certain languages, submissive verb constructions. A submissive verb construction includes an element called a submissive verb or operator. Its function is to encode affected-

3.5 Attribution of control and verbal derivation 147

ness*, the participant role of the grammatical subject. As an ontological concept, affectedness is parallel to and, as claimed in Section 3.3, reinterpretable in terms of the control construct (see Chapter 6). Accordingly, the submissive verb construction can be regarded as a strategy for encoding an alternation in the basic predicate's attribution of control.

There are other strategies for encoding alterations in the attribution of control inherent to a basic predicate, and one in particular has been mentioned at the outset of the preceding section (and in Section 3.2.2). Processes of morphological derivation yielding either enhanced-control or diminished-control (decontrol) variants of basic predicates occur in some languages or, sometimes, in entire language groups. In two which will be overviewed below, highly productive processes of this sort have been documented.

The first to be included in our brief survey is Acehnese, an Austronesian language of Indonesia. Its system of verbal derivation is discussed by Durie 1985, 1987, 1988.

According to Durie 1987, the organization of the basic verbal lexicon in Acehnese is active–stative. It has been mentioned earlier that active–stative patterning is commonly manifested through an alternation in the shapes of nominal or pronominal elements. For instance, the opposition of subjective vs objective S-indexing crucial to the active–stative patterning in Chocho (Section 3.2.2) is encoded through a contrast between suffixal and enclitic pronominals.

In Acehnese, the corresponding encoding is through proclitic vs enclitic pronominals. Both derive from independent pronouns (such as *gopnyan* in 26a, b below, and *lôn* in 26a). However, unlike the independent pronouns from which they arise, clitics participate in an alternation in S marking which establishes the active–stative patterning. Illustrations of this patterning are (26a, b) and (27a, b) (from Durie 1987: 369).

(26) a. Gopnyan geu- mat lôn
      he/she   3   hold me (full pronoun)
      'She holds me'

   b. Gopnyan ka   lôn- ngieng -geuh
      he/she completive aspect 1   see   3
      'I saw him/her'

(27) a. Geu- jak gopnyan
       3   go   he/she
       'He/she goes'
   b. Gopnyan rhët -geuh
      he/she   fall   3
      'He/she falls'

In (26b), the proclitic and the enclitic surrounding the verbal base respectively index A and P. The predicate is transitive. Intransitives may index S either through A or through P clitics, but these are not assigned interchangeably. In (27a), the A proclitic indexes an S. On the other hand, in (27b), the P enclitic indexes the S.

The selection of S-indexing pronominals is determined by the intransitive predicate's semantic classification. Intransitive action verbs, like "go" in (27a), tend to be A-inflecting, while intransitive nonaction verbs, like "fall" (accidentally)" in (27b), tend to be P-inflecting. According to Durie, such behavior is symptomatic of active–stative patterning.

However, supplementing the Acehnese mechanism of proclisis and enclisis is a rich system of verbal derivation. In particular, the language has several verbal prefixes which alter the participant relations of core arguments to basic verbs. Among these prefixes, Durie 1985, 1987 focuses on two, *teu-* and *meu-*. He associates these prefixes respectively with decontrol and augmented-control variants of basic predicates.

The first of these, *teu-*, may be affixed either to basic transitives or to subjective-inflecting basic intransitives. Added to a transitive predicate base, it yields a derived intransitive which construes with one core argument corresponding to the basic verb's P. The b-examples in (28) and (29) (from Durie 1985: 46, 49, 50) illustrate *teu*-marked decontrol alternates of the basic transitive predicates in the a-examples.

(28) a. Si   Ali ji- timbak si   Mat
        title Ali 3 shoot title Mat
        'Ali shot Mat'
     b. Teu- timbak -geuh baroe
        teu- shoot   3   yesterday
        'He was (accidentally) shot yesterday'
(29) a. Lôn- crôh pisang
        1   fry banana
        'I fry bananas'

3.5 Attribution of control and verbal derivation

b. Pisang nyan ka   teu- crôh
   banana that completed aspect *teu-* fry
   'The bananas are already fried'

However, *teu-* is not merely a detransitivizer. As Durie 1987: 386 explains, it is productively added "to any verb which takes an Actor, deriving an intransitive verb with an Undergoer." Thus when added to an agentive* (subjective-inflecting) intransitive base, it yields an objective-inflecting (undergoing*) derived predicate.

As an illustration, Durie cites the basic verb *döng* 'stand'. This verb is agentive (assigns an agent as a logical subject) and, accordingly, is subjective-inflecting. However, the derived form *teu-döng* is objective-inflecting and assigns a nonagent, undergoing subject. Moreover, its denotation contrasts with that of the basic predicate; *döng* means 'stand,' but the derived predicate means 'be upright.' Since both are, however, intransitive, *teu-*'s function in this instance is not detransitivization (reduction in the basic verb's valence).

Rather, *teu-* seems to encode more than one function. Although in the b-examples of (28) and (29), it does mark detransitivization, in the case of "stand" it marks an alteration in the inherent temporal sense of the predicate – the derived predicate, a stative, is a variant of a nonstative base. But observe that, in all instances, *teu-* encodes an alteration in the subject's participant role. Whereas the basic predicate is subjective-inflecting in that it assigns an agent as logical subject, the derived variant is objective-inflecting in that it assigns an undergoer.

Accordingly, the function of *teu-* seems most aptly treated under the rubric of decontrol or diminished control. In Acehnese, a single marker serves for encoding two kinds of alternations: a change in the lexical class of a verb from agentive to undergoing (e.g. in the case of "shoot" and "fry," respectively illustrated in 28 and 29); or a change in lexical class from control to non-control (in the case of "stand/be upright"). That both alternations receive the same encoding suggests that both belong to a unified category. In terms of the control construct Figure 3.1, this can be accounted for by associating negative subject control jointly with two terms: non-control and undergoing. These terms are opposed to control and agentivity, which can be assigned to a contrasting category positively marked for subject control. Thus, in the figure, a left branch of the scheme receives a negative value for subject control, as contrasted with a positive value for its right sister.

150 *Control and voice*

The decontrol prefix *teu-* has a counterpart in the augmented-control prefix *meu-*. Like *teu-*, *meu-* attaches to either transitive or intransitive verbal bases. Unlike *teu-*, however, *meu-* is added only to intransitives which are objective-inflecting, not subjective-inflecting. Also, unlike *teu-*, *meu-* yields only subjective-inflecting, not objective-inflecting, derived intransitives, whether added to transitive or intransitive bases.

As an illustration of *meu-*'s effect on a basic transitive predicate, Durie 1985: 48 offers the contrast between *som* 'hide, put away' and the derived subjective-inflecting detransitive variant *meu-som* 'hide oneself.' Further, illustrating the use of *meu-* in encoding subjective-inflecting agentive variants of objective-inflecting basic intransitives, Durie 1987: 390 cites the contrast between the undergoing basic predicate *seunang* 'be happy' and the derived variant *meu-seunang* 'celebrate, have a party.'

In the last instance note that, whereas "be happy," the basic predicate, is objective-inflecting (undergoing), the derived counterpart is subjective-inflecting (agentive). In addition, *meu-* alters basic temporal semantics in a manner converse to *teu-*, in this instance deriving a nonstative variant of a basic predicate which is stative.

As with *teu-*, so with *meu-* it seems inapt to describe what is going on merely as valence reduction or detransitivization. Rather, *meu-* is converse in its function to *teu-*. Applied to basic non-control predicates, it derives control counterparts; while applied to basic undergoing (objective-inflecting) predicates, it derives agentive (subjective-inflecting) counterparts. The behavior of *meu-* is therefore consistent with the assignment of a positive value for subject control jointly to the agent and control categories in Figure 3.1.

In sum, *teu-* and *meu-* are complementary in distribution and function. The former is added only to basic predicates, transitive or intransitive, which express actions and assign agentive basic subjects. Added to such predicates, the function of *teu-* is to derive objective-inflecting decontrol variants. Conversely, *meu-* is added only to basic predicates, transitive or intransitive, which either assign undergoer subjects or express nonactions (non-control predicates). Its effect, in either instance, is to derive subjective-inflecting augmented-control variants. It follows then that one of the functions of derivational morphology in Acehnese is to encode alterations of a basic predicate's inherent attribution of control.[10]

Control-encoding derivational processes also occur in languages of

3.5 Attribution of control and verbal derivation

the Salishan family, spoken along the northwest coast of North America at the USA–Canada border. Thompson 1985 is an important source on the system of augmented and diminished control in one Salishan language, Thompson River Salish.[11]

According to Thompson, there are two distinct semantic classes of intransitive basic lexical predicates in Thompson River Salish. One class is exemplified by the predicates "fall" and "turn," respectively illustrated in (30a, b) (from Thompson, p. 394). Thompson 1985 refers to these as "limited control" intransitives. The second class is exemplified by "walk" in (31a, b) (from Thompson, p. 397), which belongs to a class referred to as "control roots." Since verbs of the former class generally are undergoing intransitives, while verbs of the latter class comprise agentive intransitives, it seems apt to regard the subclassification of intransitives in this language as a form of unaccusativity.

(30) a. K^{w}ís -kn
       fall   1SG S
       'I fell'
    b. Slə́k -kt
       turn 1PL S
       'We're turned around (confused as to direction)'
(31) a. X^{w}esít -kt
       walk   1PL S
       'We walked'
    b. X^{w}esít -m   -t -∅ -m
       walk relational suffix TR 3 P 1PL A
       'We walked to him'

As noted in Sections 3.2.1–2, unaccusativity is covert, in the sense that unaccusative/unergative oppositions are not explicitly marked (in contrast to active–stative patterning, which is encoded explicitly through nominal morphology). Likewise, the organization of Thompson River Salish intransitives into two subclasses is covert; it is encoded by the verbs' contrasting participation in derivational processes.

According to Thompson 1985, intransitives of the "walk" or "control root" (agentive) class yield derived stems by suffixation of certain stem extensions, such as the relational extension -m in (31b). Also, transitives are often derived from bases of the same class by suffixation of a stem extension -t (glossed by Thompson as "transitive"), which cooccurs with the relational extension in (31b). Neither of these behaviors extends to intransitive bases of the "limited control" (undergoing) class illustrated in (30a, b).

Thompson observes that the transitive suffix -*t* is added not only to transitives derived from basic intransitives, but sometimes to basic transitives as well. Illustrations are the a-examples of (32) and (33) (32a, b are from Thompson, p. 391, and 33a, b are from Thompson, p. 392). In the absence of further derivation, a transitive verb to which the -*t* suffix is added denotes an action, or an event presupposing the animacy and intentional participation of some participant (the agent). However, in some instances, a derivational suffix -*s* may precede -*t*, as the b-examples of (32) and (33) illustrate. When a verbal stem is derived by a combination of the two suffixes, its sense is that the action denoted by the basic verb is accomplished either accidentally or as a result of a struggle (rather than by normal skill and effort). These special readings are indicated in the glosses to (32b) and (33b).

(32) a. K'ətx^w -e -t -∅ -és
 sever directive extension TR 3 P 3 A
 'He (intentionally) cut it off'
 b. K'ətx^w -s -t -∅ -és
 sever -*s* TR 3 P 3 A
 (i) 'He cut it off accidentally'
 (ii) 'He ultimately managed to get it cut off'
(33) a. C'ək -t -∅ -és
 use up TR 3 P 3 A
 'She (intentionally) used up the last of it (e.g. food)'
 b. C'ək -s -t -∅ -és
 use up -*s* TR 3 P 3 A
 (i) 'She ran out of it'
 (ii) 'She managed to use it up'

Thompson, who glosses the -*s* suffix as "causative," comments on its semantics thus: "The traditional notion *nonvolitional* covers only part of the semantic sphere represented and fails to capture the generalization ... both notions – doing something accidentally and accomplishing it with difficulty – share the feature of *limited control*. Someone acting by mistake lacks full control; likewise someone who has to struggle to do the same thing" (p. 393) (emphasis in original).

Transitive verbal bases extended by -*s* remain transitive, but the extended and basic forms vary semantically in a way reminiscent of –

3.5 Attribution of control and verbal derivation   153

though not precisely parallel to – the contrast of undergoing vs agentive transitives ("limited control" vs "control root") discussed earlier (examples 30, 31).

It turns out that the same suffix -*s* also occurs on transitive bases derived from undergoing ("limited control") basic intransitives, either accompanied or not by the transitive marker -*t*. Examples are (34a, b) (from Thompson, p. 394). In these instances, the basic predicate's logical subject corresponds to an object of the derived predicate. Thus compare (34a, b) respectively with (30a, b). While predicates derived as shown in (34a, b) are semantically action predicates, they nonetheless encode the basic subject's diminished outcome control. In sum, the -*s* extension is added to transitive agentive predicates, and its function in all instances (*pace* Thompson, who characterizes it as "causative") is apparently to encode diminished control.

(34) a. Kʷís -s -cm -s
    fall -*s* 1 P 3 A
    (i) 'She accidently caused me to fall'
    (ii) 'She managed to make me fall'
  b. Səlk -s -t -éy -s
    turn -*s* TR 1PL P 3 A
    (i) 'They accidentally got us turned around (confused as to direction)'
    (ii) 'They managed to confuse us'

The suffix -*s* is just one of several Thompson River Salish stem extensions which alter the inherent control sense of basic lexical predicates. Similar in function is another, formally reduplicative suffix (as Thompson, p. 401, describes it, "the stressed vowel and following consonant of the stem are copied and inserted directly after that sequence [with regular phonological adjustments . . .]").

Thompson glosses this suffix as OC (for "out-of-control"). He notes that it may be added to all kinds of verbal bases. For instance, it is added to both agentive and undergoing intransitives, as illustrated respectively in the b-examples of (35) and (36) (35a, b and 36a, b are from Thompson, p. 402).

(35) a. Nóxʷ -∅
    run 3 S
    '(Animal) runs'

b. Nóx̣ʷ -ox̣ʷ -∅
   run   OC   3 S
   '(Animal) is forced to run (because of natural catastrophe, a pursuer, etc.)'

(36) a. ʕʷóy̓t -kn
       sleep 1SG S
       'I went to sleep'
    b. ʕʷóy̓t -iʔ -t -kn
       sleep OC   1SG S
       (note discontinuous allomorph of root)
       (i) 'I was put to sleep, anesthetized'
       (ii) 'I finally managed to get to sleep'

Clearly, the function of the reduplicative suffix in the b-examples relates to diminished control.

To this point, only stem-forming suffixes encoding diminished control have been illustrated. However, Thompson River Salish also has suffixes encoding augmented control. An example is a suffix having alternate shapes -*ix* and -*íyx*. Glossed by Thompson as "autonomous," it is added only to undergoing intransitive bases, deriving stems with meanings similar to those of agentive intransitives. Illustrations are (37) (compare the earlier examples 30b, 34b) and (38a) (from Thompson, pp. 401, 402–3). As (38b) illustrates, stems derived by this suffix, like ordinary agentive intransitive bases, may become input to the reduplicative decontrol stem forming process described immediately above.

(37) Səlk -íyx   -kt
     turn autonomous 1PL S
     'We turned around of our own accord'
(38) a. Tét̓ -ix   -∅
        extend autonomous 3 S
        'He stood up' (*tet̓*- 'long object extends straight')
     b. Tét̓ -ət -ix   -∅
        extend OC autonomous 3 S
        'He managed to stand up'

Since none of the suffixes so far discussed consistently alters either the number or types of arguments associated with verbal bases, none seems analogous to a derived voice marker (compare the Acehnese derivational affixes discussed in n. 10). However, other control-encoding suffixes in Thompson River Salish do encode valence alternations.

One instance is a suffix -(ə́)m which can be called a control detransitivizer. It has a non-control counterpart -nwéɬn. Each of these is usually (though not invariably) added to a transitive basic predicate, and each derives a verbal stem with a valence in which the basic P is suppressed. Thompson 1985 refers to the former suffix as "middle," while the latter he terms a "decontrol middle." Predicates derived with either suffix are actional and agentive, but the first encodes no change in the base predicate's control, while the second encodes diminished outcome control. Respective illustrations are (39) and (40) (from Thompson, pp. 409, 411).

(39) Sk -ə́m -kn
    club -(ə́)m 1SG S
    'I did some clubbing'
(40) ʔuqʷeʔ -nwéɬn -∅
    drink -nwéɬn 3 S
    (i) 'He managed to get a drink'
    (ii) 'He drank (something undesirable) unintentionally'

Since these suffixes alter the valence of the base to which they are added, their effects are reminiscent of voices (as Thompson's use of the term "middle" is evidently intended to indicate). But what seems most remarkable is that a single detransitive marker evidently will not do. Rather, Thompson River Salish has two detransitivizing stem extensions, one associated with control, the other with decontrol.[12]

In light of this, Thompson avers that "control distinctions comprise an independent system in Salish grammatical structure" (p. 413). As we have observed, basic intransitives are organized into two classes (essentially, unaccusative and unergative) depending on their inherent control semantics (undergoing vs agentive). However, the inherent semantics of basic predicates may be altered by the addition of augmented-control and decontrol stem-deriving extensions. These extensions are added not only to intransitive, but also to transitive verbal bases. Valence-altering stem extensions also occur; significantly, they tend to have both control and decontrol alternates. Thus there occurs a highly elaborated mechanism of verbal derivation in Salishan languages, among whose functions is the encoding of alterations in a basic predicate's inherent attribution of control.

156 *Control and voice*

It should be added that derivational processes which encode altered attribution of control are said to occur outside Salishan as well, e.g. in neighboring languages. According to Levine 1980, in the Wakashan language Kwakwala, contrasting stem-deriving suffixes -*suʔ* and -*ł* respectively mark detransitive control and non-control alternates of basic transitive predicates.

Given the totality of evidence discussed in the present section (and see Klaiman to appear), it can be concluded that morphological derivation represents one among several universal strategies whereby the verbal lexicon of a natural language may encode the oppositions schematized in Figure 3.1, the control construct.

3.6 The grammaticization of control

Control is not a voice category, although it is significant to the organization of at least one voice type, basic voice (Section 3.3). Several behaviors which this chapter has surveyed grammaticize the control construct. They include certain patterns of lexical classification and categorization, both covert and overt, such as basic voice, verbal derivation, and anaphoric control.

Since these behaviors involve strategies for encoding categories of control – yet no one strategy need encode all distinctions allowed for by the control construct (Figure 3.1) – it is feasible for more than one control-encoding strategy to cooccur in a system. This is the case, for instance, in Acehnese (see above, Sections 3.2.2 and 3.5), where active–stative patterning coexists with productive processes of control-encoding verbal derivation.

Consider another case. An Iroquoian language, Cherokee, affords an intriguing instance in which two control-encoding mechanisms seem to occupy distinct domains of a system. This language has an unusual core nominal-indexing system described by Scancarelli 1987a, 1987b.

According to Scancarelli, the Cherokee verb indexes (shows concord with) core arguments through a system of pronominal prefixes. These prefixes are organized into two sets, called Set A (alternatively, the "agent" or "subjective" set) and Set B (alternatively, the "patient" or "objective" set).

Cherokee has both A-inflecting and B-inflecting intransitive lexical predicates. They are organized into distinct semantic classes as suggested by (41a, b) and (42a, b) (from Scancarelli 1987a: 6). In each of the following examples, pronominal prefixes are in italic type.

(41) **intransitive A-inflecting**
 a. *k*aliːskiːʔa
 'I'm dancing'
 b. *k*awoːniha
 'He's speaking'

(42) **intransitive B-inflecting**
 a. *u*ːhnaːlvha
 'He's angry'
 b. *tu*ːhyvːstoyska
 'He's sneezing'

An intransitive predicate's classification as A- or B-inflecting seems to be determined by its agentive or undergoing semantics, as (41a, b) and (42a, b) respectively suggest. So far, then, the system appears to be active–stative.

The agreement marking of transitive predicates will now be considered. As (43a) below shows, an A or transitive subject is ordinarily indexed on a verb by an A prefix. Moreover, A and B prefixes cannot cooccur on a single verbal base.

However, Cherokee manifests a split pattern conditioned by tense. In certain tenses – loosely speaking, the nonstative tenses – all predicates are B-inflecting. In the case of a transitive predicate which is A-inflecting in a stative tense, there appears in a corresponding nonstative tense form a B agreement prefix, which indexes not the logical subject, but the logical object, as illustrated in (43b) (43a, b are from Scancarelli 1987a: 3).

(43) a. **stative tense**
 *k*vːhniha (*k*=1SG A)
 'I'm hitting it'
 b. **nonstative tense**
 *aːkw*vːhnilvːʔi (*aːkw*=1SG B)
 'He/it hit me'

The Cherokee system seems to be active–stative given, first, the semantic distinction between A- and B-inflecting intransitives, illustrated in (41a, b) and (42a, b); and given, secondly, the transitive agreement pattern illustrated in (43a, b), such that A pronominals index A or transitive subjects, B pronominals index P or transitive objects. Moreover, the specific type of this system seems to be split S-marking as opposed to fluid S-marking (see above, Section 3.2.2).

The twist is that, on transitive verbal bases, the selection of A vs B pronominal agreement depends on the relative animacy of core arguments. This is not apparent in nonstative tenses, which are always B-inflecting, but it is apparent in stative tenses. The pattern can be seen by comparing (43a) with (44) (from Scancarelli 1987a: 3). In the former, the A or transitive subject is A-indexed; in the latter, the P or transitive object is B-indexed, and there is no agreement with the transitive subject or A. According to Scancarelli, the selection of A- over B-indexing in (43a) reflects the logical subject's superior "animacy" (in the present work's terms, ontological salience) ranking in comparison with the logical object. Conversely, in (44), the selection of B- over A-indexing reflects the logical object's superior ranking in comparison with the logical subject.

(44) **stative tense**
a:*k*wv:hniha (*a:kw*=1SG B)
'He's hitting me'

In Cherokee, then, there seem to be three different patterns of agreement – one for intransitives, another for nonstative transitives, and a third for stative transitives. Among intransitives, the agreement pattern is reminiscent of an active–stative system. Among nonstative transitives, pronominal agreement markers index the logical subject. The pattern among stative transitives, however, seems to involve relative ranking of referents for potentiality of agency; the ontologically superior core argument, according to the scheme in Figure 3.3, is indexed by pronominal agreement on the verb. This pattern of agreement might be said to index ontological subject*, in contrast to logical subject.

The behavior of Cherokee stative transitives is reminiscent of certain voice systems in which verbal marking is sensitive to ontological statuses. In particular, Cherokee stative transitive agreement appears to follow a pattern typical of voice systems of the inverse* type. Although inverse voice is not examined in detail until the next chapter, it may be noted here that Cherokee appears to manifest, in distinct domains, a combination of active–stative lexical patterning together with some form of inverse voice behavior, which is sensitive to ontological

3.6 The grammaticization of control

salience, as the succeeding chapter discusses. Like Acehnese, then, Cherokee furnishes evidence for the combinability within a system of distinct control-sensitive patterns.

Before concluding, it is relevant to recapitulate a question raised in Section 2.2, regarding the devices needed in a formal grammar to account for voice behaviors. As mentioned earlier, one possible account involves a particular formal device, a theta-feature. This is a semantic property which may accrue to some nominal position in the predicate–argument structure* of a verb's lexical entry.

One may invoke this device by reinterpreting a theta-hierarchy* along the lines noted above, Section 3.0 (i.e. agent > benefactive > experiencer > theme > locative) as a scale of (descending) ontological control. Then a theta-feature [±control] may be assigned to nominal positions in a predicate–argument structure in accord with the theta-hierarchy (subject to any special stipulations occasioned by the individual predicate). As noted in Section 2.2, an account roughly along these lines (involving a feature we have claimed is reinterpretable in terms of control, [±affected]) has been suggested by previous writers (Rappaport & Levin 1986).

In Section 2.2, doubt has already been expressed about the feasibility of an analysis incorporating a theta-feature. Moreover, the present chapter's survey of control-encoding systems makes additional problems apparent. For one, it does not appear that marking nominal positions in lexical structure with a binary feature will be adequate, since control is not a simple dichotomy. Some systems surveyed above in this chapter (such as Cupeño and Alabama) encode intermediary control statuses.

Also, in some systems, attribution of control seems to be independent of thematic role organization. To cite a specific instance, in the language Alabama, which has been briefly discussed in Section 3.2.2, certain verbs assign two distinct core theta-roles having equivalent attribution of control. In such instances, the verb shows agreement with its core arguments through markers from one and the same set. Hardy & Davis to appear: 13 furnish the example *chi-cha-malosti* (2SG II-1SG II-love) 'I like/love you.' Equivalent attribution of control for transitive core arguments is also possible in some inverse systems, which are explored in the following chapter. However (thanks to the condition of uniqueness* or distinctness*; see Section 1.5), a verb cannot assign two thematically equivalent arguments. But since control can be attributed equivalently to two arguments, it follows that grammaticized attribution of control is independent of theta-role structure.

A different formal treatment of control semantics is proposed in an analysis of a syntactic phenomenon known as obligatory control[13] by Farkas 1988a. Farkas posits a special two-place relation RESP at the level of logical structure (the level at which relations between participants and situations are specified). RESP is an abbreviation for "responsibility relation," a concept similar to ontological controller status. According to Farkas, RESP holds between a participant i and a situation s "just in case i brings s about" (p. 36). Farkas argues that, while the RESP relation may devolve upon thematic-level agents or structural subjects, it is nonetheless not reducible to either agent or subject. Also, she claims that an adequate account of obligatory control is not reducible to conditions involving only thematic or nominal structure statuses, but must take into consideration the RESP-relation.

It seems plausible that, as Farkas claims, control (as an ontological construct) pertains to relations between participants and situations. It also seems plausible that a grammatical system may require access to information about such relations, not necessarily in regard to obligatory control alone. Whether this information is best captured formally at the logical-structure level of representation or in some other way remains to be considered. The question of devices required in a formal account of grammatical voice will be further pursued in Chapter 6.

4 Inverse voice systems

4.0 Preliminaries: ontology, head-marking and the inverse type

This chapter has the following principal objectives: (a) to survey a group of voice systems, inverse voice* systems; (b) to enumerate and, as far as possible, account for a group of properties that, in addition to inverse voice, define inverse type* languages; and (c) to identify the characteristics that make direct–inverse a subtype of pragmatic voice* and that distinguish these systems from voice systems of other types.

The preceding chapters have been largely devoted to delineating the basic* from the derived* voice type, with emphasis on clarifying the character of the former. In Chapter 1, derived* voice has been characterized as a strategy for relating structural configurations. That is, derived voice encodes a mapping from one class of configurations, which are basic, to a second class of configurations, which are nonbasic, and which can be accounted for by derivation.

By contrast, basic* voice systems do not involve mappings or formal correspondences of structural configurations. Active–middle systems exemplify the basic voice type par excellence. As discussed in Chapter 2, these systems encode alterations in the participant role of the argument which the verb assigns as subject. In particular, they encode affectedness*, or correspondence vs noncorrespondence of the subject with the locus of the action's principal effects.

As discussed in the preceding chapter, basic voice has an additional dimension. It is among several strategies which may encode the organization of lexical verbs according to attribution of control*. In basic voice systems, attribution of control is grammaticized as a feature of a verb's inherent or lexical meaning. But in addition, control is a construct*, or a psychological pattern of expectancies about the nature of the world, the nature of events therein, and the relations of partici-

162 Inverse voice systems

pants to both. Accordingly, though it may be grammaticized as a feature of verbal semantics, the basis of attribution of control is ontological.

To recapitulate, according to Chapter 3, basic voice grammaticizes attribution of control. But the ontology of verbally denoted situations may be grammaticized through other types of voice as well, though not necessarily in the same way. Attribution of control in basic voice systems is a feature of the real-world situations that a predicate denotes, i.e. of its inherent semantics. However, an alternative way in which the ontology of situations may be grammaticized, rather than on the basis of a predicate's inherent semantics, may be on the basis of a predication's pragmatics. This chapter and the next survey the organization of some voice systems which seem to operate on this basis.

In Chapter 1, several such systems have been surveyed under the rubric of pragmatic voice*. This term applies to voice systems in which alternations of verbal marking encode the variable assignment to a verb's arguments of some special pragmatic status or salience. Chapter 1 mentions two particular varieties.

First, a pragmatic voice system may be driven by information-structure* salience. That is, the index or encoding of some nominal position may reflect the corresponding argument's prominence in the information structure of a discourse, such as its topicality. This class of pragmatic voice systems is surveyed in Chapter 5 under the rubric of information-salience* voice.

The present chapter concerns a different class of pragmatic voice systems. In these systems, alternations of verbal shape encode alternating assignments to nominal positions of a somewhat different kind of salience, ontological salience*.

The ontological salience of a nominal reflects its referent's relative importance in the concerns of the speaker and hearer, either in relation to the discourse situation, or in relation to the universe of objects in general. To clarify this, it is useful to reconsider the examples from the Algonquian language Plains Cree cited above, Chapter 1 (25a, b), reproduced here for convenience as (1a, b).

(1) a. Ni- sēkih -ā   -nān atim
       1   scare theme **DIRECT** 1PL dog
       'We scare the dog'
    b. Ni- sēkih -iko   -nān atim
       1   scare theme **INVERSE** 1PL dog
       'The dog scares us'

4.0 Preliminaries: ontology, head-marking and the inverse type

It will be recalled from Section 1.4 that the alternating assignments of verbal voice elements (theme signs) -*ā* and -*iko* in (1a) and (1b) encode alternations in the logical subject's and logical object's assignments to statuses of ontological salience and nonsalience. That is, the logical subject and object are assigned to the corresponding ontological statuses of subject and object either directly (as in 1a) or inversely (1b).

The ontological status of an argument depends on the relationship of its referent to the discourse situation. Since a speech act participant (SAP), a first or second person, has greater prominence in the concerns of a typical speaker and hearer than a non-SAP or third person, in (1a, b), "we" is more salient than "dog." As a result, the combination of logical subject "we" and logical object "dog" drives direct voice assignment in (1a); while in (1b), the combination of nonsalient "dog" and salient "we," as respective logical subject and object, drives the assignment of inverse voice. Note that in transitive predications such as (1a, b) there is no marking, apart from voice, of the core nominals' logical relations.

The present chapter surveys a number of systems with direct/inverse alternations. (They will sometimes be referred to, for simplicity, as inverse* systems.) Section 4.1 investigates some behaviors reminiscent of inverse voice in Korean. Section 4.2 treats inverse voice and some features of the inverse type in several Apachean languages.

Section 4.3 is an excursus on differences and parallels between inverse voice and derived voice. Many previous writers consider inverse a special variety of passive, some assuming that inverse voice amounts to passivization conditioned by an animacy or potentiality of agency hierarchy. Despite the parallels between passive and inverse, there are also significant differences. Section 4.3 discusses this, enumerating several factors which distinguish direct–inverse from derived voice alternations such as active/passive.

Section 4.4 surveys Algonquian languages, which are currently the best-studied inverse language group. Also discussed in Section 4.4 is a nominal category that interacts with direct vs inverse in some inverse systems, obviative* (or fourth person*). Some less-investigated Amerindian languages of the Tanoan and Salishan groups are discussed in Section 4.5, with individual subsections 4.5.1 devoted to Arizona Tewa, 4.5.2 to other Tanoan languages, and 4.5.3 to Tanoan's implications for the characterization of the inverse type. In addition, Section 4.5.3 discusses problematical aspects of the systems treated in Section 4.5. It also summarizes the chapter's findings.

164 *Inverse voice systems*

Before embarking on the systems survey, some discussion is in order concerning the relationship of voice to other morphosyntactic behaviors typical of inverse systems. As several recent writers (to be cited shortly) have observed, inverse systems tend to be characterized by a group of features, including but not limited to voice.

For instance, inverse languages show a characteristic encoding of the relations between a transitive predicate and its core arguments, illustrated above in (1a, b). One of the core arguments, the first person, is indexed on the verb jointly by a personal prefix *ni-* and by a plurality suffix *-nān*. The other argument, "dog," is not indexed by an overt verbal marker. It appears as a nonbound or independent nominal (*atim*). Notice that the shape of this nominal does not vary, nor do the shapes of the (bound) indices of the first person, although the logical relations of the core arguments are reversed in (1a) and (1b). Moreover, these relations are encoded neither by overt nominal case* nor by markers of nominal concord on the verb. In both examples, the sole encoding of the logical relations of the arguments is the verbal voice marking.

By contrast, in noninverse languages, nominal case may have the function – sometimes in conjunction with verbal concord – of encoding core argument relations (see Moravscik 1978: 233ff. for some discussion). Without belaboring the point, it may be worthwhile to compare (1a, b) with parallel examples from a case language.

Notice that in the Latin examples (2a, b), a signal of the reversal of predicate–argument relations is the reversal of nominative and accusative case assignments. Together with verbal concord, the case marking indexes the first person argument's assignment as logical subject of (2a), logical object of (2b), and the third person argument's assignment as logical object of (2a), logical subject of (2b).

(2) a. Ego   videō canem
      I-NOM see-1   dog-ACC
      'I see the dog'
    b. Canis   videt mē
      dog-NOM see-3 me-ACC
      'The dog sees me'

Note too that, in an inverse system, the relative linear positions of nominals in a predication do not affect the interpretation of the nominal relations. This is illustrated in (3a–f), from a sister language of Cree,

4.0 Preliminaries: ontology, head-marking and the inverse type

Ojibwa (Chippewa). All possible permutations of the order of independent words are shown. According to the source of these examples, Delisle 1973: 73, Ojibwa does have a preferred word order which (3a) exemplifies. However, the other examples (3b–f) are also acceptable, differing from (3a) only in "changes of emphasis" but not in information content[1] – every example in (3a–f) means 'The woman sees the man (or men)' (note that the personal prefix *o-* in every example indexes "woman"). This confirms the earlier observation that alternations of predicate–argument relations are signaled in inverse systems by voice marking alone. (See below, n. 2).

(3) a. Ikwe   o- wābam -ā   -n   ininiw -ān
       woman   3 see   **DIRECT** OBV man   OBV
    b. Ikwe ininiwan owābamān
    c. Ininiwan ikwe owābamān
    d. Ininiwan owābamān ikwe
    e. Owābamān ininiwan ikwe
    f. Owābamān ikwe ininiwan

We have now investigated two morphosyntactic characteristics correlated with direct–inverse voice. The coincidence of this, together with certain other behaviors to be discussed later, may be said to characterize an inverse type* of language. Several writers, noting this, have proposed that inverseness may be related to some fundamental parameter in language typology. Two viewpoints in particular seem worth noting. One refers to a parameter of configurationality*, while the other is based on a typological opposition of head- vs dependent-marking*.

Configurationality* has been proposed as a parameter according to which languages may differ, yielding two types, configurational and non-configurational. Although writers do not agree on the precise character of the parameter (compare e.g. Hale 1983 and Jelinek 1984), they generally have in mind a distinction in syntactic organization having to do with hierarchical vs nonhierarchical structure.

According to some writers, the presence or absence of verb phrase (VP) as a structural entity is crucial to defining configurationality. This assumes that, in a configurational language, subjects are governed at the level of the sentence, objects at the level of VP; or in other words, subject is a relation borne by a nominal outside VP, object by a nominal in VP's scope. The presence of VP thus defines a hierarchical structure.

On the other hand, in the syntax of a non-configurational language, structural relations are organized differently. In particular, there is no need to posit a VP, a constituent which distinguishes the verb's scope over different nominal positions. The result is a structural type in which distinctions of "inner" vs "outer" core nominals have no basis in structural government. Predication structures in non-configurational languages are said, rather, to be "flat" or nonhierarchical.

According to Jelinek 1985: 171, "we find a high correlation between the ... [non-configurational] language type and the occurrence of 'exotic' (non-accusative) case-marking systems – ergative, 'three-way,' 'inverse' and the so-called 'active/stative' case systems." Several features that Jelinek associates with non-configurationality happen to be typical of inverse languages. Not only do they include the limited degree to which case figures in encoding nominal relations, but also the relative freedom of word order. According to Jelinek, in non-configurational languages, word order is generally not determined by grammatical relations and is frequently free.[2]

In addition, according to Jelinek 1984, 1985, independent nominals in non-configurational languages generally do not bear markings of their logical relations in predications. Also, they are statistically infrequent. Data from inverse languages has already been cited which bears out the first of these observations (note the unmarked and invariant shapes of the core nominals "dog" in 1a, b and "woman" and "man" in 3a–f). Moreover, according to Jelinek, in non-configurational languages the essential function of encoding core nominals is typically fulfilled by bound pronominals or clitics. Instances already furnished are the (nonomissible) person prefixes *ni-* in (1a, b) and *o-* in (3a–f). The latter also occurs as a marker of the possessor role in possessive dependencies, such as (4) in Ojibwa, where it indexes the argument "Fred." (Example 4 is from Dunnigan, O'Malley & Schwartz 1978: 12.)

(4) Fred o- māmāy -an
    Fred 3 mother OBV
    'Fred's mother'

Jelinek 1984, 1985 argues for reinterpreting configurationality in terms of an argument type parameter. This notion can be explained as follows.

In configurational languages, core arguments (e.g. subject and object) are encoded by independent nominals, whose relations to predicates are defined by government (hierarchical-structure relations). In

4.0 Preliminaries: ontology, head-marking and the inverse type 167

non-configurational languages, on the other hand, independent nominals rarely surface and, when they do, are not marked for their logical relations. Accordingly, they can be classified as optional adjuncts. Therefore, in non-configurational languages, the arguments are those nominal elements which occur obligatorily; that is, the arguments are the bound pronominals or clitics.

A different theory of inverse and other patterns has recently been proposed. This proposal is stated in terms of a dichotomy of head- vs dependent-marking* (Nichols 1986). While this dichotomy implicates many of the same behaviors that Jelinek 1984, 1985 associates with configurationality, it differs in its theoretical basis.[3] Whereas configurationality is based on relations of structural government, head- vs. dependent-marking is defined on the basis of dependency.

As just noted, government is defined in terms of hierarchical-structure relations. Dependencies, however, exist in the logical relations between arguments and predicators. According to Nichols 1986, there are two ways in which dependencies may be marked: either on the predicator, i.e. the head of a phrase or clause; or on the dependent, i.e. a nonpredicator (argument) or nonhead.

Dependencies occur at the phrase, clause or sentence level. For instance, a possessive predication such as (4) (or its English counterpart, *Fred's mother*) represents a dependency at the level of the phrase. The possessor nominal represents the dependent in relation to the possessed, which is the head. Notice that, whereas in the English the dependency is encoded (by the clitic *'s*) on the dependent (the possessor nominal *Fred*), in the corresponding Ojibwa example (4), the dependency is encoded (by the prefix *o-*) on the head.

Similarly, dependencies at the level of the clause are usually marked in inverse languages upon the head, or the predicate, and not upon dependents or arguments. This has been observed earlier. By contrast, in head-marking languages the same dependencies may be encoded on arguments, or properly speaking, on nominals (e.g. by means of case* affixes, adpositions or clitics).

Other instances of head–dependent relations are noted in Nichols 1986: 57ff., although the preceding suffices for purposes of the present discussion. It appears that the head-/dependent-marking perspective provides some insight into the character of inverse systems. For instance, variation within the inverse type (this will be documented in the sections to follow) is consistent with the nature of the parameter, i.e.

its defining endpoints on a continuum, rather than an absolute dichotomy. In a given language, both head- and dependent-marking patterns may cooccur, although typically one or the other predominates (see Nichols). Moreover, the parameter predicts or is consistent with some typical inverse behaviors, such as free word order (according to Nichols 1986: 104, "head-marking languages have the greatest freedom of choice as to word order"). And although this could alternatively be accounted for as an aspect of non-configurationality, in some instances head-/dependent-marking seems to provide greater insight or is more predictive.

For example, head-/dependent-marking associates with inverse languages more than one strategy for encoding "which clause actant stands in which of the relations marked on the verb – a problem unknown to dependent-marking languages, in which each noun bears a mark of its own function in the clause" (Nichols 1986: 112). One strategy is to restrict the number of overt, nonbound or independent nominals per clause. Not only does this typify inverse systems but, according to Nichols, is extremely common in head-marking languages generally, although it is not specifically implied or predicted by configurationality.[4]

An alternative strategy typical of head-marking languages is to "set up a rigid hierarchy of animacy, definiteness, or the like, to determine which actant is eligible for the subject slot, which for the direct-object slot, and which for the indirect-object slot" (Nichols 1986: 112). In fact, there is considerable evidence that the organization of an inverse system depends critically on a hierarchy of nominal statuses.

For instance, in the Plains Cree direct/inverse alternates (1a, b), the theme marking facilitates recovery of the core argument logical relations because it presupposes a scale of ontological salience. Of the two theme categories, the direct (see 1a) encodes action proceeding in an ontologically expected direction. This means the action proceeds from a more salient participant (e.g. an SAP or speech act participant, a first or second person argument) to a less salient participant (e.g. a non-SAP, or third person argument). The opposing theme category, the inverse (see 1b), encodes action proceeding in a manner inverse to the ontologically expected direction, or from a less salient (e.g. non-SAP) to a more salient (e.g. SAP) participant.

To account for the voice alternation in (1a, b), a simple nominal

4.0 Preliminaries: ontology, head-marking and the inverse type

status hierarchy may be adduced. It is shown in (5) (where *SAP* again stands for *s*peech *a*ct *p*articipant).

(5) **Algonquian person-referencing hierarchy** (first version)

SAP > non-SAP

It will be shown later (Section 4.4) that (5) is, at best, an approximation of the salience hierarchy for systems of the Algonquian family (the family to which Plains Cree, the language illustrated in 1a, b, belongs). Some salience hierarchy is essential to the organization of every inverse system, although it may differ from system to system in its details. In every inverse system surveyed below, the operative hierarchy is some partial version of the scale of potentiality of agency or animacy hierarchy which has been introduced in Figure 3.3. It is reproduced below in (6). As noted in the previous chapter, this hierarchy amounts to a scale of ontological salience, providing a basis for the account of grammaticized attribution of control.[5]

(6)

1st person pronominal	2nd person pronominal	3rd person pronominal	proper noun	human common noun	animate common noun	inanimate common noun

←──

It will be recalled that the basis of the head-/dependent-marking parameter is the notion of dependency, defined in terms of logical relations between arguments and predicators. In conformity with this, the terms subject and object are invoked through the balance of the present chapter in the sense of logical statuses, not syntactic roles. The utility of this will become apparent as the discussion develops.

However, in addition to logical subject and object, the succeeding treatment will also refer to statuses of ontological subject* and ontological object*. These statuses accrue to nominals in respect of their relative ontological salience within a predication, according to the operative scale of ontological salience for the particular system (based on and in conformity with the hierarchy in 6). The significance of ontological subject and object statuses to the account of voice in inverse systems will become apparent over the course of the chapter.

Head-/dependent-marking, it will be recalled, is not an absolute dichotomy, but a parameter of variation between extremes or idealized types. Languages may be head- or dependent-marking to a degree,

170 *Inverse voice systems*

subject to the preponderance of one or another type of marking in different dependencies. An argument will be developed over the course of this chapter that inverseness is likewise manifested by degrees of conformity to a type.

Due to space considerations, some inverse systems are not included in the survey to follow, such as Wakashan systems of the Pacific Northwest (see Whistler 1985 for some discussion) and Chukotko-Kamchatkan languages of Siberia (see Comrie 1980, 1981a). Both have been noted earlier (Section 1.4). However, systems that are included for discussion below bear out the diversity of the inverse type. Its manifestations vary, ranging from systems with lexically restricted inverse voice alternations (e.g. Korean, see Section 4.1) to more productive systems in which direct/inverse voice alternations are robust, cooccurring with certain nonvoice behaviors characteristic of the inverse type (see Section 4.4 on Algonquian languages).

A crucial finding to emerge from the survey is that a system's degree of conformity to the inverse type is related to the morphosyntactic strategies it has available for allocating the encoding of certain functions. For instance, one behavior characteristic of various inverse systems (to be discussed in detail in Sections 4.2 and 4.4) is obviation* or fourth person* marking. Essentially, obviation is a subclassification of third person nominals according to their referents' relative ranking for ontological salience. In effect, systems with an obviative may have four ontologically ranked categories of person (obviative, proximate, first and second).

It will be demonstrated below that the presence of an obviative correlates with absence of nominal case*. That is, while no inverse language productively uses case morphology to encode core argument relations, residual core nominal case marking (restricted to inverse predications in which at least one core nominal is third person) occurs in inverse systems lacking an obviative. On the other hand, robust inverse systems, such as Algonquian systems (see Section 4.4), never manifest core nominal case, and always have an obviative. It is argued below that the presence or absence of obviation is a determinant of a system's strictness of conformity to the head-marking type. But for the time being, it may merely be noted that there is some correlation between voice behavior in inverse systems and a nonvoice behavior, obviation. The details of this and other correlations are explored later.

Before proceeding to the survey of systems, one final point is worth mentioning. Obviation in inverse languages is sometimes treated as a strategy for tracking nominal referents through discourse (see e.g. Haiman & Munro 1983a: xi).[6] It is not coincidental that discourse structure has a bearing on the organization of these systems. As noted earlier, one aim of this chapter is to distinguish the inverse from the basic and derived voice types. Basic voice, it has been claimed in the preceding chapter, is operative in the lexicon, since it amounts to a pattern of organization of a system's lexical verbs. Derived voice, by contrast, is operative in syntax; it encodes relations between verbs and nominals in predication structures (which may be lexical or clausal, depending on the model of structural analysis one assumes).

The discussion which follows is intended to show that pragmatic voice, in contrast with both basic and derived voice, is operative at the level of discourse. In the present chapter, this will be shown to hold of one class of pragmatic voice systems, inverse systems. Moreover, in support of this, it will be demonstrated that the nominal salience statuses crucial to the account of the inverse type, ontological subject and object, have reality not in the structures of predications, but in the relations between denoted events and the situation of discourse.

4.1 Korean

Patterns reminiscent of direct–inverse behaviors occur in Korean but are marginal, being confined to a small subclass of the lexical verbs. Other manifestations of the inverse type are lacking. Despite this, the system illustrates, in a rudimentary way, how alternations of direct vs inverse voice operate.

In fact, in some respects Korean seems to model the simplest possible sort of direct–inverse system. Imagine a language in which core nominals of transitive predicates may be assigned statuses of ontological subject or ontological object depending on their superior vs inferior ranking for ontological salience. Suppose further that one determinant of this ranking is a simple scale along the lines of that given above in (5) (based on, and abstracted from, the ontological salience hierarchy in 6). The scale assigns no mutual ranking to SAP arguments; but it ranks any SAP argument superior to any non-SAP argument.

It will be assumed further that, in this system, non-SAP core arguments are also mutually ranked. Their ranking is determined according to certain real-world properties of their core referents, especially animacy. This is consistent with the hierarchy in (6).

Moreover, where two non-SAP core arguments of a predicate are ontologically similar, they are equivalent in ontological salience. Accordingly, either may be assigned higher ontological salience, i.e. ontological subject status, although only one argument can bear this status per predication (the other, by default, must be assigned a status of nonsalience, i.e. ontological object status).

Finally, only some lexical predicates participate in the marking of direct vs inverse voices; the system is lexically restricted.

Modern Korean is a system with the properties just outlined. The following overview is based on the detailed summary presented in Klaiman 1984.

In Korean, a limited number of transitive verbal bases participate in a morphological alternation consisting of zero stem marking vs suffixation of a special stem formant. The basic shape of this formant is *-hi*. In Korean, as in many languages, the grammatical subject controls assignment of nominative case and verbal concord, and subject status may, in principle, accrue either to the logical subject or logical object of a participating verb. In the latter case, *-hi* appears.

This alternation of stem forms is illustrated in (7) (from Klaiman 1984: 341).

(7) a. Kɨ-nɨn   kɨ kəs -il   ic-ci
       he-NOM T that thing-objective forget-nominalizer
       mos   hanta
       not-can does
       'He is not forgetting that thing'
    b. Kɨ   kəs-ɨn   kɨ -eke ic-hi-ci   anh-nɨnta
       that thing-NOM T he by   forget-*hi*-nominalizer is-not
       'That thing is not being forgotten by him'

Alternates such as (7a, b) readily resemble actives and passives because their morphosyntactic and meaning relations are regular, as in an active/passive alternation. However, such alternates only arise if the ontological salience (attribution of control) of both core arguments is equivalent. This occurs, for instance, if the predicate has an inherent non-control semantics, as does "forget" in (7).

If, on the other hand, the predicate has a control semantics (i.e. if, in the parlance of the preceding chapter, the predicate denotes an action*), then either the unmarked or -*hi*-marked stem occurs, depending on which core argument, the logical subject or the logical object, is ontological subject, or receives the superior attribution of control.

Examples (8)–(10) (from Klaiman 1984: 333–4) illustrate this. The first of these shows that, in Korean, one can speak of a man chasing a ball (8a), but not of a ball being chased by a man (8b). (9a, b) show that either of two inanimate objects, a car or a taxi, can be spoken of as chasing or being chased by the other. (10a, b) show that, where an inanimate core argument is the logical subject, and an animate (in this case, SAP) argument is logical object, the former cannot be portrayed, so to speak, as acting on the latter. In such predications, the animate is generally the perceived controller, hence it is the ontological subject. Accordingly, the inverse or -*hi* form (10b) tends to be preferred over the direct or unmarked form (10a).

(8) a. Namca -ka   koŋ -ɨl   cchoch -ko issəyo
       man   NOM ball   objective chas   -ing is
       'A/the man is chasing a/the ball'
   b.*Koŋ -i   namca -eke cchoch-ki-ko issəyo
       ball NOM man   by   chase-*hi*-ing is
       'A/the ball is being chased by a/the man'

(9) a. Kɨ thɛksi -ka   cə cha -lɨl   ccoch -ko issəyo
       that taxi NOM that car objective chas   -ing is
       'The taxi is chasing the car'
   b. Cə cha -ka   kɨ thɛksi -e   ccoch -ko issəyo
      that car NOM that taxi   by   chas   -ing is
      'That car is being chased by the taxi'

(10) a.*Sikan -i   na -lɨl   ccoch -ko issəyo
        time   NOM I   objective chas -   ing is
        'Time is chasing me'
    b. Na -nɨn   sikan -e   ccoch-ki-ko issəyo
       I   NOM T time   by   chase-*hi*-ing is
       'I am being chased by time (feel pressured by lack of time)'

Examples (10a, b) notwithstanding, in certain instances control may be attributed to inanimate over animate participants.

Consider, for instance, a situation in which a person is injured by an automobile which he or she is not driving and, accordingly, cannot control. Here the vehicle may be analyzed as exercising no less control in the situation than the victim. Correspondingly, it is possible for either the inanimate or the animate argument of the predicate to be assigned the status of ontological subject. In accord with this, Korean speakers judge as grammatical both (11a) and (11b) (from Klaiman 1984: 335–6).

(11) a. Kɨ cha -ka   kɨ salam -ɨl   pat -assta
       that car NOM that man   objective strike past
       'The car struck the man'
    b. Kɨ salam -i   kɨ cha -e pat-hi-əssta
       that man   NOM that car by strike-*hi*-past
       'The man was struck by the car'

Incidentally, among Korean speakers there is a certain amount of intersubjective variation regarding attribution of control. As a result, speakers occasionally differ over the grammaticality of unmarked (direct) vs marked-stem (inverse) alternates.

For instance, according to Klaiman 1984: 337, younger Korean speakers seem more inclined than older speakers to accept (12a) as a plausible alternative to (12b). Both sentences depict a situation in which a man as logical object is pitted against a machine as logical subject. Presumably, speakers of a younger, more mechanically and technologically oriented generation are more willing than their elders to credit such an exotic mechanical entity as a robot with ontological control equivalent to that of a person. This is consistent with their readiness to accept (12a) as well as (12b).

(12) a. Kɨ lopothɨ -ka   cə salam -ɨl   ccoch -ko issəyo
       that robot   NOM that man   objective chas is -ing is
       'The robot is chasing the man'
    b. Cə salam -i   kɨ lopothɨ -e(ke) ccoch-ki-ko issəyo
       that man   NOM that robot   by   chase-*hi*-ing is
       'The man is being chased by the robot'

Many further details of the verb stem alternation in Korean are covered in Klaiman 1984. However, the preceding suffices to give some idea about the nature of direct–inverse voice.

Note that in Korean, ontological subjecthood devolves alternately upon either the logical subject or the logical object of certain predications. As a result, both direct and inverse forms are grammatical. Relevant instances above include (7a, b), (9a, b), (11a, b) and (for younger Korean speakers) (12a, b). In most instances, such direct/inverse alternates are restricted to 3:3 predications, i.e. occur only provided both core arguments are non-SAP or third person. Later, this will be shown to hold as well in other systems.

The fact that these alternates do occur, not just in Korean but also elsewhere, may appear to comprise evidence that systems of this sort are akin to the active–passive in type. While active–passive and direct–inverse behaviors are parallel to an extent, their differences are no less significant. This will be argued below (Section 4.3). Meanwhile, it is vital to consider systems in which, unlike Korean, alternations of direct and inverse voices are not lexically restricted, but productive.

4.2 Apachean languages

As just observed, the alternation of unmarked and -*hi* verbal stem counterparts in Korean is not productive. Only a relatively small number of verbs participate (see Klaiman 1984 for details). Accordingly, inverse patterning may be considered marginal in Korean.

On the other hand, there are inverse languages in which all transitive verbs, in principle, participate in direct/inverse alternations. To be sure, this does not imply that all verbs alternate formally for voice. The alternation is conditioned by ontological subject and object assignments, which may depend, in turn, not only on the properties of the situation that a verb denotes in any particular use, but also on the verb's inherent semantics. Therefore not all verbs can be expected to alternate, even though all participate in the system of alternations.

Restrictions on voice alternations vary somewhat from system to system. In some inverse systems, voice alternations may occur in transitive predications where both core arguments are SAP (these are traditionally referred to by Algonquianists as local predications). In other systems, however, only nonlocal predications, predications with at least one non-SAP argument, potentially alternate for voice (subject to the conditions alluded to in the last paragraph).

However, some inverse systems are restricted in that transitive verbs potentially alternate for direct and inverse voices only if both core arguments are non-SAP. This kind of inverse system is observed in a subfamily of the Athapaskan languages of North America, Apachean. Among recently documented Apachean inverse systems are Jicarilla Apache (Sandoval 1984) and San Carlos Apache (Shayne 1982).

The most extensively documented Apachean inverse system is that of Navajo. Authors generally agree on the description of Navajo voice, though not on its analysis. Several characterize the Navajo system either as passive or passive-like (Hale 1973, Creamer 1974). Others, however, do not describe the system in these terms (Frishberg 1972), and one writer explicitly disputes the active/passive analysis (Witherspoon 1977, 1980). Moreover, at least one writer proposes labeling the Navajo voice system inverse (Jelinek 1985: 172). In the present section, the primary aim is to show that Apachean systems are congruent with the inverse type as characterized above in Section 4.0.[7]

First, some particulars of Apachean morphosyntax deserve note. In Apachean clause structures, a prefix indexing logical subject obligatorily appears on the verbal base (although its shape in the third person may be zero). If the base is transitive, an object-encoding prefix may precede the subject prefix in the verbal complex, which in turn precedes the root.

A treatment of Apachean voice alternations must take special account of two object prefixes. These have the basic shapes *yi-* and *bi-*. Either one of these may, in principle, index third person (non-SAP) logical objects (or logical indirect objects of ditransitive verbs; see Jelinek 1990: 5). But according to Shayne 1982: 381, the logical subject of a predicate must also be third person or non-SAP (and indexed by zero) when either *yi-* or *bi-* is assigned. As a result, Apachean voice alternations are only manifested in 3:3 predications.

The Navajo a- and b-examples in (13)–(14) (from Witherspoon 1980: 5) and (15) (from Creamer 1974: 34) illustrate this. As (13a, b) show, *yi-* and *bi-* may alternate provided the two core arguments of the verb are comparable ontologically, or are similar in attribution of control. In such instances either argument, logical subject (13a) or logical object (13b), may be assigned the status of ontological subject. An independent nominal assigned this status is usually positioned leftmost in the clause, as these examples show.

In some predications, core nominals diverge in ontological status, with the result that only one voice is possible. This is illustrated by (14a, b) and (15a, b).

(13) a. łį́į́'   dzaanééz yi-ztał
       horse mule   kicked
       'The horse kicked the mule'

    b. Dzaanééz łį́į́' bi-ztał
       mule   horse kicked
       'The mule was kicked by the horse'
(14) a. At'ééd tó yodlą́ą́'
       girl   water drank
       'The girl drank the water'
    b.*Tó   at'ééd bodlą́ą́'
       water girl   drank
       'The water was drunk by the girl'
(15) a.*Awéé'chí'í diné yi-ztał
       baby   man kicked
       'The baby kicked the man'
    b. Diné awéé'chí'í bi-ztał
       man baby   kicked
       'The man was kicked by the baby'

Several writers (Hale 1973, Creamer 1974, Frishberg 1972) attribute the patterning in (13)–(15) to the relative animacy of the core arguments. By their accounts, (13a) and (13b) are both grammatical because both core arguments are equally animate. In (14a, b), on the other hand, subject and object statuses are respectively assigned to inanimate and animate core arguments. Since, however, subjects cannot be outranked by objects for animacy, the ungrammaticality of (14b) follows.

But as Witherspoon 1977, 1980 points out, an account along these lines fails to explain certain examples, such as (15a, b). Here both core arguments are equivalent in animacy, yet only one voice form is acceptable; there is no such alternative as (15a).

According to Witherspoon, what drives the system is not animacy but attribution of control. (15a), he claims, is odd not so much as a matter of poor grammar but as a matter of ontological absurdity. The example has a connotation – impermissible in the Navajo view of things – that the baby undertook to kick the man. Witherspoon argues that this encoding of the situation is impossible since, in the Navajo perspective, the man has greater control, and can be kicked by the baby only through his own inattention or inadvertence. Correspondingly, the sole acceptable formulation is (15b), in which "man" is explicitly encoded as a subject.

Some comments of Witherspoon 1980: 9–10 on the ontology of Navajo transitive predications are worth citing in full.

178 *Inverse voice systems*

If we go back to the sentence ... łį́į́' hastiin yiztał *the horse kicked the man*, we find that this is an unacceptable sentence. It is not just poor grammar; it is, in fact, an impossibility in the Navajo world. In the Navajo view of the world horses cannot take it upon themselves to kick men, for men are more intelligent than horses. Navajos would explain this by saying that it is not within the intellectual capabilities of the horse to conjure up a plan by which he decides that he does not like some man and decides that when the man comes near him the next time, he will give the man a swift kick. Navajos say the behavior of horses is more spontaneous than that and that they are not capable of long-range planning.

The conclusion we can draw from this is that if a man gets kicked by a horse, it is his own damn fault for not using the intelligence with which he was born. Horses kick men because men allow themselves to be kicked by being in the wrong places, and horses kick because men tickle their legs or bellies, hurt them, or scare them. It is the man who, in the ultimate sense, caused the horse to kick him and it was he who was in the wrong place when the horse kicked. Therefore, in the Navajo view of the world, when a man gets kicked by a horse, there is only one way to describe such an event:

   ... hastiin łį́į́' biztał
   (man) (horse) (it-it-kicked)

The sentence should be translated *the man let* (or *caused*) *the horse to kick him*.

Witherspoon's views on Navajo attribution of control are confirmed by other writers. For instance, Shayne 1982: 389, 387, writing on the closely related San Carlos Apache, cites the examples in (16)–(17):[8]

(16) a. Izee   ncho'í gídí yi-yeshį
      medicine bad   cat killed
      'Poison killed the cat'
   b. Gídí izee   ncho'í bi-yeshį
      cat medicine bad killed
      'The cat was killed by poison'
(17) a. Hastin   tłį   yi-yeshí
      old age/old man horse killed
      'The old man/[*old age] killed the horse'
   b. Tłí hastin   bi-yeshí
      horse old age/old man killed
      'The horse was killed by old age/[*the old man]'

Shayne, like Witherspoon, argues that animacy is an inadequate explanation for the pattern of voice alternations. As evidence, she points out that while (16a) is acceptable in the reading 'Poison killed the cat,' (17a) is not acceptable in the reading 'Old age killed the horse.' Observing that *hastin* in both examples means both 'old age' and 'old man,' she claims that an adequate account must appeal to attribution of control.

In her account, the acceptability of (16a) is due to the fact that a deadly chemical may be construed as not inferior in control to a living animal which succumbs to its effects. In other words, the animal may be perceived as having no power to resist the poison. But according to Shayne, in (17a) where *hastin* is construed as 'old man,' "the old man is considered to be a potent agent of the event of killing. The goal . . . is not seen as having contributed to its realization" (p. 397). On the other hand,

where *hastin* means 'old age,' a different picture emerges. Old age is not a separate entity that acts on the horse in some way to kill it. It is an inherent characteristic of the horse itself. Through the process of maturing, the horse eventually becomes old and dies as a result . . . Therefore, *bi-* is prefixed to the verb, indicating that the 'goal' somehow participated in the event.

In other words, "old age," unlike "old man," does not comprise an independent locus of control. Therefore, "old age" cannot be encoded as ontological subject in (17a). Rather, this status can only devolve upon "the horse," as the grammaticality of (17b) confirms.

It is worth asking at this point how Apachean voice alternations can be accounted for formally and, in particular, whether grammatical relations (relational subject, relational object) should be invoked. From the data it appears that the bound pronominals *yi-* and *bi-* always index ontological, not logical, objects of transitive predicates. The choice between the two depends on the logical status of the indexed argument – *yi-* being selected when the ontological object coincides with logical object, *bi-* being selected when the ontological object coincides with logical subject. The contrast between *yi-* and *bi-*, then, is due to the fact that they index distinct logical relations. Note that standard treatments, e.g. of Navajo, classify both as object pronominals, since both occur in the same position within the Apachean verbal complex – a position associated with one and the same ontological status, ontological object. Relational statuses of subject and object seem to have no bearing on this.

Moreover, since case morphology is lacking, the grammatical relations of independent nominals cannot be recovered from their forms, as these are invariant (this is confirmed by 13–17). To be sure, at the clause level, there are preferred vs marked linear word orders. (See Saville-Troike & McCreedy 1979 and Frishberg 1972 for some discussion of alternative word orders in Navajo.) But preferred order does not seem to be sensitive to grammatical relations. As (13)–(17) illustrate, where both core arguments of a transitive clause are encoded by independent nominals, clause-initial position tends to be occupied by ontological (not logical or relational) subject.

In sum, morphological or coding evidence does not support the existence of relational statuses of subject and object independent of ontological subject and object. In Apachean languages, voice alternations, word order and selection of bound pronominals appear sensitive only to logical and ontological statuses. They furnish no evidence for the reality of a grammatical relation subject, as distinct from and independent of ontological subject.[9]

We will now summarize the characteristics, apart from voice, which relate Apachean systems to the inverse type. As (13)–(17) confirm, Apachean languages are predominantly head-marking, with core arguments obligatorily indexed by bound pronominals in the verbal complex. Also, independent nominals bear no marking of core relations to predicates. To be sure, independent nominals are sometimes governed by postpositions (see Young & Morgan 1987: 26ff. for illustrations); but the relations encoded through postpositional marking are noncore. There is no specific marking of independent nominals for the core relations they bear to predicates. In addition, and as also noted above, there is a preferred linear order of elements within the clause. However, like Algonquian (see above, examples 3a–f), the Apachean clause has variant word orders (for discussion, see Saville-Troike & McCreedy 1979 and Frishberg 1972, both dealing with Navajo). Accordingly, word order is not a reliable criterion for the assignment of nominal statuses or relations.

Apachean languages, in common with certain other inverse systems, have one special feature. This is the obviative* or, as writers often term it, the fourth person*. Elements specific to this function occur in various Apachean languages. For instance, Kiowa-Apache has a bound pronominal *go-* (Bittle 1963: 91). A corresponding element is identified by Hoijer 1971: 76 in Chiricahua Apache.

Akmajian & Anderson 1970, Young & Morgan 1987: 9, Thompson 1989 and Jelinek 1990 discuss the fourth person in Navajo. Fourth person marking consists of a bound pronominal which occurs in place of the third person (ontological) object pronominals *yi-* and *bi-*.

According to the cited authors, the fourth person's function is to encode maintenance of a particular nominal as either subject or object over a series of clauses in a discourse. Generally, the referent of the fourth person must be human as well as non-SAP. Young & Morgan 1987: 9 comment: "In narratives, the ... [fourth person object] pronoun serves to distinguish between two third persons, and is usually applied to the main character along with any other figure who gains prominence at some point in the story (more than one character may thus be represented by the ... [fourth person object] pronoun at some point)."

The Navajo fourth person pronominal has either of two shapes, depending on whether it indexes an ontological subject or an ontological object. If the former, the shape is *j-/dz-*, and if the latter, the shape is *h-*. Illustrations, respectively, are (18a, b) from Akmajian & Anderson 1970: 4. (PRO in glosses indicates an overtly unfilled core argument position.)

(18) a. Jáan Mary yi-zts'ǫs ńt'éé' Bill 'éi / ∅   Baa' dzi-
       John Mary   kissed but   Bill that (he) Baa   4 SUBJ
       zts'ǫs hałní
       kissed said
       'John kissed Mary but Bill said that PRO (= John) kissed Baa'
    b. Baa' Chii yi- zts'ǫs ńt'éé' Kii Baa' ∅   ná- ho-   díłts'in
       Baa Chee   kissed but   Kee Baa (him)   4 OBJ hit
       nízin
       thinks
       'Baa kissed Chee but Kee thinks that Baa hit PRO (= Chee)'

Although the referent of the Apachean fourth person pronominal is generally human, in non-Apachean inverse systems, obviative or fourth person indices may refer to nonhumans. However, even in these systems, the referent of an obviative must usually be animate. This will be clarified in the discussion of Algonquian inverse systems in Section 4.4.

Meanwhile, the following section addresses one significant issue in the formal account of direct/inverse voice alternations.

4.3 Passive vs inverse voice

By this point in the presentation, most readers will be mindful of the parallelism to actives and passives of such alternate voice forms as (19)–(20) (corresponding to the Plains Cree examples 1a, b and Navajo 13a, b above, respectively):

(19) a. Ni- sēkih -ā   -nān atim
       1   scare theme **DIRECT** 1PL dog
       'We scare the dog'
   b. Ni-sēkih -iko   -nān atim
      1   scare theme **INVERSE** 1PL dog
      'The dog scares us'
(20) a. łíí' dzaanééz yi-ztał
       horse mule   kicked
       'The horse kicked the mule'
   b. Dzaanééz łíí' bi-ztał
      mule   horse kicked
      'The mule was kicked by the horse'

It has been observed earlier that many transitive predications do not display both a- and b-, or direct and inverse, alternate forms. This does not entail, however, that one could not treat the alternation as active/passive. One could claim that, in the relevant systems, the passive is sensitive to hierarchy (6), or to some scale of salience based thereon, which constrains the distribution of voice alternates.

Is there any compelling ground, then, for distinguishing the direct–inverse type from derived voice? In fact, many writers cited in the preceding section and in the following two sections assume not.

At this point, it seems appropriate to confront this issue. It is true that there is some parallelism between inverse voice and the passive. However, this does not justify placing too much emphasis on the similarities while overlooking any differences. The remainder of this section details three specific differences between active–passive and direct–inverse, differences that, to the present writer, seem critical.

Among these differences, that which seems most crucial to distinguishing inverse from derived voice is the factor of valence alteration. As discussed in Section 1.1, derived voice alternations virtually always involve valence reduction. Passivization, in particular, involves detransitivization*. In cross-language surveys of passives (e.g. Shibatani 1985,

4.3 Passive vs inverse voice

Keenan 1985), virtually no exceptions to this are reported. Generally, passivization either suppresses or grammatically downgrades the argument assigned as subject by the basic (unpassivized) predicate, either eliminating it from the valence or reassigning it as an oblique or adjunct.

But exactly the opposite holds in direct–inverse voice systems. There is no valence reduction and there is no suppression or grammatical downgrading of logical subjects. In passives, the most obvious sign of valence reorganization is formal intransitivity. But inverse voice forms, like direct voice forms, are formally transitive.

For instance, in Apachean languages, an inverse form (e.g. 20b in Navajo), like a direct form (e.g. 20a), has an element occupying the object pronominal position of the verbal complex, a sign that the verb is transitive. Comparing (20b), a *bi*- form, with (20a), a *yi*- form, yields evidence of no overt downgrading, defocusing or deemphasizing of either core argument.

Navajo does have detransitives, or intransitives derived from basic transitives. However, they are formally distinct from inverse forms (*bi*-forms) and, according to Jelinek 1990: 3, they "exclude the Inverse alternation." (See also Haile 1926, Thompson 1989.) Interestingly, detransitivization is often formally signaled in Navajo by means of the subjective and objective fourth person pronominals, which have been discussed and illustrated in the preceding section (examples 18a, b).[10]

In Algonquian languages, derived intransitives are also distinguished from inverse voice forms. This is illustrated by (21a, b), direct and inverse alternates from the language Algonkin (due to Henderson 1971: 33). In these examples, the predicate is transitive, demonstrating concord (for number) with both core arguments. As the examples show, concord marking does not vary depending on whether the form of the predication is direct or inverse. Accordingly, in the inverse (21b), there is no formal evidence of detransitivization. Algonkin does have detransitive or derived intransitive predications, as illustrated in (22c) (from Henderson, p. 39). But this example is distinct in shape both from the corresponding direct (22a) as well as the corresponding inverse (22b). Note further that, ironically, the voice marking of the detransitive (22c) turns out to be not inverse, but direct. (See Henderson for additional forms and paradigms.)

(21) a. Ni- wāpam -ā   -nān -ik
      1   see   **DIRECT** 1PL 3PL
      'We see them'

  b. Ni- wāpam -iko   -nān -ik
    1   see   **INVERSE** 1PL 3PL
    'They see us'
(22) a. O- wāpam -ā   -n
    3   see   **DIRECT** OBV
    'He sees the other'
  b. O- wāpam -iko   -n
    3   see   **INVERSE** OBV
    'The other sees him'
  c. Wāpam -ā
    see   **DIRECT**
    'He is seen'

  As a second ground for distinguishing direct–inverse from active–passive voice systems, we will now argue that analyzing the inverse as a passive results in an account which is unnecessarily complex. It is less simple than an account which recognizes the distinctness of the two and treats them as manifestations of separate voice types.

  Assuming that inverse voice forms result from passivization, special conditions must apply in the case of nonreversible predications. By this is meant predications unlike (19a, b) and (20a, b). These are reversible, or can appear in alternate voices, because both core arguments are animate. Generally, in inverse systems, the animacy of both core arguments is a precondition for a transitive predicate to alternate in both voices. It is usually not possible for a predication to alternate for voice if one argument is animate and the other inanimate.

  Applying a passivization analysis to inverse systems, accordingly, entails that the passive rule is restricted in one class of languages, inverse languages, to predications whcih have animate logical objects. That is, these languages resemble such European languages as English in having passives of expressions like "We frighten them" or "We flatter them," but differ in not having passives of expressions like "We smoke them," "We sow them," or "We weave them." A formal treatment can, of course, handle this by appealing to a nominal status hierarchy along the lines of (6) (or some version thereof) in order to stipulate the special conditions on passivization that apply in inverse languages. But a formal treatment of inverse voice forms as nonpassives, while likewise appealing to a hierarchy of ontological salience, does without a rule of passivization. Accordingly, on the grounds of simplicity, a nonpassivization account is to be preferred.[11]

The third argument against treating inverse as a derived voice is based on the fact that direct and inverse voice alternates do not express equivalent propositional content. Derived voice alternates usually preserve propositional content. Generally, active/passive counterparts bear this out. On the other hand, direct/inverse alternates such as (19a, b), (20a, b), (21a, b) and (22a, b) do not preserve propositional content.

Perhaps the clearest way of presenting this argument is by laying out, side by side, corresponding direct/inverse and active/passive counterparts. In (23), the a- and b-examples are equivalent to (19a, b) above; they respectively illustrate direct and inverse alternates. The a'- and b'- examples are a corresponding active and passive pair.

(23) a. Ni- sēkih -ā -nān atim
        'We scare the dog' (**DIRECT**)
    a'. WE scare THE DOG
    b. Ni- sēkih -iko -nān atim
        'The dog scares us' (**INVERSE**)
    b'. THE DOG is scared BY US

Notice that the b- and b'-examples of (23) are converse, not equivalent, in propositional content.

A passivization rule accounts for a regular difference in overt form between pairs of expressions that are identical in propositional content. But the requisite rule for direct/inverse alternates such as (23a, b) must take account of the fact that pairs of expressions which differ regularly (and in fact are converse to one another) in propositional content converge in overt form (except for the alternation of voice marking).[12]

We conclude that passive and inverse differ in their functional basis, and that a passivization analysis of direct/inverse voice alternations is inappropriate. Some of the points raised in the present section are reinforced in the following, which surveys what are currently the best-investigated systems of the inverse type, Algonquian systems.

4.4 Algonquian languages

Algonquian languages are spoken in Canada and the USA from the Atlantic coast as far west as Wyoming (site of the westernmost representative, Cheyenne). The family has over a dozen principle representatives[13] belonging to several subgroups. However, genetic relations within Algonquian are less than clear at the present time.[14]

Although Algonquian languages are currently the best-studied languages of the inverse type, they, like other inverse systems, are subject to conflicting analyses. One writer proposes analyzing Algonquian languages as ergative (Hewson 1987); others treat them as active–passive (Rhodes 1976, Weaver 1982, Jolley 1981, 1982); and a few writers propose altogether different accounts (Russell 1987; Perlmutter & Rhodes 1988; Piggott 1989). At least one writer advocates treating Algonquian inverse systems as manifesting a distinctive voice type (Dahlstrom 1986c).

Below, the Algonquian system of direct vs inverse voices is construed as one part of an extremely elaborate morphosyntactic system, a system in which various features of verbal valence*, including core argument relations, are encoded through the morphology of the verbal complex. Accordingly, a brief summary of verbal morphology is an important preliminary to understanding the present work's view of Algonquian voice.

In discussing the morphology of the Algonquian verb, specialists invoke a term "nucleus." This refers to the verbal base to which inflectional affixes are added. Although a nucleus is not coterminous with a verbal root, the distinction between the two will be held in abeyance until later.

The minimal verbal complex contains a nucleus which may be preceded by one of three mutually exclusive pronominal prefixes indexing the person of a core argument (first, second, or third). Whether or not it bears a prefix, a nucleus is obligatorily followed by one or more suffixes. These suffixes have a variety of functions. For instance, a core argument's grammatical number may be encoded by a suffix (although not by a prefix).

To illustrate, consider the contrast between the Cheyenne singular *nánaaʔe* 'I died/am dying' and the corresponding plural *nánaēme* 'We (exclusive) died' (from Leman 1979: 27). In both examples, the first person prefix is *ná-*, while the nucleus "sleep" is *na*. The suffixes encode the core argument's number. Or consider the contrast in the Cree singular vs plural forms *mihkwāw* 'It is red' and *mihkwāwa* 'They are red' (from Dahlstrom 1986c: 34). The nucleus "be red" belongs to a valence class whose members assign an inanimate as their sole core argument (the inanimate intransitive or II class; see below). Predicates of this class never assign prefixes of person. However, the number of the core argument is indicated by the alternation of singular vs plural suffixes *-w* and *-wa*.

The category of obviation* is likewise suffixal. Number suffixes precede obviatives in the verbal complex. Obviation is further discussed later in this section.

In addition to suffixes of number and obviation, a nucleus may be extended by a suffix of direct or inverse voice. A verbal stem formed with such a suffix is called a theme. Summing up what has been said so far, in the Algonquian verbal complex, the usual order of elements (leaving aside affixes of tense and mood/modality) is as shown in (24):[15]

(24) (a) pronominal prefix – (b) verbal nucleus – (c) theme sign – (d) number – (e) obviation

We will now momentarily leave aside the morphology of the verb to discuss certain grammatical classes.

Algonquian nominals are organized into two classes, or as they are usually termed, genders. In the majority of instances, a nominal's classification depends on the referent's natural animacy, although there are exceptions (see e.g. 25a, ii below). (Also, on the ontology of Algonquian gender classification, see Craik 1982 and Vaillancourt 1980.) Number inflections are organized into paradigms depending on the lexical gender (animacy) of the host nominal. This is illustrated by the Cree examples (25a, b), from Wolfart & Carroll 1981: 20–1 (note that plural inflections are in italic type):

(25) a. **animate**
    (i) iskwēsis 'girl,' iskwēsis*ak* 'girls'
    (ii) ospwākan 'pipe,' ospwākan*ak* 'pipes'
  b. **inanimate**
    (i) astotin 'cap', astotin*a* 'caps'
    (ii) mōhkomān 'knife', mōhkomān*a* 'knives'

Verbal nuclei are likewise organized into two classes, animate and inanimate, within each of two valence sets, transitive and intransitive. The animacy classification of an intransitive nucleus depends on the gender of its core argument. Generally, inanimate intransitive (II) nuclei are not preceded by prefixes of person. By contrast, animate intransitive (AI) nuclei may be preceded by person prefixes, frequently the same prefixes which accrue to transitive animate (TA) nuclei. (26a, b) are Cree illustrations of AI nuclei and person prefixes (from Dahlstrom 1986c: 68).

(26) a. Ni- pimipahtā -n
      1   run   1SG
      'I run'
    b. Ni- pimipahtā -nān
      1   run   1PL
      'We (exclusive) run'

Transitive nuclei are likewise divided into two classes, transitive inanimate (TI) and transitive animate (TA).[16] The animacy classification of a transitive verb is determined by the gender of one of its core arguments (specifically, the ontological object).

For nuclei of the TI class, inflections of number and person index only logical subjects. The selection of TI inflections in itself indexes the inanimate gender of the logical object; there is no specific index of its number. Note in the Ojibwa and Cree examples (27a, b) and (28a, b) (respectively from Goddard 1967b: 71 and Wolfart & Carroll 1981: 68) that the shape of the verbal complex is constant despite alternations in the logical object's number.

(27) a. O- tēpwētt -ān
      3   believe   TI 3SG
      'He believes it/them'
    b. Ki- tēpwētt -ānān
      2   believe   TI 21PL
      'We (inclusive) believe it/them'
(28) a. Pēyak wāskahikan ni- wāpaht -ēn
      one   house   1   see   TI 1SG
      'I see one house'
    b. Nīso wāskahikan -a   ni- wāpaht -ēn
      two   house   PL 1   see   TI 1SG
      'I see two houses'

Three of the Algonquian verb classes, II, AI and TI, have now been examined. The fourth and final class, the transitive animate (TA) class, is of principal concern for present purposes, since it is the only class which forms themes (inflecting stems) by alternating direct and inverse theme signs.

However, before discussing TA themes in detail, it is important to note that a great deal of information about valence* – the number and kinds (gender classes) of arguments with which an Algonquian verb construes – is encoded below the level of the inflecting stem within the structure of the verbal nucleus. Let us look briefly at this.

To be complete, an Algonquian verbal nucleus must include not only a lexical root (or, in the parlance of Algonquianists, an initial), but also some additional element. Optionally, a root may be followed by a kind of element called a medial. Obligatorily, however, a root or root plus medial must be followed by another element, a final. The nucleus of an Algonquian verb complex thus conforms to a formula "root (medial) final" (Goddard 1967b: 66).

Medials are sometimes likened to incorporated nominals. An illustration is the Ojibwa medial -āpikk-, which, when added to the root šašš- 'slip,' yields a base šaššāpikk-, meaning 'to slip on stone' (Denny 1978b: 300). Medials are of less interest to the present discussion than finals, to which we now turn.

One class of finals, termed abstract finals, is of particular interest for the following reason. A predicate may pertain to more than one valence class – inflecting in more than one paradigm, II, AI, TI, or TA – depending on which abstract final appears in the nucleus.

For instance, Goddard 1967b: 66 observes that the Fox root sanak- 'be difficult' may be assigned either of the abstract finals -esi or -at. A nucleus terminating in the former is an AI nucleus, and a nucleus terminating in the latter is an II nucleus. Correlated with this is a difference in lexical sense: sanakesi-wa (where -wa is a suffix of the AI paradigm encoding singular number) means 'he is difficult' (the shape of the third person prefix is zero). Contrastingly, sanakat-wi (where -wi is a suffix of the II paradigm encoding singular number) means 'it is difficult.'

From available literature on the semantics of Algonquian abstract finals (e.g. Denny 1977, 1978a, b, 1983a, b, 1984), it appears that these elements subsume many of the functions expressed in non-Algonquian languages by nominal case and markers of verbal valence* or transitivity*. Moreover, although by its inherent semantics an Algonquian lexical root may conform to a given valence class, it is the abstract final following the root in the verbal nucleus which determines the predicate's inflecting class, the paradigm or paradigms which it selects.

The shape of the Algonquian verbal nucleus, then, imparts a great deal of information about the valence of the predication, exclusive of the information indexed by affixes of number, person, or theme.

However, rich as the morphology of the nucleus is, for TA (and only for TA) verbs it is the theme sign, added to the nucleus to form an inflecting stem, that conveys one essential item of information. In the applicable part of the TA person–number paradigm (to be clarified below), it is the theme sign that encodes vital information as to which of the core arguments is assigned which logical status, subject or object.

The part of the TA paradigm in which theme signs furnish this information is illustrated in (29) below with examples from Cree. It should first be noted that, in Algonquian languages, inflectional paradigms of the verb are grouped into several sets termed orders. The common orders include the imperative, the conjunct and the independent. The first can be overlooked for present purposes. The examples to follow illustrate the third of these, the independent order; while the conjunct order will not be illustrated until later (when obviation is discussed).

In the independent order, a TA stem may alternate for direct and inverse theme marking under particular conditions. For instance, direct and inverse may be encoded when both core arguments are SAP (have first or second person reference). This class of forms is traditionally called local (also sometimes known as SAP or as "you-and-me" forms). The illustrations in (29a–f) (from Wolfart & Carroll 1981: 73 and Dahlstrom 1986c: 47–9) are based on the TA nucleus *wāpam* 'see':

(29) a. Ki- wāpam -iti -n   'I see you (SG)'
     b. Ki- wāpam -iti -nāwāw 'I see you (PL)'
     c. Ki- wāpam -i -n   'You (SG) see me'
     d. Ki- wāpam -i -nāwāw   'You (PL) see me'
     e. Ki- wāpam -iti -nān   'We (exclusive) see you (SG/PL)'
     f. Ki- wāpam -i -nān   'You (SG/PL) see us (exclusive)'

It is unnecessary to discuss the morphology of these forms in detail to observe that the logical relations of the first and second person arguments are exhaustively disambiguated by the pattern of inflection. That is, in (29a–f), the verbal complex encodes each logical combination of first and second person as subject and object in a formally distinct way. The sole ambiguity resides in the number of the second person argument in (29e) and (29f), apparently due to the fact that in local forms, only one plurality suffix (represented in these instances by *-nān*, the first person plural suffix) can be assigned per verbal complex.

Observe, too, that the logical relation of a second person core argument in an SAP form seems to be determined by eliminating whatever logical status is already encoded for the first person. The occurrence or nonoccurrence of a suffix identifying the first person as logical subject (-*iti*, which both Dahlstrom and Wolfart & Carroll gloss as 'inverse') makes the inference possible. If and only if this suffix does not appear – that is, if there occurs, in its stead, the direct theme suffix -*i* – the second person core argument is construed as the logical subject.

Finally, note that in each local or SAP form in (29), the assigned person prefix is *ki-*, or second person. In fact, whenever a transitive predicate is local, assigning only first and second person core arguments, then second person rather than first person prefixes are invariably assigned, not just in Cree, but in Algonquian languages in general.[17]

Most Algonquianists account for this by assigning the second person a superior position on the hierarchy of ontological salience. This amounts to reversing the two leftmost positions on the ontological salience hierarchy (6) (see again n. 5). Although (5) has been offered earlier as an approximation, it now seems appropriate to restate the salience hierarchy for Algonquian languages as shown in (30).

(30) **Algonquian person-referencing hierarchy for TA predicates**
(second version)
2 > 1 > non-SAP

It must, however, be conceded that the revised hierarchy (30) is, again, only an approximation of the operative scale of ontological salience for Algonquian. A further revision will be proposed shortly.

We will now consider TA nonlocal forms. Like TA local forms, these, too, are subject to the alternation of direct vs inverse theme marking. It will be recalled that a TA verb is nonlocal if it has at least one core argument with third person or non-SAP reference.

The a- and b-examples of (31)–(39) illustrate a variety of nonlocal direct and inverse forms, again from Cree, again in the independent order, and again with the nucleus *wāpam* 'see.' (31)–(35) are direct forms, while (36)–(39) are inverse. (31–9 are due to Wolfart & Carroll 1978: 70, 72 and Dahlstrom 1986c: 43, 53.)

(31) a. Ni- wāpam -āw
     1   see   1SG
    'I see him'
   b. Ni- wāpam -āw -ak
     1   see   1SG 3PL
    'I see them'

(32) a. Ki- wāpam -āw
    2   see   1SG
    'You (SG) see him'
  b. Ki- wāpam -āw -ak
    2   see   1SG 3PL
    'You (SG) see them'
(33) a. Ki- wāpam -āwāw
    2   see   2PL
    'You (PL) see him'
  b. Ki- wāpam -āwāw -ak
    2   see   2PL   3PL
    'You (PL) see them'
(34) Ni- / Ki- wāpam -imāwa
    1   2   see   OBV SG
    'I/you (SG) see him (OBV)'
(35) a. Wāpam -ēw
    see   3 OBV
    'He (PROX) sees him (OBV)'
  b. Wāpam -ēw   -ak
    see   3OBV 3PL
    'He (PROX) sees them (OBV)'
(36) a. Ni- wāpam -ik
    1   see   **INVERSE**
    'He sees me'
  b. Ni- wāpam -ikw   -ak
    1   see   **INVERSE** 3PL
    'They see me'
(37) a. Ki- wāpam -ik
    2   see   **INVERSE**
    'He sees you (SG)'
  b. Ki- wāpam -ikw   -ak
    2   see   **INVERSE** 3PL
    'They see you (SG)'
(38) a. Wāpam -ik
    see   **INVERSE**
    'He (OBV) sees him (PROX)'
  b. Wāpam -ikw   -ak
    see   **INVERSE** 3PL
    'They (OBV) see him (PROX)'

(39) a. Ni- wāpam -iko   -yiwa
       1   see   INVERSE 3OBV (SG)
       'He (OBV) sees me'
    b. Ki- wāpam -iko   -yiwa
       2   see   INVERSE 3OBV (SG)
       'He (OBV) sees you'

If one compares (31)–(35) with (36)–(39), it is apparent that in the second group of examples, the verbal complex includes the inverse theme sign *-iko/-ik(w)*. It therefore seems that inverse marking is assigned in nonlocal forms of the TA paradigm when either of the following conditions holds: (a) a non-SAP logical subject cooccurs with an SAP (1, 2 person) logical object; or (b) the logical subject belongs to a special subcategory of the third person, the obviative, while the logical object does not (compare 38a, b and 39a, b with 34). Neither condition is met in nonlocal forms with direct (zero) theme marking, such as (31)–(35).

The role of obviation in theme selection prompts a further revision in the ontological salience hierarchy. Originally stated in (5), this hierarchy has been restated in a noninitial but still provisional form in (30). Its further revised form is (40), which is the present work's final version of the ontological salience hierarchy for Algonquian.

(40) **Algonquian person-referencing hierarchy for TA predicates**
     2 > 1 > 3 nonobviative (proximate) > 3 obviative

In order to understand what this hierarchy entails and how it operates, a detailed examination of obviation* is called for. This will occupy the balance of the present section.

It has been mentioned in Section 4.0 that, in certain inverse systems, two subclasses of the third person category are distinguished. One of these is nonobviative or, as often termed by Algonquianists, proximate; the other is obviative or, as sometimes termed, the fourth person (see again the discussion of Apachean in Section 4.2).[18]

In an Algonquian TA predication, an obviative core argument may cooccur with a core SAP argument, as (34) illustrates. Aside from this, an obviative may comprise the sole core argument of an intransitive. This is illustrated in the Ojibwa example (41) below.

If both core arguments of a TA predication are third person, a constraint general to Algonquian languages comes into play as follows: at least one of the core nominals must be obviative.[19] This is illustrated, again in Ojibwa, by (42a, b). (41 and 42a, b are from Dunnigan, O'Malley & Schwartz 1978: 8, 9–10.) Note that, in each of these examples, the obviative marking on the nominal is cross-indexed or duplicated in the verbal complex.

One additional domain for obligatory obviation is the possessive construction. Where both the head and dependent of the possessive are third person, the former bears obviative marking, whether the construction occurs in isolation (43a, b) or corresponds to an argument in a clause (44). (These examples, once more in Ojibwa, are from Dunnigan, O'Malley & Schwartz, p. 12. 43a is equivalent to 4 above).[20]

(41) Wākośś -an   ayāw -an   imā
     fox   OBV   be   OBV   there
     'The fox is there'

(42) a. Wākośś   o- wāpam -ān   piśiw -an
        fox (PROX) 3 see   OBV   lynx OBV
        'The fox sees the lynx'

    b. Piśiw -an   o- wāpam -ikōn   wākośś
       lynx OBV 3 see   INVERSE + OBV fox (PROX)
       'The lynx sees the fox'

(43) a. Fred o- māmāy -an
        Fred 3 mother OBV
        'Fred's mother'

    b. O- māmāy -an
       3 mother OBV
       'His mother'

(44) Fred o- wāpam -ān   o- māmāy -an
     Fred 3 see   OBV   3 mother OBV
     'Fred$_i$ sees his$_{i,j}$ mother'

Although obviation is only required under specific conditions (which 42–4 exemplify), there is no prohibition against the obviative being assigned to both non-SAP core nominals of a TA predication. To be sure, examples of this sort are uncommon. However, Dahlstrom 1986c: 54 provides illustrations in Cree of both the direct and inverse forms of a TA 3OBV:3OBV predication. These are reproduced below in (45a, b). Notice that in each predicate there occur two obviative suffixes, one indexing each core argument.

(45) a. Wāpam -ē -yi -wa
    see **DIRECT** OBV SG OBV
    'He (OBV) sees him (OBV)'
  b. Wāpam -iko -yi -wa
    see **INVERSE** OBV SG OBV
    'He (OBV) sees him (OBV)'

Examples (45a, b) may be likened to active/passive pairs "He sees him" and "He is seen by him," since in information content, they are virtually interchangeable. In Algonquian, TA 3OBV:3OBV forms seem to be the only instances in which a predication can be expressed either in the direct or in the corresponding inverse shape. The significance of this will be noted below in Sections 4.5.1 and 4.5.2.

It has been observed that Algonquian languages manifest a constraint against two proximate third person nominals cooccurring in a TA predication. As a result, if one core argument of a TA 3:3 predication is proximate, the other is invariably obviative. Illustrations are (42a, b) and the earlier (35a, b) and (38a, b). In these examples, the effects of the constraint are clear. From a purely structural standpoint, however, the constraint seems difficult to motivate.

The situation may be clarified, however, if one takes into account the proper glossing of the examples. The furnished glosses obscure the fact that, in a transitive predication, the two core arguments are never of equal prominence in the speaker/hearer's attentions. Rather, one is always backgrounded in salience relative to the other. Obviation is a strategy for grammaticizing this.

Accordingly, rather than the gloss 'He (PROX) sees him (OBV)' given in (35a), a more accurate rendering would be 'He sees the other.' Similarly, rather than the gloss 'He (OBV) sees him (PROX)' given in (38a), a more accurate rendering would be 'The other sees him.' (These are, in fact, the glosses provided in the original source of the examples.) It follows that (35a) and (38a) are not equivalent in information content; they are not like typical active and passive counterparts. Note too that, where (35a) is formally direct, (38a) is formally inverse.

In (38a) (and in 38b, 42b), the inverse is assigned because the logical subject is less central to the speaker/hearer's attentions at this point in the discourse than the other core argument, the logical object. As a result, the denoted situation proceeds in the ontologically inverse or unexpected direction, since a proximate third person as logical object

196 *Inverse voice systems*

outranks an obviative as logical subject. That proximate and obviative third person subclasses interact in this way with the system of direct and inverse voice assignment is reflected in the ontological salience hierarchy (40).

It has been noted in the preceding section that the functions of obviation go beyond the domain of the clause. The present section would, therefore, be incomplete without some remarks on the obviative's role in discourse.

Goddard 1984: 273 characterizes this role as one whereby "subjects and objects are kept straight and different participants in a section of narrative may also be kept distinct." In the preceding section, the Apachean obviative has been associated with a similar function (see again the Navajo examples 18a, b).

For these reasons, at the level of discourse the obviative is often regarded as fulfilling a function of core nominal reference-tracking. In noninverse systems, nominal reference-tracking is sometimes accomplished through other strategies. At this point, it may be useful to compare several.

In many languages, nominal reference-tracking is accomplished by the use of anaphoric elements. In the English examples (46a, b), the pronouns in italic type fulfill this function.

(46) a. John showed Joe a picture of *him*
    b. John showed *him* a picture of Joe

While *him* can construe with either *John* or *Joe* as a possible antecedent in (46a), neither of these can antecede *him* in (46b). This difference is due to a complex system of rules sensitive to relations of structural government. It is largely in languages that one might characterize as configurational*, such as English, that pronominal antecedence can be construed as a reference-tracking strategy.

In some languages, nominal reference-tracking is a function of derived voices. For instance, the English passive sometimes has a reference-tracking function, as illustrated in (47a, b). In languages with a distinct pattern of case* organization, ergative* (ergative–absolutive) languages, a similar function may be fulfilled by a different derived voice, the antipassive*. For instance, the antipassive's reference-tracking function in Dyirbal, an Australian language of ergative–absolutive type, is illustrated in (48a, b) (from Comrie 1988: 10–12).

(47) a. The man hit the woman and ∅ ran away (∅ = the man)
  b. The woman was hit by the man and ∅ ran away (∅ = the woman)
(48) a. Balan   jugumbil   banggul
     class FEM ABS woman-ABS   class MASC ERG
     yara -nggu balga -n,   ∅ baninyu
     man ERG hit   nonfuture came-nonfuture
     'The man hit the woman and ∅ came here' (∅ = the woman)
  b. Bayi   yara   bani -nyu,   bagul
     class MASC ABS man-ABS come nonfuture   class FEM DAT
     jugumbilgu   ∅ balgalnganyu
     woman-DAT   hit-nonfuture ANTI
     'The man came here and ∅ hit the woman' (∅ = the man)

Some languages manifest a different reference-tracking strategy, in which verbs are variably inflected for categories of switch-reference and same-reference. In this sort of system, the alternation of inflections within a discourse unit encodes whether the subject of one predicate is the same as or different from the subject of another.

Systems with this reference-tracking strategy are called switch-reference* systems. Illustrations from a Papuan language, Usan, appear in (49a, b) (from Haiman & Munro 1983a: ix).

(49) a. Ye nam su -ab   isomei
     I tree cut same SUBJ   I-went-down
     'I cut the tree and went down'
  b. Ye nam su -ine   isorei
     I tree cut different SUBJ   it-went-down
     'I cut the tree down'

Switch-reference seems to be a fairly common reference-tracking strategy in languages which meet the characterization of non-configurationality* (see again Section 4.0). This is presumably due to their having so-called flat structure, i.e. their lacking structural government. Languages with structural government, configurational languages, often track reference through anaphora, as noted above.

Moreover, a switch-reference strategy may sometimes be complementary to a derived voice reference-tracking strategy. This appears to be the case, for instance, in Australian languages. Those which have switch-reference lack an antipassive derived voice, and vice versa (Peter Austin, personal communication).

The distinction of proximate/obviative marking in the Algonquian third person is likened by several authors (see e.g. Dahlstrom 1986b: 53; and Haiman & Munro 1983: xi) to a kind of switch-reference strategy confined to one person category. That is, over a discourse unit containing multiple predications, obviation may serve to disambiguate the logical relations of non-SAP or third person core arguments.

To be sure, a discourse unit may be of indeterminate length. It may comprise a single sentence, or may extend over indefinitely many contiguous sentences of a narrative. It is even possible, in principle, for a new discourse unit to begin between clauses in mid-sentence (Goddard 1984; Dahlstrom 1986c: 127ff.). This is because a discourse unit's length is not determined structurally, but depends on discourse considerations such as attention flow (see DeLancey 1981), and information structure.

Often, however, the Algonquian obviative's reference-tracking function is evinced within units as small as individual sentences. In such instances, the obviative may be associated with one of the paradigm sets or orders of the Algonquian verb, the conjunct order.

As noted earlier, the conjunct contrasts with two other major Algonquian orders, the imperative and the independent. Frequently, conjunct order predications are related to independent order predications in a manner reminiscent of (though not entirely isofunctional to) the relations of subordinate and main clauses in a language like English. That is, there may be some correlation (though not absolute identity) between the conjunct order and the encoding of background information (as there may be some correlation, if not absolute identity, between subordination and encoding of background information in non-Algonquian languages, e.g. English).

In a discourse unit consisting of a single sentence containing one independent order and one conjunct order clause, the alternation of proximate vs obviative marking frequently functions as a reference-tracking strategy by disambiguating the logical relations of non-SAP arguments. The Cree examples (50a, b) (from Dahlstrom 1986b: 53) illustrate this.

(50) a. John kiskēyihtam ē-āhkosit
John knows-TI independent order be sick (3 PROX conjunct order)
John$_i$ knows that he$_{i, \neq j}$ is sick'

b. John kiskēyihtam   ē-āhkosiyit
John knows-TI independent order be sick (3 OBV conjunct order)
'John$_i$ knows that he$_{\neq i, = j}$ is sick'

In (50b), the obviative in the conjunct clause cannot corefer with the proximate in the independent clause. This is because, within the discourse unit defined by a proximate and a conjunct clause, nominals marked unalike for proximate/obviative status may not corefer. By contrast, in (50a) both the conjunct and independent clause nominals are proximate, and they must corefer.

This furnishes some idea as to how the alternation of proximate vs obviative marking of non-SAP nominals encodes their sameness or distinctness of reference within minimal discourse units. Over larger units, the obviative's reference-tracking functions seem more elaborate than we have space to examine here (see Dahlstrom 1986c: 127ff. and Goddard 1984 for detailed discussion). Still, certain conclusions about the character of obviation seem warranted.

For instance, obviation does not seem to be merely sensitive to the ontological ranking of non-SAP nominals within predication structures. In some instances, the obviative's assignment also seems to reflect extra-structural factors. As suggested earlier, among these are attention flow and information structure. It is also highly likely that discourse cohesion is a factor.

Invariably, however, the obviative represents a locus of ontological nonsalience. Moreover, the determination of a nominal's salience or nonsalience depends on its status relative to the situation of the discourse, i.e. as SAP (first or second person, the latter ranking above the former; see again 40) vs non-SAP – with the latter subcategorized for degrees of nearness to (proximate) vs distance from (obviative) the concerns of speaker and hearer.

Another way of looking at this is to think of proximate and obviative not as two subcategories of the third person, but as two distinct persons, where by "person" is meant a status of ontological salience. From this perspective, Algonquian languages could be said to lack a third person category. Rather, the number of persons is four – listed in order of decreasing ontological salience these are second, first, proximate and obviative.

4.5 Tanoan languages

As discussed in the preceding section, personal prefixes in the Algonquian verbal complex encode ontological, not logical, subjects. To encode the logical relations of transitive core arguments, there is a special strategy, voice marking. It operates, however, only in TA predications. These facts can be captured by informal rules along the lines of (51) for person encoding and (52) for voice marking (both are due to Klaiman 1991b).

(51) **Algonquian person encoding**
Assign to the verbal theme (voice-marked nucleus) the person prefix compatible with the person status first, second or third of its ontological subject.

(52) **Algonquian voice marking**
In a transitive animate (TA) predication, affix to the nucleus the inverse theme sign if there is a discrepancy in the content of the ontological and logical subject positions. Affix the suffix of direct voice in case of coincidence in the ontological and logical subjects.

According to (51), only ontological subjects are indexed by person markers, and according to (52), the logical status of a core argument may be encoded by voice (but not by person) marking. Consistent with this, the assignment of person prefixes in Algonquian systems displays a striking constancy. That is, in animate predications, whether transitive or intransitive, the person index generally does not vary, provided the ontological subject is constant.

The Algonkin examples in (53a–c) (from Henderson 1971: 30–1) illustrate this. These predications are, respectively, TA direct, TA inverse, and animate intransitive, or AI. Note that the ontological subject of each example is the second person, and each example identically begins with the second person prefix *ki-*.

(53) a. Ki- wāpam -ā
    2SG see   **DIRECT**
    'You see him/her'
  b. Ki- wāpam -ik
    2SG see   **INVERSE**
    'He/she sees you'

c. Ki-   pimosse
   2SG   walk
   'You walk'

This pattern of ontological subject indexing is characteristic not only of Algonquian, but also of certain non-Algonquian systems to be surveyed in the following two sections.

Most previous writers do not classify these systems as inverse (see, however, Whistler 1985). We therefore embark on their analysis with the caveat that what is proposed below is not a standard view. At the present stage of research, moreover, the systems in question are highly controversial. The reader is accordingly advised that many observations presented below in the form of assertions should be construed as inbetween hypotheses and conjectures – certainly not as proven facts. Regarding many crucial features of these systems, reliable facts are simply unavailable at the present time. Nevertheless, to provide some foundation for future headway in the analysis of these systems, it would seem useful to marshal as much evidence as possible supporting their congruence with the inverse type.

Although discussed below as inverse systems, there are certain characteristics distinguishing these from other systems of the inverse type. To clarify, imagine a system similar to Algonquian, but with a unified third person category and no proximate/obviative opposition. It follows that, in a TA 3:3 predication, neither core argument outranks the other in ontological salience. Consequently, all TA 3:3 predications are, in principle, reversible, alternating for both voices, direct and inverse.

Such a system requires a special strategy for recovering the logical relations of core arguments in TA predications. Since both core arguments are of equal ontological ranking, the logical relations cannot be recovered by recourse to an ontological salience hierarchy.

With this in mind, one hypothetical possibility for recovering logical relations might be by alternations in shapes of third person pronominals. This occurs in Apachean (see again Section 4.2). The systems surveyed below, however, manifest an alternative strategy. This is restricted case* marking, i.e. a strategy of assigning case (oblique marking) to certain core nominals (specifically, inverse logical subjects; see below).

Another distinctive characteristic of these systems is the pattern of voice marking in local predications. In Algonquian, direct forms of verbs may assign overt stem markers or theme signs, and inverse forms always do. Furthermore, as the earlier Cree examples (29a–f) illustrate, TA local forms may alternate for theme marking. By contrast, in the systems surveyed below, local predications are either direct in form or inverse in form. Which voice is selected varies from language to language, but in each system, exactly one voice is assigned in all local forms.

Most inverse systems with the characteristics just outlined belong to one Amerindian language group, the Tanoan languages. However, the illustrations in (54)–(57), showing the characteristics just outlined, are selected not from a Tanoan language, but from a little-investigated Salishan language, Lummi. These examples are due to Jelinek & Demers 1983: 168 (their analysis differs, however, from that suggested here).

Notice that there is no element glossed as an obviative in any of the Lummi examples. However, the b-examples of (54) and (55) include an element -ŋ, which is glossed as inverse.[21] (55a, b) are direct/inverse 3:3 counterparts. Observe that in the inverse, (55b), the logical subject is non-obviative, but is governed by a prepositional element ə. In general, in inverse predications, this element marks the nominal corresponding to the logical subject, in conformity with the above discussion. Finally, as (56) and (57) illustrate, all TA local predications are formally direct, never inverse.

(54) a. **DIRECT**
*– – –
'The man knows me/you'
b. **INVERSE**
x̣či -t -ŋ -sən / -sxʷ ə cə swəyʔqəʔ
know TR -ŋ 1   2   by the man
'I am/you are known by the man'

(55) a. **DIRECT**
x̣či -t -s   cə swəyʔqəʔ cə swiʔqoʔəɫ
know TR 3 TR SUBJ the man   the boy
'The man knows the boy'
b. **INVERSE**
x̣či -t -ŋ cə swiʔqóʔəɫ ə cə swəyʔqəʔ
know TR -ŋ the boy   by the man
'The boy is known by the man'

(56) a. **DIRECT**
    x̱či   -t   -oŋəs -sən
    know TR 1/2   1
    'I know you'
  b. **INVERSE**
    * _ _ _
    'You are known by me'
(57) a. **DIRECT**
    x̱či   -t   -oŋəs -sx^w
    know TR 1/2   2
    'You know me'
  b. **INVERSE**
    * _ _ _
    'I am known by you'

Having briefly illustrated the typical characteristics of this special inverse subtype with data from Lummi, our discussion now moves on to the systems which are the main focus of the present section, Tanoan systems.

Below, Section 4.5.1 concerns inverse patterning in Arizona Tewa. Several additional Tanoan systems are surveyed in Section 4.5.2. Lastly, Section 4.5.3 discusses some implications of Tanoan's controversial status in relation to the inverse type.

Tanoan is the name of a group of languages spoken today in New Mexico and Arizona. Davis 1979 is a useful survey of some of the grammatical literature, while Kroskrity 1977 provides information on the history of the family and the status of its speakers.

Tanoan has three major branches: Tewa, Tiwa and Towa. Tewa is spoken on the Hopi First Mesa in northern Arizona, where it is known as Arizona Tewa (AT). There are also communities of Tewa speakers in New Mexico (e.g. at the pueblo of San Juan); here the designation of the speech is Rio Grande Tewa. Tiwa is divided into a northern branch, represented by the speeches of the pueblos of Taos and Picurís, and a southern branch comprising Southern Tiwa (ST), spoken at Sandía and Isleta pueblos in New Mexico. The single surviving community of Towa speakers is at the New Mexico pueblo of Jemez.

The Tanoan languages whose voice behaviors will be considered below are AT, ST, Picurís and Towa (Jemez). AT differs in its voice behavior from the others, and it will be examined first.

4.5.1 Arizona Tewa

The Arizona Tewa (AT) data below and some of the observations concerning it are due to Kroskrity 1985. At first glance, AT may seem unpromising for a survey of voice behaviors, because it lacks overt verbal morphology specific to the encoding of voice alternations. However, AT does have an elaborate inventory of person prefixes which obligatorily appear on verbal bases. It will be argued below that the pattern of assignment of AT person affixes does relate to the encoding of voices, being isofunctional to a direct–inverse voice system.

Other Tanoan languages also have elaborate person-indexing morphology, but in AT the organization of the paradigms is somewhat different. One AT paradigm is called by Kroskrity 1985 "stative"; a second is called "active"; and a third, "passive." These paradigms are reproduced in Figure 4.1 respectively as Set I, Set II and Set III.

Before proceeding, it should be noted that Figure 4.1 includes only paradigms for animate intransitive and transitive animate predications. AT has additional paradigms for reflexives and possessives. Also, Tanoan languages generally have distinctive paradigms for nonindicatives (e.g. imperatives) and for transitive inanimates and ditransitives. These can be overlooked for immediate purposes.

We shall now consider the functions of the AT paradigms that Kroskrity 1985 calls active and passive, corresponding respectively to Sets II and III in Figure 4.1. In an intransitive predication, a person prefix may be selected from Set I. In a transitive predication, the prefix is selected from one of the remaining sets, Set II or Set III, although not from both (two prefixes of person may not cooccur in a verbal complex).

Prefixes of Set II index person and number of logical subjects. But there is an important condition on their assignment: they occur only when the logical object is third person. Thus the Set II forms are so distributed as to cover about the range of instances that are expressed through direct voice forms in Algonquian languages.

An illustration is (58) (from Kroskrity, p. 313). Here nothing in the shape of the verbal prefix indexes the number of the logical object. However, since the prefix belongs to Set II, the person of the object must be third.

(58) Nɛ́'i kʷiyó dó-   tay
    this woman 1SG II know
    'I know this woman'

	Person and number of logical subject								
	1SG	1DU	1PL	2SG	2DU	2PL	3SG	3DU	3PL
SET I	'o-	ga-	gi-	'ų-	da-	'i-	na-	da-	di-
SET II	dó-	'án-	'í:-	ná:-	den-	'obí:n-	mán-	den-	dí-

		Person of logical subject		
		1	2	3
SET III	Person–number of logical object			dí-
	2SG	wí-	dí-	wó:-
	2DU			wó:bén-
	2PL			wó:bé-
	3SG			'ó:-
	3DU			'ó:bén-
	3PL			'ó:bé-

Note: Subscripted hooks denote nasalization.

Figure 4.1 Some Arizona Tewa person prefix paradigms, based on Kroskrity 1985

An example illustrating Set III person marking is (59) (from Kroskrity, p. 311). Set III forms are also confined to transitives, but their range of distribution is nearly complementary to Set II. That is, a Set III prefix is selected just when the logical subject is not of higher status than the logical object (relative to a salience hierarchy to be stated shortly). (59) illustrates an instance when only Set III forms can be selected: when the logical object outranks the logical subject. It will be recalled that this is the same range of instances in which inverse marking is assigned in Algonquian languages.

(59) Hę'i sen -di   'ų   wó:-   k^{h}ęgen -'án
     that man OBL   you   3:2SG III help   completive
     'That man helped you'

Below, set II forms, such as (58), will be labeled direct, and set III forms, such as (59), will be labeled inverse. It has been observed earlier of Lummi (54b, 55b) that independent nominals representing logical subjects of inverse predications display some form of case marking. Also, it has been stated that this applies to all languages of the inverse subtype under discussion. As (59) illustrates, in AT, an element -di/-dí fulfills this function.[22] However, logical objects of AT inverse predications are not case marked, nor are core nominals of direct predications (see 58).

Since in AT, the subject relation is marked (by -di/-dí) only in TA inverse predications, it follows that local predications must be formally inverse. This is demonstrated in (60a, b) (from Kroskrity 1985: 311). Independent pronouns corresponding to respective first and second person logical subjects in (60a, b) are marked with -di/-dí, indicating that the predications are inverse. This is the reason for including the prefixes wí- and dí-, which respectively index 1:2 and 2:1 person categories in (60a, b), in the inverse or Set III inflectional paradigm of Figure 4.1.

(60) a. ų   na:n -di   wí-   tay
        you   we   OBL   1:2 III know
        'We know/recognize you'
     b. Na: 'ų   -di   dí-   k^{w}ek^{hw}ę di
        I   you   OBL   2:1 III shoot
        'You shot me'

The AT facts discussed so far can be summarized in a few simple statements. For instance, (61) (equivalent to the earlier 5) is the hierarchy of ontological salience for AT (also valid for other Tanoan languages surveyed in Section 4.5.2, as well as for Lummi). In addition, (62) states an AT person indexing rule, while rule (63) captures the distribution of -*di*/-*dí*.

(61) SAP > non-SAP
(62) **AT person encoding**
In a transitive predication, an ontological subject may be indexed on the verb by a Set II prefix in case it coincides with logical subject and the predication is not local. An ontological subject can be indexed by a Set III prefix provided it coincides with other than logical subject.
(63) **AT case marking**
In an inverse predication (i.e., where the verb selects an agreement prefix of Set III), an independent nominal corresponding to ontological object, or properly speaking to logical subject, receives oblique marking.

As noted earlier, prefix sets II and III are both assigned in TA predications, but are nearly complementary or mutually exclusive. Set III prefixes occur either in local transitive predications, as illustrated in (60a, b), or in nonlocal predications in which a non-SAP (third person) logical subject is ontologically outranked by an SAP (1, 2 person) logical object, as illustrated in (59). Such predications do not have Set II alternate forms. By contrast, Set II, not Set III, prefixes are selected in nonlocal predications in which an SAP logical subject cooccurs with a non-SAP logical object, such as (58). In sum, for all classes of predications described in this paragraph, alternations of Set II and Set III forms are impossible.

However, one class of instances remains, 3:3 predications. When both core arguments, logical subject and logical object, of a transitive predicate have non-SAP or third person referents and are animate (and, according to Kroskrity 1985: 315, are of equivalent definiteness), then the predicate may alternately assign Set II or Set III prefixes. In terms of the analysis assumed here, this means that transitive animate (TA) 3:3 predications have direct and inverse counterparts. In fact, these represent the only class of predications in AT which permits alternate (direct/inverse) voice encodings,[23] thus comprising the only domain in which Sets II and III prefixes are not complementary, but overlap in distribution. (64a, b) illustrate this (from Kroskrity, p. 309).

208   *Inverse voice systems*

(64) a. Hę'i sen nę́'i 'enú mán- kʰʷę́di
       that man this boy 3SG II hit
       'That man hit this boy'
    b. Nę́'i 'enú hę'i sen -di 'óː- kʰʷę́di
       this boy that man OBL 3:3SG III hit
       'That man hit this boy' (glossed by Kroskrity 1985: 309 as 'This boy was hit by that man')

Assuming, as the present analysis does, that the AT system is inverse, its pattern of person prefix assignment appears isofunctional to the alternation of *yi-* and *bi-* ontological object-encoding prefixes in Apachean (Section 4.2), or to the alternation of direct vs inverse theme signs in Algonquian (Section 4.4). However, AT and the other systems of its inverse subtype have one special feature, the assignment of case to inverse logical subjects. We propose to relate this feature to AT's lack of an obviative person category.

The logic of this is as follows. In inverse systems with an obviative – e.g. Apachean and Algonquian – core nominals are not assigned overt case. Rather, in these systems, core logical relations in TA 3:3 predications are recovered through the alternation of morphological voices (however these may be encoded). Given their lack of core nominal case, these systems can be regarded as conforming closely to the head-marking type discussed earlier (Section 4.0).

On the other hand, in its limited use of case marking to disambiguate core nominal relations in inverse 3:3 predications, AT (along with Lummi, discussed at the outset of Section 4.5, and along with the other Tanoan systems later discussed in Section 4.5.2) seems to represent a different kind of inverse system, one which is less strictly head-marking. Furthermore, one might think of the rule of core nominal case assignment as a cost to this sort of inverse system for lacking an obviative.

Such an analysis is admittedly unprecedented. One might prefer an alternative view of matters as follows: since logical subjects of TA 3:3 predications are assigned oblique case, a marked voice form, such as (64b), represents a derived voice. In Kroskrity 1985, this seems to be one of the motives for glossing Set III forms as passive.

In weighing these alternatives, it will be vital to consider what the second one, the passivization analysis, entails. As observed earlier, in Section 4.3, derived voices in general, and passives in particular, are strategies of detransitivization*. That is, derived voice rules like passive typically alter, and specifically reduce, basic valence*. As also noted in Section 4.3, inverse voice forms differ in that they generally preserve the transitivity of their direct counterparts.

If AT Set III forms are presumed passive, then 3:3 forms marked with -di/-dí, such as (64b), would necessarily be detransitive counterparts of transitives, such as (64a). But that is not all; a passivization account also implicates detransitivization in local forms such as (60a, b), since their logical subjects also are assigned di/-dí marking.

This seems problematical. Local forms appear to be both semantically and logically transitive, not intransitive. The case marking of their logical subjects can be accounted for by rule (63) without assuming any alteration of the verbal valence.

Leaving aside local forms, if 3:3 Set III forms were passive, then one would expect them to have morphosyntactic behavior similar to that of intransitives. AT does have formal detransitives, or intransitives derived from transitives. For instance, in examples (65a, b) below (from Kroskrity, p. 309), the detransitive (65b) is formally related to the transitive (65a). As might be anticipated, (65b) assigns a person prefix from Set I, a paradigm characterized above as intransitive. (Kroskrity 1985 labels this paradigm stative; but each instance he furnishes of a nonreflexive, nonimperative basic intransitive predicate turns out to select its agreement prefix from this paradigm. Example 65c below, from Kroskrity, p. 314, is an illustration.)

(65) a. Naːm -bí   sayáː   'enú mán- 'owídi
       we   GEN grandmother boy 3:3 II bathed
       'Our grandmother bathed the boy'
    b. 'eː-p'up'íːle   na-   'owídi -tíː
       child-newborn 3SG I bathe detransitive
       'The newborn child was bathed'
    c. Walabi -'í'í -dí   na-   mɛ
       Walpi   there OBL 3SG I go
       'He went from Walpi'

As the data suggests, AT detransitives are formally distinct from inverse forms. Inverse forms, unlike detransitives, do not assign Set I person prefixes; their person prefixes are from a different paradigm, Set III. In addition, inverse forms do not cooccur with markers of detransitivization, such as the suffix -tí in (65b). Set III forms appear to have

210 *Inverse voice systems*

no particular morphosyntactic affinities with intransitives. Consequently, there seems to be no formal ground for identifying them with passives.

Kroskrity 1985, however, raises several objections to an inverse analysis. (Among Tanoanists, he is the only one known to the present writer who does discuss the possibility that AT may have inverse rather than passive voice.) According to Kroskrity, AT is too dissimilar typologically from Algonquian systems to be amenable to one and the same voice account. Here in their entirety are his comments (Kroskrity, p. 319):

> First, Tewa has no 'direct/inverse' contrast in its verbal morphology. Second, the pronominal prefix in Algonkian remains the same in both inverse and direct constructions; it simply indexes the participant which is higher in animacy. Finally, and perhaps more important, Algonkian languages like Fox never have a transitive construction in which agent and patient are equal in animacy, and thus capable of the stylistic alternation available in AT 3/3 constructions. These significant differences show that the inverse pattern hardly provides a suitable framework for understanding the data.

The points raised above will now be briefly discussed.

First, it is unclear in what sense Kroskrity asserts that Tewa verbal morphology lacks a direct/inverse contrast. As earlier stated, the opposition of AT Set II and Set III prefixes, so integral to the verbal morphology of the language, is isofunctional to an alternation of direct vs inverse voice.

It is true that AT lacks a specific morpheme of inverse voice. But all that seems to follow from this is a rationale for the fact that, unlike Algonquian-type inverse systems, this language has an elaborate system of person-encoding prefixes. Other Tanoan languages do have inverse voice suffixes (see Section 4.5.2). In these systems, correspondingly, the shapes of person prefixes do not, as in AT, exhaustively differentiate core nominal logical relations.[24] It is not clear why it seems to be Kroskrity's view that an alternation of direct vs inverse voice must be encoded by a specific inverse voice morpheme, as this is lacking not only in AT, but also in Apachean, discussed earlier (Section 4.2).

Apachean also affords evidence, in its *yi-/bi-* opposition, that in an inverse system, it is possible for a given person category to be indexed in alternate forms. This is significant in respect of Kroskrity's argument that, in Algonquian inverse systems, pronominal prefixes do not vary in shape according to nominal–predicate relations, but simply index the person of the nominal corresponding to the ontological subject.

Although Kroskrity treats this as an argument against assigning AT to the inverse type, all that seems to follow from it is that Algonquian manifests one way of encoding inverse patterning, while Apachean languages and at least one Tanoan language manifest others.

Kroskrity's final argument is the putative fact that Algonquian languages do not demonstrate TA 3:3 predications with core arguments of equivalent "animacy" (ontological salience, in the present work's terms). This claim, however, is inaccurate, as demonstrated by the earlier Algonquian (Cree) examples (45a, b), repeated here for convenience as (66a, b).

(66) a. Wāpam -ē   -yi   -wa
      see   **DIRECT** OBV SG OBV
      'He (OBV) sees him (OBV)'
   b. Wāpam -iko   -yi   -wa
      see   **INVERSE** OBV SG OBV
      'He (OBV) sees him (OBV)'

(66a, b) comprise corresponding direct and inverse forms. As noted earlier, such counterparts occur in Algonquian only in TA 3:3 predications in which both core arguments are obviative. They refute Kroskrity's characterization of Algonquian predication structures as invariantly irreversible.

All inverse systems, in fact, permit direct/inverse counterparts of transitive predications provided both core arguments belong to the system's minimum ontological salience category. The difference between Algonquian systems and AT in this regard turns out to be the latter's lack of an obviative person category, not its alleged nonconformity with the inverse type.

4.5.2 Other Tanoan languages

As noted on p. 203, other Tanoan languages differ from AT in voice patterning. The present section discusses several of the non-Tewa Tanoan languages, including Picurís, Southern Tiwa (ST) and Towa (or Jemez). One of these, ST, has already been illustrated in Section 1.2, examples (6)–(8).

AT has several features in common with its non-Tewa sisters. For instance, in each of these languages, the verbal complex assigns no more than one person prefix, which indexes the ontological subject. Also, special case elements are assigned to independent nominal logical subjects of Set III (inverse) predications. Among these elements, AT -di/-dí (see 64a, b) has already been illustrated (also the Lummi counterpart ə; see 54b, 55b). In the non-Tewa Tanoan languages, corresponding elements include Picurís -pa (see below, 69b) and ST -ba (see Chapter 1, 6b; also 75b below). Like the corresponding case element in AT, these originate as markers of noncore nominal statuses, especially instrumentals.

Picurís, ST and Towa (Jemez), however, differ from AT in certain respects. For instance, they do not have distinct person paradigms for direct and inverse predications. Instead, for nonreflexive, nonimperative transitive predications, each of these languages has only one set of person prefixes. Recall that, in AT, the logical relation of the ontological subject is usually unambiguous, since the prefix is selected from one of two distinct sets, Set II or Set III. Lacking alternate prefix sets, however, the non-Tewa Tanoan languages require some other strategy or means of recovering core nominal logical relations.

The strategy in question consists of the assignment of a theme sign in one of the voices. For instance, in ST, the verbal complex may contain a suffixal theme sign -che; it has been illustrated in Chapter 1 (6b), and appears as well in the b-examples of (75)–(77) below. In Picurís, the corresponding element is -mía, illustrated in the b-examples of (67)–(69). At this point, the status of these theme signs bears comment.

Examples (6a, b) in Section 1.2 illustrate two forms of an ST predication "The ladies saw the babies." The second example, (6b), includes the theme sign -che. In Chapter 1, this element was tentatively labeled a detransitivizing marker, and it was suggested that the alternation of forms in (6a, b) reflects a rule of derived voice. A similar analysis has also been proposed for Picurís -mía (see below). However, on several grounds, a reanalysis now seems in order.

One of these grounds is distributional: the theme signs in question occur only in TA predications. As noted in Section 4.3, ordinary derived voices, such as the passive, are generally not so restricted. Furthermore, these theme signs have virtually the same distribution as the Set III person prefixes in AT, with local predications furnishing the sole exceptions (these are discussed shortly). This is clear from descriptive accounts of the languages concerned.

For instance, Zaharlick 1982: 45, assuming Picurís -mía to be a marker of passivization, describes the distribution of supposed actives and passives as follows:

4.5 Tanoan languages

(a) When subject and ... direct object are both third person, either active or passive sentences will occur, i.e. passive is optional.
(b) When subject and ... direct object are both non-third person ... [or] ... when subject is non-third person and ... direct object is third person, active sentences will occur and passive is not possible.
(c) When subject is third person ... and direct object is non-third person, passive is required.

The distribution of forms described above is illustrated by the Picurís examples (67)–(70) below. All are TA predications; (67)–(69) are nonlocal, while (70a, b) are local.

Note that in the nonlocal forms, Set II prefixes are assigned. This holds whether the action is direct, i.e. proceeds in the ontologically expected direction, or whether it is inverse, i.e. proceeds in the opposing direction. Thus in (67) and (69), identical prefixes are assigned in the a- and b-examples. (The alternation of first person singular prefixes *ti*- and *ta*- in 68a, b will be accounted for shortly.) The logical relations of the core arguments must be disambiguated by means other than person indexing. This is achieved by the alternation of zero (direct) vs marked (inverse) themes. Accordingly, in the inverse or b-examples of (67)–(69), the verbal complexes include the theme sign *-mía*. (Examples 67–68 are from Zaharlick 1982: 41, 40; example 69 is from Zaharlick, pp. 35–6.)

Note that theme marking is absent in the local forms (70a, b) (these examples are due to Zaharlick 1982: 41). As this suggests, local predications in Picurís, unlike AT, are not formally inverse, but direct. Moreover, in local predications, the person prefixes belong to a special paradigm. They do not come from the transitive paradigm, or Set II, as can be ascertained by the Picurís person prefix paradigms for nonlocal forms in Figure 4.2 (based on Zaharlick 1982: 47, fns. 3, 4). According to Zaharlick, the Set I prefixes in the figure are assigned in intransitive predications, while the Set II prefixes are assigned in (nonlocal) transitives.

(67) a. **DIRECT**
Sənene 'a-   mǫn   -'ạn
man   2SG I = 2SG:IIA see   past
'You saw the man'

    b. **INVERSE**
       'a-   mǫn -mia -'ąn sənene -pa
       2SG I = 2SG:IIA see -*mia* past man   OBL
       'The man saw you'

(68) a. **DIRECT**
       Sənene ti-   mǫn -'ąn
       man   1SG:IIA see past
       'I saw the man'
    b. **INVERSE**
       Ta-   mǫn -mia -'ąn sənene -pa
       1SG I see -*mia* past man   OBL
       'The man saw me'

(69) a. **DIRECT**
       (Sənene) ∅-   mǫn -'ąn
       (man)   3SG I = 3SG:IIA see past
       'He (the man) saw him'
    b. **INVERSE**
       ∅-   mǫn -mia -'ąn (sənene -pa)
       3SG I = 3SG:IIA see -*mia* past (man   OBL)
       'He (the man) saw him' (glossed by Zaharlick 1982: 35–6 as 'He was seen by him [the man]')

(70) a. (Ną) 'ą- mǫn - 'ąn
       (I)   1:2 see   past
       'I saw you'
    b. ('ę) may- mǫn -'ąn
       (you) 2:1   see   past
       'You saw me'

As mentioned, nonlocal transitive predications in Picurís assign prefixes of Figure 4.2, Set II. However, in this set, only the prefixes listed in the row headed Object class A (hereafter to be referred to as IIA prefixes) are relevant to the present discussion. It is these prefixes which are assigned in TA predications, such as the earlier (67)–(69). Prefixes listed under the headings Object class B and Object class C, non-TA prefixes, are included for completeness, but are not central to the discussion to follow, as our principal focus is on predications which exhibit alternations of morphological voice – i.e. TA (nonlocal) predications.[25]

Comparing what has been said so far about voice and person assignment in Picurís with the AT facts given in the preceding section, one might conclude that the differences between the two systems involve matters of detail, not a distinction in fundamental type. Whereas AT has opposing direct and inverse TA prefix sets, Picurís (together with the other non-Tewa Tanoan languages) manages with a single set, the IIA prefixes in Figure 4.2. Correspondingly, theme marking in the Picurís verbal complex distinguishes direct and inverse forms. The only other obvious difference in the systems involves the treatment of local predictions. As shown above, whereas local predictions are formally inverse in AT, in Picurís (and in the other non-Tewa Tanoan languages; see e.g. Rosen 1990: 8 on ST), they are formally direct.

Nonetheless, earlier writers (such as Zaharlick 1982 on Picurís; see the earlier citation from that work) generally treat inverse forms as passives. Writers on this and the other non-Tewa systems seem to be supported in their view by one significant aspect of the distribution of person prefixes: the person prefixes in certain corresponding direct and inverse forms seem to be selected from distinct transitive and intransitive sets.

This can be illustrated by returning to the Picurís examples (68a, b), repeated here for convenience as (71a, b). Notice that in the direct predication (71a), the person prefix is a IIA prefix. However, in the corresponding inverse (71b), the prefix is from Set I. This is significant because, as some writers observe (e.g. Zaharlick 1982 on Picurís, and Rosen 1990 on ST), the affixes assigned in basic intransitive predications come from Set I. Accordingly, if one compares (71b) with (71c) (from Zaharlick 1982: 37), it appears that a TA inverse form assigns the same person prefix as an intransitive having an identical ontological subject. Since this suggests that the -mía or marked voice form in (71b) is detransitive, one might feel justified in concluding that it may be a passive.

(71) a. Sənene ti-   mǫn -'ąn
        man   1SG:IIA see   past
        'I saw the man'
    b. Ta-   mǫn -mia -'ąn sənene -pa
        1SG I see -mia past man   OBL
        'The man saw me'
    c. Ta- me -'ąn
        1SG I go past
        'I went'

	Person and number of logical subject							
	1SG	1DU	1PL	2SG	2DU	2PL	3SG	3DU	3PL
SET I	ta-	'ąn-	'i-	'a-	mąn-	mą-	∅-	'ąn-	'i-
SET II Object class A	ti-	'ąn-	'i-	'a-	mąn-	mą-	∅-	'ąn-	'i-
Object class B	pi-	pąn-	pi-	'i-	pąn-	pi-	'i-	pąn-	pi-
Object class C	ta-	ko-	'o-	kąm-	mąm-	'ąm-	ku-	mu-	'u-

Note: Subscripted hooks denote nasalization.

Figure 4.2   Some Picurís person prefix paradigms, based on Zaharlick 1982

4.5 Tanoan languages

It is true that, holding the ontological subject constant, person prefixes in TA inverse forms and intransitives generally coalesce. In fact, this is valid not only in Picurís, but also in ST and in Towa (Jemez).

However, unlike (71a–c), there are many instances in which person prefixes coalesce not just in corresponding animate intransitive or AI and TA inverse predications, but in corresponding TA direct predications as well. For instance, compare (71a–c) with (72a–c). (Examples 72a, b are based on the earlier 69a, b, while 72c is from Zaharlick 1982: 36.) Each of (72a–c) bears an identical (zero) prefix indexing the third person singular ontological subject.

(72) a. Ø-   mǫn -'ąn
　　　3SG I = 3SG:IIA see   past
　　　'He/she saw (unspecified) third person'
　　b. Ø-   mǫn -mia -'ąn
　　　3SG I = 3SG:IIA see -*mia* past
　　　'(Unspecified) third person saw him/her'
　　c. Ø-   me -'ąn
　　　3SG I go   past
　　　'He/she went'

Moreover, (72a–c) is neither a fluke nor an isolated case. For example, the very same pattern is repeated in (73a–c) (respectively from Zaharlick 1982: 41, 40, 37; note that 73a, b are related to 67a, b). An alert reader may notice that this pattern resembles that found in Algonquian languages, as discussed above, Sections 4.4, 4.5. It is worth comparing (73a–c) with a parallel set of Algonquian forms. These forms, taken from the language Algonkin, have appeared earlier, in (53a–c); they are reproduced for convenience in (74a–c).

(73) a. (Sənene)   'a-   mǫn -'ąn
　　　(man)   2SG I = 2SG:IIA see   past
　　　'You saw him (the man)'
　　b. 'a-   mǫn -mia -'ąn (sənene -pa)
　　　2SG I = 2SG:IIA see -*mia* past (man   OBL)
　　　'He (the man) saw you'
　　c. 'a- me -'ąn
　　　2SG I go past
　　　'You went'

(74) a. Ki-   wāpam -ā
        2SG   see   **DIRECT**
        'You see him/her'
    b. Ki-   wāpam -ik
        2SG   see   **INVERSE**
        'He/she sees you'
    c. Ki-   pimosse
        2SG   walk
        'You walk'

As noted above, in Tanoan languages, the coalescence of person marking in intransitive and TA inverse forms has been taken by some earlier writers as evidence that the inverse forms are passive. However, the finding that person marking coalesces not just in these forms alone, but also in TA direct forms as well, seriously weakens this position.

It has been noted in Sections 4.4 and the first part of Section 4.5 that consistency in person prefix assignment in forms such as (74a–c) is normative for Algonquian. How normative is the parallel patterning in (72a–c) and (73a–c) for Tanoan? One might speculate that, in Picurís, instances such as (72) and (73) are exceptional, while the earlier (71a–c) illustrates the norm.

However, for predications which assign IIA prefixes, it is actually the patterning in (71a–c) which is exceptional. That is, in predications of this class, the norm is for ontological subjects to coincide for person indexing in all three forms, animate intransitive, TA direct, and TA inverse alike.

This can be confirmed by comparing the Set I prefixes in Figure 4.2 with the prefixes in Set IIA. In each instance, holding constant the person and number of the ontological subject, no difference occurs in the shapes of the Set I and Set IIA prefixes, the sole exception being the first person singular.

This suggests that the Picurís paradigms in Figure 4.2 can be restated with greater economy by collapsing Sets I and IIA. The exceptional person marking in (71a) can be accounted for by a special rule stipulating variation in the shape of the first person singular ontological subject prefix in TA direct forms (Klaiman 1991b provides a statement of this rule).

An account along these lines is consistent with the view of inverseness developed in the present chapter. According to this view, in the inverse

4.5 Tanoan languages

type, verbal morphology is sensitive to ontological, not logical core relations. Voice variation is a strategy found in inverse systems for recovering the logical relations of core arguments. It is needed because the assignment of person prefixes indexing ontological subjects of animate predications of all types (direct, inverse or intransitive) tends to be consistent. However, the degree of this consistency does vary from system to system within the type.

Algonquian languages appear to be the most consistent in person prefix assignment. They are also among the most strictly head-marking inverse systems, lacking as they do independent nominal case as a means of disambiguating core logical relations. In Algonquian, ontological subject indexing in animate predications both transitive and intransitive displays a sameness which is virtually absolute, largely without the occasional paradigm exceptions that typify less consistent systems, such as Picurís. The less consistent systems are, not coincidentally, also the inverse systems that are less strictly head-marking, i.e. the ones that do assign core nominal case.

Parallel behavior in more than one Tanoan language supports this view. For instance, the pattern of distribution of person prefixes in Picurís is duplicated in ST.

The ST examples (75)–(77) given below illustrate this. These examples are parallel to the earlier Picurís examples (71)–(73). (Examples 75a, c are from Rosen 1990: 683, 672; 75b is from Allen & Gardiner 1981: 296; 76b is from Allen, Frantz, Gardiner & Perlmutter 1990: 332; 76a, c are from Allen & Gardiner 1981: 293; and 77a–c are respectively from Allen, Gardiner & Frantz 1984: 295, Allen & Frantz 1978: 12, and Rosen 1990: 672.) The relevant person prefix paradigms for ST are presented in Figure 4.3 (the forms are due to Rosen 1990: 673). In the figure, notice that the erstwhile Set I (intransitive) prefixes and Set IIA (TA or transitive animate) prefixes coincide, once again, in every category except the first person singular.

(75) a. (Seuanide) ti- mū -ban
     (man)   1SG:IIA see past
     'I saw him (the man)'

   b. (Seuanide -ba) te- mū -che -ban
     (man   OBL 1SG I see **INVERSE** past
     'He (the man) saw me'

  c. Te- mî - ban
    1SG I go past
    'I went'
(76) a. ∅-   mū -ban
    3SG I = 3SG:IIA see past
    'He/she saw (unspecified) third person'
  b. ∅-   mū -che -ban
    3SG I = 3SG:IIA see **INVERSE** past
    '(Unspecified) third person saw him/her'
  c. ∅- mî -ban
    3SG I go past
    'He/she went'
(77) a. (Seuanide) a-   mū -ban
    (man) 2SG I = 2SG:IIA see past
    'You saw him (the man)'
  b. (Seuanide -ba) a-   mū -che -ban
    (man OBL) 2SG I = 2SG:IIA see **INVERSE** past
    'He (the man) saw you'
  c. A- mî -ban
    2SG I go past
    'You went'

Towa (Jemez), too, has very similar patterning, as revealed by the person prefix paradigms in Figure 4.4 (from Myers 1970: 65, 63). But this system differs in certain details. Note that the first person singular prefixes in Sets I (animate intransitive) and II (TA) coincide in shape. As the figure shows, the Towa (Jemez) prefix forms diverge in just the second and third person duals.[26]

The evidence furnished in this section from the three non-Tewa systems, Picurís, ST and Towa, supports the assertion of a fundamental congruity between Tanoan systems and the Algonquian pattern of person indexing. That is, where the organization of these systems diverge appears to be in strictness of conformity to head-marking, rather than in voice organization. In addition, the evidence presented above supports identifying direct–inverse as a type of system in which person encoding is sensitive to ontological, rather than logical, nominal statuses.

Moreover, systems with specific inverse voice elements (theme signs) share some consistency in shapes of person markers indexing ontologi-

Person and number of logical subject

	1SG	1DU	1PL	2SG	2DU	2PL	3SG	3DU	3PL
SET I	te-	in-	i-	a-	men-	ma-	∅-	in-	i-
SET II Object class A	ti-	in-	i-	a-	men-	ma-	∅-	in-	i-
Object class B	bi-	imim-	ibi-	i-	mimim-	bibi-	i-	imim-	ibi-
Object class C	te-	kin-	kiw-	ku-	men-	mow-	u	in-	iw-

Figure 4.3 Some Southern Tiwa person prefix paradigms, based on Rosen 1990

Person and number of ontological subject

	1SG	1DU	1PL	2SG	2DU	2PL	3SG	3DU	3PL
SET I	u-	*i-*	e-	*a-*	mo-	ba-	∅-	*ii-*	e-
SET II 3SG ontological object	u-	*i-*	e-	*a-*	m*a-*	ba-	∅-	*i-*	e-

Note: Italic type denotes nasalization.

Figure 4.4 Some Towa (Jemez) person prefix paradigms, based on Myers 1970

221

222 *Inverse voice systems*

cal subjects, whether in animate predications intransitive or transitive, direct or inverse. On the basis of this chapter's survey of systems, it seems that the tendency for this behavior is strong in the Tiwa and Towa branches of Tanoan; while in Algonquian systems, it is virtually absolute.

4.5.3 Tanoan systems and the inverse type

In Section 4.5 so far, evidence has been presented of certain congruities between the pattern of voice and person marking in Tanoan languages and the inverse type. As noted earlier, this is a nonstandard view. Generally, prior writers analyze these systems as manifesting some kind of derived voice, particularly a passive (although Perlmutter 1989 analyzes the ST inverse as a different derived voice, an antipassive).

The preceding sections furnish evidence that not inconsequential difficulties attend any derived voice analysis of Tanoan systems. The inverse account, however, entails certain difficulties of its own. It cannot be hoped that, with the present work, Tanoan voice and related behaviors will cease to be controversial.[27]

For instance, voice analysis in Tanoan languages (apart from Tewa) is complicated by the fact that, while the fundamental patterning of these systems may be direct–inverse, nonetheless certain derived voice processes appear to operate. In this connection, it should be observed that Figures 4.2–4.4, the respective prefix paradigms for Picurís, ST and Towa (Jemez), have scope only in basic (nonderived) predications. There are distinct paradigms for predications which are nonbasic, i.e. derived.

Consider, for instance, Picurís. According to Zaharlick 1982: 47, apart from the Set I and Set II prefixes shown in Figure 4.2, this language also has a distinct Set III. Its forms are assigned in ditransitive predications. They simultaneously index two logical relations, subject and indirect object.

According to Rosen 1990: 673–4, ST likewise has a special ditransitive paradigm (exclusive of the prefix sets in Figure 4.3), as well as yet another paradigm for a class of predications termed "intransitive plus dative" (or "1::3"). Respective illustrations of ST ditransitive and 1::3 forms have already been given in Section 1.2 (7a, b) and (8a, b). For convenience, they are reproduced below as (78a, b) and (79a, b).

(78) a. Ti-   khwien- wia -ban 'ī - 'ay
       1SG:3SG animate dog   give past you to
       'I gave the dog to you'
   b. Ka-   khwien- wia -ban
       1SG:2SG/3SG animate dog   give past
       'I gave you the dog'
(79) a. Seuan -ide   ∅-   wan -ban na -'ay
       man   SG animate 3SG animate   come past I   to
       'The man came to me'
   b. In-   seuan- wan -ban (na)
       1SG/3SG animate   man   come past (I)
       (gloss as in 79a)

Note that, in (78b), the person prefix, glossed 1SG:2SG/3SG animate, is not selected from the paradigm in Figure 4.3, but belongs to the distinct paradigm that Rosen 1990 terms ditransitive. And in (79b), the person prefix, glossed 1SG/3SG animate, is likewise not from Figure 4.3, but belongs to the 1::3 paradigm. (See Rosen or, alternatively, Allen, Frantz, Gardiner & Perlmutter 1990 for the complete paradigms.)

Because in (78) and (79), the a- and b-examples are formal alternates and preserve propositional content, one plausible way of accounting for them would be to posit rules deriving the latter from the former, i.e. derived voice rules. A derived voice treatment seems particularly apt because, as noted in Section 1.2, the b-alternates reflect reductions in the valence* of the a-counterparts.

There is, however, one complicating factor: a highly elaborate system of noun incorporation which interacts with person prefix assignment. Note, for instance, that in the ST examples (79a, b), the nominal "man" is unincorporated and incorporated, respectively. Noun incorporation was already alluded to in the discussion of ST in Section 1.2. Moreover, as Zaharlick 1982 notes, it is also a factor in the analysis of derived voice alternates in Picurís.

Owing in part to the complicated conditions on noun incorporation in ST, there is currently no consensus of opinion as to how best to analyze its system of derived voices (compare the radically different accounts proposed by Allen, Frantz, Gardiner & Perlmutter 1990, and by Rosen 1990). However, and although now is not the occasion to embark on a complete review of these matters, there does seem to be evidence that in systems of this kind, derived voices coexist with a basically inverse pattern of organization.

For instance, in ST, the effect of the derived voice rules respectively illustrated in (78) and (79) is to alter the assignments of arguments to positions in the verb's inherent or lexically assigned valence*. Thus the argument "you" is an oblique in (78a), but evidently is a core nominal (object) in (78b); while "I," similarly, is an oblique in (79a), but appears to be a core nominal (subject) in (79b).

What is most significant about such examples is that the reassignments of arguments among core and noncore positions are constrained by the basic direct–inverse pattern of the system. Thus in example (80b) below, a derived object ontologically outranks the logical subject. Consequently, unlike (80a) without the derived voice rule, (80b) is necessarily inverse rather than direct. On the other hand, where a derived subject is ontologically outranked by the logical subject, as in (81), then in keeping with the basic patterning, the inverse form (81b) is not possible; the predication can only be expressed in a direct form (81a). (Examples 80a, b, 81a, and 81b are, respectively, from Allen & Frantz 1978: 14; Allen, Frantz, Gardiner & Perlmutter 1990: 325; and Allen & Frantz 1986: 401.)

(80) a. Liorade ∅-   khwien- wia -ban na -'ay
       lady   3SG II   dog   give past I   to
       'The lady gave a dog to me'
    b. Liorade -ba   in-   khwien- wia -che -ban
       lady   OBL   1SG/3SG animate   dog   give -che past
       'I was given a dog by the lady'

(81) a. Seuanide ta-   khwien- wia -ban
       man   1SG:3/3SG dog   give past
       'I gave the man the dog'
    b.*A-   khwien- wia -che -ban na -ba
       3SG/3SG animate   dog   give -che past I   OBL
       'He was given the dog by me'

Without extending the discussion, we wish to suggest, on the basis of the above, that Tiwa languages host more than one type of voice. A number of other systems in which different voice types cooccur have already been discussed in previous chapters. It appears that in some

Tanoan languages, similarly, derived voice processes may coexist with a basic pattern which is direct–inverse.

The present chapter will conclude with some general observations on inverseness. Emerging from the above survey of Apachean, Algonquian, Tanoan and other systems is an image of a well-defined type within which there exists some scope for variation in specific behaviors. Moreover, it seems that this variation reflects an interplay between (a) certain functions characteristic of the type and (b) the availability of strategies within individual systems for their encoding. (82a, b) summarize some parameters of variation to which this chapter's survey of inverse systems attests.

(82) a. Existence or absence of a specific inverse voice morpheme, which in turn determines, respectively, whether person indices are constant, or vary in shape to encode alternate assignments of arguments to ontological statuses.
b. Existence or absence of an obviative person category, which in turn determines whether logical subjects of inverse TA predictions are unmarked or marked, respectively, for case.

In addition to these parameters of variation, the present chapter has yielded other significant generalizations about inverse systems, thus potentially contributing to a refinement of present views of the inverse type. Perhaps the survey of systems has helped especially in establishing what the type is not.

For example, inverse typology does not consist in the mandatory presence of morphology specific to direct voice; nor to inverse voice; nor to an obviative subcategory of the third person. None of these is required in a direct–inverse system; AT, in particular, does without all three.

What inverse systems do manifest, as a class, is the characteristic of head-marking and a tendency – absolute in Algonquian languages, strong in Tanoan – for person prefixes specific to intransitive animates (as contrasted with transitive animates) to be lacking.

In addition, this chapter has established certain hallmark traits of direct–inverse systems – traits whose extendability to language groups outside Salishan (Lummi), Algonquian and Tanoan may be tested in future research. These hallmark traits are the following three:

(83) a. Person indexing and voice are mainly driven ontologically, not

thematically and not by reference to nominals' relational or logical statuses.
b. The tendency is strong or absolute for coincidence in the shapes of verbal person-indexing elements in both transitive and intransitive predications having identical ontological subjects, irrespective of voice.
c. Above all, direct–inverse systems are characterized by coincidence in form, except for voice marking, of transitive animate predications which are converse to one another in propositional structure.

5 *Information-salience voice systems*

5.0 Preliminaries: clausal pragmatics and informational salience

Chapters 3 and 4 distinguish two types of nonderived voice, each type grammaticizing the ontology of verbally denoted situations in a distinct way. This distinction arises because the kind of ontological salience nominals are assigned in predications is determined by the level or domain of structure at which the grammaticization of control occurs. That is, nominals are assigned salience in respect of their (relative) status either in predication structures or in the structure of discourse.

Chapter 3 discusses one type of ontological salience termed attribution of control*. This variety of ontological salience arises from, or is a feature of, meanings inherent to lexical predicates. In voice systems which encode alternate nominal-position assignments of this sort of control, the voice patterning reflects the semantic classification of the system's lexical predicates. As Chapter 3 discusses, languages evince various strategies for encoding attribution of control, including one particular voice type, basic voice*.

But according to Chapter 4, ontological salience has an alternative basis in the relationship of a verbally denoted situation's participants to the world of the discourse. This kind of ontological salience does not inhere in verbal semantics. Rather, variable salience assignments accrue to a predication's nominals in respect of their referents' centrality or noncentrality to speaker/hearer concerns, interests and expectations. Since this sort of ontological salience is driven by factors external to a predication's content, i.e. by discourse factors, its basis is not semantic, but pragmatic. Accordingly, systems of verbal alternations that encode this sort of ontological salience are classified as a distinct voice type, pragmatic voice*. The preceding chapter has surveyed one class of pragmatic voice systems, inverse* systems.

But there also occurs another class of pragmatic voice systems.

228 *Information-salience voice systems*

Rather than encoding a nominal referent's ontological salience in discourse structure, systems of this class have a somewhat different basis. In these systems, alternations of verbal morphology encode nominals' relative centrality or noncentrality to the discourse's informational objectives. Since nominal salience of this sort arises in or is determined at the level of discourse information structure, it can be termed informational or information-structure* salience.

Probably every language has strategies for encoding discourse informational salience and for assigning it to elements of structural units, such as clauses. However, the morphosyntax of a given language may or may not be sensitive to such strategies. The present chapter is concerned with systems in which alternating assignments of nominal information-salience statuses are encoded overtly in morphosyntax by alternations of verbal shapes, i.e. by contrasting voices of the verb. Pragmatic voice systems of this type are surveyed below under the rubric of information-salience voice*. Alternatively, they may be termed, loosely, focus* systems.

This usage reflects one of the typical senses in which the term "focus" is invoked in recent grammatical theory. Theoreticians use this term and others, especially "topic," in reference to various statuses of information-structure salience. Both terms are used, as well, by authors of descriptive studies of particular languages, including several whose information-salience systems are surveyed in this chapter.[1]

The following survey is confined to two distinct, genetically unrelated, language groups, each of which contributes evidence for the reality of an information-salience or focus voice type. First, in Section 5.1, Mayan languages will be discussed, using data primarily from one representative language, K'ekchi. Subsequently, Section 5.2 surveys the recently much-discussed voice systems of Philippine languages, using data primarily from Cebuano, and secondarily from Tagalog.

5.1 Mayan languages

In Mayan languages, information-salience voices coexist with derived voices. Moreover, in many Mayan languages, more than one kind of derived voice occurs. This is significant because the information-salience voices, which encode alternating assignments of nominal salience, usually interact with the morphosyntax of one or more derived voices.

This can be clarified by illustrating some typical Mayan derived voice behaviors. The discussion that follows will primarily center on one language, K'ekchi. At the outset, however, it is convenient for purposes of illustration to use data from a different language, Mam (as documented in England 1983).

Mam typifies Mayan languages in two pertinent respects. First, it exemplifies a pattern of case organization called ergative–absolutive (or, simply, ergative*), which has been explained earlier (Section 2.4). Secondly, like many Mayan languages, it manifests a derived voice which is robust only in languages with ergative–absolutive case organization, the antipassive*. In addition, and thirdly, Mam is representative of a large set of Mayan languages in which there occurs more than one kind of derived voice (Larsen & Norman 1979: 361), since it (like K'ekchi, to be discussed below) also has a passive.

Illustrations of Mam derived voices are given in (1a, b) and (2a, b) below. The a-examples illustrate ordinary, or direct, transitive constructions. The b-example in (1) is the passive counterpart of the a-example, while the b-example in (2) is an antipassive counterpart of (2a). (Examples 1a, b are from England, p. 201. 2a, b are from England, p. 212; 2b also appears in Baker 1988: 129.)

(1) a. Ma   ∅-   jaw   t-   tx'ee?ma   -n
       tense 3SG ABS AUX   3SG ERG   cut   directional
       cheep tzee?
       José   tree
       'José cut the tree'
    b. Ma   ∅-   tx'eem -at   tzee? t-   u?n
       tense 3SG ABS   cut   passive   tree   3SG ERG   by-RN
       cheep
       José
       'The tree was cut by José'

(2) a. Ma   ∅-   tzaj   t-   tzyu   -?n   cheep
       tense 3SG ABS AUX   3SG ERG   grab   directional José
       ch'it
       bird
       'José grabbed the bird'
    b. Ma   ∅-   tzyuu   -n   cheep t-
       tense 3SG ABS   grab   ANTI   José   3SG ERG
       i?j
       patientive RN ch'it
                      bird
       'José grabbed the bird'

Mayan languages belong to the head-marking* type, which has been explained in the preceding chapter (Section 4.0). Accordingly, in these languages core nominal logical relations are indexed primarily by bound pronominals in the verbal complex. In Mam, as in Mayan languages generally, these pronominals are organized into two sets or paradigms. One, the absolutive, indexes P or logical objects of transitives, as well as S or intransitive subjects; while A or logical subjects of transitives are indexed by a separate paradigm, the ergative. (Below, the terms ergative and absolutive are used both in reference to core nominal case categories, as well as in reference to the distinct pronominal prefix sets which index these categories.)

As noted, Mayan languages tend to have multiple voices, especially derived voices. The difference between one of these, the passive, illustrated in (1b), and the antipassive, illustrated in (2b), is as follows. Under passivization, a logical nonsubject, in this instance the object, takes on properties characteristic of (basic) subjects (such as case assignment and government of verbal person indices). By contrast, with antipassivization the transitive subject takes on properties typical of the (basic) object. Since in an ergative language the same morphological behaviors accrue to transitive object (P) as to intransitive subject (S), one effect of antipassivization is to dissociate the transitive subject (A) from its usual case assignment, the ergative, and reassign it to the absolutive. (However, for an alternative portrayal of antipassivization, see Kozinsky et al. 1988: 653ff.)

These characteristics are borne out in the respective passive and antipassive b-examples of (1) and (2). First, note that in the b-examples certain nominals are preceded by a prefix indexing agreement for person, attached to an element called a relational noun (glossed as RN). The complex made up of a person-indexing prefix plus a relational noun governs the following nominal much like an oblique preposition. Thus in a passive, e.g. (1b), the relational noun functions much the same as the agentive marker *by* in English; while in an antipassive, e.g. (2b), the relational noun is analogous to the dative case, used in many ergative languages to mark logical direct objects of antipassives (see e.g. the Dyirbal illustration in Section 4.4, 48b). In Mayan passives and antipassives, moreover, a nominal representing a logical subject or object which is governed by a relational noun is not indexed within the verbal complex.

Accordingly, both derived voices, passive and antipassive, are associated with alterations of person indexing in the verbal complex, as (1) and (2) illustrate. In a basic transitive, such as (1a), the A is indexed by an ergative verbal prefix, while the P is indexed by an absolutive prefix. But in the corresponding passive, the verb is suffixed by a voice marker (-*at* in 1b), and the sole core nominal is the logical object or P ("tree" in 1b). This nominal alone has core status, since it alone is indexed by a verbal person prefix, which continues to be selected from the absolutive set. The A of a passive, by contrast, has noncore status, as shown by its overt marking with a relational noun and its failure to govern a verbal person index.

In the antipassive, the patterning is similar. Once again, the verb takes a special suffix (-*n* in 2b). However, and crucially, in the antipassive the P or logical object ("bird" in 2b), not the A, is noncore, being governed by a relational noun. Also, the sole core nominal, indexed in the verbal complex by a prefix (again of the absolutive, not ergative set), is not the logical object or P, but the logical subject or A ("José" in 2b). This can be confirmed by comparing (2b) with (3) (from England 1983: 212). In the latter, the verbal prefix registers singular number, and cannot index the P, which is plural.

(3) Ma   ∅-   tzyuu -n   cheep
    tense 3SG ABS   grab   ANTI   José
    ky-   iʔj   ch'it
    3PL ERG   patientive RN   bird
    'José grabbed the birds'

Now that the main properties of the Mayan antipassive have been illustrated, the discussion turns to the encoding of nominal informational salience assignments; that is, to pragmatic voice. Although other Mayan languages will be discussed eventually, most of this section is devoted to relevant behaviors in a single language, K'ekchi. The discussion is based largely on a sketch of this language's voice and voice-related morphosyntactic patterns by Berinstein 1985 (although other K'ekchi sources have also been consulted, including Freund 1976 and Pinkerton 1976a).

The aims of what follows are twofold: first, to provide evidence for nominal information-salience statuses; and secondly, to show how alternative assignments of these statuses to eligible nominal positions in the clause are encoded through the morphosyntax of antipassivization.

Writers on K'ekchi (and on some of its sisters) distinguish two antipassive constructions with different morphosyntactic properties. Antipassives, as noted above, are somewhat analogous in their effects to passives. However, while the passive's typical effects include either downgrading or suppression of logical subjects, the antipassive affects the status of logical objects. Some Mayanists apply the term absolutive antipassive to an antipassive in which the P or logical object is suppressed or overtly absent.

Where the P is not suppressed, however, its formal treatment may vary. In some languages, including K'ekchi, there are distinct antipassives which diverge in the formal treatment of (unsuppressed) P nominals.

In one such nonabsolutive antipassive, illustrated for K'ekchi below in (4), the P is overtly downgraded. Typically, it is governed by a relational noun which, as remarked earlier, has the effect of marking the governed nominal as noncore or oblique. The Mam example (2b) above also illustrates this kind of antipassive.

But in the other nonabsolutive antipassive, illustrated by the K'ekchi example (5), there is no explicit case marking of the P. Its noncore status is inferred only from the absence of any bound pronominal indexing it in the verbal complex (the sole bound pronominal in ex. 5 indexes the A, "the men," instead). (Both examples 4 and 5 are from Berinstein 1985: 219).[2]

(4) Eb li cuink x- e'- sic' -o -c
PL the man tense 3PL ABS pick ANTI aspect
r- e li cape
3SG ERG DAT RN the coffee
'The man picked the coffee'

(5) X- e'- sic'- -o -c cape li cuink
tense 3PL ABS pick ANTI aspect coffee the men
'The men picked coffee'

A number of Mayanists call attention to the distinction between the two kinds of downgrading (or nonabsolutive) antipassives illustrated in (4) and (5). The former is usually referred to under the rubric of focus antipassive, while the latter is referred to by some writers (e.g. Dayley 1981: 13) as an incorporating antipassive. The differences between these types are two. First, the morphosyntactic treatment of P differs in the way already described. Secondly, in the second kind of downgrading antipassive, the incorporating antipassive, the P – "coffee" in (5) – is invariably nonreferential. Compare the same argument glossed (referentially) as "the coffee" in (4). (The term "nonreferential" will be clarified below.)

Both antipassives illustrated in (4) and (5) differ from passives in that passivization does not affect the P's basic case assignment as an absolutive. In an antipassive, by contrast, the absolutive case is reassigned from the P to the A. This is typical of antipassives in languages in general. Moreover, in any ergative language having an antipassive derived voice, particular morphosyntactic properties tend to devolve upon absolutives – case and government of verbal concord are two that have already been alluded to above, and in some languages there are others. One effect of antipassivization is to make absolutive properties accessible to A of transitives.

But in many Mayan languages, K'ekchi included, another vital property of the absolutive is that it must be assigned to any nominal which has a certain status of informational salience within the clause. This relates to the distinction in downgrading (nonabsolutive) antipassives, since only one kind, the focus antipassive illustrated in (4), presupposes this type of information salience. To understand how this works in K'ekchi we need to consider what statuses of informational salience occur in the language.

Berinstein 1985 distinguishes two statuses of informational salience, which she calls topic and focus (hereafter salience-T and salience-F or, in glosses, simply T and F).[3] She cites various formal properties which distinguish each kind of salience, a few of which will now be noted.

One is a difference in linear position. A nominal assigned salience-T appears clause-initially, while a nominal assigned salience-F occurs preverbally. Since the neutral order of major nonbound elements in the K'ekchi clause is Verb–Object–Subject (VOS), it follows that if both salience-T and salience-F are assigned within a clause, the former nominal occurs clause-initially, and the latter afterward, preceding the verbal complex. An illustration of this is (6) (from Berinstein, p. 91).

(6) [Li che'] [r-   iq'uin   li   ch'ich'] x-
    the tree T 3SG ERG with-RN F the machete tense
    0-   yoq'u -e'   cui'
    3SG ABS cut   passive *cui'*
    'As for the tree, with the machete it was cut'

In (6), the element *cui'* marks the site of extraction of an instrumental which is assigned salience-F. It may also mark the extraction site of a locative assigned salience-F, such as "dry land" in (7). (7 is from Berinstein, p. 89.) *Cui'* does not, however, mark extraction sites of nominals assigned salience-T, and thus comprises a further test for distinguishing the two kinds of salience.

(7) [Chaki ch'och'] li   cuanqu -eb   cui'
     dry   land F that exist   3PL ABS cui'
     'It was dry land that they were on'

Apart from differences in formal encoding, the two nominal salience statuses differ somewhat in function, or in the type of informational salience each represents. Salience-F nominals, according to Berinstein, "are generally contrastive or emphatic" (p. 93), while salience-T nominals basically comprise "what the sentence is about" or "the theme of the discourse" (p. 92).

Moreover, certain rules which relate to pragmatics at the level of the clause are sensitive to salience-F but not to salience-T. This is true not just in K'ekchi, but in a sizable class of Mayan languages (to be enumerated later). For instance, a nominal must be assigned salience-F, but not salience-T, in order to be emphasized. In K'ekchi the sign of this is an emphatic particle *ha'*, shown in (8) (from Berinstein, p. 94). In addition, a nominal must be assigned salience-F, but not salience-T, to be relativized upon, as illustrated in (9) (from Berinstein, p. 109). Finally, salience-F, but not salience-T, is required for a nominal to be questioned, as in (10), where the *cui'* marking the extraction site confirms that salience-F is involved (this example is from Berinstein, p. 89).

(8) Ha'   li   ic   x-   ∅-   in-   lok'
    EMPH the chili tense 3SG ABS 1SG ERG buy
    'That chili, I bought'

(9) Na'bal li   nequ- e'-   xic r-   iq'uin
    many   that tense 3PL ABS go   3SG ERG with-RN
    aj   ilonel nequ- e'-   cam
    noun classifier seer   tense 3PL ABS die
    'Many of those that go to the shaman die'

(10) C'a'ru x-   ∅-   e'x-   yoc' cui'
     what   tense 3SG ABS 3PL ERG cut   cui'
     'What did they cut it with?'

The relevance of voice to the rules illustrated in (8)–(10) (hereafter called F-sensitive rules) is due to the fact, noted above, that the salience to which these rules are sensitive, salience-F, devolves only upon nominals assigned absolutive case. In other words, an ergative nominal may not be assigned salience-F (except, in K'ekchi, when it antecedes a reflexive). Salience-T may accrue either to an absolutive (as shown in 6) or to an ergative. But for ergatives, the only allowable salience assignment is salience-T and not salience-F, as demonstrated by the contrasting grammaticality of (11a, b) (from Berinstein, p. 91).

(11) a. [Laj   lu']   [oxib chi ch'ich']   x-
         noun classifier Pedro T three of machete F tense
         0-   x-   yoc' cui' li che'
         3SG ABS 3SG ERG cut *cui'* the tree
         'Pedro, with three machetes he cut the tree'
   b.*[Oxib chi ch'ich']   [laj   lu']   x-
       three of machete T noun classifier Pedro tense
       0-   x-   yoc' li che'
       3SG ABS 3SG ERG cut the tree
       'With three machetes, Pedro was the one who cut the tree'

Since in basic transitives, the A or logical subject is assigned ergative case, it follows that an A requires special treatment to receive salience-F, and thus be made accessible to F-sensitive rules. It turns out that passive, although reassigning A from ergative to oblique, does not make it available for salience-F. The only way an A can be assigned this salience is to be reassigned from ergative to absolutive by antipassivization.[4]

Moreover, this does not apply just in K'ekchi. According to Larsen & Norman 1979: 356–9, a constraint against F-sensitive rules targeting ergative A holds throughout the languages of the Mamean subgroup of Mayan (including both Mam, which has been discussed above, and Ixil, which will be discussed later). It also applies in the Kanjobalan subgroup (e.g., in Jacaltec) and the Quichean subgroup (which includes Cakchiquel, Tzutujil, Pocomam, and the language presently of central interest, K'ekchi). Moreover, Larsen & Norman state that in all the languages affected by the constraint, the usual means of making ergative A accessible to F-sensitive rules is antipassivization.[5]

At this point it is appropriate to clarify how voices, specifically the focus and incorporating antipassives, relate to the two kinds of informational salience. In the incorporating antipassive, the kind illustrated in

236   *Information-salience voice systems*

(5), the P has the status of an unmarked absolutive, is nonreferential, and may not be assigned informational salience. However, the A may be assigned either kind of salience or neither. (5) is an instance where no salience is assigned; while (12) (from Berinstein, p. 221) illustrates a focus antipassive in which the A is assigned salience-F (obligatorily so, since it is questioned).

(12) Ani ta̱-   ∅-   lok' -o   -k   cua
     who tense 3SG ABS buy ANTI aspect tortillas
     'Who will buy tortillas?'

Compare this with the focus antipassive, the kind illustrated earlier in (4). In a focus antipassive, the logical subject or A is invariably assigned salience-F (as confirmed by the preverbal position of A, "the men," in 4). Since no more than one nominal can be assigned a given salience status per clause, the P or logical object may never be assigned salience-F in a focus antipassive. But it may be assigned salience-T; this is illustrated in (13) (from Berinstein, p. 198).

(13) [Li   tumin] [lain]   x-   in-   q'eu
     the money T first person F tense 3SG ABS give
     -o   -c   acu-   e   r-   e
     ANTI aspect 2SG ABS DAT RN 3SG ERG DAT RN
     'The money, I was the one who gave it to you'

To sum up, either the incorporating or the focus antipassive has the effect of blocking the P or logical object (basic absolutive) nominal from being assigned salience-F. In the incorporating antipassive, this correlates with the P's morphosyntactic downgrading, whereby it becomes insusceptible to any informational salience assignment. On the other hand, in a focus antipassive, salience-T is available for assignment to various arguments, including the P, but salience-F is always assigned to A, and is therefore inaccessible to P or any other nominal.

In our discussion of the interplay of K'ekchi case and voice assignments, there is one factor which has not yet been adequately explained, referentiality. It has been noted above that in incorporating antipassives, the P is invariably nonreferential, although the meaning of this has yet to be clarified.

According to Berinstein 1985: 224, a particular use of a nominal is nonreferential if inserting any of the following would automatically change the nominal's contextual meaning, or result in ungrammaticality: a definite article, number expression, noun classifier, or possessive. In her wording, "A nonreferential noun in K'ekchi cannot cooccur with a definite article, numeral, noun classifier, or possessive affix" (p. 224). Nominals which cannot be qualified in any of the ways just described are referential. (Note that K'ekchi proper nouns cooccur with qualifiers, such as articles and classifiers.)

To illustrate, the nominal "coffee" in (4), being qualified with a definite article, is referential. However, in (5), the same nominal cannot be qualified, as this would both alter the meaning and render the construction ungrammatical. Accordingly, in (5), this nominal is nonreferential.

The significance of referentiality for present concerns is that a core nominal – an S, A or P – may be assigned either absolutive or ergative case in K'ekchi only if it is referential. A nonreferential A may be expressed as the downgraded or suppressed nominal of an antipassive. A nonreferential P may be expressed as an unmarked absolutive, which is possible only in an incorporating antipassive. Accordingly, in an incorporating antipassive such as (5), antipassivization is not an option, but occurs obligatorily. (If, on the other hand, P is referential, then the incorporating antipassive is not an option, but disallowed.)

Interestingly, there is one other option for the formal treatment of a nonreferential core nominal, be it S, A or P. The nominal may simply be assigned either salience-T or salience-F. In fact, unless a predication with a nonreferential A is passivized, or unless a predication with a nonreferential P is antipassivized, a nonreferential A or P must be assigned either salience-T or salience-F.[6]

The obligatory assignment of salience to an S is illustrated below by the contrasting grammaticality of (14a, b); to a P, by (15a, b); and to an A, by (16a, b) (these examples are respectively from Berinstein, p. 240, p. 228, and pp. 242–3). In (16b), antipassivization is required because the salience assigned to the A is salience-F; this follows from the earlier-mentioned constraint against assigning salience-F to an ergative A.[7]

(14) a. *Nequ- e'- cuobac tz'i'
      tense 3PL bark dog
      'Dogs bark'
   b. Tz'i' nequ- e'- cuobac
      dogs tense 3PL bark
      'Dogs, they bark'

(15) a. *X-   ∅-   ka-   tz'iba hu
         tense 3SG ABS 1PL ERG write letter
         'We wrote letters'
    b. Hu   x-   ∅-   ka-   tz'iba
         letter tense 3SG ABS 1PL ERG write
         'Letters we wrote'
(16) a. *Qu-   in-   e'x-   tiu hix
         tense 1SG ABS 3PL ERG bite jaguar
         'Jaguars attacked me'
    b. Hix   qu-   e'-   ti'   -o   -c   cu-
         jaguar tense 3PL ABS bite ANTI aspect 1SG ERG
         e
         DAT RN
         'They were jaguars that attacked me'

As the above examples show, being assigned informational salience may allow a nonreferential core nominal to preserve its absolutive or ergative case assignment. But otherwise, such a nominal must cede its absolutive or ergative case assignment through passivization or antipassivization, respectively.

We will now attempt to sum up what has been established so far about voice and informational salience in K'ekchi, with a view to broadening the discussion shortly in order to take in other Mayan systems.

In terms of the voice typology of the present work, passive and antipassive both belong to the derived voice type. In some languages, these voices play significant roles in the organization of discourse (as suggested in the discussion of nominal reference-tracking in the preceding chapter, Section 4.4). Accordingly, both passive and antipassive may have certain effects in pragmatics beyond the level of the clause.

However, in Mayan languages, derived voices also seem to have effects on pragmatics at the clause level. Specifically, derived voices affect the pragmatic status of certain arguments – A in the case of the passive, P in the case of the antipassive – by restricting their accessibility to a well-defined information-salience status, salience-F. Interestingly, this is achieved in one derived voice, the focus antipassive, by assigning salience-F to a nominal status other than P, i.e. to the A. A plausible way of looking at this is that both passive and antipassive regulate the conditions under which A and P either are assigned salience or are accessible to salience assignments.

Moreover, in regulating salience assignments in this way, antipassive and passive also regulate the accessibility of core nominals to F-sensitive processes, i.e. emphatic fronting, question and relativization, illustrated in (8)–(10). As noted earlier, this holds not only in K'ekchi (the language shown in these examples), but in a large class of Mayan languages. Accordingly, derived voices in these languages do not merely alter core nominals' relational statuses or case category assignments. Insofar as they regulate nominal assignments to statuses of informational (pragmatic) salience, they take on the character of pragmatic voice processes.

Now, broadening the discussion, we need to reconsider and amplify on the richness of voice inventories in Mayan languages. As discussed earlier, Mayan languages generally have antipassives. In fact (according to Dayley 1981: 48), antipassives are undocumented in only two languages of the family. Typically, a Mayan language has more than one formally distinct antipassive. In addition, Mayan languages usually have passives. From individual language descriptions (e.g. Mam, as documented in England 1983; Jacaltec, as in Craig 1977; Tzutujil, as in Dayley 1985; and Tzotzil, as in Aissen 1987), it also appears that it is not unusual for more than one passive to occur per language.

Moreover, in many Mayan languages the inventory of voices goes beyond passives and antipassives alone. We will briefly consider two other derived voices commonly found in these languages.

For instance, a survey of Mayan voice systems by Dayley 1981 documents the frequency of a type called a referential voice. This voice entails assignment of the absolutive to certain kinds of arguments other than logical subjects (A) and objects (P). For instance, according to Dayley 1985: 48, the referential voice in Chol targets any of the following semantic roles: dative, benefactive, malefactive and possessor.

According to Aissen 1987: 104ff., in Tzotzil there is a corresponding voice targeting approximately the same semantic roles. Under her account, formulated in terms of relational grammar (RG) as well as arc pair grammar (APG), the effect of this voice is to assign absolutive to a basic (in her parlance, initial-stratum) indirect object, thereby dissociating this case from the basic (initial-stratum) direct object. Incidentally, in Tzotzil and various other Mayan languages having a referential voice, passive can apply to its output, deriving an intransitive with the referentially derived absolutive nominal as subject.

According to Dayley 1985, the referential voice in Chol is encoded by a suffix -*b'e*, while according to Aissen, the corresponding Tzotzil suffix is -*be*. Interestingly, a suffix of similar shape occurs in a number of Mayan languages encoding a distinct kind of voice, which writers usually term instrumental voice. This voice targets nominals bearing the instrument semantic role. Its effect is to assign informational salience to these nominals, as a result of which they occur in preverbal position within the clause.

Apart from assigning informational salience, the effects of the instrumental voice on the targeted nominal vary from system to system. In some systems, a targeted instrumental becomes an absolutive; in others, it becomes an unmarked nonabsolutive; while in still others, it is overtly oblique. All three possibilities are realized within the Quichean subgroup alone. This is demonstrated by the respective Quiche, Tzutujil and Cakchiquel examples (17), (18) and (19) (from Dayley 1981: 28).

(17) Ch'iich' x- ∅- sok -b'e
machete tense 3SG ABS wound instrumental voice
-r aw- eech
passive 2SG ERG RN
'It was a machete you were wounded with'

(18) Machat x- in- choy -b'e -x
machete tense 1SG ABS cut instrumental voice passive
-i
mode
'It was a machete I was cut with'

(19) R- ik'in jun machät x-
3SG ERG with-RN a machete tense
i- sok -b'e -x
1SG ABS wound instrumental voice passive
'With a machete I was wounded'

Let us see how the effects of instrumental voice vary in the three illustrated languages. In the Quiche example (17), there is only one core nominal, and the predicate is a derived intransitive. The instrumental voice assigns informational salience to the nominal "machete." This nominal is indexed within the verbal complex by a prefix of the absolutive paradigm and, accordingly, is an absolutive. In Tzutujil (18), on the other hand, the instrumental voice likewise assigns informational salience to an instrumental nominal, but that nominal does not acquire the morphosyntactic properties of an absolutive. To be sure, it may be overtly unmarked, as in (18); but according to Dayley 1981: 28, it cannot be an absolutive since, as the example shows, the instrumental nominal is not indexed within the verbal complex (the prefix indexes not "machete," but the logical object "I"). Finally, in the Cakchiquel example (19), the instrumental voice assigns salience to the instrumental nominal without in any way affecting its morphosyntactic status. This follows because not only is the nominal in question not indexed in the verbal complex, but it also remains overtly oblique (i.e., is governed by a relational noun). It follows that, in an instance such as (19), the instrumental voice functions purely as a pragmatic index, i.e. a marker of informational salience assignment, without encoding any role-remapping or derived voice function at all. This point is significant, as we will soon see.

Despite its variable effects on the case marking and verbal indexing of instrumentals from language to language, there is one effect always associated with the instrumental voice: an alteration in the basic predication's pragmatics. That is, the instrumental voice makes an otherwise inaccessible theta-role, the instrument, accessible to the F-sensitive processes of emphatic fronting, question and relativization. These instrumental voice functions are respectively illustrated in the Tzutujil examples (20b–d) (compare 20a, a basic transitive without instrumental voice). (20a–d are from Dayley 1985: 215–17.)

(20) a. Jar aachi x-   0-   uu-   choy
       the man tense 3SG ABS 3SG ERG cut
       chee? tza?n/chee machat
       wood with   machete
       'The man cut wood with a machete'

   b. Jar aachi machat x-   0-   0-   choy
      a   man   machete tense 3SG ABS 3SG ERG cut
      b'e   -ej   ja chee?
      instrumental voice verb class the wood
      'It was a machete the man cut the wood with'

   c. Naq x-   0-   a-   b'an
      what tense 3SG ABS 2SG ERG do
      -b'e   -ej
      instrumental voice verb class
      'What did you do it with?'

d. Ja nuutee? x- ∅- uu- loq' kikop
the my-mother tense 3SG ABS 3SG ERG buy cacao
n- ∅- ∅- b'an -b'e
tense 3SG ABS 3SG ERG make instrumental voice
-j chaqijya?
verb class chocolate
'My mother bought cacao with which she makes chocolate'

In connection with (20a–d), Dayley 1985: 217 comments, "the instrumental voice is to instruments as the focus antipassive is to agents." But it is not so certain that the two voices are parallel in their effects; for while the focus antipassive invariably makes an A or logical subject absolutive, instrumental voice does not invariably have this effect on instrumental arguments, nor do these always acquire the full set of properties associated with basic absolutives. It is noteworthy that in none of the Tzutujil instrumental voice examples of (20b–d) is the instrumental role indexed by an absolutive prefix within the verbal complex.

Other voices, too, sometimes vary in their effects from one Mayan language to another. For instance, we have noted that it is usual for the A of a focus antipassive to be indexed within the verbal complex by an absolutive prefix. However, according to Mondloch 1981: 13, in two languages – Jacaltec and Ixil – the focus antipassive results in the A's fronting, but not in its reassignment as an absolutive. Rather, the P retains absolutive status; if expressed by a nonbound nominal it is unmarked, and it is the P that is indexed by the absolutive prefix in the verbal complex. Also, in Quiche, the rule of pronominal prefix assignment in focus antipassives does not invariably target A. (For discussion of this highly complicated rule, see Mondloch, pp. 221ff.)

Variability in prefix and core nominal case assignment in Mayan marked voices is significant to the present discussion for the following reasons. The less a marked voice confers upon a targeted nominal the morphosyntactic properties of an absolutive, the less it affects that nominal's basic morphosyntactic relation. As a result, the rule's effects may be limited to the domain of clausal pragmatics. In certain Mayan systems, some voice alternations appear to be exclusively pragmatic in their functions, signaling virtually nothing except alternate informational salience assignments to nominals in the clause. The Tzutujil instrumental voice has been mentioned in this regard above.

5.1 Mayan languages

One Mayan language in which there seems to have evolved a virtual separation of pragmatic from derived voices is Ixil. Illustrations of Ixil pragmatic voices have been cited earlier in Section 1.4 (26), (27). At this point, it is appropriate to examine the system in a little more detail.

According to Ayres 1983, most Ixil marked voices, other than the passive, index the assignment of informational salience (which Ayres calls focus) to some nominal position or status. The only nominal status which cannot be indexed for informational salience in this way, according to Ayres, is P.

The reason the system operates in such a way is that, apart from passive, none of the marked voices is used exclusively to encode alterations in nominal morphosyntactic relations. Essentially, what these voices encode is the thematic status of the nominal which is assigned informational salience. Furthermore, voices other than the passive all interact with F-sensitive rules, which once again comprise emphatic fronting, question and relativization.

The Ixil examples in (21)–(24) illustrate this. (21a) illustrates a basic transitive predication, and (21b) is its focus antipassive counterpart (both examples are from Ayres 1983: 27). The first example is transitive, since an ergative prefix appears in the verbal complex. By contrast, the second example has no such prefix (the form *in* at the beginning of the example is an independent or nonbound pronominal). However, there is no evidence that the morphosyntactic statuses of core nominals as such are altered. This follows since "I" and "you" in (21b) maintain the respective ergative and absolutive case assignments they bear in the basic transitive (21a). (See Ayres, pp. 27–9 for further discussion.)

Now consider (22a, b) (from Ayres, p. 42). (22b) illustrates an instrumental voice predication based on the ordinary transitive (22a). Neither the logical subject nor the logical object (respectively "you" and "me") appears to alter its basic morphosyntactic status in these examples, since both are indexed by elements of identical case and shape in the verbal complexes of (22a) and (22b) alike.

(23a, b) illustrate another oblique voice, the locative voice (these examples are from Ayres, pp. 26, 25). In this voice, informational salience is assigned to certain kinds of noninstrumental obliques. For instance, the focused nominal in (23b) is a goal. If one compares the ordinary transitive counterpart in (23a), one again finds no formal evidence that voice alters the basic morphosyntactic statuses of the clause's core nominals. Specifically, note that the ergative prefix in the

244 *Information-salience voice systems*

verbal complex indexes just the logical subject "you" in both examples; there is no prefix indexing logical object in either. Moreover, the shape of the oblique (*s we* 'to me') is invariant – all that changes is its linear position (it is fronted in 23b), showing that its pragmatic status is altered, although apparently not its morphosyntactic status.

By contrast, the Ixil passive does entail alterations in core nominal morphosyntax, including case assignments. Notice that in an active (24a) and the corresponding passive (24b), there is variation both in the indexing of core nominals within the verbal complex, as well as in the case marking of independent nominals. (24a, b are from Ayres, p. 22.)

(21) a. Kat   in-/un-   q'os axh
     aspect 1SG ERG hit 2SG ABS
     'I hit you' (Chajul and Nebaj dialects)
   b. In   kat   q'os -on   axh
     1SG ERG aspect hit   ANTI 2SG ABS
     'It was I who hit you' (Chajul and Nebaj dialects)
(22) a. A-   k'oni in   ta'n uula
     2SG ERG shoot 1SG ABS with sling
     'You shot me with a sling' (Chajul dialect)
   b. Uula a-   k'oni -b'e   in
     sling 2SG ERG shoot   instrumental voice 1SG ABS
     'It was a sling that you shot me with' (Chajul dialect)
(23) a. Kat   o-   oya ∅   u b'oob'al s we
     aspect 2SG ERG give 3SG ABS the hat   to me
     'You gave the hat to me' (Nebaj dialect)
   b. S we kat o-   oya kat   ∅   u   b'oob'al
     to me aspect 2SG ERG give voice 3SG ABS the hat
     'To me you gave the hat' (Nebaj dialect)
(24) a. Kat   t-   il ∅   ixoj naj
     aspect 3SG ERG see 3SG ABS she he
     'She saw him' (Nebaj dialect)
   b. Kat il -ax   ∅   naj ta?n ixoj
     aspect see passive 3SG ABS he by   she
     'He was seen by her' (Nebaj dialect)

The Ixil nonpassive voices illustrated in (21)–(23) appear distinct in function from the passive voice illustrated in (24) since, as noted, they do not seem to encode alterations in the morphosyntactic (i.e., case) statuses of core nominals. Rather, what these voices principally encode are alternating assignments of informational salience (focus) among certain noncore nominal positions. As a result, their effect is to signal alternations in the assignment of informational salience within the clause.

In sum, the main function of Ixil nonpassive voices is to encode alterations not in basic clausal morphosyntax, but rather, in clausal pragmatics. In this sense, they are appropriately considered pragmatic, not derived voices.

5.2 Philippine languages

Languages of the Austronesian family are spoken in an enormous area of the Pacific Basin and the Indian Ocean, extending from Taiwan and Polynesia westward as far as Madagascar. Essays in Sebeok 1971b offer details of the membership and geographical extent of this family.

Philippine languages comprise one branch of a subgroup within Austronesian, Malayo-Polynesian. A voice system common to many Philippine languages has intrigued scholars over the past several decades, and its implications for grammatical theory are the subject of a recent controversy involving both Philippinists and non-Philippinists. This variety of voice and its theoretical implications are of interest to the present work as well, and will now be discussed.

To put the discussion into a typological perspective, however, it will be useful to first recapitulate some of the preceding section's findings regarding pragmatic voices in Mayan. Mayan languages usually have more than one kind of informational salience assignable to core and noncore nominals of clauses. Typically, too, a Mayan language will have more than one derived voice. In most Mayan languages, the indexing of informational salience and the voice system may operate independently. That is, salience may be assigned in clauses where no voice rule applies, and, conversely, the application of a voice rule does not necessarily entail assignment of salience to one of the clause's nominals.

However, a Mayan language typically has at least one derived voice which regulates the assignment to core nominal positions or statuses of one particular kind of salience (often referred to by Mayanists as "focus"). In turn, it is this kind of salience that, in language after language, obligatorily accrues to any nominal targeted by a particular set of rules, earlier called focus-sensitive (F-sensitive) rules. These rules comprise the same set in all Mayan languages: emphatic fronting, question and relativization. Furthermore, focus is related to the pragmatics of discourse, because any focused nominal is referential, i.e. is either definite or can be governed by certain qualifiers which restrict the scope of its reference. For this reason, one can characterize Mayan languages as encoding certain pragmatic functions through derived voices. And in a small subset of these languages, of which Ixil is representative, the essential function of most voices is pragmatic. That is, alternations of verbal voice principally encode alternative information-salience (focus) assignments to particular nominal positions or statuses in the clause.

We can now compare the situation in a different language group, Philippine languages. The balance of the present chapter comprises a survey of some Philippine systems.

In a Philippine clause, the verbal complex usually includes one from among a limited set of indices. These are bound elements which alternate in indexing particular nominal positions or statuses. Some recent writers use the term focus to refer to these indices, but Philippine linguistics has an older tradition (e.g. Bloomfield 1917, Blake 1925) in which they are termed voices, and this terminology will be followed below. Alternations of voice correlate in Philippine languages, as in Mayan, with alternating assignments of informational salience to particular nominal positions or statuses. Moreover, as in Mayan languages, so too in Philippine languages, there is more than one status of informational salience to which clausal nominals may be assigned. However, only one particular information-salience status is indexed by the system of verbal voices.

Intriguingly, in Philippine languages, this status is also picked out by a particular set of rules, prominent among which are three corresponding to the F-sensitive rules in Mayan: emphatic fronting, question and relativization. In addition, focus in Philippine languages, like F-salience in Mayan, accrues just to referential (usually definite) nominals. In sum, Philippine and Mayan pragmatic voices seem to differ not so much as a matter of fundamental organization or type, but in functional consistency. That is, whereas Mayan voices usually have derived in addition to pragmatic functions, Philippine voices generally are purely pragmatic in their functions. This is the case because the only status or property a nominal is assigned by virtue of verbal voice indexing in Philippine systems is focus, or informational salience, as will be shown below.

Most of the following illustrations will be drawn from one Philippine language, Cebuano (for which the principal sources consulted are

Shibatani 1986, 1988a and 1988b). Occasionally other, related systems will be compared (including Tagalog, which is one of the best-investigated Philippine languages).

In each of the Cebuano illustrations (25a–d) below (from Shibatani 1988a: 88–9), the verbal complexes include markers of different voices. The verbal voice forms in (25a–d) are respectively labeled Actor (A), Goal (G), Directional (D), and Instrumental (I), according to the participant role of the indexed nominal. While some writers attribute a larger number of voices to certain Philippine languages (see, for instance, Schachter & Otanes 1972 and Naylor 1975 on Tagalog), the four shown in (25a–d) are adequate for purposes of illustration. (In these examples, the nominals which are focused are glossed in **boldface**.)

(25) a. Ni-   hatag   si   Juan sa libro sa bata
        A voice give   Focus   Juan G book D child
        '**Juan** gave the book to the child'
    b. Gi-   hatag   ni Juan ang   libro sa bata
        G voice give   A Juan Focus   book D child
        'Juan gave **the book** to the child'
    c. Gi-   hatag -an   ang   bata ni Juan sa libro
        D voice give   D voice Focus   child A Juan G book
        'Juan gave **the child** the book'
    d. I-   hiwa ang   kutsilyo sa mangga ni Maria
        I voice cut Focus knife   G mango A Maria
        'Maria cut the mango with **the knife**'

Like most Mayan languages (see Dayley 1981: 14, 64), Philippine languages have verb-initial word order as the neutral word order (Shibatani 1988a: 88). In contrast to Mayan languages, however, there is no necessary linear word order rearrangement in a Philippine language when a nominal is focused, as (25a, b) illustrate.

Another difference is that in Philippine systems such as Cebuano and Tagalog, unlike Mayan systems, indices of the case or other morphosyntactic statuses of core nominals usually do not occur within the verbal complex. Rather, one nominal is indexed per clause and the index is the voice. The voice marking is often prefixal, as in (25a, b, d); occasionally the marking is of some other sort, such as an ambifix (as in 25c) or a suffix (Tagalog, for instance, has suffixal voice indices). But however the voice may be encoded in the verbal complex, the nominal position

248 *Information-salience voice systems*

indexed by the voice is usually reconfirmed by an element or particle preceding the focused nominal. These particles are glossed in (25a–d) as Focus. (More will be said later on the coindexing relation between focus and voice markers.)

In each of (25a–d), one independent or nonbound nominal is focused (indicated by **boldface**). This is the maximum number of focused nominals allowed per clause. The focus particles are of varying shapes according to the governed nominal's participant role. These particles are, in (25a), an A or actor focus particle; in (25b), a G or goal focus particle; in (25c), a D or directional focus particle; and in (25d), an I or instrumental focus particle. Note that, in each of (25a–d), the focus particle replaces, as it were, the case particle that normally precedes the relevant nominal when it is not focused.

Clearly, voice and focus are integral to Philippine sentence organization. With this established, it is now convenient to consider in greater detail the interrelations of Philippine focus and voice. The first thing to consider will be how participant roles, thematic role structure and nominal subcategorization interrelate in focus assignment.

Focuses do not directly index any one of the categories just mentioned. Rather, focus is among several formal categories of the noun, categories which, for convenience, may be considered categories of case*. Moreover, the shape of a focus particle may vary depending on the sort of nominal to be indexed[8] – specifically, depending on whether it is a personal name, personal pronoun, common noun, or demonstrative.

This is clarified in Figure 5.1, based on form classes in Cebuano (reproduced from Shibatani 1988a: 86, 87, Tables 1 and 2). (In this figure, the terms "Focus" and "Voice" replace Shibatani's original terms, respectively "Topic" and "Focus.")

As Shibatani notes, and as shown in Figure 5.1 (I), Cebuano person pronouns show four forms apiece, personal names show three, and common nouns and demonstratives show just two.

In the figure, (II), the nominal form classes are mapped onto three categories: focus, genitive and oblique. These categories effectively comprise cases. The cases, in turn, map onto functional categories (or nominal participant roles) and onto categories of verbal voice as shown. According to the figure, (II), the participant roles of actor and goal, when unfocused, are assigned to a single case category, the genitive; while recipient, direction, location and instrument, when unfocused, are

I

Form labels	Focus	Genitive	Oblique	Gloss
Personal names	si Juan	ni Juan	kang Juan	'Juan'
Person pronouns	siya	iya/niya	kaniya	'he'
Common nouns	ang bata	sa bata	sa bata	'child'
Demonstratives	kini	niini	niini	'this'

II

Form categories	Functions (participant roles) (the following except Possessor)	Voice categories
Focus	Possessor	
Genitive	Actor (agent)	Actor voice
	Goal (patient)	Goal voice
	Recipient	
Oblique	Direction	Directional voice
	Location	
	Instrument	Instrumental voice

Figure 5.1 Mappings of nominal functions, case categories, verbal voices and form classes in Cebuano, based on Shibatani 1988a

assigned to a different case category, the oblique. Again, the shape of the focus particle assigned in each case category depends on the status of the nominal as set forth in (I) of Figure 5.1.

At this point, one matter worth clarifying is the functions of Philippine case particles. Although these mark nominals for case categories, their functions do not precisely parallel the typical functions of non-Philippine cases. In the first place, focus, i.e. locus of informational salience, is uncommonly treated as a case in other languages; but formally, it does comprise a case in Philippine languages. And in the second place, the Philippine case particles, other than focus, may be supplemented by additional means for marking the participant role of the governed nominal. For instance, in the Cebuano example (26) below (from Shibatani 1988a: 93), a preposition *gikan* "from" clarifies the location role of the oblique (directional case) nominal "wall." Conversely, nominals unmarked for case are sometimes prepositionally governed. Thus in (27) (from Shibatani, p. 110), notice the prepositional marking of the case-unmarked nominal "hand and foot."

(26) ... Gi-   kawat   ko   kining sundang gikan sa
      G voice grabbed first person A Focus bolo   from   D
      bungbong
      wall
      '... I grabbed **this bolo** from the wall'

(27) Nanganak   kadto ang   usa ka magtiayon ug bata
      gave birth-A voice once Focus one   couple   G child
      nga   walay kamot ug tili
      linking particle without hand   and foot
      'Once **a couple** gave birth to a child without limbs'

Philippine nominal focus is relevant to our present concerns because Philippine voices index focus. More precisely speaking, the voices index the participant roles of nominals which are focused, or assigned clause-level informational salience. As mentioned earlier, focus is only one sort of informational salience which obtains at the level of the clause (others will be alluded to later). However, focus plays a unique role in Philippine morphosyntax, since it is the only salience indexed by the system of voices.

There is, in fact, a large body of literature by Philippinists concerning focus and focus functions (including Dahl 1978; Griño 1973; Kess 1975, 1976; Llamzon 1973; McKaughan 1973; Naylor 1975, 1978; Schachter

1976, 1977; and more). While this literature may help to some extent in clarifying what focus is, it perhaps is more successful in clarifying what focus is not. Possibly this is due to the fact that current linguistics offers a very limited framework for the study of information structure, notwithstanding a growing interest in this topic, particularly in relation to discourse pragmatics (for instance, see essays in Tomlin 1987 and references therein).

One thing which research on Philippine languages seems to have already established is that Philippine focus has unique properties, making it distinct from some kinds of informational salience found in non-Philippine languages. For instance, focus is not the same as a status referred to in some Western-language studies as "theme," meaning the part of a sentence's information structure which is most presupposed, or contributes the least to the development of the discourse. Themehood in this sense does not, for example, accrue to the focus in the example (28) below (see Naylor 1975: 14 for further discussion).

Also, although some Philippinists allude to it as "topic," the kind of information salience represented by the Philippine focus is very different from the status referred to by the same term by writers on a number of non-Philippine languages, a case in point being Japanese. Shibatani 1986: 37–8 discusses this in the context of a story about a character Annie, whose birthday is approaching, and her friend Jiji who plans to give her a present. In English the story concludes, "There was a book that Annie liked at the store. So, Jiji gave the book to Annie." Speakers of Philippine languages typically translate this story assigning the focus to the last clause's goal participant role, as in the Cebuano example (28) (from Shibatani, p. 38). However, according to Shibatani, in the Japanese version the locus of informational salience or topic, marked by a topic particle *wa*, more naturally devolves upon the actor ("Jiji") than upon the goal ("the book").

(28) Busa, gihatag   ni Jiji ang   libro sa Annie
     so   gave-G voice A Jiji Focus book D Annie
     'So, Jiji gave **the book** to Annie'

Interestingly, there are also important differences between Philippine focus and the informational salience termed salience-F in the preceding section's discussion of Mayan languages. For instance, according to Section 5.1, salience-F is generally emphatic or contrastive. However, this does not necessarily hold of focus in Philippine languages (although it is possible to impart contrastive emphasis to a focused nominal, as will be illustrated below).

Loosely, the function that focus does serve in Philippine languages can be described as follows. According to Naylor 1975: 16ff., the Philippine focus is a signal of how an argument, in relation to a predicate, is to be construed as contributing to the continuity of the unfolding discourse. Accordingly, the referent tends to be strong in the attentions of the speaker/hearer, either because its relevance has been established earlier in the discourse (for instance, this holds of "book" in 28), or because its referent is part of the speaker and hearer's mutually shared background knowledge. Generally, this would not hold of nominals assigned salience-F in Mayan.

On the other hand, like salience-F in Mayan languages, focus in Philippine languages represents a locus of referentiality. Usually, a nominal assigned focus must be referentially definite. In many Philippine languages, nominals which may be glossed alternately as definite or indefinite when unfocused are glossed as definite when focused (see Schachter 1976: 495 for Tagalog examples and discussion).

It was noted in the preceding section that nonreferential nominals in Mayan languages such as K'ekchi might be assigned informational salience (either salience-T or salience-F), and that, in fact, this is one way of satisfying a constraint against assigning core cases (ergative and absolutive) to nonreferential nominals (see again examples 14–16). In Philippine languages, nonreferential nominals are never assigned focus (and sometimes are not assigned overt case; see again 27). Also, as earlier mentioned, focused nominals in Philippine languages are usually definite. In the relatively rare instance in which a nondefinite nominal is focused, it is qualified, and so its reference is restricted and not indefinite. Shibatani 1988a: 111 furnishes the following Cebuano example illustrating a nondefinite but qualified (quantified) nominal in focus.

(29) ... Iyang na- kita ang usa ka sinaw nga
 he-A G voice saw Focus one shiny linking particle
 awa nga adunay puronpurong
 fish linking particle there-is-crown
 '... he saw **a shiny milkfish** wearing a crown'

(29) is typical of the conditions under which focus may be assigned to nondefinite nominals in Philippine languages. These conditions have been studied in detail for Tagalog (with many comments as well on

Cebuano) by Adams & Manaster-Ramer 1988. Like (29), all their examples contain (and according to these authors, p. 88, "have to contain") a quantifier which, as stated before, establishes the reference of the nominal as restricted, hence not indefinite and so not nonreferential.

Among the several parallels between Mayan F-salience and Philippine focus, perhaps the most striking is the earlier-noted fact that this nominal status is targeted by focus-sensitive rules. Moreover, in Philippine languages these rules include emphatic fronting, question and relativization, i.e. just the rules which are F-sensitive in Mayan. But before offering illustrations of these rules in Philippine languages, it is important to substantiate the link between focus and the voice system.

In Philippine languages, unlike Mayan languages, the selection of verbal voice does not comprise a condition on the accessibility of various nominals to focus assignment. Rather, most kinds of constructions require one nominal to be in focus, with verbal voice serving to coindex that nominal's participant role. Although, as a result, there is a characteristic one-to-one relation between voice and focus, a few qualifications should be noted.

In Philippine systems, one generally does not find instances in which a focus fails to be coindexed by the corresponding voice in the verb. The converse, however, may obtain. That is, there are instances in which, despite the verb's indexing a particular voice, no overtly focused nominal appears in the clause. According to Shibatani 1986: 25–9, there are several specific conditions under which this occurs. A typical class of instances is meteorological expressions. An illustration is the Hiligaynon example (30) (from Wolfenden 1975: 101), in which a case-marked nominal does cooccur in the clause with the voice-indexed verb, but is not focused.

(30) Magaulan   pa karon sa gabi
     will rain-A voice yet now   D night
     'It will rain yet tonight'

Also, examples occur in which there is neither overt voice nor focus. In fact, according to Shibatani 1986: 28ff., this is characteristic of two kinds of clauses. One kind is existential clauses, which are often used to introduce a discourse, as illustrated in the Cebuano example in (31) (from Shibatani, p. 29). The second kind is nominalizations; nominalized clauses never include overt markers of voice or focus. This is illustrated by another Cebuano example in (32) (from Shibatani, p. 25).

(31) Diha kadtoy usa ka bata nga ginganlag Juan Pusog
     exist once one child linking particle named Juan Pusog
     'Once there was a child named Juan Pusog'

(32) pag-   dagan ni   /*si   Juan
     nominalization run GEN / Focus Juan
     'running by Juan'

Since focus selection always determines the assignment of voice in the verbal complex, while voice may not always determine focus, it seems reasonable to treat voice as a kind of anaphoric category. That is, Philippine voices coindex nominal focus assignments but, unlike voices in Mayan languages, do not drive them.

Nonetheless, like Mayan, Philippine languages do have focus-sensitive rules, as stated earlier. Shibatani 1986: 45ff. comments on the remarkable overlap in the rules which, in each family, turn out to be sensitive to voice-indexed statuses of informational salience (focus). As he observes, not only in Mayan, but also in Philippine languages, rules of question, relativization and emphatic fronting (in his parlance, clefting) are all sensitive to focus.

To see this, first consider the Cebuano examples (33a, b) (from Shibatani 1986:49) illustrating the question rule. (33a), in which a focused nominal is questioned, is grammatical; by contrast, (33b), with a questioned nonfocused nominal, is ungrammatical.

(34a, b) (from Shibatani, p. 46) is a pair of Cebuano examples respectively showing focused and unfocused nominals targeted by the relativization rule. The former is grammatical, the latter ungrammatical.

(33) a. Unsa ba   ang [gi-   basa sa bata]
        what question Focus G voice read A child
        '**What** did the child read?'
     b.*Kinsa ba   ang [gi-   basa ang   libro]
        who question Focus G voice read Focus book
        'Who read **the book**?'

(34) a. ang   bata nga   [ni-   basa ug libro]
        Focus child linking particle A voice read G book
        '**the child** who read a/the book'

5.2 Philippine languages

b.*ang   libro   nga   [ni-   basa ang   bata]
Focus book linking particle A voice read Focus child
'the book that **the child** read'

Philippine languages also have rules of emphatic fronting. Some of these rules do not target focused nominals alone. However, illustrations of some emphatic-fronting processes which are focus-sensitive are given for Cebuano in (35) (from Shibatani 1988a: 131) and for Tagalog in (36) (from Schachter & Otanes 1972: 486; also cited by Shibatani, p. 131). The illustrated processes differ in certain properties. For instance, in the Cebuano example, the focused nominal is simply fronted; while in the Tagalog example, it is followed by an emphatic particle *ay*.[9]

(35) Si   Maria gi-   higugma ni Juan
     Focus Maria G voice love   A Juan
     '**Maria**, Juan loves'

(36) Ang   sulat   ay   tinanggap ko kahapon
     Focus letter EMPH arrive   I   yesterday
     '**The letter**, it arrived yesterday' (formal style)

According to Shibatani 1988a: 133ff., emphatic fronting sometimes interacts with certain morphosyntactic behaviors, such as control of gapping. In the Cebuano example (37b) (from Shibatani, p. 134), a nominal which has been targeted by emphatic fronting acquires this property. Otherwise, it ordinarily accrues only to the participant role of actor (as illustrated in 37a). This is noteworthy because assignments of morphosyntactic properties to various nominal statuses have significant implications for defining the basic structural organization of a system, a matter to which the discussion is about to turn.

(37) a. Ni-   kumusta si   Juan ni Pedro ug   ni-
       A voice greet   Focus Juan G Pedro and A voice
       haluk ni Maria
       kiss   G Maria
       'Juan greeted **Pedro** and $\emptyset$ (= Juan) kissed Maria'

     b. Si   Pedro ni-   kumusta si Juan niya ug
       Focus Pedro A voice kissed   A Juan him and
       ni-   haluk ni Maria
       A voice kiss   G Maria
       '**Pedro** Juan greeted and $\emptyset$ (= Pedro, ≠Juan) kissed Maria'

In recent Philippine linguistics, the distribution of morphosyntactic properties among nominal statuses in clause structures has been a central issue in a major program of inquiry into the typology of subject and the definition of subject properties, a program initiated by Schachter 1976, 1977. For the present work's purposes, the definition of subject is not at issue. However, it is relevant to note, as Schachter's research and that of others has established, that in Philippine languages some morphosyntactic properties devolve upon focused nominals; others devolve upon actors (whether focused or unfocused); and still others (such as emphatic fronting in Kapampangan; see n. 9) devolve alternately upon focused nominals or unfocused actors. (There may also be properties which devolve upon other statuses altogether, as 37b suggests; but this will be left aside for present purposes. Also, the following discussion leaves aside properties that are purely morphological or semantic, as opposed to morphosyntactic.)

Figure 5.2 lists morphosyntactic properties which research on Philippine languages has established are sensitive, respectively, to focus, actor or actor/focus.[10]

The distribution of morphosyntactic properties over pragmatic (i.e., focus) vs non-pragmatic (i.e., actor) statuses – to which Schachter 1976, 1977 alludes under the rubric of reference-related vs role-related properties – has inspired competing claims about the basic structural organization of Philippine languages. These claims and counterclaims merit some critical attention at this point in our discussion.

According to one school of thought, non-Actor voices in Philippine languages are nonbasic, or derived. This view is due to the observation, captured in Figure 5.2, that the single nominal status upon which a plurality of morphosyntactic properties devolves is the focused actor. According to this view, the Actor voice is, accordingly, basic.

The view just described is, in fact, part of the tradition of descriptive research on Philippine languages. Non-Actor voices are labeled passives in the earliest studies of Philippine syntax by Western writers, e.g. Bloomfield 1917 and Blake 1925. Recent writers who maintain this viewpoint include Bell 1983 on Cebuano, as well as Keenan 1976b and Randriamasimanana 1986 on Malagasy (not a Philippine, but a Malayo-Polynesian language).

A second and more recent viewpoint (represented *inter alia* by Payne 1982 and by Cooreman, Fox & Givón 1984) is that the dominant voice in Philippine languages is antipassive, and that the basic structural

Focus-sensitive properties
relativizable
can be directly questioned
floats quantifier
functions as a controller and as a gap in the *samtang* "while"-clause
raisable out of the *nga* subordinate clause

Actor-sensitive properties
deleted in imperatives
antecedes reflexives

Actor-/focus-sensitive properties
functions as a controller and as a gap in coordinate as well as in complement structures
emphatic fronting

Figure 5.2   Focus-, actor- and actor-/focus-sensitive properties in Philippine languages, based on Shibatani 1988a: 125, 1988b: 107

organization of these languages is, accordingly, ergative–absolutive. This view is based on an observation that in certain of these languages, a statistical plurality of morphosyntactic properties devolves upon logical objects of transitives (i.e., upon the participant role of Goal), since Goal voice happens to be statistically most common in these languages. But some writers are cautious about accepting this view. For instance, Foley & Van Valin 1984: 134ff., 176, 178, after a careful and critical examination of data, declare themselves unable to reach a definite conclusion as to the fundamental accusativity or ergativity of Philippine systems as a class.

On the other hand, some writers (e.g. Shibatani 1988a, 1988b; De Wolf 1988) have looked at the issues and arrive at certain definite conclusions about the fundamental structural organizations of Philippine languages. Shibatani's views are especially carefully grounded and deserve a brief discussion here.

Shibatani holds that it is implausible to treat the sort of voice found in Philippine languages as any kind of derived voice, passive or antipassive. His main argument rests on markedness: whereas in languages in general, derived voices are more marked than their active counterparts, one finds on examining Philippine languages that there seems to be no one voice that is consistently marked or unmarked relative to some particular other.

In addition, Shibatani notes that suppression or downgrading of agents (actors) is typical in passives. Conversely, suppression or downgrading of themes or patients (goals) is typical in antipassives. But, he claims, in Philippine languages no particular nominal position is characteristically downgraded or suppressed in any voice. On the contrary, in Philippine languages, each voice indexes a participant role's foregrounding or informational salience.

These and other arguments of Shibatani[11] seem cogent and compelling, as does his conclusion: that there is no specific derived voice with which Philippine focus indexing (voice) merits identification. The one function indisputably associated with Philippine voice is that of indexing the participant role of a nominal assigned informational salience, or the focused nominal. In general, this is not a central function of derived voices.

In this connection, it is noteworthy that Philippinists are unable to agree on the definition of subject. That is, in Philippine languages there seems to be no single participant role (case), thematic relation or syntactic status to which a plurality of significant morphosyntactic properties accrues. Schachter 1976, 1977 examines relevant data and concludes that subject properties are divided over two nominal statuses; i.e., that actor and focus both qualify as kinds of subjects. However, Shibatani 1988b: 108ff. decides on the basis of the same evidence that the best generalization is as follows: actor and focus are not subjects, but approach a subject prototype, with the focused actor being the nearest thing to a prototypical subject for these systems.

As this shows, the applicability of the notion of subject to Philippine systems is in dispute. But if this is so, then it seems especially dubious to associate Philippine voices with strategies for moving nominals in and out of subject position – which is what derived voices amount to.

To sum up, in Philippine languages, pragmatic (informational) salience is significant, being crucial to a variety of morphosyntactic behaviors. In these languages, verbal voice functions as an index of nominal salience assignments. In fact, the alternating voices of the verb serve purely to index alternating assignments of informational salience to nominal positions. The case is similar in a minority of Mayan languages alluded to in the preceding section (e.g. Ixil); while in other Mayan languages, derived voices combine with their characteristic or essential functions (i.e., as passives and antipassives) the further function of regulating information-salience assignments.

Focus or information-salience voice comprises a strategy for indexing the alternating assignments to nominals of certain statuses, informational salience statuses, which pertain to clausal pragmatics. Based on the present chapter's survey, this class of systems appears to have reality as a distinct type under the rubric of grammatical voice.

6 Toward a theory of voice

In some current grammatical theories (see Klaiman in preparation), the category of voice is regarded as encoding alternative allocations of nominals among positions in structural configurations. Many researchers associate the idea of voice most particularly with verbally marked alternations of nominal assignments affecting the content of one structural position, the subject position (see Chapter 1, n. 16). This view of matters is reflected in one writer's characterization of voice as "a strategy to move NPs in and out of subject position" (Barber 1975: 16), as noted earlier (Section 1.2).

The issue of subject's universality has been debated in recent grammatical research. In some languages, it is clear that a status of subject can be identified by an exclusive coincidence upon some one structural position of a group of significant morphosyntactic properties. This has been discussed in Section 1.2 (see examples 9, 10).

However, in subsequent chapters of the present work, a variety of voice types have been surveyed. Among these there are several systems having productive voice alternations in the absence of any well-defined subject status. For instance, Section 5.2 has discussed voice behaviors in Philippine languages. Philippine languages are characterized by elaborate systems of alternating voices, but lack an uncontroversially defined subject relation. Another instance worth noting in this connection is Sanskrit. Despite its well-known and robust system of obligatory active/ middle marking in most paradigms of the verb, this language apparently has no morphosyntactically verifiable subject relation or status (see again Chapter 1, n. 18). In view of these facts, it appears overly restrictive to define voice in terms of alternations involving variable assignments of nominal arguments to the status of subject.

In opposition to the majority of current theories, the present work has taken the position that it is not necessary that a language be organized in terms of grammatical relations such as subject in order to demonstrate

Toward a theory of voice 261

some type of voice behavior. Consistent with this, voice has been characterized above (Section 1.0) as a category encoding alternations in the configurations of nominal statuses with which verbs are in particular relationships. This characterization assumes that the configurations in question may be identified in different systems with different levels of grammatical organization, not necessarily the level of structural relations alone. Accordingly, the investigation of voice has a typological dimension. One aim of the present work has been to provide the study of voice typology with a substantial and worthwhile beginning. This has been the purpose of the survey of systems in Chapters 2–5.

The purpose of this chapter, however, is to make a beginning in voice's formal analysis; that is, to discuss possibilities for adapting grammatical theory so as to account for the category in its rich diversity of manifestations. To this end, it seems apt to note one feature that is evidently common to the various kinds of voice systems surveyed above.

It does appear that different types of voice are sensitive to different levels of grammatical organization; this much is clear from the survey. But in general, any voice system seems to make reference to some scale or relative ranking of nominals according to their assigned statuses at a relevant or applicable level of grammatical organization for the given system. Moreover, voice alternations, in some way, recur to or index hierarchically superior nominal statuses.

Consider, for instance, the derived voice type. As discussed earlier, a derived voice system amounts to a strategy for encoding the alternating assignments of different arguments of a verb to a single structural position, that of subject. Subject, moreover, cross-linguistically outranks alternative statuses of the same order (such as object, indirect object, oblique and so forth) in regard to a variety of formal properties (Keenan & Comrie 1977). Similarly, in systems with another kind of derived voice, antipassive*, the core nominal status to which nominals are alternately assigned is the absolutive (see Section 5.1); and in these systems, it is the absolutive that manifests an analogous sort of superiority over other nominal statuses of the same order, such as the ergative.

If nominal statuses encoded or coindexed by other voice types likewise manifest superior ranking over other statuses at the relevant organizational levels (i.e. levels other than that of structural relations), then the possibility exists that, for all its typological diversity, voice can be furnished with an analysis validating its oneness as a grammatical category.

In order to clarify this point, we may compare derived voice with a different voice type, the focus* voice type. As noted earlier, in Philippine languages, the existence of a morphosyntactically verifiable subject relation is debatable, and these languages exemplify focus voice. The focus type is also manifested in languages of the Mayan family (see Section 5.1). Focus voice alternations do not reassign nominals among relational statuses, i.e. among subject and nonsubject positions, but rather are sensitive to the information structure of the clause or sentence. In such systems, moreover, there may occur more than one grammatically significant status of informational salience.

As Chapter 5 has observed, in Mayan and Philippine systems alike, grammatically significant informational salience statuses include focus and topic. Of these two, the status upon which a plurality of or the most significant grammatical behaviors devolves or devolve is the focus (see Chapter 5, n. 1).

One could loosely state a principle of voice marking for systems of the focus type as follows:

(1) Coindex on the verb the participant role (e.g. Actor, Goal, Instrument or other) corresponding to the nominal position which is focused.

A statement along these lines may basically sum up the pattern of voice marking in pure focus voice systems, such as Philippine systems and a minority of Mayan systems (e.g. Ixil; see Section 5.1). There are, to be sure, other systems where focus voice interacts with derived voice behaviors. This occurs, for instance, in the majority of Mayan languages (as discussed in Section 5.1). For such systems, a statement along the lines of (1) will not be adequate.

Be that as it may, just as subject in derived voice systems has hierarchical superiority over all comparable (i.e. relational) statuses, so focus in information-salience voice systems outranks or is hierarchically superior to other statuses of the same order (at the level of information structure). This follows since, as just observed, a greater number of significant grammatical properties converge upon focus than upon other informational salience statuses.

Plausibly, then, what is common to different types of voice systems may be that wherever voice alternations occur, they encode alternative assignments of arguments to positions which have superior ranking at some grammatically significant level of organization, be it that of relational structure, information structure or some other level. (One alternative level which will be taken up momentarily is ontological structure.)

Let us now explore, in a tentative way, how this insight can be extended to an account of other voice types. First we shall take up the inverse* voice type, earlier surveyed in Chapter 4. It will be recalled that, in this type, voice alternations are sensitive to statuses of ontological salience. It is assumed that this salience pertains to a particular level of grammatical organization, ontological structure. After considering the inverse type, we will consider how ontological structure might also be invoked in the account of another major voice type, basic* voice systems.

In inverse systems, voice alternations have scope only in transitive predications, as discussed in Chapter 4 above. In some inverse systems, voice alternations may be restricted to transitive predications with at least one animate core argument, i.e. transitive animates (again see Chapter 4).

Whatever the domain of direct/inverse voice alternations in a given system, in general, core referents of the relevant class of predications are ranked for positions on a hierarchy of ontological salience. The details of the hierarchy may vary with individual systems although, in general, ontological salience hierarchies conform to some subscale of the hierarchy of potentiality of agency, or animacy hierarchy, shown earlier in Chapter 4, example (6) (= Chapter 3, Figure 3.3). Occasionally, individual systems may deviate from this hierarchy in certain particulars (as noted in Section 4.4).

Also as noted in Chapter 4, in a transitive predication, the core argument receiving the highest attribution of salience according to the applicable scale for the system can be termed the ontological subject*. A core argument of the predication which receives lower attribution of control is termed ontological object*. The voice alternation indexes the relationships of ontological statuses of subject and object to certain independently defined positions at some level of organization (characterized in Chapter 4 as logical statuses; but see below). Having reviewed this, we may now consider how ontological structure and ontological salience, conceptions fundamental to the analysis of inverse systems, might be handled in a formalized account.

For this purpose, we will invoke an assumption of Farkas 1988a: 33 (and authors cited therein) regarding the relations between logical predicates and ontological structures. This assumption is that a verbal idea can be associated with a set S of (possible) situations s. In each s, there are individuals having properties and occupying various relations.

A given S or situation-set can be equated with the ontological structure of the corresponding lexical predicate (verb). For the analysis of an inverse system, the relevant ontological structures will be those of predicates which are subject to voice variation, i.e. transitive or, in some systems, transitive animate predicates.

It is assumed that, in an inverse system, participants in an s are ranked according to the ontological salience hierarchy particular to the system, and that the relative rankings of core nominals determine statuses of ontological subject and object. Now, for every s or situation, we can define a set P of *potential controllers*. P consists of all participant roles in s ranked higher than the lowest ranking or status according to the system's ontological salience hierarchy.

We shall also introduce a relation of *actual controller*. Actual controller is defined as a two-place relation holding between a participant p and s just in case certain conditions hold. Tentatively, we suggest these conditions are approximately as follows:

(2) a. The realization of s depends crucially on the participant role of p; and
   b. s is *possibly intentional* (as discussed by Farkas 1988a: 36), meaning that it is compatible with p's intentional involvement in s.[1]

One of the ways in which ontological structure, as just conceptualized, is relevant to the analysis of inverse systems is that it imposes a constraint on argument structure, a constraint evinced in all inverse systems. This is as follows: in a predication involving a predicate of the relevant (potentially voice-alternating) class (e.g. transitive or transitive animate, depending on the system; note too that, in some systems, you-and-me or local are excluded from the voice variation), two core arguments may be of equivalent ontological salience only if set P, the set of potential controllers, is null.

The constraint just stated entails that, in the class of predications where voice alternations have scope, core nominals may not be of equivalent ontological salience. The remaining class consists of predications in which both core arguments are of the lowest ontological salience category. As discussed earlier (Chapter 4), it is only these predications (e.g. 3OBV:3OBV in Algonquian languages, 3:3 predications in certain other inverse systems) which alternate formally for both voice categories, direct as well as inverse. The stated constraint accounts for the fact that, outside of this class, other predications are not expressible in alternate voices.

With the above view of ontological structure, one can now formalize an account of inverse voice behavior without appealing (as earlier in Chapter 4) to logical statuses of subject and object. Instead, a condition on inverse voice encoding can be stated in the following terms:

(3) Assign the index of the marked (inverse) voice to the verb in case the actual controller in s coincides with the ontological object. Assign the index of the unmarked (direct) voice in case the actual controller in s coincides with the ontological subject.

Notice that condition (3) formulates the basis for voice assignments purely in terms of one level of grammatical organization, the ontological level. This eliminates the need to refer to an additional level of organization, such as the logical-structure level. One reason this seems desirable is that the ontological status invoked instead, that of actual controller, may also be useful in a formal account of other voice systems. Systems of the basic voice type (to be discussed shortly) are an instance in point. As will be shown, both these and systems of the inverse type share the characteristic of grammaticizing some nominal status related to the ontological construct of control*.

Under the account of direct-inverse systems in (3), voices encode alternate participant role assignments (controller vs non-controller) to ontological subject. The ontological subject, for its part, is defined in terms of the relatively superior ranking of some nominal in a given predication for ontological salience, according to the salience hierarchy which applies in the particular system. Thus an inverse system is driven by or sensitive to some nominal status which is superior relative to some scale or hierarchy.

This bears out the earlier suggestion that, in general, some hierarchically superior nominal status figures in the organization of any voice system. To be sure, the level of grammatical organization relevant to the hierarchical ranking of nominals is not the same in all types of voice systems. But it is the fact that the system is sensitive to some hierarchically superior nominal status which supports the direct-inverse type's affinity with voice behaviors in general.

Let us now consider, once more in an exploratory and tentative way, how something along the lines of the above conception of ontological structure might lend itself to a formal account of voice systems of another type, basic* voice systems. These are the most complex voice systems to come within the scope of the present work's systems survey. Not one, but two of the present work's earlier chapters (Chapters 2, 3) concern this type. It will be recalled that, according to Chapter 3, basic voice pertains to the level of lexical organization. Correspondingly, in basic type (as contrasted with inverse type) systems, all lexical predicates (rather than some) are subject to overt voice marking.

In discussing basic voice systems, we shall henceforth rely on an assumption that thematic or theta-role* structure is relevant to the organization of systems of this type. Theta-roles, moreover, can be ranked according to a scale or theta-hierarchy*. A partial version of this hierarchy might be suggested as follows (following Bresnan 1987, Kiparsky 1987): agent > beneficiary > theme/patient > location, etc., as noted earlier (Section 3.0).

Notice that this scale can be construed as a grammaticized hierarchy of *potentiality of control* in the sense that, the higher a participant role ranks on the scale, the greater the likelihood of its meeting the criteria defining *actual controller* set forth earlier. The significance of this will be clarified shortly.

In developing a basis for a formal analysis of basic voice systems, we assume, once more, that any predicate is associated with a situation-set S of possible situations *s*, and that participant roles can be defined on the basis of properties of participants in a given *s*. To illustrate, corresponding to a use of a predicate, such as *agitate*, there may be some *s* in which there is one participant in the role of that which effects agitation, and/or one participant in the role of that which is agitated, etc.

We shall now make one special assumption in regard to a class of predicates common to all basic voice systems. As noted in Chapter 2, related neuter* and transitive* predicates occur in many languages. In languages with basic voice systems, they comprise a subclass of the active/middle alternating verbs.

Here it will be assumed that distinct situation-sets S do not accrue to transitive and neuter alternates. Rather, there is a common S for both the neuter and its correlated transitive. Moreover, the set of participant roles in any *s* associated with the neuter corresponds to a subset of the set of participant roles for an *s* associated with the transitive counterpart. Thus in the case of the English verb *bend*, there is one situation-set or S, and this S specifies one participant role corresponding to that which effects bending, as well as a second participant role corresponding to that which bends. In a given situation *s* corresponding to a use of the neuter (intransitive) verb *bend*, there occurs one participant in the second role assigned by the transitive, the role of that which bends, but none in the first. Thus, as stated, the neuter's participant role-set is a subset of that of the correlated transitive. It is assumed, then, that there is no distinction in neuter vs transitive situation-sets at the level of ontological structure; S is the same for both a neuter and the related transitive predicate. Note that this assumption is independent of an assumption, stated above in Chapter 2, that at a distinct level, i.e. in the lexicon, corresponding neuter and transitive verbs are furnished with separate but related lexical entries.

Now it will be assumed that in basic voice systems, every S, every situation-set associated with a given lexical predicate, has a set P of *potential controllers* comprising all participant roles whose ontological ranking is higher than that of the lowest-ranking status on the relevant ontological salience hierarchy for the given system. The definition of the potential controller set or P is the same in basic voice systems as has been stipulated earlier for inverse systems, except that for the latter, potential controller is defined relative to an *s* or individual situation (rather than to an S or situation-set).

Also, for every *s* in S, a *controller-set* C can be defined as follows. Set C for any *s* consists of any participant role or roles that are in P, or comprise potential controllers, and which have the highest ranking in *s* relative to the applicable ontological salience scale for the given system. Thus in *Max agitated Maxine*, both participant roles corresponding to *Max* and *Maxine* are in C; while in *I agitated the solution*, only the first participant role, that of *I*, is in P. It follows that the participant role of *I* ontologically outranks that of *the solution*, and accordingly, the former alone is in C.

In accounting for basic voice systems, one must provide for certain two-place relations in the ontological structures associated with lexical verbs. One of these is a relation of *actual controller*. This relation is defined for basic voice systems as for inverse systems; see (2a, b) above. Given the characterization of actual controller, it follows that a participant in the actual controller relation is invariably an element of C, the *controller-set* (defined above).

It is assumed that the grammaticization of the actual controller relation takes place in such a way that, in any single predication, there can be just one controller. Thus a situation in which Max agitates Maxine may, in principle, be grammaticized with either Max or Maxine assigned a controller status, but not both simultaneously. (Clearly this point applies not just to basic voice systems, but also to the earlier-discussed inverse systems as well.)

In addition, we define a second two-place relation of *affected entity* as follows. This relation holds between an s and a participant p in s provided the following conditions are met:

(4) a. The set P is not a null set (i.e., the situation is in principle controllable); and
   b. the principal effects of s accrue to p.

The affected entity relation is obviously very critical in the formal account of basic voice systems. For this reason, a few illustrations are useful at this point.

First, consider a predication *Max agitated Maxine*. Here condition (4a) holds, because the action is in principle controllable. Also, *Maxine* fulfills condition (4b). Accordingly, the participant role corresponding to *Maxine* is assigned the relation of affected entity. In the same way, affected entity status accrues to *Maxine* in *Maxine suffered/arose/pondered/spoke*, since again condition (4a) holds – the action is controllable – and the affected entity remains *Maxine*.

In *Max bent the bow*, the participant role corresponding to *the bow* is assigned the relation of affected entity. This occurs because condition (4a) is fulfilled – the action is in principle controllable – and because condition (4b) applies to *the bow*, which represents the participant role that sustains the principal effects. In the corresponding neuter *The bow broke*, again, condition (4a) is met because the situation is controllable in principle. That is, the set P of potential controllers in S is not null (bearing in mind that the S of the neuter predicate is equivalent to the S of the corresponding transitive, as asserted above). The affected entity relation accrues to the participant role of *the bow* in this instance.

On the other hand, no affected entity relation occurs in an instance such as *The door creaked*. The reason is that the verb, which is not neuter, relates to a situation-set S in which there is a null set P of potential controllers. Correspondingly, the action is non-controllable in principle, i.e. condition (a) is not met, so there can be no affected entity.

With this theoretical groundwork, we can now consider what conditions apply in the assignment of voice categories, active and middle, in a basic type system. Here no attempt is made to account for all logically conceivable variations. But two possibilities that seem worth considering are stated in (5a, b).

(5) a. Assign middle marking just when the status of subject in the predicate's *logical structure* coincides with a nominal position representing the relation of *affected entity*; active otherwise.
 b. Assign middle marking just when the *thematically superior core theta-role* assigned by a *basic* predicate coincides with a nominal position representing the relation of *affected entity*; or when the basic predicate's thematically superior theta-role is not assigned as a core syntactic relation; active otherwise.

Although the a- and b-statements in (5) may appear similar, they have different implications. To the extent that the distribution of voices in a given basic voice system is not idiosyncratic but follows some principle, (5a, b) each accounts for a somewhat different pattern of voice assignment. We will consider each in turn.

Statement (5a) approximately describes the distribution of active and middle voices in one of the basic voice systems discussed in Chapter 2, Tamil. The wording of (5a) takes account of the fact that affected entity status devolves upon some nominal position that a verb assigns, not upon its referent. This is another way of saying that in Tamil, a participant role is individuated to an argument position, not to the referent thereof. The accuracy of this for Tamil has already been noted in Section 2.2. As observed there, in Tamil the middle (Weak) voice is never assigned in case subject and nonsubject arguments in a predication coincide referentially (see again Chapter 2, examples 37–40).

Moreover, (5a) is consistent with another significant fact about Tamil voice (also discussed above in Section 2.2). This is the fact that passive variants of basic or nonpassive predications generally preserve the latter's active or middle (i.e., Strong or Weak) voice assignment. Consistent with this, (5a) refers to logical, as contrasted with relational, subject.

On the other hand, statement (5b) more nearly characterizes the sort of basic voice system found in classical Indo-European. It will be recalled from Section 2.3 that, in a language like Sanskrit, the activeness or passiveness of a lexical structure is a factor in basic voice assignment. The thematic relation which an active verb assigns as its superior core theta-role does not comprise a core nominal in a corresponding passive. The latter invariably inflects in the middle, not the active. (5b) takes account of this by stipulating middle voice assignment when the logically superior theta-role of a lexical predicate is morphosyntactically downgraded or suppressed, i.e. by passivization.

Statement (5b) also accounts for middle voice assignment in nonpassives. In so doing, it invokes the theta-hierarchy* alluded to earlier. It has already been mentioned that the theta-hierarchy can be construed as a scale of potentiality of agency, i.e. a measure of the likelihood that a participant p in some situation s (where s relates to a use of a particular lexical verb in a predication) will fulfill the relation of *actual controller* that has been defined earlier.

This suggests a basis for resolving a problem noted earlier (Section 2.2) and reintroduced later (Section 3.6), the problem of how affectedness and control are related or in what sense they are interdefinable as ontological statuses. Clearly, the affected entity relation is not definitionally equivalent to controller. However, in basic voice systems, affected entity is grammaticized in such a way that middle voice encodes its assignment just when it devolves upon the thematic status of a predication that has the greatest potentiality of fulfilling the *actual controller* relation, the thematically superior theta-role. As this implies, a basic voice system, like other voice systems, recurs to a hierarchically superior nominal status, that of thematically superior argument; the voice marking encodes this nominal's role as the maximal potential controlling role in the s, the affected entity.

This ties in with the middle's affinity as an inherent* voice (i.e. a voice specific to nonalternating or *media tantum* predicates) for predicates having a deponent* (control-presupposing), as contrasted with a nondeponent, semantics (a tendency earlier discussed in Chapter 2). It may now be observed that the invariant middleness of deponents can be construed, plausibly, as reflecting grammaticization of the principle that affected entity correlates with the scale embodied by the theta-hierarchy, i.e. a scale of grammaticized potentiality of control. In this way is suggested and proposed a principled basis for asserting that control, an ontological construct, plays a significant role in the organization of basic voice systems.

Now let us summarize the material covered in the present study. In Chapter 1, we have identified the scope of voice phenomena by proposing a nonrigorous typology of voice behaviors organized into three broad classes: derived, basic and pragmatic (with the latter subcategorized into two sets – inverse systems, and information-salience or focus systems). In the subsequent four chapters, we have proceeded to survey some systems of each class, identifying a number of their salient and recurrent characteristics. The present chapter does not purport to have formulated a theory of voice, but merely to have mentioned some directions that might be pursued in the future to this end. The author hopes that, for all its tentativeness, the present study might provide a fruitful basis for an enhanced understanding of an intriguing grammatical category whose nature has long seemed obscure.

Notes

1 The study of voice

1 The reader may consult a separate work (Klaiman in preparation) on the treatment of voice in several current grammatical models.
2 A homophonous sense of the term voice relates to articulatory properties of speech sounds. In fact, the two senses of the term are historically connected (see Lyons 1968: 372). Throughout the present work, the term voice is invoked only as a designation for a grammatical category, not in reference to speech sounds or acoustics.
3 Some writers (e.g. Benveniste 1971a) continue to use the term diathesis today, although usually not strictly in reference to the morphological manifestations of voice, but rather with reference to possibilities for different syntactic arrangements involving a given predicate and a set of arguments. By contrast, some current writers (e.g. Tesnière 1959: 242ff.) think of voice more in terms of processes for reorganizing the content of syntactic positions in the sentence. See the discussion of diathesis* in the main text below, Section 2.1.
4 This tradition persists, explicitly or implicitly, in some recent works. For instance, the following definition presents this view explicitly: "Voice is an overt grammatical category basically pertaining to transitive verbs. The function of voice is to indicate the relationship the verb has with its arguments" (Dayley 1981: 11). The same viewpoint is sometimes implicitly expressed when voice alternations are associated with a verb's relationships with two arguments, as in the following definition from a linguistics dictionary: "A **category** used in the **grammatical** description of **sentence** or **clause** structure, primarily with reference to **verbs**, to express the way sentences may alter the relationship between the **subject** and **object** of a verb" (Crystal 1980: 378, s.v. *voice$_2$*; emphasis in original).
5 A formalism for specifying alternate voice forms of sentences is included in the case grammar model of Fillmore 1968. This model has contributed to the development of current grammatical theory by influencing syntacticians to consider the place in grammatical organization of semantic roles* (which Fillmore refers to as cases). However, the idea that the semantic roles of nominals have relevance for syntax does not originate with Fillmorean case grammar (as its author acknowledges). Rather, it has considerable antiquity

outside the Western grammatical tradition, notably in Sanskrit grammar (see Cardona 1974).

6 In recent literature, terms for voices which signal A-omission are various; they include "middle," "mediopassive" (Grady 1965), and "patient–subject constructions" (van Oosten 1977). Similarly, there are a variety of terms for voices involving P-omission, including "medioagentive" (Jacobsen 1985: 183), "antipassive" (Heath 1976: 203) and "agentive" (Smith-Stark 1978). One of the goals of the present work is to inject some clarity into what is currently an area of confusion, although not by trying purely to standardize nomenclature related to voice, but by exploring its typology.

7 In English, there is a contrast between instances such as (5b), *Baseballs are thrown*, and instances such as *Baseballs throw smoothly*. In the former, the P can be characterized as assuming some relation basic to A, thereby entailing a "disruption" in basic verb–nominal relations. This type is a rearrangement marked voice. The latter type of construction, on the other hand, involves the obligatory suppression of A; note the ungrammaticality of **Baseballs throw smoothly by Babe Ruth* or (as a counterpart to 3b) **Se rompió la ventana por ellos*. However, suppression of A does not adequately distinguish the omission from the rearrangement type of marked voice in all languages, since many languages have rearrangement marked voices of the type shown in (5b), but without the option which English has of expression A overtly. English constructions of the type *Baseballs throw smoothly* are not only stylistically marked but also lexically restricted; only certain basically transitive verbs occur in such constructions. They are discussed by some writers under the rubric of middle verbs*, although traditionally, the same verbs have the designation neuters*. (See Klaiman 1991a.)

8 In the main text, the usage of the terms "normal" and "disruption" follows that of Smith-Stark 1978: 184, fn. 4: "voice categories are used to mark the alteration of the *normal* relations between a verb and its arguments" (emphasis in original); also Dayley 1981: 11: "A *change in voice* involves a disruption of the basic transitive relationship, along with overt morphological or syntactic marking of such a change" (emphasis in original).

9 Although it is not covered in the above discussion, a fully complete scheme would include the antipassive*, which could be represented as a rearrangement marked voice of the format $Vt \sim A$ *(oblique P)*. The antipassive is further discussed in the main text, in Section 1.4 and in Chapters 3 (ns. 7, 8) and 5.

10 It is doubtful that one argument can assume the semantic role basic to another: "We know of no clear cases in which derived subjects become, e.g. agents" (Keenan 1976a: 324) (and see Johnson 1977a: 681). Likewise, it is hard to imagine a voice alternation whereby a nominal which is not a basic A (transitive subject) can assume that status – particularly since, as the main text, Section 1.1 notes, rearrangement marked voices usually entail valence reduction.

11 Through the balance of the present chapter, terms such as Subject, Object, etc. have upper case initials when referring to grammatical relations. This is

done to distinguish grammatical relations from other conceptions of subject, object and so forth (such as logical subject and object).

12 Because the idea of universalness is all too often problematic (see e.g. Dryer 1982, responding to O'Grady 1980), it is worth emphasizing that the "universal" in the term universal grammar does not imply statistical predominance nor recurrence in all languages. Rather, it is based on the observation that some grammatical behaviors are selected over logically conceivable alternative behaviors under particular conditions. When a particular behavior is favored, in this sense, over any other behavior which might qualify as a logical alternative choice, it may be considered universal as discussed by DeLancey 1981: 629–30: "while they do not occur in all languages, only these patterns occur in any language." Universal grammar concerns the description and explication of grammatical phenomena which are universal in this way. As a research program, its study does not presuppose any particular model of grammatical description nor any specific formal theory, although individual grammatical theories and descriptive models often claim to be better suited than others to the goals of universal grammar.

13 The relational hypothesis (as contrasted with relational grammar proper) has more proponents than would be feasible to list here. However, representative works include Keenan 1975, Comrie 1976, Keenan & Comrie 1977, Johnson 1977b, Frantz 1979 and Postal 1986. On relational grammar proper, the following sources may be consulted: Johnson 1979 (an accessible, if dated, introduction); Perlmutter 1980 (a concise overview); Johnson & Postal 1980 (a detailed outline of a variety of relational grammar called arc pair grammar); Blake 1990. In addition, essays in the relational formalism are collected in Perlmutter 1983, Perlmutter & Rosen 1984, and in Postal & Joseph. Also, there is a detailed bibliography of relational grammar in Dubinsky & Rosen 1987.

14 According to Allen, Frantz & Gardiner 1981: 6 and Allen, Gardiner & Frantz 1984: 303, n. 20, in an instance such as (7b), the verbal prefix actually references three arguments. It does so in accord with a general fact of Southern Tiwa agreement that any transitive verb must be marked for agreement with the basic Object, regardless of what relation the corresponding nominal may assume in the clause or sentence as a result of role-remapping rules. This peculiarity of Southern Tiwa agreement is indicated in the gloss to (7b), following the practice of the above-cited authors, by a colon before the agreement feature for the basic Indirect Object, as contrasted with a slash before the agreement feature for the basic Object. (See the following note.)

15 Although it assumes grammatical relations, the role-remapping account of voice which has been outlined in the main text differs from the treatment of voice rules in standard relational grammar. In particular, many conventions of the relational formalism have been overlooked. A few of the discrepancies may be mentioned here. The statuses termed Subject, Object and Indirect Object in the main text respectively correspond to relational gram-

mar R-signs 1, 2 and 3. The operations schematized in Figure 1.4 (ii)–(iv) correspond respectively to the relational rules of 2-1 Advancement; 3-2 Advancement (roughly coterminous with what earlier transformational grammars term "dative movement"); and Oblique-1 Advancement (the particular variety illustrated in the main text corresponds to relational grammar's Locative-1 Advancement). In a relational grammar analysis, these rules would be illustrated in a standard notational format (relational network) such as a stratal diagram; Figure 1.4 instead relies on an *ad hoc* notation. Also, the notation in Figure 1.4, unlike that of relational grammar, fails to reveal what status accrues to an argument whose basic grammatical relation has been assumed by some other argument (such as the basic Subject in ii and iv and the basic Object in iii). Relational grammar assigns to such a nominal a relation called chômeur. Accordingly, in the glosses to the Southern Tiwa examples (6)–(8) of the main text, slash precedes the referential features of chômeurs, while colon precedes those of nonchômeurs (see the preceding note).

16 An objection may be raised at this juncture by the grammarian who prefers to take a broader view of voice, seeing the category as embracing all rules or operations which affect the valence with which a verb is lexically associated, not just those alterations which involve the content of the subject position. Proponents of this school would include in the category of voice certain rules or processes which are not allowed for under the definition of voice in the main text above, such as rules for forming morphological causatives and other kinds of applicative* constructions (which are described in the main text below, Section 2.1). Although in principle there is no barrier to defining the category in the way just suggested, the present work will take a narrower view by not including applicatives under the rubric of voice. (I am nevertheless grateful to B. Comrie for some thought-provoking discussions of this issue.)

17 To be sure, not all nominals assigned to the grammatical relation Subject in basic structures are Agents. Also, not all nominals linked to the role Agent are necessarily agentive (in the sense discussed by Cruse 1973) in the same manner or degree. For instance, *the man* has different semantic roles in *The man inherited the money* and *The man tore up the money*, although it may be considered an Agent in each. In both of these examples the same holds of the patientiveness of *the money*. On the problem of specifying the content of semantic roles, see the main text below, Section 1.5.

18 The Classical Sanskrit passive of the present tense conjugation is an instance in point. Its characteristic is the stem formant *-ya* added to verbal bases. This passive, illustrated below in (ib) (compare the corresponding active ia), always inflects in the middle, never the active. Observe that, in the active, the basic or logical subject occurs in the nominative case and governs verbal concord (ia); while in the corresponding passive (ib), the basic or logical object has the morphological properties associated with the subject, and the latter, if expressed, appears in the instrumental case.

(i) a. Devadattaḥ   kaṭam   karoti
    Devadatta-NOM mat-ACC makes-3SG **ACTIVE**
    'Devadatta makes a mat' (= main text 12a)
  b. Kaṭo   Devadattena   kri -ya -te
    mat-NOM Devadatta-INST make -ya 3SG **MIDDLE**
    'A mat is made by Devadatta'

Although it may appear that passive alters the content of the grammatical relation Subject, in actuality, such a status is not crucial to many syntactic processes in the language. For instance, consider the finite conjunct expression (iia) and a corresponding complex construction, called a serial verb or gerundial expression, in (iib):

(ii) a. (Sā)   pāṇāv   ādatte tato sā   mām   karṣati
    (she-NOM) hand-LOC takes then she-NOM me-ACC drags
    'She takes (my) hand and then she drags me'
  b. Pāṇāv   ādāya   sā mām   karṣati
    hand-LOC having-taken she me-ACC drags
    'Having taken (my) hand she drags me'

In Sanskrit traditional grammar, the construction illustrated in (iib) is said to be sanctioned when two or more syntactically linked clauses share an argument. This argument must have the grammatical status *kartṛ*, a term which most Western interpreters translate as 'agent.' In (iia, b) the *kartṛ* is *sā* 'she.' In both examples, this nominal has the usual subject properties (nominative case and government of verb agreement).

Both juncts in (iib) are active. However, it is possible to passivize one junct, as shown below in (iii). But note that passivization has no effect on the clause-adjoining rule. Each junct must have the same *kartṛ* regardless of its active or passive form. In (iii), passivization of the second junct does not alter the antecedence of the argument "she." The first person argument (logical object) does not acquire that status, although as a result of passivization it does acquire the usual subject morphological properties. Example (iii) means just the same as (iib), 'She takes (my) hand and drags me,' not 'Taking (her) hand, I am dragged by her' (= 'I take her hand and she drags me').

(iii) Pāṇāv   ādāya   kṛṣ -ya -māṇas
    hand-LOC having-taken drag -ya present PTCPL SG MASC
    tayā   'ham
    by her-INST I-NOM

Most Classical Sanskrit rules of interclausal syntax are like the rule illustrated in (iib) and (iii), whose operation is unaffected by passivization. This is to say that most Sanskrit syntactic processes are sensitive to roles such as Agent, but not sensitive to grammatical relations such as Subject (see Klaiman 1987a and references therein for further discussion). Consistent with this, as Cardona 1976: 1 mentions, ancient Sanskrit grammarians speak of nothing on the order of the modern notion Subject, in the sense of a syntactic status which can be mapped and remapped over various semantic roles. (Concerning the *kāraka* or nominal statuses to which traditional Sanskrit grammars ascribe a major role in the morphosyntax, see Cardona 1974, Hook 1976.)

To be sure, one can analyze the Sanskrit alternation of unmarked vs *-ya*- marked verbal stems as a manifestation of role-remapping voice by treating the nominal position which receives nominative case and controls verbal agreement as Subject. The point of the present discussion is, however, that the relevance of such a relation Subject to the illustrated clause-adjoining rule and to other rules is limited. In general, grammatical relations such as Subject are not prominent in the organization of the syntax in this language.

19 "R" in glosses to (21)–(23) can be associated with either of two functions which Arnott 1970 attributes to distinct extensions, the Reflexive and the Retaliative. The former usually applies to verbs denoting "actions which it is unusual for a Fulani to perform on himself" (p. 342), such as "shave" (example 21) and "dress hair" (example 22). The Retaliative extension applies to verbs denoting actions done by different parties in turn, e.g. *Baaba foodʼa ŋgo, kaaŋgaadʼo foodʼ-t-oo ŋgo* 'The father pulls it, and the madman pulls it in turn' (p. 343). In the main text, Arnott's Reflexive and Retaliative extensions are treated as one morpheme (glossed "R"), since both have the same shape. It may be noted that there is a formally distinct Reciprocal extension (Arnott, pp. 357–9) denoting actions in which two parties participate with mutual effect; or actions in which more than one participant is acted on with mutual effect (e.g. "join (things) together," "mix (things) up"). According to Arnott, only active inflections accrue to the Reciprocal extension, except in instances of the second (mutual effect) type where active and passive inflections may alternate. For further discussion of Fula extensions (including their relationship to the morphosyntax of applicative* constructions), see below, Section 2.1.

20 Theta-role hierarchies (or the equivalent) have been proposed by Gruber 1965 and Fillmore 1968 (as part of a case grammar model which conflates theta-roles with the notion of case*), by Jackendoff 1972, and by Foley & Van Valin 1984, *inter alia*. Kiparsky 1987 assumes a theta-role hierarchy which lists, in descending order, a set of "actant roles" (including Cause, Means, Goal); the Theme role; and "path roles" (including From, Via and To). In addition, the theory posits two features, [Affected] and [Volitional], with which theta-roles interact. Specifically, it is claimed that, in the grammaticization of logical structures, theta-roles can accrue to argument positions, fusing with one or both of these features, or with each other. (See also Comrie 1981b: 51ff.)

2 Middle voice and basic voice systems

1 In connection with this, Lyons 1968: 373 comments on the relations of the Indo-European middle and passive as follows: "the opposition of voice in

Greek is primarily one of active *v.* middle. The passive was a later development (as it was in all the Indo-European languages)." Other Indo-Europeanists, however, do not concur. Thus Kuryłowicz 1964: 74, 76 states that the active/passive alternation has historical primacy in Indo-European over the active/middle. He avers that "The term *mediopassive*, used with reference to the I.E. category in question, implies a secondary *middle* function besides the primary passive one . . . the true middle is only a semantic variety of the active voice" (emphasis in the original). For more on active, middle and passive in Indo-European see the main text below, Section 2.3.

2 Kuryłowicz, however, emphatically dissociates himself from this view: "To look for an underlying *reflexive* (hence also *reciprocal*) value of the I.E. middle is to depend on its translation into English, German, and so on" (1964: 74; emphasis in original).

3 The infinitive ending *-de* in (3a, b) is distinctive to the Fuuta Tooro dialect since, in Gombe, the corresponding element is *-ki*.

4 Extensions vary somewhat from dialect to dialect. Only extensions common both to Gombe and to Fuuta Tooro Fula are discussed in the main text below. The same extensions, incidentally, happen to be shared by Adamawa Fula, a dialect spoken in parts of Nigeria and Cameroon (Stennes 1967: 132–5).

5 Applicatives are a feature that Fula shares with many Bantu languages outside the Niger-Congo group, such as Chi-Mwi:ni, described by Kisseberth & Abasheikh 1977, Marantz 1982a: 12, 1982b: 331; Kinyarwanda, described by Kimenyi 1980; and other Bantu languages, discussed e.g. by Hyman & Duranti 1982. Applied constructions also occur in Uto-Aztecan (see Comrie 1982 on Huichol); Bahasa Indonesia (Chung 1976); Niuean, a Polynesian language (Seiter 1979); and in some of Fula's sister languages in the West Atlantic subgroup of Niger-Congo, e.g. Wolof (Njie 1982: 196–200) and hu-Limba (Berry 1960).

6 In the present discussion, biclausality refers only to the overt occurrence of two predicates within one construction. On the question of the underlying monoclausality or biclausality of morphological causative constructions in languages generally, see Davies & Rosen 1988.

7 From available sources it is not clear to what extent a simple radical's voice potential can be increased by the cooccurrence of more than one applicative extension. Arnott 1970: 27 notes that it is rare, but possible, for as many as three non-prepositionally-marked object nominals to follow a radical which has been extended by two or more extensions, as in (i). He does not comment on the voice potential of such a form.

(i) 'o maɓɓ -it -ir -an -ii
he close Reversive Modal DAT General Past **ACTIVE**
Bello yolnde hakkiilo
Bello door care
'He opened (unclosed) the door with care for Bello'

8 The Fula causative differs from the other applicatives discussed in that a

nonsimple radical derived by this extension takes only active primary voice. Radicals derived by other applicatives can occur in nonactive primary voices, as shown in (ia, b) (from Arnott 1970: 354) and (iia, b) (from Arnott 1970: 349).

(i) a. 6e   'umm -ake
       they rise   General Past **MIDDLE**
       'They rose up'
   b. 6e   'umm -an -ake   habre
       they rise   DAT General Past **MIDDLE** fight
       'They rose up for a fight'
(ii) a. 'o joodˊ -ake
        he sit   General Past **MIDDLE**
        'He sat down'
     b. 'o joodˊ -or -ake   hakkiilo
         he sit   Modal General Past **MIDDLE** care
         'He sat down with care (carefully)'

Although a causative extended radical invariably has active primary voice, the causative extension may accrue to simple radicals whose primary voice is nonactive. Thus a counterpart to the periphrastic causative (7b) of the main text is the morphological causative *Mi darnii aali* 'I stopped Ali.' Though this example is active, the corresponding simple radical "stop," illustrated in (7a) of the main text, takes middle primary voice.

An important difference between the causative and the other applicative extensions illustrated in the main text is that only one passive is derivable from a causative extended radical. Professor Arnott (personal communication) provides the illustrations *Puccu yarii ndiyam* 'The horse drank water,' *'o yarnii puccu ndiyam* 'He gave water for drinking to the horse,' *Puccu yarnaama ndiyam* 'The horse was given water to drink,' but **Ndiyam yarnaama puccu* 'The water was given to the horse for drinking.'

9 The radical *kirs-/hirs-* 'slaughter' is one of a large number of Fula radicals which vary their shapes according to the number (singular or plural) of the grammatical subject (Arnott 1970: 204). Thus, compare (9b) with (9a) and (9c). Other such radicals include *hokk-/ndokk-* 'give' in (25a, b) and *yerd-/ŋgerd-* 'trust' in (26a, b).
10 Interestingly, adding *wudere* 'cloth' to the end of this expression results in ungrammaticality (Professor Arnott, personal communication).
11 Arnott 1956: 141, 1970: 259 furnishes some examples as follows, where *-a* is an active nonfinite stem element and *-o* is a corresponding middle element:

wel -a	'be pleasant, sweet'	wel -o	'please'
mett -a	'be unpleasant'	mett -o	'displease'
endˊ -a	'be kind'	endˊ -o	'be kind to'
wodˊdˊ -a	'be distant'	wodˊdˊ -o	'go far from'

12 P or invariantly passive-inflecting simple radicals comprise a defective class having only a few members – interestingly enough, "all referring to a physi-

cal or mental abnormality, or to strong desire" (Arnott 1970: 412). Examples gleaned from Arnott (personal communication), Arnott 1956, 1970 and Sylla 1979, 1982 amount to the following: *hooý-/weel-* 'be hungry'; *faat-* 'be foolish'; *suun-* 'be covetous'; *yoom-* 'hanker, long (for)'; *yinn-* 'be mad'; *baarr-* 'be impotent'; *haang-* 'be crazed'. However, these may not all reliably be one-voice radicals. Professor Arnott (personal communication) advises that, with the exception of the last radical listed, he has come across instances of each of these (albeit rare; some only in dictionaries) in which the radical is inflected nonpassively.

13 It may be noted, as an interesting aside, that the two semantic groupings of A verbs described in the main text criss-cross the unaccusative/unergative* distinction posited by Perlmutter 1978: 162. According to Perlmutter, adjectival verbs (the first group of A verbs discussed in the main text) are unaccusative, while *Schallwörter*, or verbs expressing natural cries (the second discussed group), are unergative. However, not all writers concur. For instance, Harris 1981 treats the latter verbal class as unaccusative, in contrast to verbs expressing volitional acts of sounding (as in making music or articulate speech), which she classes as unergative. For more on unaccusativity, see Section 3.2.1 in the main text.

14 This recalls the well-known association of English middle* verbs with noneventual semantics: while such a form, expressing a nonpunctual temporal sense, is grammatical, e.g. *The floor waxed well*, compare the following form with a punctual sense, which is ungrammatical: **The floor waxed once/twice/yesterday/when I waxed it*. In other languages, too, the middle may have an affinity with noneventuality or with nonpunctual aspect. For instance, it is well known that the stative use of the perfect aspect in archaic Greek often correlates with middle inflections. To illustrate, the perfect of the verb *persuade* in Homer means "believe" and is inflected in the middle (B. Comrie, personal communication). For further discussion see the main text below, Section 2.3. Also, on the relationship between transitivity* and telic/atelic* temporal meaning, see Hopper & Thompson 1980.

15 In the Fuuta Tooro dialect the form of the Reciprocal extension is *-ondir*. Gombe has two corresponding forms, *-indir* and *-ootir*, illustrated respectively in (25b) and (26b) of the main text. According to Arnott 1970: 359, they are distinguished chiefly in that the latter is more often added to simple radicals which have middle primary voice. (See also Chapter 1 of the main text, n. 19.)

16 This is the middle imperative termination in Fuuta Tooro. For the Gombe Fula counterpart see Figure 2.1.

17 Apart from the instance in (19b) of the main text, Arnott 1956: 137 cites the following radicals associated with this unextended middle function: *yiiw-* 'bathe,' *liir-* 'dry in the sun,' *lall-* 'rinse,' *sulm-* 'wash the face,' *fin-* 'apply antimony to,' *meet-* 'put a turban on,' *ɓorn-* 'dress,' *wif-* 'fan,' *ɗabb-* 'put fomentation on,' and other verbs of grooming or dressing (roughly equivalent to the class Haiman 1983: 803 terms "introverted" verbs).

18 Geniušienė 1987: 126, however, assumes that this type does represent a

structural reflexive. She posits a diathesis containing an indirect object which coincides in reference with the other core argument, the subject. (This analysis recalls Barber's 1975 analysis of Greek middle voice functions discussed above in Section 1.3.) The present work does not follow this analysis, however, since it seems implausible for Fula. This is due to the fact that the radical which illustrates the relevant function in (20b), res-, has no potential for assigning an indirect object. This radical is not trivalent, but bivalent (Professor Arnott, personal communication). Accordingly it is assumed that, whatever may be the correct diathesis representation of the middle voice type in (20b), it is not a structural reflexive.

19 According to Paramasivam 1979: 75, n. 3, a count of verbs beginning with [a] in one Tamil lexicon reveals that some 58.6 per cent alternate for both categories. The remainder are invariantly Weak or invariantly Strong.

20 Numbers in parentheses after examples in the present section refer to page numbers in the published version of Paramasivam's thesis (Paramasivam 1979). Tamil examples which bear no indication of source are from the present author's own data, elicited from informants.

21 In this section and the following, the terms differential* and inherent* do not (as in the preceding section on Fula) refer to functions of primary vs non-primary voices of verbs, but have a slightly different sense. Below, the term inherent refers to the functions a voice expresses as an invariant voice, i.e. a voice of active-only inflecting or of middle-only inflecting verbs. Correspondingly, the term differential refers below to the functions a voice expresses when it accrues to verbs which inflect in more than one basic voice.

22 Except (39) and (40a), all these examples contain the auxiliary verb *koḷ* 'take.' Some Tamil grammarians refer to this as a reflexive verb, although Kemmer 1988: 278ff. (a work which concerns extended functions of reflexive morphemes in both their synchronic and diachronic characteristics) classes this verb (or rather, its reflex in another, closely related Dravidian language) as a "middle marker." But as noted in the main text, none of the examples in the present discussion inflects in the Weak (middle) voice.

23 This subclass is reminiscent of certain intransitive verbs termed "ingestive" in studies of modern Indo-Aryan languages (see Klaiman 1982c and references therein). It should be noted that several Tamil verbs which seem semantically consistent with this class unaccountably turn out to be invariant Strong verbs; e.g. *mō* 'smell (TR),' *kuṭi* 'drink, inhale,' and *pār* 'see.'

24 However, according to Smyth 1974: 195, active terminations do occur on passive stems in Greek aorists. According to Burrow 1973: 354, active terminations also sometimes accrue to passive stems in Iranian (Avestan and Old Persian). Moreover, occasional instances of this sort in Sanskrit are noted by Whitney 1973: 277, para. 774.

25 Speijer 1973: 239 notes that in many Sanskrit verbs where reciprocity is denoted, the preverb *vyati-*, illustrated in (55), occurs.

26 According to Smyth 1974: 375, the preverb *dia-* in (56) (related to a preposition meaning "through") is "common in the reciprocal middle." It seems parallel to the Sanskrit preverb *vyati* - (preceding note).

Notes to Chapter 2

27 The specific rules of the Sanskrit grammar for which commentaries furnish the a- and b-examples in (58) and (59) are respectively I.iii.20 *aṅo donāsya viharaṇe*, I.iii.36 *sammānanotsañcanācāryakaraṇajñānabhṛtiviganavyayeṣu niyaḥ*, I. iii.18 *parivyavebhyaḥ kriyaḥ* and I.iii.37 *kartṛsthe cāśarīre karmaṇi*.

28 According to Geniušienė 1987: 257, the middle form in (60b) can be alternatively expressed by the active verb in collocation with a reflexive clitic (*me dirumpo*). This active–reflexive construction, she states, has historically replaced the middle in Romance. The construction in question is a probable source of the neo-middle constructions alluded to in the main text, illustrated in (52a–c).

29 The passive function of -*ya* may originate in its earlier function as a marker of telic neuter intransitive verbs. The forms in (66b, i–vi) all belong to one of ten traditionally recognized conjugational classes of Sanskrit roots, Class Four. The characteristic of this class is the formation of the present stem in unaccented -*ya*: "The fourth class contains some 130 roots which form their present by means of the suffix *ya*: e.g. *kupyati* 'is angry,' *krudhyati* 'id.,' *tuṣyati* 'is pleased,' *yudhyati* 'fights,' *vidhyati* 'pierces' . . . *dīvyati* 'plays,' *hṛṣyati* 'rejoices,' *tapyate* 'is hot,' *paśyati* 'sees,' *nahyati* 'ties' " (Burrow 1973: 330). In the earliest Sanskrit, the formal passive in -*ya* was accented, and therefore was distinguished from the unaccented -*ya* characteristic of Class Four verbs. But in the period between Vedic (the earliest stage of Sanskrit) and the Classical language, distinctive accentuation was largely lost, resulting in a number of Class Four middles being readily reinterpreted as formal passives. In this connection, note that in the list of verbs just cited, two (*paś*- 'see' and *nah*- 'tie') are basically transitive but become intransitive in the middle: *paśyate* 'is seen' and *nahyate* 'is tied.' Thus in the middle inflection, the meaning of these verbs is passive. See Burrow for more on the historical development of the formal passive in Sanskrit (and on the development of the formal passive in Greek, see Smyth 1974: 218–19).

One further fact is worth noting in connection with (66b, i–vi). According to Rosen 1984: 56, both neuter intransitives in -*ya* as well as Sanskrit -*ya* passives are initially unaccusative, having an initial Object but no initial Subject in their structural representations. The formant -*ya* occurs, in Rosen's view, "as a marker of 2-1 Advancement." However, since many Sanskrit middles without -*ya* (such as those in 63b, i–iii) are also neuter, and since, in general, Sanskrit -*ya*-marked forms inflect in the middle, it would seem apt to identify the marker of the putative 2-1 Advancement as the middle category, rather than as -*ya*. At all events, treating -*ya* as a marker of unaccusativity is implausible (*pace* Rosen), since the same marker is characteristic of all Class Four verbs, including some which are basically transitive (e.g. the verbs "see" and "tie" just discussed).

30 In the next sentence, Wheelock adds, "In origin these were probably reflexive verbs," thereby echoing Bopp's theory (discussed earlier in the present section) that the r element is historically a reflexive marker.

31 Schwyzer 1950: 225 notes that most verbs of the *activa tantum* class in Greek do, in fact, accept middle terminations in the future tense. This recalls the

behavior of Fula A(M)P radicals, verbs which inflect in the middle only in noneventual temporomodal categories (see again Section 2.1).

32 Some roots alternately inflect in Class Four as well as in some other conjugational class. A few of these roots vary for voice inflection according to class; they take active inflections as Class Four verbs and middle inflections otherwise. Examples include *vriḍate* (Class One middle) / *vridyati* (Class Four active) 'is ashamed, is bashful, feels modest' and *svedate* (Class One middle) / *svidyati* (Class Four active) 'sweats, perspires.'

33 The semantic reflexive function accrues to every reflexive form in Geniušienė's survey. The sole exceptions are constructions with a characteristic -*s* in two modern Northern Germanic languages, Swedish and Norwegian (the former is illustrated in the main text, examples 52a–c). Although in theory, this -*s* historically derives from a reflexive, Geniušienė observes (pp. 345, 347) that constructions in which it occurs do not express the semantic reflexive function. Rather, in just these languages, the semantic reflexive is expressed by a distinct construction.

34 One way of conceptualizing this type is to think of active–stative systems as grammaticizing the lexical distinction of *unaccusative** vs *unergative** verbs. This and alternative views of active–stative typology are considered in Section 3.2.2.

3 Control and voice

1 The term agent* as used in this chapter obviously differs from the same term's designation of a particular semantic role (see Chapter 1, Figure 1.5). Also, agent in the present chapter's usage is not exactly the same as the notion "actor," which is invoked as a counterpart to "undergoer" in one current grammatical theory, role and reference grammar. Actor in role and reference grammar is "the argument of a predicate which expresses the participant which performs, effects, instigates, or controls the situation denoted by the predicate." This contrasts with undergoer, "the argument which expresses the participant which does not perform, initiate, or control any situation but rather is affected by it in some way" (Foley & Van Valin 1984: 29). In role and reference grammar, logical subjects of non-control predicates are generally classified as actors, e.g. *the sun* in *The sun emits radiation*. However, under the control scheme proposed in this chapter, such an argument is neither an agent nor an undergoer, but is simply the logical subject of a non-control (nonaction) predicate.

2 In the words of Thalberg 1972: 49, "various forms of inactivity rank as deeds. If an energetic businessman relaxes from his normal routine, and sits motionless in his easy chair all the afternoon, has he not done something? At any rate, we would not dismiss his inactivity as something that befell him. On the other side, people to whom things are happening are not always passive. The victim of a robbery might struggle vigorously with the hold-up man."

3 The distinction between outcome and agenda control seems particularly relevant to the well-known experiments on obedience to authority carried

out by Stanley Milgram at Yale University (Milgram 1974). Unwitting subjects of these experiments were asked to deliver shocks to perceived victims. The shocks were bogus but were believed by the experimental subjects to be real. The subjects evidently perceived the locus of agenda control to be external, since they reported feeling obligated to comply with instructions to deliver shocks, notwithstanding absence of threat or other compulsion. However, the locus of outcome control was evidently perceived by the subjects as internal, since they frequently asked the experimenter for reassurance about the responsibility for any potential effects of the shocks on the perceived victims.

4 In addition to these classes, Thalberg (pp. 69ff.) also recognizes several sets of "philosophically significant" (p. 71) near analogs to the predicates listed in Class Three. These near analog predicates denote success or failure in the manner of performing actions. One group includes *miss, bungle, botch, blunder, fail*; a second includes *misjudge, miscalculate, misidentify*; and there is a third group including *perfect, complete, conclude* and *succeed*. For the purposes of the present discussion, however, Thalberg's near analog predicates can be overlooked.

5 In addition, Figure 3.4 indicates an affinity between unaccusative predicate concepts and certain lexically inherent temporal senses of verbs, i.e. Aktionsart*; this is reflected in (A) (e)–(f) of the figure. In this connection, it is noteworthy that one writer, Van Valin 1987, 1990 reinterprets unaccusativity as an encoding of a verbal category opposition based on inherent temporal meaning or Aktionsart (see his work for details). Also, concerning the inherent aspectual semantics of English middle (neuter) verbs, see Fagan 1988.

6 Where both the logical subject and logical object of the corresponding basic transitive predicate are animate, then if the logical subject is suppressed, the derived objective intransitive may alternatively have either a detransitive (passive) or a reflexive reading. Thus in principle, according to Mock 1982 (1980): 21–2, an alternative gloss of (2b) is 'I buy myself.'

7 Antipassive* derived voices occur in a number of languages of the ergative* case marking type. Given that active–stative patterning has traditionally been characterized as a "split" type of ergativity (see the main text below), one might expect a derived voice in an active–stative language such as Chocho to have the characteristics of an antipassive. However, the Chocho derived voice illustrated in the main text is not an antipassive. An antipassive involves derivation from a transitive lexical predicate of an intransitive which construes with an absolutive (objectively marked) A and assigns an oblique (if not suppressed) P. In the Chocho derived voice, however, the derived intransitive is objective-inflecting – the sole core nominal indexed on the verb is P – and it assigns an oblique (if not suppressed) A. In fact, Chocho, an active language, has no antipassive; and in general, antipassive derived voices seem uncharacteristic of active–stative systems. (For more on the distinction between ergative and active behaviors, see the main text below; and for more discussion of antipassivization, see Chapter 5.)

8 As Section 5 observed in the preceding note, ergative–absolutive systems

often have anti-passive* derived voices. One function of such voices is to derive intransitives from transitive verbal bases (see Chapter 5 for exegesis and illustrations). But processes for deriving one inflecting class of intransitives from another seem more typical of active than of ergative systems. Illustrations from an active language, Acehnese, will be furnished below in the main text, Section 3.5.

9 Given the distinctness of active–stative patterning from ergative case organization, there is no reason in principle why the two cannot cooccur in one language; and Dahlstrom 1983 shows that in some instances, they do. In the systems she describes, active patterning prevails when a predicate construes with SAP (first and second person) core arguments, while the patterning elsewhere is predominantly ergative (manifesting, however, ergative/absolutive splits of the usual kinds).

10 Although the two Acehnese prefixes discussed in the main text are not markers of detransitivization *per se*, they do encode an alternation of participant roles within a basic predicate's valence. In a sense, they encode rearrangements in the kinds (if not, in all instances, the number) of arguments with which the predicate construes. For this reason, there seems to be an affinity between these elements and markers of derived voice. In connection with this, and although there is no absolute demarcation in natural languages between morphological processes of inflection and derivation (see Payne 1985), it is interesting to note that, cross-linguistically, different voice types tend to be encoded through distinct types of morphological processes. Specifically, derivational morphology seems to be a favored strategy for encoding derived voices. By contrast, as shown in Chapter 2, basic voice alternations are more typically encoded by means of inflection, i.e. by opposing paradigms of middle vs active inflectional endings.

11 Other works on control encoding in Thompson River Salish include Carlson & Thompson 1982, Thompson 1979a, 1979b and Thompson & Thompson 1981. In addition, Thompson 1985 cites a number of works on the control marking system in other Salishan languages. A few salient items in this area are Saunders & Davis 1982 and Davis & Saunders 1986, 1989 on Bella Coola; Mattina 1982 on Colville-Okanagan; and Hess 1973 on Puget Salish.

12 There are no corresponding suffixes specifically marking control and decontrol detransitive neuters, i.e. derived intransitives which assign a sole core nominal corresponding to the P of the basic (transitive) predicate, with the basic A suppressed. However, other suffixes of the control-altering class sometimes have this effect. For instance, OC forms sometimes function as neuter detransitives, as in (i) below (from Thompson, p. 420). Such a form has a decontrol reading, but a neuter detransitive with a control reading can be encoded through some other suffix. Interestingly, for this purpose the suffix which seems most often used is the reflexive, as (ii) illustrates (from Thompson, p. 412).

(i) K'ətx^w -úx^w -∅ (cf. main text, 32a, b)
    sever   OC   3 S
    'It has gotten severed (somehow)'

(ii) Qəm -e   -cút   -kt
    warm directive extension reflexive 1PL S
    'We warmed (ourselves) up'

13 Obligatory control (termed functional control in lexical–functional grammar) refers to the phenomenon of clauses manifesting suppressed or "missing" nominal positions; it is related to anaphoric control (discussed above in Section 3.4). An instance of obligatory control would be a phonetically unrealized subject whose reference is supplied by some nominal position in a containing or matrix clause. For example, ∅ in *John asked Mary ∅ to go* represents a controlled subject position. Obligatory control, to be sure, is a kind of anaphoric process. As such, this type of control is distinct from the behaviors discussed in this chapter under the rubric of the control construct. Nevertheless, it is not unfeasible that a device which figures in a formal account of an anaphoric process, e.g. obligatory control, may prove relevant to the formal account of ontological control.

4 Inverse voice systems

1 It is noteworthy that the category glossed "obviative" OBV both in verbal as well as nominal forms of (3a–f) does not comprise a case of concord marker, nor does it encode the logical relation between an argument and a predicate. Its function is explained later, Sections 4.2, 4.4.
2 Free or relatively unconstrained word order also occurs in some configurational languages, particularly those having elaborate case morphology. An instance in point is Latin, illustrated in (2) of the main text. In each example, the words could be rearranged six different ways without affecting the predication's content.

According to Jelinek 1984: 73, independent nominals in free word order languages tend to display one or more of the following characteristics: (i) they bear no grammatical relations; (ii) their case marking shows their grammatical relations; or (iii) their order reflects pragmatic factors. Both (ii) and (iii) hold in Latin and some other configurational languages. However, Jelinek claims that free word order in non-configurational languages is due to (i), an absence of independent nominal arguments. This is discussed under the rubric of the argument type parameter in the main text below.
3 As Scancarelli 1987b: 368–9 observes: "The pronominal argument languages described by Jelinek correspond roughly to those languages in which the clause-level relationships between verbs and nominals are marked on the head (the verb), rather than the dependents (the nouns), of the constituent (the clause). The lexical argument languages correspond roughly to those languages in which the clause-level relationships between verbs and nominals are marked on the dependents." In this connection, see also Dahlstrom 1986a.
4 Under the argument type parameter of Jelinek 1984, 1985, arguments in non-configurational languages consist of bound pronominals, while independent nominals are not arguments, but optional adjuncts. However,

in principle, there is no restriction on the number of optional elements per predication. Accordingly, there seems to be no reason why a non-configurational language cannot allow every clause to include as many optional independent nominals as obligatory bound pronominals.
5 Subsequent discussion will reveal that the ranking of the two leftmost statuses on hierarchy (6) is not universal. See the overview of Algonquian below, Section 4.4.
6 Some non-Algonquianists speak of obviation specifically as a nominal reference-tracking strategy, not necessarily in connection with inverse systems (see Farkas 1988b for an illustration of this usage). In an inverse system, one function of the obviative is reference-tracking (see below, Section 4.4). But in addition, the obviative of an inverse system has an important function within simple predications, signaling assignments of unequal degrees of ontological salience to third person core nominals. See the main text below, Sections 4.2, 4.4.
7 For detailed arguments against treating the Navajo voice system as active–passive, see Witherspoon 1977, 1980 and Klaiman 1988. Also, see the remainder of the present section as well as the following section in the main text.
8 Some comparable Navajo examples are cited in Elgin 1973: 172.
9 Nonmorphological or behavioral evidence might help determine whether relational subject and object have reality in Apachean grammar and, if so, whether they correlate with other, ontological and/or logical, nominal statuses. In existing literature such evidence is not, however, easy to find. Nonetheless, Sandoval 1984 offers some relevant data from Jicarilla Apache. It concerns anaphoric binding in complex constructions.

According to Sandoval (p. 185), in example (i) below, barring heavy pause between *Bill* and the adjunct phrase following it, the subject ($\emptyset$) of the adjunct is anaphorically bound by *Bill*, not by *John*. Note that in (i), the main clause verb is a *yi-* form, and the first and second nominal positions in the clause are respectively interpreted as logical subject and object.

On the other hand, where the main clause verb is a *bi-* form, as in (ii), the anaphoric binding works as follows. The first and second nominal positions in (ii) correspond, respectively, to logical object and subject. Without heavy pause following the latter (*Bill*), the adjunct's subject is interpreted, once more, as anaphorically bound by the noninitial nominal. But in (ii), in contrast to (i), this nominal, *Bill*, is the main-clause logical subject, not the logical object.

(i) John Bill $\emptyset$ łį́ naabiyégo yį́į́łtsą́
John Bill   horse riding   saw
'John$_i$ saw Bill$_j$ $\emptyset_{=j, \neq i}$ riding a horse'

(ii) John Bill $\emptyset$ łį́ naabiyégo bį́į́łtsą́
John Bill   horse riding   saw
'Bill$_i$, $\emptyset_{=i, \neq j}$ riding a horse, saw John$_j$'
(= 'John$_j$ was seen by Bill$_i$ $\emptyset_{=i, \neq j}$ riding a horse')

On the basis of this data, anaphoric binding in -*go* adjuncts can be accounted for as follows: the adjunct's subject is anaphorically bound by the logical object of a *yi-* predicate and by the logical subject of a *bi-* predicate. This is not, however, the simplest possible analysis. It would be simpler to state that the binding is controlled by a particular syntactic position in the main or nonadjunct clause, the clause-second position (occupied by *Bill* in both i and ii). Accordingly, anaphoric binding in -*go* adjuncts could be adduced as behavioral evidence for the reality of a relation object, which coincides with ontological object (but is distinct from logical object). Whether Apachean also affords behavioral evidence for a relation subject is unknown to the present writer, and bears investigating.

10 The fourth person pronominals, in their detransitive use, often carry a nuance of the speaker's politeness or deference to the (overtly unspecified) referent. See Young & Morgan 1987: 9, 76–7 for further discussion.

11 Klaiman 1991b (superseding Klaiman 1989) offers a tentative version of such an account for Algonquian and for certain Tanoan languages. Incidentally, note that by assuming the alternative account with a rule of passivization, it not only becomes necessary to stipulate the rule's restriction from applying in predications with inanimate logical objects, but also its obligatory application in predications with inanimate logical subjects, e.g. (17b) of the main text. For particulars of one such account proposed by a previous writer, see the main text below, Section 4.5.2.

12 Similarly, the following Navajo *yi-* and *bi-* alternates (based on the main text, examples 20a, b) are converse, not identical in propositional content:

(i) łį́į́' dzaanééz yi-ztał
  'The horse kicked the mule'
(ii) łį́į́' dzaanééz bi-ztał
  'The mule kicked the horse' (= 'The horse was kicked by the mule')

It is worth noting that the main-text argument has force not only in distinguishing inverse from passive, but also in distinguishing inverse from derived voices in general, such as oblique passives and antipassives. The logic of this is that derived voices in general, not just passives, usually do not alter basic propositional content, but rather suppress or downgrade logical subjects. Given this, one can conclude that inverse is to be distinguished from all kinds of derived voices (*pace* Perlmutter 1989, who argues for reanalyzing an inverse voice in a Tanoan language as antipassivization).

13 Teeter 1967 discusses the past and current status of the Algonquian languages. According to his statement (pp. 3; 5, n. 13), the major representatives of the family today are, in alphabetical order: Arapaho, Blackfoot, Cheyenne, Cree, Delaware, Fox (Mesquakie), Malecite-Passamaquoddy, Menomini, Micmac, Natick-Narragansett, Ojibwa (Chippewa), Penobscot-Abnaki, Potawatomi and Shawnee. The main text cites only a selection of available descriptive materials on some of these languages. Certain additional works, which have provided valuable background information for our survey, are noted below. (For furnishing a copy of one of these works, Dahlstrom 1986c, the author is indebted to Amy Dahlstrom.)

Notes to Chapter 4   289

General: Goddard 1967a, 1967b; Bloomfield 1971; essays in Sebeok 1973; Delisle 1973; Teeter 1973; Frantz 1976; Dunnigan, O'Malley & Schwartz 1978; Denny 1977, 1983a, 1984; Jolley 1983; Hewson 1987; Rhodes 1987.
Blackfoot: Frantz 1966, 1967; Fox & Frantz 1979.
Cheyenne: Russell 1987; Leman 1979–1980.
Cree: Dahlstrom 1986b, 1986c; Ellis 1962, 1971; Jolley 1981, 1982; Wolfart 1973, 1978; Wolfart & Carroll 1973, 1981.
Delaware: Voegelin 1971; Goddard 1979.
Fox: LeSourd 1976; Goddard 1984; Dahlstrom 1986a.
Malecite-Passamaquoddy: Teeter 1971.
Menomini: Bloomfield 1962.
Micmac: Williams & Jerome 1979.
Ojibwa: Rogers 1975, 1976; Denny 1978b; Grafstein 1981; Rhodes 1976, 1980.
Potawatomi: Hockett 1939, 1966; Erickson 1965.

14 Also unclear at this time is the status of one language not discussed in the main text of the present work, Michif or French Cree. It is classified, by some writers, as a Creole; by others, as a mixed language; and by still others, as an Algonquian language. Relevant sources include Weaver 1982, 1983; Rhodes 1977, 1986; Papen 1987; Thomason 1987; and Thomason & Kaufman 1988.

15 Not addressed in the main text is whether affix categories (a) and (d) in (24) are to be considered bound pronominals or markers of agreement (concord). According to Jelinek 1985, the elements in question comprise arguments of the predicate, not agreement markers (see again Section 4.0 of the main text). Moreover, in their treatment of Blackfoot, Fox & Frantz 1979 furnish independent arguments against an agreement marker analysis of these elements. Treating them as agreement markers, furthermore, seems inapt for another reason. Verbs of the class to which e.g. Cree "be red" pertains, the II (inanimate intransitive) class, often express situations – such as atmospheric events – that have no participants. These predicates cannot construe with independent nominals. However, they may be assigned affixes, such as suffixes of number (see again the discussion of the predicate "be red" suffixed by singular/plural -*w* and -*wa* immediately above in the main text). Thus if one treats the affixes in question as agreement markers, one must proceed to the undesirable conclusion that in some instances they may lack antecedents, or be unbound.

16 Generally, if a transitive predicate assigns either a beneficiary or a goal theta-role in addition to a theme, the former is treated as a core argument to the exclusion of the latter. This occurs not only in Algonquian and Apachean (see the discussion of Navajo in Jelinek 1990), but is also said to be characteristic of other inverse systems (see Whistler 1985: 240; 259–60, n. 13).

17 This is confirmed by the shapes of nonlocal forms indexing inclusive "we" (you and me), e.g. *Ki-wāpam-ā-naw* 'We (inclusive) see him'; *Ki-wāpam-ā-naw-ak* 'We (inclusive) see them' (where -*ak* is a plural suffix of the third

person); *Ki-wāpam-iko-naw* 'He sees us (inclusive)' (where *-iko* is an inverse theme sign). By contrast, if a first person plural suffix cooccurs with the first person prefix *ni-* rather than the second person prefix *ki-* and the predication is nonlocal, then the form is glossed with exclusive rather than inclusive "we"; e.g. *Ni-wāpam-ā-nān* 'We (exclusive) see him,' *ni-wāpam-iko-nān* 'He sees us (exclusive).' (The preceding forms are from Wolfart & Carroll 1981: 72.) For some discussion of the relative ranking of the Algonquian second and first persons, see Zwicky 1977 and Jolley 1983.

18 According to Dahlstrom 1986c: 145, n. 1, the earliest use by an Algonquianist of the term "obviative" occurs in Cuoq 1866. However, Weaver 1982: 22 states that a term "to obviate" appears in a grammatical description of Cree by Howse 1844: 125, from which the following passage is cited:

When two 'third' persons (both of them *agents*, or both of them *patients*) meet together, this relational form serves to distinguish the *accessory* or dependent, from the *principle* [sic – present author] or leading 'third' person – the relative from the absolute agent, &c. – thus *obviating* (emphasis mine – DW), by shewing their relative position, the ambiguity which would otherwise arise from the meeting of several third persons in the sentence.

Regardless of the origin of the term, it is true, as Weaver states, that its use has become generalized in Algonquian studies since the Bloomfield era. As noted in the main text, writers on other families, such as Apachean, often discuss the same behavior under the rubric of the fourth person.

19 This constraint might more accurately be ascribed to the level of discourse rather than to clause-level syntax. In general, within a given discourse unit, a maximum of one proximate nominal occurs. The problem is specifying the boundaries of the Algonquian discourse unit. One discourse unit may change over to the next either at or within the boundaries of such structural units as sentences. For further comment, see the main text below.

20 In addition to the nearer obviative or ordinary fourth person, some Algonquianists posit a further obviative or fifth person category. In Cree, according to Dahlstrom 1986c: 25, the further obviative is indexed on predicates by a suffix *-im*. On nominals, the further obviative index has the basic shape *-eyi*; it may be followed by an (ordinary) obviative suffix. In (i) below (from Wolfart 1978: 257), the second further obviative is illustrated; note that *-eyi* is in italic type. Both of the further obviatives (also in italic type) appear in (ii) (from Dahlstrom 1986c: 55).

(i) okimāw o- kosis -a   o- tēm *-iyi* -wa
    chief   3 son   3SG OBV 3 horse *-eyi* 3SG OBV
    'the chief's son's horse'

(ii) Wāpamēw iskwēwah   ēh- wayawiyit   ē-
     saw-OBV woman-OBV go out-3SG OBV be
    kī- nipah*im*iht   onāpēm*iyi*wah
    killed-conjunct order-*im* her husband-*eyi*-3SG OBV
    'He saw a woman come out, a woman whose husband had been killed'

The analysis of the supposed further obviative or fifth person elements is controversial. Wolfart 1978 observes that they occur only in possessives. On this ground he argues that, while they may serve as markers of nominal reference-tracking, they do not mark obviation proper. In his view, whereas an obviative represents a subcategory of the third person, these elements do not; hence they are not commensurate with the ordinary obviative or fourth person. In the main text, following Wolfart, it is assumed that Cree has only one obviative.

21 According to Jelinek & Demers, p. 182, -ŋ in Lummi also encodes decontrol variants (see again Section 3.5) of basic intransitive predicates.

22 As functions marked by this element, Kroskrity 1978 lists the instrumental, instrumental-source, locative-source and comitative; also (according to Kroskrity 1985: 314) the benefactive. The first three of these functions are respectively illustrated in (i)–(iii) (from Kroskrity, p. 25). Not illustrated below, but discussed by Kroskrity, are certain other functions encoded by this element in stative complement clauses and in negative expressions.

(i) E:nu pe -dí a:yu mán- k^{hw}ę́di
    boy stick with girl 3SG II hit
    'The boy hit the girl with a stick'

(ii) Na: k'u: -ʔiʔi -dí dó- k'ege -ʔan
     I rock there with/from 1SGII build house past
     'I built a house out of rock'

(iii) Na:bah -ʔiʔi -dí ʔo- mɛ
      field there from 1SG I go
      'I went from the field'

According to Kroskrity 1978: 28, the invariant meaning of -di/-dí is "associational": it "associates its NP argument with the predication or one of the arguments of the simple sentence in which it occurs." Outside of the inverse construction, then, nominals marked with this element are generally noncore. It seems plausible that the extension of this element's functions to the marking of various grammatically backgrounded nominal statuses may have a natural basis, consistent with its encoding the locus of lesser ontological salience – the logical subject – in inverse constructions.

23 This does not entail that Set II and Set III forms of 3:3 predications are equivalent pragmatically or can be used interchangeably in discourse. See Kroskrity 1985 for some discussion.

24 To clarify, in AT 3:3 predications, the shapes of person prefixes in direct and inverse counterparts (such as 64a, b in the main text) are distinct. However, in other Tanoan languages, e.g. Picurís and Southern Tiwa (ST) (discussed in the following section of the main text), the shapes of person prefixes in corresponding predications are equivalent; the third person prefix in both direct and inverse alternates is zero. This is illustrated by subsequent examples in the main text, e.g. (69a, b) in Picurís and (76a, b) in ST. For some additional, parallel examples in other persons, see (67a, b) in Picurís and (77a, b) in ST.

25 This statement fudges on two facts: (i) some TI or transitive inanimate

predications do assign person prefixes from the row headed Object class A in Figure 4.2, Set II; and (ii) plural TA predications select person prefixes from the row headed Object class B, not A, in Figure 4.2, Set II.

In both Picurís and ST, there are three noun classes, designated by Tanoanists as i, ii and iii. All nominals in class i are animate, while ii and iii comprise subclasses of inanimates. In the verbal complex, singulars and plurals of the three noun classes are indexed by person prefix categories A, B and C according to the following scheme (from Allen, Frantz, Gardiner & Perlmutter 1990).

A = iSG or iiSG
B = iPL or iiiSG
C = iiPL or iiiPL

It follows that A and B prefixes are both assigned in TA predications; only C prefixes are not. However, available descriptive materials on Tanoan languages afford relatively few examples of transitive predications with B or C prefixes. Furthermore, the A prefix subparadigm of Set II (or its equivalent) has a special status, not only in Picurís but also in ST and Towa (Jemez). See the main text below for clarification.

26 In Towa (Jemez), no nominal classes A, B, C are distinguished (see preceding note). Set II paradigms index the ontological object for first, second or third person, and for singular, dual or plural number. Note that Figure 4.4, Set II, lists only Towa (Jemez) forms which index third person singular ontological objects. This subparadigm corresponds to the Set IIA prefixes in Picurís (Figure 4.2) and ST (Figure 4.3). For complete Towa paradigms, see Myers 1970: 63–5, Appendix I.

27 One problem confronting an inverse treatment of Tanoan languages is that of accounting for case marking in TA 3:3 predications, such as the AT examples (64a, b). That TA 3:3 inverse forms (e.g. 64b) require special (case) marking to disambiguate core logical relations seems plausible enough on the face of matters. However, in corresponding direct TA 3:3 forms (e.g. 64a), core logical relations are expressed by no overt case marking, but by rigid word order, with logical subject nominals preceding logical objects. This does not apply in the inverse (Kroskrity 1990: 13). It is unclear why a case-marking strategy should occur only in inverse, but not in direct, TA 3:3 forms.

Another problem for an inverse analysis is that, in some Tanoan languages, the parallelism of intransitive, direct and inverse person prefixing breaks down when the ontological subject is plural. This is not a problem in AT, which has distinct intransitive, direct and inverse prefix sets. Nor do plurals seem to pattern differently from singulars in Towa (Jemez) (judging by the paradigms in Myers 1970). However, in Tiwa, it is when ontological subjects are singular in number that one encounters parallel sets such as Picurís (72a–c) and (73a–c) or ST (76a–c) and (77a–c). By contrast, when the ontological subject is plural, the direct and inverse forms may assign distinct prefixes. This is illustrated in the ST examples (6a, b) in Section 1.2. If one advocates an inverse analysis over a passivization analysis for these systems, such forms are highly problematical, because the prefixes assigned in the relevant (inverse) forms (e.g. *i-* in 6b) appear indistinguishable from the plural prefixes assigned in intransitives (see Figure 4.3).

5 Information-salience voice systems

1 Following some traditional views of sentential pragmatics (e.g. the Prague School), certain current grammatical formalisms recognize and even ascribe to universal grammar one or more informational salience roles or statuses. For present concerns this is significant, since it is consistent with assuming, as we do, that verbal voice alternations may be among the strategies available to languages for encoding alternate information-salience assignments. Two current formalisms which include information-salience statuses among their primitives of structural representation are lexical–functional grammar (LFG) and relational grammar (RG). Although a full overview of these models cannot be furnished in the present work, their respective treatments of information-salience statuses (e.g. topic* and focus*) do merit the briefest of summaries here.

In LFG, the inventory of fundamental statuses or grammatical functions (GFs) which nominal positions may be assigned includes, along with SUBJ, OBJ and so forth, two statuses FOCUS and TOPIC. LFG treats these (along with one other, the adjunct GF or ADJ) as members of a class of "inner argument" GFs. This term refers to functions that (unlike SUBJ, OBJ, etc.) cannot be mapped onto theta-roles in lexical structures directly. Rather, these GFs accrue to theta-roles which are already assigned to outer-argument GFs, according to Bresnan & Mchombo 1987: 746, 753. This work accounts for verb–nominal agreement in Chicheŵa, a Bantu language, by invoking both FOCUS and TOPIC.

Likewise, topic (TOP) and focus (FOC) are two fundamental nominal statuses in relational grammar or RG (and in another, closely related formalism, arc pair grammar; see Johnson & Postal 1980). They are included, along with Question (Q) and Relative (REL), in a class of relations called Overlay relations. Unlike other relations such as subject (1), object (2) and indirect object (3), RG treats Overlay relations as optional to the organization of particular languages; some do without Overlay relations entirely. Moreover, even in languages where they occur, Overlay relations cannot arise in the most fundamental level of structural representation, i.e. in initial strata. They originate, rather, in noninitial strata as replacements for non-Overlay relations (Berinstein 1985: 10ff.; Aissen 1987).

From the fact that different authors use the terms focus and topic, it should not be assumed that loci of informational salience which are distinguished in different languages under these labels necessarily coincide in specific properties or behaviors. This will be clarified in the discussion of Mayan and Philippine systems in the main text below (Sections 5.1 and 5.2, respectively). Even the fact that each of two leading models, LFG and RG, invoke such informational salience statuses does not entail that exactly the same properties and behaviors accrue cross-linguistically to nominals which either formalism treats as focus or topic. Rather, researchers in more than one model seem to have arrived at the tacit consensus to treat under the rubric of focus any status of informational salience to which a language's morphosyntax is sensitive or which it overtly encodes, while labeling as topic any secondary or less morphosyntactically prominent status of informational salience.

2 In (4) and (5) (and subsequent K'ekchi examples) in the main text, underlining represents Berinstein's convention for indicating segmental length. For arguments that the P is nonabsolutive in both kinds of antipassives illustrated in (4) and (5), see Berinstein, pp. 221ff., 246ff.

3 While the overview of K'ekchi grammar by Pinkerton 1976a also invokes two statuses bearing the same names, it gives very different characterizations of them from Berinstein's. Only the latter's account of K'ekchi informational salience is followed in the main text below.

4 Working within an RG framework, Berinstein accounts for the facts outlined in the main text by invoking a constraint that a chômeur cannot be assigned informational salience (either salience-F or salience-T). She also proposes that an ergative cannot be assigned salience-F (in her parlance, it cannot bear a "narrow overlay" relation) unless it also heads an absolutive arc. (The last stipulation accounts for the fact, noted in the main text above, that ergatives can be assigned salience-F just when they antecede reflexives.) See her work for details of this account.

5 Significantly, Larsen & Norman offer arguments that it is (absolutive-marked) A and P, not the absolutive case *per se*, that F-sensitive rules target. See their work, p. 361, for details.

6 Berinstein 1985: 231 accounts for this by a constraint she terms the referentiality constraint. According to it, ergative A and absolutive P or S, when nonreferential, must be assigned salience.

Note incidentally in this connection that, according to Freund 1976: 31, a K'ekchi verb may bear an ergative prefix indexing A only if the P is referential. However, this is counterexemplified in the main text below by (15b).

7 According to Berinstein 1985, a nonreferential A may retain its basic ergative case assignment if it is topicalized, omitting the necessity of antipassivizing. However, her work includes no illustration supporting this.

8 Occasionally a focus category assigns focus particles of varying shapes, while other times, focus particles of more than one category coalesce in shape. Correspondingly, on occasion a voice is encoded by alternative verbal indices, or the shapes of indices for distinct voices coalesce. For a table illustrating this for Tagalog, see Naylor 1975: 37.

9 Tagalog also has emphatic fronting without *ay*, which Schachter & Otanes 1972: 493 term "contrastive inversion." On this and other strategies for emphasizing or topicalizing Tagalog nominals, see Schachter & Otanes, pp. 485ff.

In some Philippine languages, some kinds of nonfocused nominals may be accessible to emphatic fronting. An instance is Kapampangan, in which emphatic fronting targets either of two statuses: focused nominals (whatever their participant roles), or nonfocused actor nominals. The former is illustrated in (i), the latter in (ii) (from Mirikitani 1972: 151; also cited by Shibatani 1988a: 131). In both instances, emphatic fronting is indicated by the particle *ing*.

(i) Ing   mangga seli   ne   ning lalaki king tindahan
Focus mango bought-G voice he-it A   boy   D   store
'**The mango**, the boy bought it at the store'

(ii) Ing   lalaki seli   ne   ing   mangga king tindahan
Topic boy   bought-G voice he-it Focus mango D   store
'The boy, he bought **the mango** at the store'

10 It should be noted that the properties listed in the last group of the figure, actor-/focus-sensitive properties, do not all necessarily accrue alternately to actors or focused nominals in every Philippine language. In particular, the last property listed, emphatic fronting, is purely a focus-sensitive property in at least two languages, Cebuano and Tagalog, as illustrated in (35) and (36) in the main text. This is different from the situation in Kapampangan (see preceding note).

11 Shibatani 1988a: 97ff. also attacks the validity of the statistical grounds, mentioned in the main text above, for claiming that Philippine systems exemplify an ergative–absolutive type. In his view, it is dubious to treat a statistically dominant voice, i.e. the Goal voice, as indicative of basic case assignment. Rather, basic case is manifested in forms which lack overt voice and focus, such as nominalizations (illustrated in the main text, 32). If one compares transitive and intransitive nominalizations, it will be observed that the transitive object or P does not coalesce in basic case assignment with the intransitive subject or S, because the former is typically assigned goal case, while the usual case of the latter is actor. Thus where overt voice is absent, the patterning of morphological cases typical of ergative–absolutive systems fails to materialize.

It may be noted, moreover, that the supposed statistical prevalence of Goal voice over other voices is not observed in all Philippine languages. Goal voice is statistically prevalent in some systems, but not in others. For instance, according to a count reported in Shibatani 1988a: 96, the proportion of Actor voice is slightly higher than that of Goal voice in Cebuano. Again, for more on these and other issues in the analysis of the basic structural organization of Philippine languages, see Shibatani 1988a, 1988b.

6 Toward a theory of voice

1 Note that, for a participant *p* to be considered a controller of some situation *s*, it is not necessary that the participant intend specifically to bring *s* about. See Farkas 1988a: 36; and see above, Section 3.2.

Bibliography

Abbreviations

BLS   Proceedings of the *n*th Annual Meeting of the Berkeley Linguistics Society. Berkeley: Berkeley Linguistics Society.
CLS   Papers from the *n*th Regional Meeting, Chicago Linguistic Society. Chicago: Chicago Linguistic Society.
PNAC   Papers of the *n*th Algonquian Conference. W. Cowan, ed. Ottawa: Carleton University.

Adams, K. L. & A. Manaster-Ramer. 1988. Some questions of topic/focus choice in Tagalog. *Oceanic Linguistics* 27.1/2: 79–101.
Aissen, J. L. 1987. *Tzotzil clause structure*. Dordrecht: Reidel.
Akmajian, A. & S. Anderson. 1970. On the use of fourth person in Navajo, or Navajo made harder. *International Journal of American Linguistics* 36.1: 1–8.
Allen, B. J. & D. G. Frantz. 1978. Verb agreement in Southern Tiwa. In J. Jaeger *et al.* (eds.) *BLS 4*, 11–17.
    1983a. An impersonal passive in Southern Tiwa. Summer Institute of Linguistics, University of North Dakota Sessions, *Work Papers* 27, 1–9. Huntington Beach, CA: Summer Institute of Linguistics.
    1983b. Advancements and verb agreement in Southern Tiwa. In Perlmutter 1983b, 303–14.
    1986. Goal advancement in Southern Tiwa. *International Journal of American Linguistics* 52.4: 388–403.
Allen, B. J., D. G. Frantz & D. B. Gardiner. 1981. Phantom arcs in Southern Tiwa. In J. P. Daly & M. H. Daly (eds.) Summer Institute of Linguistics, University of North Dakota Sessions, *Work Papers* 25, 1–10. Huntington Beach, CA: Summer Institute of Linguistics.
Allen, B. J., D. G. Frantz, D. B. Gardiner & D. M. Perlmutter. 1990. Verb agreement multistratal representation in Southern Tiwa. In Postal & Joseph 1990: 321–83.
Allen, B. J. & D. B. Gardiner. 1981. Passive in Southern Tiwa. In C. Elerick (ed.) *Proceedings of the Ninth Annual Southwestern Areal Language and Linguistics Workshop*, 291–302. El Paso: University of Texas.
Allen, B. J., D. B. Gardiner & D. G. Frantz. 1984. Noun incorporation in

Southern Tiwa. *International Journal of American Linguistics* 50.3: 292–311.
Andersen, P. K. 1987. Remarks on passive morphology. Ms. To appear in B. Brogyany & R. Lipp (eds.) *Essays in linguistics and philology offered in honor of Oswald Szemerenyi on the occasion of his 71st birthday*. Amsterdam: Benjamins.
Andrews, A. 1985. The major functions of the noun phrase. In Shopen 1985, 62–154.
Arden, A. H. 1969. A progressive grammar of the Tamil language. 5th edn, revised by A. C. Clayton, reprinted. Madras: The Christian Literature Society.
Arnott, D. W. 1956. The middle voice in Fula. University of London, *Bulletin of the School of Oriental and African Studies* 18.1: 130–44.
  1970. *The nominal and verbal systems of Fula*. Oxford: Oxford University Press.
Ayres, Glenn. 1983. The antipassive 'voice' in Ixil. *International Journal of American Linguistics* 49.1: 20–45.
Bach, E. & R. Harms (eds.) 1968. *Universals in linguistic theory*. New York: Holt.
Baker, M. C. 1983. Objects, themes, and lexical rules in Italian. In Levin *et al.* 1983, 1–45.
  1988. *Incorporation: a theory of grammatical function changing*. Chicago: University of Chicago Press.
Barber, E. J. W. 1975. Voice – beyond the passive. In C. Cogen *et al.* (eds.) *BLS 1*, 16–24.
Bell, S. J. 1983. Advancements and ascensions in Cebuano. In Perlmutter 1983b, 143–218.
Benveniste, E. 1971a. Active and middle voice in the verb. In Benveniste 1971b, 145–51.
  1971b. *Problems in general linguistics*. Tr. M. E. Meek. Coral Gables: University of Miami Press.
Berinstein, A. 1985. *Evidence for multiattachment in K'ekchi Mayan*. New York: Garland.
Berry, J. 1960. A note on voice and aspect in hu-Limba. *Sierra Leone Studies* 13, 36–40.
Binkley, R., R. Bronaugh & A. Marras (eds.) 1971. *Agent, action, and reason*. Toronto: University of Toronto Press.
Bittle, W. E. 1963. Kiowa-Apache. In Hoijer *et al.* 1963, 76–101.
Blake, B. J. 1990. *Relational grammar*. London & New York: Routledge.
Blake, F. R. 1925. *A grammar of the Tagálog language: the chief native idiom of the Philippine islands*. American Oriental Series 1. New Haven: American Oriental Society.
Bloomfield, L. 1917. Tagalog texts with grammatical analysis. University of Illinois, *Studies in Language and Literature* 3.2–4. Urbana: University of Illinois.
  1962. *The Menomini language*. New Haven: Yale University Press.

1971. Algonquian. In Hoijer *et al.* 1971, 85–129.
Bopp, F. 1862. *A comparative grammar of the Sanskṛit, Zend, Greek, Latin, Lithuanian, Gothic, German, and Slavonic languages*, vol. 2. Tr. E. B. Eastwick. 3rd edn. London & Edinburgh: Williams & Norgate.
Brennenstuhl, W. 1976. What we can't do. In S. Mufwene *et al.* (eds.) *CLS 12*, 59–71.
Brennenstuhl, W. & K. Wachowicz. 1976. On the pragmatics of control. In H. Thompson *et al.* (eds.) *BLS 2*, 396–405.
Bresnan, J. (ed.) 1982. *The mental representation of grammatical relations*. Cambridge, MA: MIT Press.
  1987. On locative inversion in Chicheŵa. Stanford University Center for the Study of Language and Information, *CSLI Monthly* 2.8: 1–6. Stanford, CA: Stanford University.
Bresnan, J. & S. A. Mchombo. 1987. Topic, pronoun, and agreement in Chicheŵa. *Language* 63.4: 741–82.
Burrow, T. 1973. *The Sanskrit language*. Third edn, revised. London: Faber & Faber.
Burrow, T. & M. Emeneau. 1961. *A Dravidian etymological dictionary*. 1st edn. London: Oxford University Press.
Campbell, L. & M. Mithun (eds.) 1979. *The languages of native America: historical and comparative assessment*. Austin: University of Texas Press.
Cardona, G. 1974. Pāṇini's *kārakas*: agency, animation and identity. *Journal of Indian Philosophy* 2, 231–306.
  1976. Subject in Sanskrit. In Verma 1976, 1–38.
Carlson, B. F. & L. C. Thompson. 1982. Out of control in two (maybe more) Salish languages. *Anthropological Linguistics* 24.1: 51–65.
Chappell, H. 1986a. Formal and colloquial adversity passives in standard Chinese. *Linguistics* 24, 1025–52.
  1986b. The passive of bodily effect in Chinese. *Studies in Language* 10.2: 271–96.
Chierchia, G., B. H. Partee & R. Turner (eds.) 1989. *Properties, types and meaning*, vol. 2: *Semantic issues*. Dordrecht: Kluwer Academic.
Chu, C. C. 1973. The passive construction: Chinese and English. *Journal of Chinese Linguistics* 1.3: 437–70.
Chung, S. 1976. An object-creating rule in Bahasa Indonesia. *Linguistic Inquiry* 7.1: 41–87.
Clark, M. 1974a. Submissive verbs as adversatives in some Asian languages. In Nguyen 1974b, 89–110.
  1974b. Passive and ergative in Vietnamese. In Nguyen 1974b, 75–88.
Cole, P. & J. M. Sadock (eds.) 1977. *Syntax and semantics*, vol. 8: *Grammatical relations*. New York: Academic Press.
Comrie, B. 1976. The syntax of causative constructions: cross-language similarities and divergencies. In Shibatani 1976, 261–312.
  1978. Ergativity. In Lehmann 1978, 329–94.
  1980. Inverse verb forms in Siberia: evidence from Chukchee, Koryak, and Kamchadal. *Folia Linguistica Historica* 1, 61–74.

1981a. The genetic affiliation of Kamchadal: some morphological evidence. In Comrie 1981c, 109–20.
1981b. *Language universals and linguistic typology: syntax and morphology.* Chicago: University of Chicago Press.
(ed.) 1981c. *Studies in the languages of the USSR. International Review of Slavic Linguistics.* Current Inquiry into Language, Linguistics and Human Communication 38. Carbondale, IL: Linguistic Research, Inc.
1982. Grammatical relations in Huichol. In Hopper & Thompson 1982, 95–115.
1988. Passive and voice. In Shibatani 1988c, 9–23.
Cook, E.-D. & D. B. Gerdts (eds.) 1984. *Syntax and semantics*, vol. 16: *The syntax of Native American languages.* New York: Academic Press.
Cook, E.-D. & J. Kaye (eds.) 1978. *Linguistic studies of native Canada.* Vancouver: University of British Columbia Press.
Cooreman, A., B. Fox & T. Givón. 1984. The discourse definition of ergativity. *Studies in Language* 8.1: 1–34.
Craig, C. G. 1977. *The structure of Jacaltec.* Austin: University of Texas Press.
Craik, B. 1982. The animate in Cree language and ideology. *PNAC 13*, 29–35.
Creamer, M. H. 1974. Ranking in Navajo nouns. *Diné Bizaad Náníl'íjh (Navajo Language Review)* 1.1: 29–38.
Croft, W., H. B.-Z. Shyldkrot & S. Kemmer. 1987. Diachronic semantic processes in the middle voice. In Ramat, Carruba & Bernini 1987, 179–92.
Cruse, D. A. 1973. Some thoughts on agentivity. *Journal of Linguistics* 9.1: 11–23.
Crystal, D. 1980. *A first dictionary of linguistics and phonetics.* 1st edn. London: André Deutsch.
Cuoq, J.-A. 1866. *Etudes philologiques sur quelques langues sauvages de l'Amérique.* Montreal: Dawson Brothers.
Dahl, O. C. 1978. The fourth focus. In Wurm & Carrington 1978, 383–93.
Dahlstrom, A. 1983. Agent-patient languages and split case marking systems. In A. Dahlstrom *et al.* (eds.) *BLS 9*, 37–46.
1986a. Nominal arguments and pronominal inflection in Fox. Presented at the 61st Annual Meeting, Linguistic Society of America, New York.
1986b. Weak crossover and obviation. In V. Nikiforidou *et al.* (eds.) *BLS 12*, 51–60.
1986c. *Plains Cree Morphosyntax.* University of California–Berkeley Ph.D. diss.
Davidson, D. 1971. Agency. In Binkley, Bronaugh & Marras 1971, 3–37.
Davies, W. & C. Rosen. 1988. Unions as multi-predicate clauses. *Language* 64.1: 52–88.
Davis, I. 1979. The Kiowa–Tanoan, Keresan, and Zuni languages. In Campbell & Mithun 1979, 390–443.
Davis, P. W. & R. Saunders. 1986. Control and development in Bella Coola. *International Journal of American Linguistics* 52.3: 212–26.
1989. Language and intelligence: The semantic unity of -*m*- in Bella Coola. *Lingua* 78.2/3: 113–58.

Davis, S. (ed.) 1984. *Studies on Native American languages, Japanese and Spanish.* University of Arizona Department of Linguistics, *COYOTE Papers* 5. Tucson: University of Arizona.

Dayley, J. 1981. Voice and ergativity in Mayan languages. *Journal of Mayan Linguistics* 2.2: 3–82.

1985. Voice in Tzutujil. In Nichols & Woodbury 1985, 192–226.

DeCharms, R. 1979. Personal causation and perceived control. In Perlmuter & Monty 1979, 29–40.

1981. Personal causation and locus of control: two different traditions and two uncorrelated measures. In Lefcourt 1981, 337–58.

DeLancey, S. 1981. An interpretation of split ergativity and related patterns. *Language* 51.3: 626–57.

1985. On active typology and the nature of agentivity. In Plank 1985, 47–60.

Delisle, G. L. 1973. On the so-called fourth person in Algonquian. Stanford University Department of Linguistics, *Working Papers on Language Universals* 12, 69–83. Stanford, CA: Stanford University.

Denny, J. 1977. Semantics of abstract finals in inanimate intransitive verbs. *PNAC 8*, 124–42.

1978a. The semantic roles of medials within Algonquian verbs. *International Journal of American Linguistics* 44.2: 153–55.

1978b. Verb class meanings of the abstract finals in Ojibway inanimate intransitive verbs. *International Journal of American Linguistics* 44.4: 294–322.

1983a. Semantics of abstract finals in Algonquian transitive inanimate verbs. *Canadian Journal of Linguistics* 28.2: 133–48.

1983b. Micmac semantics: medials for noun classes. *PNAC 14*, 363–68.

1984. Semantic verb classes and abstract finals. *PNAC 15*, 241–71.

De Wolf, C. M. 1988. Voice in Austronesian languages of Philippine type: passive, ergative, or neither? In Shibatani 1988c, 143–93.

Dixon, R. M. W. 1979. Ergativity. *Language* 55.1: 59–138.

Dowty, D. 1986. Thematic roles and semantics. In V. Nikiforidou *et al.* (eds.) *BLS 12*, 340–54.

1989. On the semantic content of the notion of 'thematic role.' In Chierchia, Partee & Turner 1989, 69–129.

Dryer, M. 1982. In defense of a universal passive. *Linguistic Analysis* 10.1: 53–60.

Dubinsky, S. & C. Rosen. 1987. *A bibliography on relational grammar through May 1987 with selected titles on lexical–functional grammar.* Bloomington: Indiana University Linguistics Club.

Dunnigan, T., P. O'Malley & L. Schwartz. 1978. A functional analysis of the Algonquian obviative. University of Minnesota Department of Linguistics, *Minnesota Papers in Linguistics and the Philosophy of Language* 5, 7–21. Minneapolis: University of Minnesota.

Durie, M. 1985. Control and decontrol in Acehnese. *Australian Journal of Linguistics* 5.1: 43–53.

1987. Grammatical relations in Acehnese. *Studies in Language* 11.2: 365–99.

1988. Preferred argument structure in an active language. *Lingua* 74.1: 1–25.

Duval, S. & R. A. Wicklund. 1972. *A theory of objective self awareness*. New York: Academic Press.
Dyer, W. W. 1976. *Your erroneous zones*. New York: Funk & Wagnalls.
Efrat, B. (ed.) 1979. *The Victorian conference on northwestern languages, Victoria, B.C., Nov. 4–5, 1976*. British Columbia Provincial Museum Heritage Record no. 4. Victoria, BC: British Columbia Provincial Museum.
Ekniyom, P. 1977. The topic/comment distinction and passivization in Thai. University of Hawaii Department of Linguistics, *Working Papers in Linguistics* 9.2: 93–110. Honolulu: University of Hawaii.
Elgin, P. A. S. 1973. *Some topics in Navajo syntax*. University of California–San Diego Ph.D. diss.
Ellis, C. D. 1962. *Spoken Cree, west coast of James Bay*. Toronto: Anglican Book Center.
  1971. Cree verb paradigms. *International Journal of American Linguistics* 37.2: 76–95.
Emeneau, M. 1951. *Studies in Vietnamese (Annamese) grammar*. University of California Publications in Linguistics vol. 8. Berkeley & Los Angeles: University of California Press.
England, N. C. (ed.) 1978. *Papers in Mayan linguistics*. University of Missouri Miscellaneous Publications in Anthropology no. 6, Studies in Mayan Linguistics no. 2. Columbia: University of Missouri.
  1983. *A grammar of Mam, a Mayan language*. Austin: University of Texas Press.
Entwistle, W. J. & W. A. Morison. 1964. *Russian and the Slavonic languages*. 2nd edn. London: Faber & Faber.
Erickson, B. 1965. Patterns of person–number reference in Potawatomi. *International Journal of American Linguistics* 31.3: 226–36.
Fagan, S. M. B. 1988. The Engish Middle. *Linguistic Inquiry* 19:2 181–203.
Farkas, D. 1988a. On obligatory control. *Linguistics and Philosophy* 11.1: 27–58.
  1988b. On obviation. Presented at the 63rd Annual Meeting, Linguistic Society of America, New Orleans.
Filbeck, D. 1973. The passive in Thai. *Anthropological Linguistics* 15.1: 33–41.
Fillmore, C. 1968. The case for case. In Bach & Harms 1968, 1–88.
Foley, W. A. & R. D. Van Valin, Jr. 1984. *Functional syntax and universal grammar*. Cambridge: Cambridge University Press.
Fox, B. & P. Hopper (eds.). To appear. *Voice: form and function*. Amsterdam: Benjamins.
Fox, J. & D. G. Frantz. 1979. Blackfoot clitic pronouns. *PNAC 10*, 152–66.
Frantz, D. G. 1966. Person indexing in Blackfoot. *International Journal of American Linguistics* 32.1: 50–8.
  1967. Blackfoot paradigms and matrices. In *Contributions to anthropology: linguistics I (Algonquian)*. National Museum of Canada Anthropological Series no. 78, Bulletin 214, 140–6. Ottawa: National Museum of Canada.
  1976. Unspecified-subject phenomena in Algonquian. *PNAC 7*, 197–216.
  1979. Grammatical relations in universal grammar. Summer Institute of Ling-

uistics, University of North Dakota Sessions, *Work Papers* 23, Supplement. Huntington Beach, CA: Summer Institute of Linguistics.

1985. Syntactic constraints on noun incorporation in Southern Tiwa. In M. Niepokúj *et al*. (eds.) *BLS 11*, 107–16.

Freund, R. 1976. A sketch of K'ekchi verb morphology. In Pinkerton 1976b, 26–47.

Frishberg, N. 1972. Navaho object markers and the great chain of being. In Kimball 1972, 259–66.

Fuller, J. W. 1985. On the passive construction in Hmong. In N. Stenson (ed.) University of Minnesota Department of Linguistics, *Minnesota Papers in Linguistics and the Philosophy of Language* 10, *Papers from the Tenth Minnesota Regional Conference on Language and Linguistics, May 11–12, 1984*, 51–65. Minneapolis: University of Minnesota.

Geniušienė, E. 1987. *The typology of reflexives*. Berlin: Mouton-de Gruyter.

Gerdts, D. B. 1984. A relational analysis of Halkomelem causals. In Cook & Gerdts 1984, 169–204.

Gerdts, D. B. & K. Michelson (eds.) 1989. *Theoretical perspectives on native American languages*. Albany: State University of New York Press.

Givón, T. 1975. Cause and control: on the semantics of interpersonal manipulation. In Kimball 1975, 59–89.

1981. Typology and functional domains. *Studies in Language* 5.2: 163–93.

Goddard, I. 1967a. Notes on the genetic classification of the Algonquian languages. In *Contributions to anthropology: linguistics I (Algonquian)*. National Museum of Canada Anthropological Series no. 78, Bulletin 214, 7–12. Ottawa: National Museum of Canada.

1967b. The Algonquian independent indicative. In *Contributions to anthropology: linguistics I (Algonquian)*. National Museum of Canada Anthropological Series no. 78, Bulletin 214, 66–106. Ottawa: National Museum of Canada.

1979. *Delaware verbal morphology: a descriptive and comparative study*. New York: Garland.

1984. The obviative in Fox narrative discourse. *PNAC 15*, 273–86.

Gonda, J. 1951. *Remarks on the Sanskrit passive*. Leiden: Brill.

1960. Reflections on the Indo-European medium I. *Lingua* 9.1: 30–67.

González, A. B. (ed.) 1973. *Parangal Kay Cecilio Lopez: essays in honor of Cecilio Lopez on his 75th birthday*. *Journal of Linguistics* special monograph issue 4. Quezon City: Linguistic Society of the Philippines.

Gordon, E. V. 1957. *An introduction to Old Norse*. 2nd edn, revised by A. R. Taylor. London: Oxford University Press.

Grady, M. 1965. The medio-passive voice in modern English. *Word* 21.2: 270–2.

Grafstein, A. 1981. Obviation in Ojibwa. University of Montreal Department of Linguistics, *Montreal Working Papers in Linguistics* 16, 83–134. Montreal: University of Montreal.

Grimshaw, J. 1982. On the lexical representation of Romance reflexive clitics. In Bresnan 1982, 87–148.

Griño, E. U. 1973. Provisions for emphasis in Hiligaynon. In González 1973, 141–52.

Gruber, J. S. 1965. *Studies in lexical relations.* MIT Ph.D. diss.
Haile, Fr. B. 1926. *A manual of Navaho grammar.* Arizona: St Michael's. Reprinted 1974. New York: AMS Press.
Haiman, J. 1976. Agentless sentences. *Foundations of Language* 14.1: 19–53.
 1983. Iconic and economic motivation. *Language* 59.4: 781–819.
Haiman, J. & P. Munro. 1983a. Introduction. In Haiman & Munro 1983b, ix–xv.
 (eds.) 1983b. *Switch-reference and universal grammar.* Amsterdam: Benjamins.
Hale, K. 1973. A note on subject–object inversion in Navajo. In Kachru *et al.* 1973, 300–9.
 1983. Warlpiri and the grammar of non-configurational languages. *Natural Language and Linguistic Theory* 1.1: 5–77.
Hardy, H. K. & P. W. Davis. To appear. The semantics of agreement in Alabama. In Scancarelli & Davis to appear.
Harris, A. 1981. *Georgian syntax: a study in relational grammar.* Cambridge: Cambridge University Press.
Harvey, J. H., B. Harris & J. M. Lightner. 1979. Perceived freedom as a central concept in psychological theory and research. In Perlmuter & Monty 1979, 275–300.
Hashimoto, M. J. 1969. Observations on the passive construction. Princeton University Chinese Linguistics Project and Seminar, *Unicorn* 5, 59–71. Princeton, NJ: Princeton University.
 1988. The structure and typology of the Chinese passive construction. In Shibatani 1988c, 329–54.
Heath, J. 1976. Antipassivization: a functional typology. In H. Thompson *et al.* (eds.) *BLS* 2, 202–11.
Henderson, T. S. T. 1971. Participant-reference in Algonkin. *Cahiers linguistiques d'Ottawa* 1, 27–49.
Hess, T. M. 1973. Agent in a Coast Salish language. *International Journal of American Linguistics* 39.2: 89–94.
Hewson, J. 1987. Are Algonquian languages ergative? *PNAC 18*, 147–53.
Hill, J. 1969. Volitional and non-volitional verbs in Cupeño. In R. Binnick *et al.* (eds.) *CLS 5*, 348–56.
Hock, H. H. 1982. The Sanskrit passive: synchronic behavior and diachronic development. In P. Mistry (ed.) *Studies in South Asian languages and linguistics*, special issue of *South Asian Review* 6.3: 127–37.
 1986. 'P-oriented' constructions in Sanskrit. In Krishnamurti *et al.* 1986, 15–26.
Hockett, C. 1939. Potawatomi syntax. *Language* 15.4: 235–48.
 1966. What Algonquian is really like. *International Journal of American Linguistics* 32.1: 59–73.
Hoekstra, T. 1984. *Transitivity: grammatical relations in government-binding theory.* Dordrecht: Foris.
Hoijer, H. 1971. Chiricahua Apache. In Hoijer *et al.* 1971, 55–84.
Hoijer, H. *et al.* (eds.) 1963. *Studies in the Athapaskan languages.* University of California Publications in Linguistics vol. 29. Berkeley & Los Angeles: University of California Press.

(eds.) 1971. *Linguistic structures of native America*. 4th printing. New York: Johnson Reprint Company. Originally published 1946. Viking Fund Publications in Anthropology 46. New Haven: Yale University.

Holisky, D. A. 1987. The case of the intransitive subject in Tsova-Tush (Batsbi). In R. M. W. Dixon (ed.) *Studies in ergativity*, special issue of *Lingua* 71.1/4: 103–32. Amsterdam: North-Holland.

Hook, P. 1976. Aṣṭādhyāyī 3.4.21 and the role of semantics in Paninian linguistics. In S. Mufwene *et al.* (eds.) *CLS 12*, 302–12.

Hopper, P. & S. Thompson. 1980. Transitivity in grammar and discourse. *Language* 56.1: 251–99.

(eds.) 1982. *Syntax and semantics*, vol. 15: *Studies in transitivity*. New York: Academic Press.

Howse, J. 1844. *A grammar of the Cree language*. London: J. G. F. & J. Rivington.

Hsu, C.-L. 1974. On the relationship between the active and the passive in Chinese. *Journal of Chinese Linguistics* 2.2: 172–9.

Hubbard, P. 1985. *The syntax of the Albanian verb complex*. New York: Garland.

Hyman, L. M. & A. Duranti. 1982. On the object relation in Bantu. In Hopper & Thompson 1982, 217–39.

Ishikawa, A. 1985. *Complex predicates and lexical operations in Japanese*. Stanford University Ph.D. diss.

Jackendoff, R. S. 1972. *Semantic interpretation in generative grammar*. Cambridge, MA: MIT Press.

Jacobsen, W. H., Jr. 1985. The analog of the passive transformation in ergative-type languages. In Nichols & Woodbury 1985, 176–91.

Jacobson, P. & G. Pullum (eds.) 1982. *The nature of syntactic representation*. Dordrecht: Reidel.

Jelinek, E. 1984. Empty categories, case, and configurationality. *Natural Language and Linguistic Theory* 2.1: 39–76.

1985. Ergativity and the argument type parameter. In S. DeLancey & R. S. Tomlin (eds.) University of Oregon Department of Linguistics, *Proceedings of the First Annual Meeting of the Pacific Linguistics Conference*, 168–82. Eugene, OR: University of Oregon.

1990. Grammatical relations and coindexing in inverse systems. Presented at the Fifth Biennial Conference on Grammatical Relations, University of California–San Diego. To appear in Proceedings.

Jelinek, E. & R. A. Demers. 1983. The agent hierarchy and voice in some Coast Salish languages. *International Journal of American Linguistics* 49.2: 167–85.

Jespersen, O. 1965. *The philosophy of grammar*. New York: Norton.

Johnson, D. E. 1977a. On Keenan's definition of 'subject of.' *Linguistic Inquiry* 8.4: 637–92.

1977b. On relational constraints on grammars. In Cole & Sadock 1977, 151–78.

1979. *Toward a theory of relationally based grammar*. New York: Garland.

Johnson, D. E. & P. M. Postal. 1980. *Arc pair grammar.* Princeton, NJ: Princeton University Press.
Jolley, C. 1981. The passive in Plains Cree. *Journal of the Linguistic Association of the Southwest* 4, 161–84.
　1982. On the Plains Cree passive: an analysis of syntactic and lexical rules. In B. D. Joseph (ed.) Ohio State University Department of Linguistics, *Ohio State University Working Papers in Linguistics* 26, 1–33. Columbus, OH: Ohio State University.
　1983. Algonquian person hierarchy: Morphosyntactic or semantic? *PNAC 14*, 281–91.
Kachru, B. *et al.* (eds.) 1973. *Issues in linguistics: papers in honor of Henry and Renée Kahane.* Urbana: University of Illinois Press.
Keenan, E. L. 1975. Some universals of passive in relational grammar. In R. Grossman *et al.* (eds.) *CLS 11*, 340–52.
　1976a. Towards a universal definition of 'subject.' In Li 1976, 303–33.
　1976b. Remarkable subjects in Malagasy. In Li 1976, 247–301.
　1985. Passive in the world's languages. In Shopen 1985, 243–81.
Keenan, E. L. & B. Comrie. 1977. Noun phrase accessibility and universal grammar. *Linguistic Inquiry* 8.1: 63–99.
Kemmer, S. E. 1988. *The middle voice: a typological and diachronic study.* Stanford University Ph.D. diss.
Kess, J. F. 1975. On the semantics of focus. *Anthropological Linguistics* 17.7: 353–62.
　1976. Reconsidering the notion of *focus* in the description of Tagalog. In Nguyen 1976, 173–86.
Kierman, F. 1969. Night-thoughts on the passive. Princeton University Chinese Linguistics Project and Seminar, *Unicorn* 5, 72–78. Princeton, NJ: Princeton University.
Kimball, J. P. (ed.) 1972. *Syntax and semantics*, vol. 1. New York: Academic Press.
　(ed.) 1975. *Syntax and semantics*, vol. 4, New York: Academic Press.
Kimenyi, A. 1980. *A relational grammar of Kinyardwanda.* University of California Publications in Linguistics vol. 91. Berkeley: University of California Press.
Kiparsky, P. 1987. The thematic structure of psychological predicates. Presented at the Symposium on the Syntax and Morphology of Psychological Predicates, Third Biennial Conference on Relational Grammar and Grammatical Relations, University of Iowa, Iowa City, IA.
Kisseberth, C. W. & M. I. Abasheikh. 1977. The object relationship in Chi-Mwi:ni, a Bantu language. In Cole & Sadock 1977, 179–218.
Klaiman, M. H. 1982a. Affectiveness and the voice system of Japanese. In M. Macaulay *et al.* (eds.) *BLS 8*, 398–413.
　1982b. Defining 'voice': evidence from Tamil. In K. Tuite *et al.* (eds.) *CLS 18*, 267–81.
　1982c. Arguments against the 'ingestive verb' hypothesis. In Koul 1982, 138–45.

1983. Japanese -(r)are-: a skeptic's view òf the type one/type two controversy. *Papers in Japanese Linguistics* 9, 43–67.
1984. The grammar of doing and undergoing in Korean. Seoul National University Language Research Institute, *Language Research* 20.4: 331–43.
1987a. The Sanskrit passive in lexical–functional grammar. In B. Need *et al.* (eds.) *CLS 23/1*, 196–214.
1987b. Aktionsart, semantics, and function in the Japanese 'passive.' *Studies in Language* 11.2: 401–34.
1988. Affectedness and control: a typology of voice systems. In Shibatani 1988c, 25–83.
1989. Inverse voice and head-marking in Tanoan languages. In C. Wiltshire *et al.* (eds.) *CLS 25/1*, 258–71.
1991a. Control and grammar. *Linguistics* 29.4.
1991b. The relationship of inverse voice and head-marking in Arizona Tewa and other Tanoan languages. Presented at the Twentieth Annual Symposium (Word Order in Discourse), Department of Linguistics, University of Wisconsin–Milwaukee.
To appear. Middle verbs, middle reflexive constructions, and middle voice. *Studies in Language*.
In preparation. The treatment of voice in current grammatical theory.
Klimov, G. A. 1974. On the character of languages of active typology. *Linguistics* 131, 11–25. Reprinted from *Voprosy Jazykoznanija* 4 (1972), 3–13.
Koul, O. N. (ed.) 1982. *Topics in Hindi linguistics*, vol. 2. Delhi: Bahri.
Kozinsky, I. Š., V. P. Nedjalkov & M. S. Polinskaja. 1988. Antipassivization in Chukchee: oblique object, object incorporation, zero object. In Shibatani 1988c: 651–706.
Krishnamurti, Bh. *et al.* (eds.) 1986. *South Asian languages: structure, convergence and diglossia*. Delhi: Motilal Banarsidass.
Kroskrity, P. V. 1977. *Aspects of Arizona Tewa language structure and language use*. Indiana University Ph.D. diss.
1978. On the lexical integrity of Arizona Tewa /-dí/: a principled choice between homophony and polysemy. *International Journal of American Linguistics* 44.1: 24–30.
1985. A holistic understanding of Arizona Tewa passives. *Language* 61.2: 306–28.
1990. The art of voice: toward an understanding of Arizona Tewa voice constructions and their use in traditional narratives. Presented at the University of California–San Diego Voice Symposium. To appear in Fox & Hopper.
Kuryłowicz, J. 1964. *The inflectional categories of Indo-European*. Heidelberg: Carl Winter.
Lacey, H. M. 1979. Control, perceived control, and the methodological role of cognitive constructs. In Perlmuter & Monty 1979, 5–16.
Ladusaw, W. A. 1988. A proposed distinction between *levels* and *strata*. In Linguistic Society of Korea, *Linguistics in the morning calm, 2: selected papers from SICOL–1986*, 37–51. Seoul: Hanshin.

Langacker, R. & P. Munro. 1975. Passives and their meaning. *Language* 51.4: 789–830.
Larsen, T. W. & W. M. Norman. 1979. Correlates of ergativity in Mayan grammar. In Plank 1979, 347–70.
Le, T. D. 1976. Vietnamese passives. In S. Mufwene *et al.* (eds.) *CLS 12*, 438–49.
Lefcourt, H. (ed.) 1981. *Research with the locus of control construct*, vol. 1: *Assessment methods*. New York: Academic Press.
  1982. *Locus of control: current trends in theory and research*. 2nd edn. Hillsdale, NJ: Lawrence Erlbaum Associates.
Lehmann, W. P. (ed.) 1978. *Syntactic typology: studies in the phenomenology of language*. Austin: University of Texas Press.
Leman, W. 1979–1980. *A reference grammar of the Cheyenne language*. 2 vols. University of Northern Colorado Department of Anthropology, Occasional Publications in Anthropology, Linguistics Series no. 5. Greeley, CO: University of Northern Colorado.
LeSourd, P. 1976. Verb agreement in Fox. In J. Hankamer & J. Aissen (eds.) Harvard University Department of Linguistics, *Harvard Studies in Syntax and Semantics II*, 445–528. Cambridge, MA: Harvard University.
Levenson, H. 1981. Differentiating among internality, powerful others, and chance. In Lefcourt 1981, 15–63.
Levin, B. 1987. The middle construction and ergativity. In R. M. W. Dixon (ed.) *Studies in ergativity*, special issue of *Lingua* 71.1/4: 17–31. Amsterdam: North-Holland.
Levin, L., M. Rappaport & A. Zaenen (eds.) 1983. *Papers in lexical–functional grammar*. Bloomington: Indiana University Linguistics Club.
Levine, R. D. 1980. Passives and controllability in Kwakwala. *Glossa* 14.2: 139–67.
Li, C. (ed.) 1976. *Subject and topic*. New York: Academic Press.
Llamzon, T. A. 1973. The four focus transformations of Tagalog. In González 1973, 168–83.
Lyons, J. 1968. *Introduction to theoretical linguistics*. Cambridge: Cambridge University Press.
Manickam, V. Sp. 1972. *A study of Tamil verbs*. Annamalainagar, India: Annamalai University.
Marantz, A. 1982a. Grammatical relations and explanation in linguistics. In Zaenen 1982, 1–24.
  1982b. Affixation and the syntax of applied verb constructions. In D. P. Flickinger *et al.* (eds.) Stanford University Department of Linguistics, *Proceedings of the First West Coast Conference on Formal Linguistics*, 330–40. Stanford, CA: Stanford University.
  1984. *On the nature of grammatical relations*. Cambridge, MA: MIT Press.
Mattina, A. 1982. The Colville–Okanagan transitive system. *International Journal of American Linguistics* 48.4: 421–35.
Mattina, A. & T. Montler (eds.) 1981. *Working papers of the Sixteenth International Conference on Salishan Languages*. University of Montana Occasional Papers in Linguistics 2. Butte, MT: University of Montana.

McCawley, N. 1972. On the treatment of Japanese passives. In P. Peranteau *et al.* (eds.) *CLS 8*, 259–70.

McDonough, J. & B. Plunkett (eds.) 1987. *Proceedings of NELS [New England Linguistic Society] 17*. University of Massachusetts South College, Department of Linguistics Graduate Linguistics Students Association. Amherst, MA: University of Massachusetts.

McKaughan, H. P. 1973. Subject versus topic. In González 1973, 206–13.

McKinney, J. P. 1981. The construct of engagement style: theory and research. In Lefcourt 1981, 359–83.

Merlan, F. 1985. Split intransitivity: functional oppositions in intransitive inflection. In Nichols & Woodbury 1985, 324–62.

Michael, I. 1970. *English grammatical categories and the tradition to 1800*. Cambridge: Cambridge University Press.

Milgram, S. 1974. *Obedience to authority: an experimental view*. New York: Harper & Row.

Mirikitani, L. T. 1972. *Kapampangan syntax*. *Oceanic Linguistics* special publication no. 10. Honolulu: University Press of Hawaii.

Mock, C. 1982. Los casos morfosintácticos del Chocho. Universidad Nacional Autónoma de México Instituto de Investigaciones Antropológicas, *Anales de Antropología* 19.2: 345–78. English-language version (1980), Chocho case marking and the typology of case. Ms.

Mondloch, J. L. 1981. *Voice in Quiche-Maya*. State University of New York–Albany Ph.D. diss.

Moravscik, E. A. 1978. On the distribution of ergative and accusative patterns. *Lingua* 45.3/4: 233–79.

Moravscik, E. A. & J. R. Wirth (eds.) 1980. *Syntax and semantics*, vol. 13: *Current approaches to syntax*. New York: Academic Press.

Myers, B. J. 1970. *Towa phrase structure*. University of North Dakota M.A. thesis.

Naylor, P. B. 1975. Topic, focus, and emphasis in the Tagalog verbal clause. *Oceanic Linguistics* 14.1: 12–79.

  1978. Toward focus in Austronesian. In Wurm & Carrington 1978, 395–442.

Nedjalkov, V. P. & B. Comrie (eds.) 1988. *Typology of resultative constructions*. Amsterdam: Benjamins.

Nguyen, D. L. 1974a. A classification of verbs in Vietnamese and its pedagogical implications. In Nguyen 1974b, 191–213.

  (ed.) 1974b. *South-East Asian linguistic studies*. Research School of Pacific Studies Department of Linguistics, *Pacific Linguistics* Series C, no. 31. Canberra: Australian National University.

  (ed.) 1976. *South-East Asian Linguistic Studies*, vol. 2. Research School of Pacific Studies Department of Linguistics, *Pacific Linguistics* series C, no. 42. Canberra: Australian National University.

Nichols, J. 1986. Head-marking and dependent-marking grammar. *Language* 62.1: 56–119.

Nichols, J. & A. C. Woodbury (eds.) 1985. *Grammar inside and outside the clause: some approaches to theory from the field*. Cambridge: Cambridge University Press.

Njie, C. M. 1982. *Description syntaxique du Wolof de Gambie*. Dakar-Abidjan-Lomé: Les Nouvelles Editions Africaines.
O'Connor, M. C. 1985. Semantics and discourse pragmatics of active case-marking in Northern Pomo. In S. DeLancey & R. S. Tomlin (eds.) University of Oregon Department of Linguistics, *Proceedings of the First Annual Meeting of the Pacific Linguistics Conference*, 225–46. Eugene, OR: University of Oregon.
O'Grady, W. D. 1980. The universal character of passivization. *Linguistic Analysis* 6.4: 393–405.
van Oosten, J. 1977. Subjects and agenthood in English. In W. Beach *et al.* (eds.) *CLS 13*, 459–71.
Papen, R. 1987. Linguistic variation in the French component of Métif grammar. *PNAC 18*, 247–59.
Paramasivam, K. 1979. Effectivity and causativity in Tamil. *International Journal of Dravidian Linguistics* 8.1: 71–151. Trivandrum, India. University of Chicago Ph.D. diss., 1977.
Paterson, S. J. 1983. *Voice and transitivity*. University of London Ph.D. diss.
Payne, D. L. 1985. Inflection and derivation: is there a difference? In S. DeLancey & R. S. Tomlin (eds.) University of Oregon Department of Linguistics, *Proceedings of the First Annual Meeting of the Pacific Linguistics Conference*, 247–60. Eugene, OR: University of Oregon.
Payne, T. E. 1982. Role and reference related subject properties and ergativity in Yup'ik Eskimo and Tagalog. *Studies in Language* 6.1: 75–106.
  1984. Split S-marking and fluid S-marking revisited. In D. Testen *et al.* (eds.) *Papers from the parasession on lexical semantics*, 222–32. Chicago: Chicago Linguistic Society.
Perel'muter, I. A. 1988. The stative, resultative, passive and perfect in ancient Greek (Homeric Greek). In Nedjalkov & Comrie 1988, 277–87.
Perlmuter, L. C. & R. A. Monty (eds.) 1979. *Choice and perceived control*. Hillsdale, NJ: Lawrence Erlbaum Associates.
Perlmutter, D. M. 1978. Impersonal passives and the unaccusative hypothesis. In J. Jaeger *et al.* (eds.) *BLS 4*, 157–89.
  1980. Relational grammar. In Moravscik & Wirth 1980, 195–229.
  1982. Syntactic representation, syntactic levels, and the notion of subject. In Jacobson & Pullum 1982, 283–340.
  (ed.) 1983. *Studies in relational grammar*, vol. 1. Chicago: University of Chicago Press.
  1989. Does Southern Tiwa grammar need initial-stratum reference? Presented at the 64th Annual Meeting, Linguistic Society of America, Washington, D.C.
Perlmutter, D. M. & R. Rhodes. 1988. Thematic–syntactic alignments in Ojibwa: evidence for subject–object reversal. Presented at the 63rd Annual Meeting, Linguistic Society of America, New Orleans.
Perlmutter, D. M. & C. Rosen (eds.) 1984. *Studies in relational grammar*, vol. 2. Chicago: University of Chicago Press.
Phares, E. J. 1976. *Locus of control in personality*. Morristown, NJ: General Learning Press.

Piggott, G. L. 1989. Argument structure and the morphology of the Ojibwa verb. In Gerdts & Michelson 1989, 176–208.
Pinkerton, S. 1976a. Ergativity and word order. In Pinkerton 1976b, 48–66.
(ed.) 1976b. *Studies in K'ekchi*. University of Texas Department of Linguistics, *Texas Linguistics Forum* 3. Austin: University of Texas.
Plank, F. (ed.) 1979. *Ergativity: towards a theory of grammatical relations*. London: Academic Press.
(ed.) 1985. *Relational typology*. Berlin: Mouton-de Gruyter.
Postal, P. M. 1986. *Studies of passive clauses*. Albany: State University of New York Press.
Postal, P. M. & B. D. Joseph (eds.) 1990. *Studies in relational grammar*, vol. 3. Chicago: University of Chicago Press.
Prasithrathsint, A. 1983. The Thai equivalents of the English passives in formal writing: a study of the influence of translation on the target language. University of Hawaii Department of Linguistics, *Working Papers in Linguistics* 15.1: 47–68. Honolulu: University of Hawaii.
Ramat, A. G., O. Carruba & G. Bernini (eds.) 1987. *Papers from the Seventh International Conference on Historical Linguistics*. Amsterdam: Benjamins.
Randriamasimanana, C. 1986. *The causatives of Malagasy*. Oceanic Linguistics special publication no. 21. Honolulu: University Press of Hawaii.
Rappaport, M. & B. Levin. 1986. What to do with theta-roles. MIT Department of Linguistics, *Lexicon Project Working Papers* 11. Cambridge, MA: MIT.
Reid, D. W. & M. Ziegler. 1981. The desired control measure and adjustment among the elderly. In Lefcourt 1981, 127–59.
Renshon, S. A. 1979. The need for personal control in political life: origins, dynamics, and implications. In Perlmuter & Monty 1979, 41–63.
Rhodes, R. A. 1976. *The morphosyntax of the Central Ojibwa verb*. University of Michigan Ph.D. diss.
1977. French Cree – a case of borrowing. *PNAC 8*, 6–25.
1980. On the semantics of the instrumental finals of Ojibwa. *PNAC 11*, 183–97.
1986. Métchif – a second look. *PNAC 17*, 287–96.
1987. Inversive person marking. Presented at the Conference on Native American Languages and Grammatical Typology, University of Chicago.
van Riemsdijk H. & E. Williams. 1986. *Introduction to the theory of grammar*. Cambridge, MA: MIT Press.
Rogers, J. 1975. Prediction of transitive animate verbs in an Ojibwa dialect. *International Journal of American Linguistics* 41.2: 114–39.
1976. Coding of role information in Ojibwa. *PNAC 7*, 257–71.
Rosen, C. 1984. The interface between semantic roles and initial grammatical relations. In Perlmutter & Rosen 1984, 38–77.
1990. Rethinking Southern Tiwa: the geometry of a triple-agreement language. *Language* 66.4: 669–713.
Rosenbaum, A. S. 1986. *Coercion and autonomy: philosophical foundations, issues, and practices*. New York: Greenwood Press.
Russell, D. 1987. Person agreement in Cheyenne: a reanalysis of post-stem suffixes. *PNAC 18*, 303–19.

Saksena, A. 1980. The affected agent. *Language* 56.4: 812–26.
Sandoval, M. 1984. The syntactic function of the *yi-/bi-* alternation in Jicarilla Apache. In Davis 1984, 153–90.
Sapir, J. D. 1971. West Atlantic: an inventory of the languages, their noun class systems, and consonant alternations. In Sebeok 1971a, 45–112.
Saunders, R. & P. Davis. 1982. The control system of Bella Coola. *International Journal of American Linguistics* 48.1: 1–15.
Saville-Troike, M. & L. A. McCreedy. 1979. Topic-prominence in Navajo. Presented at the 54th Annual Meeting, Linguistic Society of America, Los Angeles.
Scancarelli, J. 1987a. Multiple determinants of split ergative morphology. Presented at the 62nd Annual Meeting, Linguistic Society of America, San Francisco.
   1987b. *Grammatical relations and verb agreement in Cherokee*. UCLA Ph.D. diss.
Scancarelli, J. & P. W. Davis (eds.). To appear. *Native languages of the Southeast: representative studies*. University of Nebraska Press.
Schachter, P. 1976. The subject in Philippine languages: topic, actor, actor-topic, or none of the above? In Li 1976, 491–518.
   1977. Reference-related and role-related properties of subjects. In Cole & Sadock 1977, 279–306.
Schachter, P. & F. T. Otanes. 1972. *Tagalog reference grammar*. Berkeley & Los Angeles: University of California Press.
Schwyzer, E. 1950. *Griechische Grammatik*, vol. 2: *Syntax und syntaktische Stilistik*. Munich: C. H. Beck'sche Verlagsbuchhandlung.
Sebeok, T. A. (ed.) 1971a. *Current trends in linguistics*, vol. 7: *Linguistics in sub-Saharan Africa*. The Hague: Mouton.
   (ed.) 1971b. *Current trends in linguistics*, vol. 8: *Linguistics in Oceania*, pt. 1: *Indigenous languages*. The Hague: Mouton.
   (ed.) 1973. *Current trends in linguistics*, vol. 10: *Linguistics in North America*, pt. 3: *Native languages of North America*. The Hague: Mouton.
Seiter, W. J. 1979. Instrumental advancement in Niuean. *Linguistic Inquiry* 10.4: 595–621.
Seligman, M. E. P. & S. M. Miller. 1979. The psychology of power: concluding comments. In Perlmuter & Monty 1979, 347–70.
Sells, P. 1985. *Lectures on contemporary syntactic theories: an introduction to government-binding theory, generalized phrase structure grammar, and lexical–functional grammar*. Stanford University Center for the Study of Language and Information. Stanford, CA: Stanford University.
Shayne, J. 1982. Some semantic aspects of *yi-* and *bi-* in San Carlos Apache. In Hopper & Thompson 1982, 379–407.
Shibatani, M. (ed.) 1976. *Syntax and semantics*, vol. 6: *The grammar of causative constructions*. New York: Academic Press.
   1985. Passives and related constructions. *Language* 61.4: 821–48.
   1986. Grammaticization of topic into subject. Presented at the Symposium on Grammaticalization, University of Oregon Department of Linguistics, Eugene, OR. In Traugott & Heine in press.

1988a. Voice in Philippine languages. In Shibatani 1988c, 85–142.
1988b. Some empirical issues in linguistic typology: a Philippine perspective. In Linguistic Society of Korea, *Linguistics in the morning calm 2: selected papers from SICOL – 1986*, 79–117. Seoul: Hanshin.
(ed.) 1988c. *Passive and voice*. Amsterdam: Benjamins.
Shopen, T. (ed.) 1985. *Language typology and syntactic description*, vol. 1: *Clause structure*. Cambridge: Cambridge University Press.
Siewierska, A. 1984. *The passive: a comparative linguistic analysis*. London: Croom Helm.
Smith-Stark, T. 1978. The Mayan antipassive: some facts and fictions. In England 1978, 169–87.
Smyth, H. W. 1974. *Greek grammar*. Revised by G. M. Messing. Cambridge, MA: Harvard University Press.
Speijer, J. S. 1973. *Sanskrit syntax*. Reprint of 1886 edn (Leiden: Brill). Delhi: Motilal Banarsidass.
Steever, S. B. 1981. *Selected papers on Tamil and Dravidian linguistics*. Madurai, India: Muttu Patippakam.
Stennes, L. 1967. *A reference grammar of Adamawa Fula*. Michigan State University African Studies Center, African Language Monographs 8. E. Lansing, MI: Michigan State University.
Sylla, Y. 1979. *Grammatical relations and Fula syntax*. UCLA Ph.D. diss.
1982. *Grammaire moderne du Pulaar*. Dakar-Abidjan-Lomé: Les Nouvelles Editions Africaines.
Tamil lexicon. 1926–1936. 6 vols. plus Supplement (1938). Madras: University of Madras.
Teeter, K. V. 1967. Genetic classification in Algonquian. In *Contributions to anthropology: linguistics I (Algonquian)*. National Museum of Canada Anthropological Series no. 78, Bulletin 214, 1–6. Ottawa: National Museum of Canada.
1971. The main features of Malecite–Passamaquoddy grammar. In J. Sawyer (ed.), University of California Publications in Linguistics vol. 65, *Studies in American Indian languages*, 191–249. Berkeley: University of California.
1973. Algonquian. In Sebeok 1973, 1143–63.
Tesnière, L. 1959. *Eléments de syntaxe structurale*. Paris: Librairie C. Klincksieck.
Thalberg, I. 1972. *Enigmas of agency: studies in the philosophy of human action*. London & New York: Allen & Unwin and Humanities Press.
Thomas, M. 1988. Submissive passives in Vietnamese. In L. MacLeod *et al.* (eds.) *CLS 24/1*, 377–90.
Thomason, S. G. 1987. Language mixture: social causes and linguistic effects. Presented at the Conference on the Social Context of Language Change, Stanford University.
Thomason, S. G. & T. Kaufman. 1988. *Language contact, creolization, and genetic linguistics*. Berkeley: University of California Press.
Thompson, C. L. 1989. Voice and obviation in Navajo. In R. Carlson *et al.* (eds.), *Proceedings of the Fourth Meeting of the Pacific Linguistics Conference*, 466–88. Eugene, OR: University of Oregon.

1990. Passives and inverse constructions. Presented at the University of California–San Diego Voice Symposium. To appear in Fox & Hopper.
Thompson, L. C. 1979a. The control system: A major category in the grammar of Salishan languages. In Efrat 1979, 156–76.
  1979b. Control in Salish grammar. University of Hawaii Department of Linguistics, *Working Papers in Linguistics* 11.1: 133–50. Honolulu: University of Hawaii.
  1985. Control in Salish grammar. In Plank 1985, 391–428.
Thompson, L. C. & M. T. Thompson. 1981. More on the control system of Thompson Salish. In Mattina & Montler 1981, 126–31.
Thurneyson, R. 1970. *A grammar of Old Irish*. Tr. D. A. Binchy & O. Bergin. Reprint, revised edn. Dublin: Dublin Institute for Advanced Studies.
Tomlin, R. S. (ed.) 1987. *Coherence and grounding in discourse: outcome of a symposium, Eugene, Oregon, June 1984*. Amsterdam: Benjamins.
Traugott, E. & B. Heine (eds.). In press. *Approaches to grammaticalization*. 2 vols. Amsterdam: Benjamins.
Truitner, N. 1972. Passive sentences in Vietnamese. In P. Peranteau *et al.* (eds.) *CLS 8*, 368–78.
Vaillancourt, L.-P. 1980. De la catégorie du genre en cris. *PNAC 11*, 33–39.
Van Valin, R. D., Jr. 1987. The unaccusative hypothesis vs lexical semantics: syntactic vs semantic approaches to verb classification. In McDonough & Plunkett 1987, 641–61.
  1990. Semantic parameters of split intransitivity. *Language* 66.2: 221–60.
Vasu, S. C. 1962. *The Aṣhṭādhyāyī of Pāṇini*, vol. 1. Reprint edn. Delhi: Motilal Banarsidass.
Verma, M. K. (ed.) 1976. *The notion of subject in South Asian languages*. South Asian Studies Publication Series, Publication no. 2. Madison: University of Wisconsin.
Voegelin, C. F. 1971. Delaware, an Eastern Algonquian language. In Hoijer *et al.* 1971, 130–57.
Weaver, D. 1982. Obviation in Michif. University of North Dakota M.A. thesis. Published 1982. In D. C. Derbyshire (ed.) Summer Institute of Linguistics, University of North Dakota Sessions, *Work Papers* 26, 174–262. Huntington Beach, CA: Summer Institute of Linguistics.
  1983. The effect of language change and death on obviation in Michif. *PNAC 14*, 261–68.
Wertheimer, A. 1987. *Coercion*. Princeton, NJ: Princeton University Press.
Westermann, D. & M. A. Bryan. 1970. *Handbook of African languages*, pt. 2: *The languages of West Africa*. Folkestone & London: Dawsons of Pall Mall for the International African Institute.
Wheelock, F. 1963. *Latin: an introductory course based on ancient authors*. 3rd edn. New York: Barnes & Noble.
Whistler, K. W. 1985. Focus, perspective, and inverse person marking in Nootkan. In Nichols & Woodbury 1985, 227–65.
Whitney, W. 1885. *The roots, verb-forms, and primary derivatives of the Sanskrit language*. Supplement to Whitney 1973. Leipzig: Breitkopf and Härtel.

1973. *Sanskrit grammar*. Reprint, 5th edn. Delhi: Motilal Banarsidass.
Williams, W. & J. Jerome. 1979. Aspects of Micmac intransitive animate inflection. *PNAC 10*, 191–202.
Witherspoon, G. 1977. *Language and art in the Navajo universe*. Ann Arbor: University of Michigan Press.
   1980. Language in culture and culture in language. *International Journal of American Linguistics* 46.1: 1–13.
Wolfart, H. C. 1973. Plains Cree: a grammatical study. *Transactions of the American Philosophical Society* n.s. 63, pt. 5.
   1978. How many obviatives: sense and reference in a Cree verb paradigm. In Cook & Kaye 1978, 255–72.
Wolfart, H. C. & J. F. Carroll. 1973. *Meet Cree: a practical guide to the Cree language*. Edmonton: University of Alberta Press.
   1981. *Meet Cree: a guide to the Cree language*. 2nd, revised edn. Edmonton: University of Alberta Press.
Wolfenden, E. P. 1975. *A description of Hiligaynon syntax*. Norman, OK: Summer Institute of Linguistics.
Woodcock, E. C. 1959. *A new Latin syntax*. Cambridge, MA: Harvard University Press.
Wurm, S. A. & L. Carrington (eds.) 1978. *Second International Conference on Austronesian Linguistics*, fascicle 1: *Western Austronesian*. Research School of Pacific Studies Department of Linguistics, *Pacific Linguistics* Series C, no. 61. Canberra: Australian National University.
Young, R. W. & W. Morgan, Sr. 1987. *The Navajo language: a grammar and colloquial dictionary*. 2nd, revised edn. Albuquerque: University of New Mexico Press.
Zaenen, A. (ed.) 1982. *Subjects and other subjects: proceedings of the Harvard conference on the representation of grammatical relations*. Bloomington: Indiana University Linguistics Club.
Zaharlick, A. 1982. Tanoan studies: passive sentences in Picurís. In B. D. Joseph (ed.) Ohio State University Department of Linguistics, *Ohio State University Working Papers in Linguistics* 26, 34–48. Columbus, OH: Ohio State University.
Zide, A. R. K. 1972. Transitive and causative in Gorum. *Journal of Linguistics* 8.2: 201–15.
Zwicky, A. M. 1977. Hierarchies of person. In W. Beach *et al.* (eds.) *CLS 13*, 714–33.

Index

action, *verbally encoded event implicating the involvement of a participant to which or to whom control is ascribed*, 110, 112, 113, 114, 118, 133, 135, 136, 138, 150, 152, 153, 155, 173, 283 nn. 1, 2, 284 n. 4; accidental, 113, 133–5, 152–3; effects of, xiii, 11, 25, 73, 75, 82, 92, 106; mental/emotive, 57, 98, 101, 133; physical, 57, 98, 100, 101, 133; reflex, 100, 102, 104, 113, 133; spontaneous, 30–1, 74, 84, 93, *see also* inchoative; verbal semantic classes
activa tantum, *see* non-middle inflecting verbs
active/middle, xiv, 24–7, 29, 44, 93, 102, 104, 105–6, 260, 266, 278 n. 1; *see also* active–middle systems; active voice; basic voice type; middle
active–middle systems, 25, 42, 43, 44, 104, 108, 112, 140, 161; *see also* basic voice type
active-only, *see* non-middle inflecting verbs
active/passive, 2, 23, 27, 163, 172, 176, 182, 185, 195, 278 n. 1; *see also* active–passive systems; passives; passive voice; passivization
active–passive systems, 175, 182, 184, 186, 287 n. 7; *see also* derived voice
active voice, 3, 49, 50, 56, 57–9, 89, 101, 105, 123, 138, 182, 195, 204, 213, 244, 269, 270, 275–6 n. 18, 277 n. 19, 278 n. 1, 279 nn. 8, 11, 282 n. 28, 283 n. 32, 285 n. 10
active–stative type, 106–8, 112, 118, 124–32, 137, 147, 148, 151, 156, 157–8, 166, 283 n. 34, 284 n. 7, 285 nn. 8, 9
activity vs passivity, 3, 113, 283 n. 2
actor, 67, 149, 248, 249, 256, 258, 262, 283 n. 1, 295 nn. 9, 10, 11
adjuncts, 286 n. 4, 293 n. 1
adversity passives, *see* submissive verb constructions

affectedness, *characteristic of a participant in a verbally encoded situation which is typically sentient, is outranked for potential control by no other participant, and upon which devolve the principal effects of the denoted event or situation*, 28, 45, 67–9, 70, 72, 74, 76–9, 80, 82, 85, 92, 101, 103, 105, 108, 109, 138, 144, 147, 161, 270, 283 n. 1; affected entity relation, 268–70; Affectee status, 76–9, 92, 159, 277 n. 20; affective/effective, 72; *see also* Weak/Strong
agency, 112, 117, 118, 120, 121, 123, 124, 134, 135, 136, 137, 139, 149, 150, 151, 153, 155, 157, 273 n. 6, 275 n. 17, 283 n. 1; *see also* potentiality of agency scale; thematic relations
agentivity, *see* agency
agreement, *see* concord
Aktionsart, *a feature of inherent verbal semantics implicating the temporal character of the denoted event or situation*, 59, 94, 95, 105, 284 n. 5; telic/atelic, *characteristic of predicates whose semantics implicates the presence/absence of a natural endpoint of the denoted situation, action or event*, 94–7, 101, 103, 105, 280 n. 14, 282 n. 29
Alabama, *see* Muskogean languages
Algonquian languages, xiv, 162, 163, 169, 170, 180, 185–99, 200–1, 208, 210, 211, 217, 219, 220, 222, 225, 287 nn. 5, 6, 288 n. 11, 288–9 n. 13, 289 nn. 13, 14, 16, 290 nn. 17, 18, 19, 20; Algonkin, 183, 200, 217; Cheyenne, 185, 289 n. 13; Ojibwa (Chippewa), 165, 166, 167, 188, 189, 193, 194, 289 n. 13; Plains Cree (Cree) 32, 162, 164, 168, 169, 182, 188, 190, 191, 194, 198, 202, 289 n. 13, 290–1 n. 20
anaphora, 254, 286 n. 13; anaphoric

315

316 *Index*

anaphora (*cont.*)
  binding, 287–8, n. 9; anaphoric control, 143–4, 156, 286 n. 13
animacy, 45, 47, 57, 59, 81, 99, 102, 103, 113, 139, 145, 152, 158, 173–4, 177–8, 181, 184, 187–9, 204, 207, 211, 214, 215, 217, 218, 219, 222, 225, 226, 263, 264, 284 n. 6, 288 n. 11, 289 n. 15, 291–2 n. 25
animacy hierarchy, *see* potentiality of agency scale
antipassive, *see* passives
Apachean languages, 163, 175–81, 183, 196, 201, 208, 225, 287 n. 9, 289 n. 16, 290 n. 18; Chiricahua Apache, 180; Jicarilla Apache, 175, 286 n. 9; Navajo, 176–81, 182, 183, 196, 287 nn. 7, 8, 288 n. 12, 289 n. 16; San Carlos Apache, 175, 178–9; *see also* Athapaskan languages; Kiowa-Apache
applicatives, 50, 51, 52, 53–4, 63, 275 n. 16, 277 n. 19, 278 n. 7, 278–9 n. 8; *see also* extensions
arc pair grammar (APG), *see* relational grammar
argument frame, *a representation of that which a verb's inherent properties contribute to the interpretations of clauses in which it appears; subsumes both valence (which see) and predicate-argument structure (which see)*, 36, 37, 39, 75; *see also* lexical representation; predicate-argument structure
argument structure, 4–5, 9, 11, 35–43, 77, 106, 159, 164; normal, 4–5, 9, 11, 273 n. 8; *see also* clause structure; linking; logical relations; valence
argument type parameter, 166, 286 nn. 2, 3, 4
arguments, 12, 73, 183, 252, 262, 272 nn. 3, 4, 273 n. 10, 277 n. 20, 283 n. 1, 285 n. 10, 286 nn. 1, 2, 3, 4, 289 n. 15; core, 4, 6, 7, 11, 36, 51, 73, 77, 156, 159, 164, 168, 170, 180, 183, 186, 193, 200, 201, 211, 219, 263, 264, 285 n. 9, 289 n. 16; noncore, 4, 11, 180, 231, 291 n. 22; *see also* logical relations; nominal positions
Aṣṭādhyāyī, 1, 82–3, 89–92, 273 n. 5, 276–7 n. 18, 282 n. 27
Athapaskan languages, 175; *see also* Apachean languages, 175
attribution of control, *see* control
Australian languages, 196, 197–8; Dyirbal, 196, 230
Austronesian languages, 35, 147, 245;
Acehnese, 147–50, 154, 156, 285 n. 10; Bahasa Indonesia, 278 n. 5; Malayo-Polynesian languages, 35, 245; (Malagasy, 256); Niuean, 278 n. 5
authority, 115, 283 n. 3; *see also* power
autonomy, 115; *see also* power
awareness, 113, 117, 119; *see also* perception

background knowledge, 252; *see also* relevance
backgrounding, 291 n. 22
Bantu languages, 278 n. 5; 293 n. 1; Chicheŵa, 293 n. 1; Chi-Mwi:ni, 278 n. 5; Kinyarwanda, 278 n. 5; *see also* Niger-Congo languages
basic voice type, xiv, 2, 24, 25, 27, 29, 35, 43, 44–6, 56, 73, 104, 112, 137–40, 161, 162, 171, 227, 263, 265, 266–70, 271, 285 n. 10; *see also* active–middle systems
biclausal, 51, 141, 278 n. 6
biuniqueness condition, 41–2; *see also* uniqueness condition
bivalent, *see* ditransitive

case, *a nominal category whereby is encoded the grammatical relationship of a nominal in a clause to the verb*, 1, 24, 25, 128, 164, 166, 170, 201, 206, 208, 219, 225, 229, 233, 236, 243, 247, 248, 250, 252, 258, 277 n. 20, 286 nn. 1, 2, 292 n. 27, 295 n. 11; absolutive, 230, 231, 233, 235, 236, 237, 238, 239, 240, 241, 242, 243, 252, 261, 284 n. 7, 294 nn. 2, 4; ergative, 34, 230, 231, 235, 237, 238, 243, 252, 261, 294 nn. 4, 6, 7; ergative/absolutive, 35, 46, 106–8, 129–30, 229, 230, 284 n. 7, 285 n. 9; *see also* ergative–absolutive systems; ergative language type; ergativity instrumental, 233, 241, 275 n. 18, 291 n. 22; nominative/accusative, 129, 130; oblique, 208, 235, 240, 241, 244, 248, 249, 250, 284 n. 7
case grammar, 37, 272 n. 5, 277 n. 20
causative, 51, 53, 72, 90–1, 135, 152–3, 278–9 n. 8; morphological, 51, 72, 275 n. 16, 278 n. 6, 279 n. 8; periphrastic, 51, 72, 279 n. 8
Cherokee, *see* Iroquoian languages
Chinese, *see* Southeast Asian languages
Chocho, *see* Otomanguean languages
choice, 114, 115, 117
Chukotko-Kamchatkan languages, 33, 170
clause structure, 4–5, 12, 20, 23, 29;

Index 317

normal, 4, 9, 11, 12, 273 n. 8; *see also* argument structure
coercion, 113, 115; *see also* control
completeness condition, 39
concord, 157–8, 164, 183, 233, 276 n. 18, 286 n. 1, 289 n. 15
configurationality, 165–7, 168, 196, 197, 286 n. 2, 286–7 n. 4; *see also* argument type parameter
conjunct order, *see* orders
control, *capacity of an individual to engage or, alternatively, to refrain from engaging in a particular action (which see); characteristic of a participant in a given situation such that (a) the situation's realization depends on the participant role (which see) in question and (b) the situation is compatible with that participant's intentional involvement therein*, 31, 45, 47, 57, 59, 81–2, 84, 100, 104, 107, 110–60, 172–4, 268, 270, 283 n. 1, 285 nn. 11, 12, 286 n. 13, 291 n. 21; agenda, 115, 145, 146, 283–4 n. 3; attribution of, 112, 118, 147, 156, 159, 161–2, 169, 176, 177–9, 227; control construct, 110–12, 120–1, 122, 137–40, 149, 156, 161, 172, 265; outcome, 115, 116, 135, 145, 146, 153, 155, 283–4 n. 3; *see also* locus of control
controller, actual, 264, 265, 266, 267, 268, 270; controller-set (C), 267; potential controller set (P), 264, 267, 268
Cupeño, 118, 132–6, 159

decontrol, *see* control
dependency, 167, 169, 286 n. 3
deponency, *characteristic of verbs expressing physical or mental dispositions presupposing the logical subject's animacy and control*, 45, 47, 59, 69, 70, 81–2, 83, 100, 102, 104, 270; deponent (in traditional grammar), 97–8; *see also* Latin, r̲ conjugation
derivation, 23, 111, 112, 127–8, 140, 147–50, 150–6, 161, 284 n. 7, 285 n. 10
derived voice, 127–8, 197–8, 208, 212, 223, 224, 225, 245, 257, 258, 284 n. 7, 285 n. 8, 288 n. 12; derived voice type, xiii, 22, 23, 34, 35, 44, 73, 143, 161, 171, 186, 208, 225, 228, 229, 238, 241, 243, 246, 256, 258, 261, 262, 271, 285 n. 10; *see also* active–passive systems
detransitivization, 18, 19, 45, 46, 50, 52, 54, 55, 57, 61, 62, 64, 76, 80, 92, 95, 97, 104, 105, 127, 148, 149, 150, 182–3,
208–9, 212, 215, 240, 273 n. 10, 284 nn. 6, 7, 285 nn. 8, 10, 12, 288 n. 10
diathesis, *a representation of the lexical structure of a verb which takes into account its alternative relationships with nominals or nominal positions*, 2, 64–9, 123, 272 n. 3; body-part, 65, 67, 68, 75, 88, 90, 104; objective decausative, 65, 66, 67, 83, 92, 104; *see also* neuters; reciprocal, 65, 66–7, 89–90; structural reflexive, 65, 67, 68, 75, 82, 89–92, 281 n. 12; transitive (ordinary), 64, 66; transitive (indirect) reflexive, 68, 75, 104
differential voices, *see* semantic functions of voices
direct/inverse, *see* inverse
direct–inverse voice systems, *see* inverse
distinctness condition, 41–2, 159; *see also* uniqueness condition
ditransitive, 4, 17, 56, 176, 222–3, 281 n. 18
downgrading, *see* suppression
Dravidian languages, 25, 46, 69, 70, 281 n. 22; Tamil, 25–6, 29, 46, 69–82, 102, 105, 106, 269, 281 nn. 19, 20, 22, 23; Tamil traditional grammars, 70
dummy, 8

English, *see* Indo-European languages
Equi, 21
ergative/absolutive, *see* case
ergative–absolutive systems, 129, 196, 257, 284–5 n. 8, 295 n. 11
ergative language type, 44, 129, 166, 186, 196, 230, 233, 284 n. 7
ergativity, 35, 72, 129–30, 284 n. 7, 285 n. 9
extensions, 29–30, 50, 51, 52, 53, 63–5, 67–9, 151, 153, 155, 277 n. 19, 278 n. 7, 278–9 n. 8; Benefactive, 51; Dative, 51, 53–4; Modal, 51, 53–4; Reciprocal, 63; Reflexive, 63, 68–9, 277 n. 19; *see also* applicatives

fluid S-marking, 125, 158; *see also* split S-marking
focus, 11, 34–5, 228, 233–7, 245–59, 262, 293–4 n. 1, 294 n. 8, 294–5 n. 9, 295 nn. 10, 11; particles (actor [A], goal [G], direction [D], instrumental [I]), 248, 250; *see also* pragmatic voice type; salience, informational
focus-sensitive (F-sensitive) rules, 234, 241, 243, 245, 246, 253, 254, 294 n. 5; emphasis, 234, 241, 243, 245, 246, 251–

focus-sensitive rules (*cont.*)
  6, 294–5 n. 9, 295 n. 10; question, 234, 241, 243, 245–6, 253, 254, 293 n. 1; relativization, 234, 241, 243, 246, 253, 254, 293 n. 1
focus systems, 33–5, 42, 43, 228, 245, 259, 262; *see also* information-salience systems; pragmatic voice type
foregrounding, 258
fourth person, *see* obviative
Fula (Fulani), 26, 29–30, 46, 47–69, 70, 95, 96, 102, 105, 106, 278 nn. 3, 4, 5, 7, 278–9 n. 8, 279 nn. 9, 10, 11, 279–80 n. 12, 280 nn. 15, 16, 17, 281 n. 18, 282 n. 21, 283 n. 31; Adamawa dialect, 278 n. 4; Fuuta Tooro dialect, 47, 48, 51, 63, 278 nn. 3, 4, 280 nn. 15, 16; Gombe dialect, 47, 278 nn. 3, 4, 280 nn. 15, 16; *see also* Niger-Congo languages
functional control, *see* obligatory control

generative-transformational grammar, 21
government, 165, 166, 167, 180, 233, 241, 246, 250, 275–6 n. 18
grammatical categories, 2, 261, 271, 272 nn. 2, 4; of the verb, xiv, 1, 2; *see also* case; mood/modality; number; person; temporal categories
grammatical relations, 1, 2, 13, 14, 20–1, 27, 142, 179–80, 226, 260, 262–3, 269, 273–4 n. 11, 274 n. 15, 277 n. 18, 286 n. 2; indirect object, 12, 14, 17, 20, 28, 31, 131, 261, 274 nn. 14, 15, 281 n. 18; object, 12, 14, 17–19, 24, 28, 51, 78, 121, 124–7, 131, 156, 165, 179–80, 224, 261, 272 n. 4, 273–4 n. 11, 274 n. 14, 274–5 n. 15, 295 n. 11; oblique, 14, 17–20, 34, 51, 127, 142, 261; subject, 12, 13, 14, 17–21, 22, 23, 24, 25, 27–8, 31, 54, 78, 83, 85, 92, 121, 124–7, 131, 142, 143–5, 147, 156, 161, 165, 179–80, 224, 256, 258, 260–2, 269, 272 n. 4, 273 n. 10, 273–4 n. 11, 274–5 n. 15, 275 n. 17, 276–7 n. 18, 281 n. 18, 286 n. 13, 288 n. 9, 295 n. 11
grammaticization, 117, 137, 161, 162, 169, 195, 227, 265, 266, 268, 270, 277 n. 20
Greek, xiv, 2, 3, 24, 27–9, 31, 47, 78, 84–92, 93, 95–100, 104, 278 n. 1, 280 n. 14, 281 nn. 18, 24, 282 nn. 29–31; Homeric, 84, 96, 280 n. 14; *see also* Indo-European languages

head-/dependent-marking, 165, 167–70, 180, 208, 219, 220, 225, 230, 286 n. 3;
head-marking type, 170, 180, 208, 219, 220, 225, 230

inchoative, *characteristic of uncontrolled events, or of verbally encoded situations presupposing no participant's control*, 45, 74, 84, 93, 102, 103; *see also* action, spontaneous
independence condition, 39
independent order, *see* orders
Indo-European languages, xiv, 9, 23, 24, 25, 26, 29, 30, 46, 78, 82–104, 105, 270, 277–8 n. 1, 278 n. 2; Balto-Slavic, 86; Celtic, 86; (Old Irish, 86); Germanic, 86, 283 n. 33; (English, 7, 21, 45, 65, 93, 96, 118, 127, 167, 196, 198, 267, 278 n. 2, 280 n. 14; German, 7, 278 n. 2; Gothic, 85, 93; Norwegian, 283 n. 33; Old Norse, 86; Swedish, 86, 283 n. 33); Hittite, 86, 93; Indo-Iranian, 84, 85, 86; (Avestan, 281 n. 24; Old Persian, 85, 281 n. 24; Indo-Aryan, 69, 281 n. 23; (Bengali, 6)); Tocharian, 86; *see also* Greek; Latin; Romance languages; Sanskrit
inflection, 24, 26, 46, 54, 70, 85, 95, 107, 111, 123, 125–32, 148–50, 157–9, 188, 190, 283 n. 32, 284 n. 7, 285 n. 10
informational salience, *see* information-salience systems
information-salience systems, 33–5, 42, 43, 228, 245, 259, 262; *see also* focus systems; pragmatic voice type; salience, informational
information structure, 33, 198, 199, 228, 251, 262, 263; *see also* background knowledge; focus; relevance; salience, informational; topic
inherent voices, *see* semantic functions of voices
instrumental voice (Mayan), *see* passives
intentionality, 113, 114, 119, 133, 135, 295 n. 1; possibly intentional *s*, 264
intransitives, *see* transitivity
inverse, xiv, 33, 193, 200, 202, 206, 209, 210, 212, 213, 215, 218, 220, 224, 225, 265, 288 n. 12, 289 n. 16, 290 n. 17, 291 n. 22; direct/inverse, 32, 171, 175, 181, 182, 185, 202, 207, 208, 210, 211, 263, 291 n. 24, 292 n. 27; direct–inverse systems, 32, 33, 42, 43, 158, 161–226, 263, 264, 265, 267, 287 n. 6, 292–3 n. 27; direct voice, 200, 202, 204, 206, 213, 215, 218, 225, 265
Iroquoian languages, Cherokee, 156–9

Japanese, *see* Southeast Asian languages

Kiowa-Apache, 180
Korean, *see* Southeast Asian languages

Latin, xiv, 2, 3, 24, 86, 93, 97, 164, 286 n. 2; r̄ conjugation, 86, 97, 282 n. 30; *see also* Indo-European languages; Romance languages
lexical entailment, 37–8
lexical-functional grammar (LFG), 41, 121, 286 n. 13, 293 n. 1
lexical representation, 22, 36–42, 76, 266–9, 270; *see also* argument frame; predicate-argument structure; valence
lexicon, 43, 44, 45, 70, 100–1, 104–7, 109, 111, 112, 113, 118, 121, 132–3, 137–40, 156, 227
linking, *identification of the semantic roles assigned by a lexical predicate with a set of nominal positions*, 11, 12, 22, 24, 38, 39, 78, 275 n. 17; *see also* argument structure
local predications, 175, 190, 191, 202, 212, 213, 264, 289–90 n. 17; *see also* person, first, second
locus of causality, 115, 116
locus of control, 114, 115, 179, 284 n. 3; *see also* control
logical relations, 4, 5, 11, 14, 36–7, 83, 118, 160, 164, 166, 167, 200, 201, 210, 219, 220, 226, 263–4, 265, 269, 286 n. 1; logical indirect object, 176; logical object, 83, 123, 142, 163, 169, 173, 174, 176, 177, 188, 190, 195, 204, 206, 207, 219, 224, 230, 236, 243, 244, 257, 274 n. 11, 275 n. 18, 284 n. 6, 287–8 n. 9, 288 n. 11; logical subject, 54, 83, 92, 104, 110, 111, 118, 119, 123, 124, 132, 134, 145, 153, 158, 163, 169, 173, 174, 176, 177, 183, 190, 195, 196, 201, 202, 204, 206, 207, 211–12, 219, 224, 225, 230, 236, 243, 244, 269, 274 n. 11, 275 n. 18, 283 n. 1, 284 n. 6, 287–8 n. 9, 288 n. 11, 291 n. 22
logical structure, *see* logical relations

markedness, 6–9, 20, 71, 86, 95, 97, 107–8, 137–8, 166, 170, 173, 174, 185, 190, 193, 200, 201, 206, 208, 213, 218, 225, 226, 241, 248, 250, 257, 265, 269, 273 n. 7, 277 n. 18, 282 n. 29, 284 n. 7, 285 nn. 11, 12
marking, *see* markedness
Mayan languages, xiv, 228–45, 246, 247, 251, 252, 253, 254, 258, 262, 293 n. 1; Kanjobalan, 235; (Jacaltec, 235, 239, 242); Mamean, 235; (Ixil, 33, 235, 242, 243–5, 246, 258, 262; Mam, 229, 230, 232, 235, 239); Quichean, 235; (Cakchiquel, 235, 240–1; K'ekchi, 228, 229, 231–8, 239, 294 nn. 2, 3, 6; Pocomam, 235; Quiche, 240, 242; Tzutujil, 235, 239, 240, 242); Tzeltal, 6; Tzotzil, 239
media tantum, *see* non-active inflecting verbs
medioagentive, 273 n. 6
mediopassive, 45, 46, 273 n. 6, 278 n. 1; *see also* Latin, r̄ conjugation
middle, 3–4, 24, 27, 29, 44–109, 123–4, 138, 155, 269, 270, 273 n. 6, 278 nn. 1, 2, 279 nn. 8, 11, 280 nn. 14, 15, 16, 17, 281 nn. 18, 22, 282 nn. 28, 29, 282–3 n. 31, 283 n. 32, 285 n. 10; catalytic function of, 90, 104; nucleonic function of, 91; *see also* active–middle systems; basic voice type; middle verbs; semantic functions of voices
middle verbs (lexical class), 45–6, 93, 124, 273 n. 7, 280 n. 14, 284 n. 5
middle-only, *see* non-active inflecting verbs
modality, *see* mood/modality
monoclausal, 51, 278 n. 6
monostratal grammars, 22, 121; *see also* multistratal grammars
mood/modality, 1, 2, 59; imperative, 280 n. 16; irrealis, 60, 61, 95–6, 105; *see also* noneventuality; temporomodal semantics
multistratal grammars, 22, 121; *see also* monostratal grammars
Muskogean languages, Alabama, 131–2, 159

negatives, 60, 291 n. 22; *see also* mood/modality, irrealis
neo-middle voice functions, *functions of elements cognate to reflexive markers which overlap those of inflectional middle voices*, 45–6, 86–7, 282 n. 28
neuters, *intransitive verbs which are in correspondence with semantically related, homophonous transitives*, 62, 66, 67, 83, 92–5, 97, 101, 103, 104, 105, 122, 123, 127, 266–8, 273 n. 7, 282 n. 29, 284 n. 5, 285 n. 12; *see also* diathesis, objective decausative
Niger-Congo languages, 26, 46, 47, 278 n. 5; West Atlantic subgroup, 26, 46, 47,

320 Index

Niger-Congo languages (*cont.*)
  278 n. 5; hu-Limba, 278 n. 5; Wolof,
  278 n. 5; *see also* Fula
nominal downgrading, *see* suppression
nominal positions, core, 156, 170, 171,
  208, 224, 230, 231, 238, 239, 245, 261,
  269, 270, 287 n. 6; noncore, 224, 231,
  245, 291 n. 22; *see also* arguments
nominal reference tracking, 171, 181,
  196–9, 287 n. 6, 291 n. 20; *see also*
  obviation; switch-reference
nominal suppression, *see* suppression
nominalizations, 253, 295 n. 11
nominative/accusative, *see* case
non-active inflecting verbs, 55, 57, 59, 70,
  72, 80–2, 83, 96, 97–104, 105, 106, 108,
  111, 138–9, 270, 281 n. 21
non-control, *see* control
non-configurational, *see* configurationality
nondeponent, *see* deponency
noneventuality, *characteristic of a verbally
  encoded situation or event which is
  irrealis and/or nonpunctual*; 61, 69, 74,
  82, 83, 95–6, 103, 105, 283 n. 31; *see
  also* mood/modality; temporal
  categories; temporomodal semantics
non-middle inflecting verbs, 55, 57–9, 66,
  70, 72, 80, 81–2, 83, 97–104, 105, 106,
  108, 111, 138–9, 281 n. 21, 282 n. 31
nonreferential nominals, 232–3, 236–7,
  238, 252, 253, 294 n. 7; *see also*
  referentiality
nonvolitional action, *see* volitionality
normal configuration, *see* argument
  structure; nominal positions
noun incorporation, 17–18, 19, 20, 223
number, 129, 183, 186–7, 189, 190, 204,
  218, 219, 231, 279 n. 9, 289 n. 15, 292
  nn. 25, 26, 292–3 n. 27

obligatory control, 160, 286 n. 13
object, *see* grammatical relations; logical
  relations; ontology
obviation, 169, 170, 171, 187, 193, 194,
  196, 287 n. 6, 291 n. 20; *see also*
  obviative; person
obviative, 163, 170, 180–1, 183, 193, 194,
  195–6, 199, 201, 202, 208, 211, 225, 286
  n. 1, 288 n. 10, 290 n. 18, 290–1 n. 20;
  see also obviation; person
ontological object, *see* ontology
ontological subject, *see* ontology
ontology, 138, 140, 144, 146, 147, 159,
  160, 162, 168, 176, 177, 179–80, 195,
  213, 220, 224, 225, 227, 265, 286 n. 13;
  ontological object, *that core argument*

*of a transitive predicate identified with
  inferior attribution of control*, 163, 169,
  171–2, 175, 179, 180, 181, 188, 207,
  208, 221, 263, 265, 292 n. 26;
ontological structure, 263–9, 271;
ontological subject, *that core argument
  of a transitive predicate identified with
  superior attribution of control*, 158, 163,
  169, 171–4, 175, 176, 180, 181, 200,
  201, 207, 210, 211, 215, 221, 263, 265,
  292 n. 27; *see also* salience, ontological
orders, conjunct, 190, 198–9;
  independent, 190, 191, 198–9
Otomanguean languages, Chocho, 124–8,
  284 n. 7; *see also* Uto-Aztecan
  languages

Pāṇini, *see* Aṣṭādhyāyī
Papuan languages, 197; Usan, 197
participant roles, *semantic or pragmatic
  statuses borne by a verb's assigned
  arguments*, 36, 42, 110, 139, 161, 248,
  250, 253, 258, 262, 264–9, 285 n. 10,
  295 n. 9
passive-only inflecting verbs, 55, 279–80
  n. 12
passive voice, 23, 29, 35, 44, 45, 50, 53–4,
  56, 78, 84–5, 95, 135, 163, 172, 176,
  182, 184, 185, 195, 204, 208–10, 212–
  13, 215, 218, 229, 230, 238, 239, 243,
  244, 257, 258, 269, 270, 275–7 n. 18,
  278 n. 1, 279 n. 8, 281 n. 24, 282 n. 29,
  284 n. 6, 288 n. 12; *see also* passives;
  passivation
passives, antipassive, xiii, 23, 34, 196,
  198, 229, 230, 231, 232, 233, 235, 237,
  238, 239, 256, 258, 261, 273 nn. 6, 9,
  284 n. 7, 284–5 n. 8, 288 n. 12, 294 nn.
  2, 7; (absolutive antipassive, 232; focus
  antipassive, 232, 233, 235, 236, 238,
  242, 243; incorporating antipassive,
  232, 235, 236, 237); impersonal passive,
  xiii, 8, 23, 84; instrumental voice
  (Mayan), 240–2, 243, 247; oblique
  passive, xiii, 23, 243, 288 n. 12;
  ordinary (personal) passive, xiii, 3, 8,
  23, 78, 230, 244; referential voice
  (Mayan), 239–40; *see also* passive
  voice; semantic functions of voices
passivization, xiii, 24, 53, 54, 78–9, 83,
  84, 98, 163, 182–5, 209, 230, 270, 275–7
  n. 18, 288 n. 11, 293 n. 27; *see also*
  passives; passive voice
patient-subject constructions, 273 n. 6
perception, 116; *see also* awareness
person, 129, 170, 186, 187, 189, 199, 200,

204, 211, 212, 218, 223, 225, 230, 291 n. 24, 291-2 n. 25; first, second (speech act participants, SAP), 125, 164, 168, 169, 171, 172, 190, 191, 193, 199, 206, 207, 213, 219, 264, 285 n. 9, 289-90 n. 17, 292 n. 26; *see also* local predications; fourth, *see* obviative; third, 164, 175, 176, 181, 191, 193, 195, 198, 199, 201, 202, 204, 207, 208, 211, 213, 265, 287 n. 6, 290 n. 18, 291 nn. 20, 23, 24, 292 n. 26; fifth, 290-1, n. 20; *see also* obviative; proximate
Philippine languages, xiv, 35, 228, 245-59, 260, 262, 293 n. 1, 295 n. 11; Cebuano, 228, 246-56, 295 nn. 10, 11; Kapampangan, 256, 295 nn. 9, 10; Tagalog, xiv, 228, 247, 252, 255, 294 nn. 8, 9, 295 n. 10; *see also* Austronesian languages
philosophy, 112, 113, 114, 116
polyadicity, *alternations of valence (which see) associated with a lexical predicate*, 45
possession, 28, 65, 67, 77, 90, 104, 125, 131, 166, 194, 204, 291 n. 20
possessives, *see* possession
potentiality of agency scale, 119-20, 122, 123, 127, 133, 139, 145, 158, 163, 168, 169, 184, 263, 270
potentiality of control hierarchy, 266
power, 114-15, 179; *see also* control
pragmatics, 162, 227, 238, 241, 242, 245, 246, 251, 256, 258, 259, 286 n. 2, 291 n. 23, 293 n. 1; pragmatic salience, 33, 42, 162, 256
pragmatic voice type, xiv, 31, 35, 43, 161, 162, 171, 227, 231, 245, 246, 271; Actor voice, 247, 249, 256, 295 n. 11; Directional voice, 247, 249; Goal voice, 247, 257, 295 n. 11; Instrumental voice (Philippine languages), 247, 249; *see also* focus; information-salience systems; inverse; salience; informational; salience, ontological
predicate-argument structure, *that part of an argument frame (which see) specifying the logical structure composed of a verb in a network of relations with arguments*, 4, 12, 14, 22, 36-7, 159; *see also* argument frame; lexical representation; valence
predications, 36, 166, 171, 172, 189, 204, 212, 213, 214, 215, 217, 218, 224, 227, 263, 264, 268, 270, 288 n. 11, 290 n. 17, 291 nn. 22, 23, 292 n. 25
prototype, 138-40

proximate, 170, 193, 195-6, 199, 201; *see also* person, third
psychology, 112, 114

radicals, 48, 50, 51, 53-61, 63, 64, 66-8, 96, 278 n. 7, 279 nn. 8, 9, 279-80 n. 12, 280 nn. 15, 17, 281 n. 18
Raising, 21
reciprocal, 28, 29, 45, 65-7, 75, 89-90, 103, 105, 277 n. 19, 278 n. 2, 280 n. 15, 281 n. 25; *see also* diathesis, reciprocal
reference-related properties, 256; *see also* role-related properties
reference tracking, *see* nominal reference tracking
referentiality, *characteristic of nominals having restricted (hence not indefinite) reference*, 237, 246, 252, 253, 294 n. 6; *see also* nonreferential nominals
referential voice (Mayan), *see* passives
reflexive, 6, 28, 29, 45, 46, 50, 62-9, 70, 75, 82, 85-9, 104, 204, 212, 277 n. 19, 278 n. 2, 282 nn. 28, 30, 283 n. 33, 284 n. 6, 285 n. 12; reflexive pronouns, 63, 88, 282 n. 28; reflexive passive, 46; semantic reflexive meaning, 64-5, 66, 68, 69, 75, 88-90, 103, 105, 283 n. 33; *see also* diathesis
reinforcement, 114, 115
relational grammar (RG), 13, 239, 274 n. 13, 274-5 n. 15, 293 n. 1; arc pair grammar (APG), 239, 274 n. 13, 293 n. 1
relational hypothesis, 13, 274 n. 13
relational noun, 230, 231, 241
relevance, 252; *see also* background knowledge; information structure
responsibility-relation (RESP), 160
role and reference grammar (RRG), 283 n. 1
role-related properties, 256; *see also* reference-related properties
role-remapping, *characteristic of a rule or process which alters the grammatical relation to which an argument is mapped in a basic (nonderived) structural configuration*, 11, 13, 14, 22, 24, 241, 274 n. 14, 277 n. 18
Romance languages, 86, 282 n. 28; French, 47; Italic, 123; (Italian, 123); Spanish, 6, 64

salience, informational xiv, 11, 33-5, 43, 162, 228, 231, 233, 234, 236, 238, 240, 241, 242, 243, 244-5, 246, 250, 251, 252, 258, 259, 262, 271, 293-4 n. 1, 294

salience, informational (cont.)
n. 6; see also focus; information-salience systems; pragmatics, pragmatic salience; ontological, xiv, 32–3, 120, 158–9, 162–3, 168–9, 170, 171, 172, 184, 191, 193, 195, 199, 201, 207, 211, 227, 263–7, 287 n. 6, 291 n. 22; see also inverse; ontology
Salishan languages, 132, 163, 225, 285 n. 11; Bella Coola, 285 n. 11; Colville-Okanagan, 285 n. 11; Lummi 202–3, 206, 207, 208, 212, 225, 291 n. 21; Puget Salish, 285 n. 11; Thompson River Salish, 151–6, 285 nn. 11, 12
Sanskrit, xiv, 1, 25, 29, 30–1, 69, 70, 78, 84, 86–91, 93–104, 106, 260, 270, 275–7 n. 18, 281 nn. 24, 25, 26, 272 n. 29; traditional grammars, see Aṣṭādhyāyī; Vedic, 84, 282 n. 29; see also Indo-European languages
semantic functions of voices, differential, 49, 50, 55, 56, 59, 60–3, 74, 80, 82, 83, 85, 92, 95, 102, 281 n. 21; inherent, 49, 50, 55, 56, 59, 61, 80, 82, 270, 281 n. 21; middle, 44–109, 138, 278 n. 1; passive, 83, 84, 88, 278 n. 1, 284 n. 6; see also middle
semantic roles, *that which the arguments assigned by a predicate individually contribute to the interpretation of a structural configuration in which that predicate appears; or alternatively, the contents of nominal positions specified in a predicate-argument structure, subsuming thematic relations*, 4, 11, 12, 22, 23, 36–8, 65, 73, 75, 83, 239, 272 n. 5, 273 n. 10, 275 n. 17, 277 n. 18, 283 n. 1; see also thematic relations
semantics, 29, 138–40, 159, 160, 162, 195, 227, 256, 263–70
situations (s), 264–5, 266–8, 270, 295 n. 1
situation-set (S), 264, 266–8
social sciences, 112
Southeast Asian languages, 140; Cambodian, 141; Chinese (Mandarin), 141, 143, 144; Chinese (non-Mandarin), 141; Hmong, 141; Japanese, 141–6, 251; Korean, 163, 170, 171–5; Lao, 141; Thai, 141; Vietnamese, 141, 143, 144
split patterning, 125, 129, 157–8, 284 n. 7, 285 n. 9
split S-marking, 125, 151; see also fluid S-marking
Strong voice, 29, 269, 281 nn. 19, 23; see also Weak voice
structural configurations, see clause structure
subject, see grammatical relations; logical relations; ontology
submissive verb constructions, 112, 140–6, 147
subordinate clauses, 129, 198
suppression, 73, 83, 183, 232–3, 257–8, 270, 273 n. 7, 284 nn. 6, 7, 288 n. 12
switch-reference, 197–8; see also nominal reference tracking

Tanoan languages, 14, 163, 200–26, 288 nn. 11, 12, 291 n. 24, 292 nn. 25, 27; Tewa, 203, 211, 212, 215, 220, 222; (Arizona Tewa, 163, 203, 204–11, 212, 213, 214–15, 225, 291 n. 24, 292 n. 27); Tiwa, 203, 222, 224, 292 n. 27; (Picurís, 203, 211–21, 222–3, 291 n. 24, 292 nn. 25, 26, 27; Southern Tiwa, 14–20, 203, 211–21, 222–4, 274 n. 14; 275 n. 15; 291 n. 24; 292 nn. 25, 26); Towa, 203, 211, 212, 217, 220–1, 222, 292 nn. 25, 26, 27; (Jemez, 203, 211, 212, 217, 220–1, 222, 292 nn. 25, 26, 27)
telic/atelic, see Aktionsart
temporal categories, 47–8, 59, 60, 95–7, 105, 129, 149, 150, 284 n. 5; infinitive, 278 n. 3; nonpunctual, 47–8, 60, 61, 95–7, 105, 280 n. 14, see also noneventuality; aspect, 1, 2, 59, 105, 129; (perfect, 95–6, 280 n. 14; progressive, 59; stative (statal), 59, 60, 96, 130, 149, 150, 157–8, 204, 209, 280 n. 14, 291 n. 22); tense, 1, 2, 59, 96, 105, 129, 157; (future, 60, 96; present, 96, 97, 275 n. 18); see also Aktionsart
temporomodal semantics, 69, 74, 82, 95, 96–7, 103, 105, 130, 283 n. 31; see also mood/modality; temporal categories
Thai, see Southeast Asian languages
thematic relations, 37–42, 76, 111, 159–60, 226, 241, 243, 248, 266, 269, 270, 277 n. 20, 293 n. 1; agent, 3, 4, 11, 12, 13, 14, 17, 21, 24, 25, 28, 31, 38, 39, 40, 41, 42, 74, 92, 93, 111, 117, 119, 120, 131, 134, 149, 152, 156, 179, 249, 258, 273 nn. 6, 10, 275 n. 17, 276 n. 18, 283 n. 1, 290 n. 18; beneficiary, 14, 38, 40, 111, 289 n. 16; direction, 248, 249; experiencer, 14, 17, 31, 38, 40, 111; goal, 179, 243, 248, 249, 251, 257, 258, 262, 277 n. 20, 289 n. 16, 295 n. 11; instrument, 14, 18, 34, 38, 40, 51, 240–2, 248, 249, 262; location, 14, 38, 40,

111, 248, 249, 250; patient, 3, 4, 11, 12, 13, 14, 17, 21, 24, 38, 40, 42, 131, 156, 249, 258, 273 n. 6, 290 n. 18; recipient, 248, 249; theme, 40, 111, 258, 277 n. 20, 289 n. 16; *see also* semantic roles
theme, 251; *see also* topic
theme signs, 163, 168, 187, 188, 189, 190, 193, 200, 202, 208, 212, 213, 220, 225, 290 n. 17
theta-feature, 159
theta-hierarchy, 39, 111, 159, 266, 270, 277 n. 20
theta-roles, *see* thematic relations
topic, 11, 33, 162, 228, 233–7, 248, 251, 262, 293–4 n. 1, 294 nn. 7, 9
topicality, *see* topic
traditional grammar, 2–4, 9, 27; *see also* Sanskrit, traditional grammars; Dravidian languages, Tamil traditional grammars
transitivity, 3, 8, 29, 44, 45, 46, 50, 57, 72, 93, 95, 104, 105, 107, 108, 111, 118, 121, 123, 125–8, 135, 137, 148–50, 151–5, 156–8, 163, 171, 172, 176, 182–3, 187–9, 204–7, 209, 212–18, 222, 225, 226, 229, 230, 231, 233, 243, 257, 263, 264, 266–7, 272 n. 4, 273 nn. 7, 8, 274 n. 14, 280 n. 14, 282 n. 29, 294 nn. 6, 7, 285 nn. 8, 12, 289 nn. 15, 16, 291–2 n. 25, 292–3 n. 27, 295 n. 11
typology, 165, 170, 245, 256, 283 n. 34; of voice, 1, 9, 11, 22, 42–3, 110, 132, 170, 238, 261, 271, 273 n. 6

unaccusative/unergative, 118, 151, 280 n. 13, 283 n. 34
unaccusative verbs, 121–4, 155, 280 n. 13, 284 n. 5; *see also* unergative verbs
unaccusativity, 112, 121–4, 137, 151
undergoer, 72, 111, 149, 283 n. 1
undergoing, 111, 112, 117, 118, 120–4, 135, 136, 137, 139, 149, 150–3, 155, 157
unergative verbs, 121–4, 155, 280 n. 13; *see also* unaccusative verbs
uniqueness condition, 41–2, 159; *see also* biuniqueness condition; distinctness condition
universal grammar, 13, 118, 260, 274 n. 12
Uto-Aztecan languages, 118, 124, 133, 135, 278 n. 5; Huichol, 278 n. 5; *see also* Otomanguean languages

valence, *the number and kinds of arguments with which a lexical predicate is associated in its argument frame (which see)*, 7, 12, 29, 44, 45, 46, 50–7, 83, 121, 154–5, 186, 188–9, 209, 223, 275 n. 16, 285 n. 10; *see also* predicate-argument structure; transitivity; verbal argument structure
valence reduction, *see* detransitivization
verb stem extensions, *see* extensions
verbal argument structure, 4, 11, 35–43, 77, 106, 159, 164; *see also* logical relations; predicate-argument structure; valence
verbal semantic classes, ingestives, 281 n. 33; expressing natural occurrences, 119, 133, 136, 145–6; expressing qualities, 57, 81; expressing ritual actions, 133; of speaking, 58, 81, 102; *Schallwörter*, 59, 101, 123, 280 n. 13
Vietnamese, *see* Southeast Asian languages
voice, *a verbal category encoding alternations in the configurations of nominal statuses with which a verb is in particular relationships*, xiii, 1, 2, 6, 9, 14, 47, 53, 113, 155, 160, 164, 175, 176, 180, 185, 186, 200, 204, 219, 220, 225, 226, 228, 236, 245, 246, 248, 250, 253, 257, 258, 259, 260–71, 272–3 nn. 1–10; 275 n. 16, 277–8 n. 1, 279–80 n. 12, 281 n. 21, 293 n. 1, 295 n. 11; *see also* basic voice type; derived voice; focus; inverse; passives; passive voice; pragmatic voice type; Weak/Strong
voice potential, 29, 50, 53, 54, 55, 278 n. 7
volitional action, *see* volitionality
volitionality, 39, 72, 114, 118, 133–6, 152, 277 n. 20, 280 n. 13

Wakashan languages, 33, 156, 170; Kwakwala, 156; Nootkan, 33
Weak/Strong, 25, 69–82
Weak voice, 29, 269, 281 nn. 19, 22; *see also* Strong voice
word order, 18–19, 164–5, 166, 168, 180, 233, 244, 247, 286 n. 2, 287–8 n. 9

Made in the USA
Lexington, KY
16 February 2012